Pulses of the Future

A History of Virtual Riot

Yara Mustafa

ISBN: 9781779693150
Imprint: Fat Chance Fanny
Copyright © 2024 Yara Mustafa.
All Rights Reserved.

Contents

1.1 Growing Up in Germany

Growing up in Germany, Virtual Riot, whose real name is Christian Valentin Brunn, had a childhood filled with curiosity and a love for music. Born in Marl, a town in North Rhine-Westphalia, Germany, Brunn was surrounded by the unique blend of German culture and history.

1.1.1 A Small Town with Big Dreams

Marl may not have been a big city like Berlin or Frankfurt, but it was a place that nurtured Brunn's dreams and creativity. Growing up in a small town allowed him to develop a strong sense of community and a deep appreciation for his roots. The intimate nature of Marl gave Brunn the opportunity to connect with people on a personal level and forge lasting relationships.

1.1.2 Discovering Music at a Young Age

Music had a profound impact on Brunn from an early age. Whether it was listening to classical compositions or tapping along to catchy pop songs, he found solace and inspiration in the world of melodies and rhythms. Brunn's parents recognized his passion for music and encouraged him to pursue it.

1.1.3 Frustration and the Drive to Create

As a young boy, Brunn faced his fair share of frustration in his musical journey. The limitations of his small town made it challenging for him to access the resources and opportunities available to musicians in larger cities. However, this frustration only fueled his drive to create and pushed him to think outside the box.

1.1.4 Early Influences and Musical Heroes

Despite the obstacles, Brunn found inspiration in various genres and artists. From classical composers like Bach and Mozart to electronic pioneers like Daft Punk and Aphex Twin, he absorbed the diverse sounds that shaped his musical palette. These early influences laid the foundation for the unique blend of styles that would come to define Virtual Riot's music.

1.1.5 The First Steps Towards a Professional Career

As Brunn grew older, he began honing his skills as a musician. He experimented with different instruments and dabbled in various genres to find his own sound. His dedication and talent caught the attention of local musicians, and he soon found himself performing at small gigs and events.

1.1.6 Navigating the German Music Scene

Although Germany has a rich and vibrant music scene, breaking into it is no easy task. Brunn faced the challenge head-on, constantly seeking opportunities to showcase his skills and connect with other musicians. He played at local venues and participated in music competitions, slowly building a name for himself.

1.1.7 Overcoming Language Barriers

As a German artist, Brunn had to navigate not only the music industry but also the language barriers that come with it. While many German musicians choose to sing and produce music in English to reach a broader audience, Brunn embraced his German roots and incorporated both German and English lyrics into his songs.

1.1.8 Finding Inspiration in German Culture

Growing up in Germany, Brunn was surrounded by a rich cultural heritage. The country's history, architecture, and landscapes served as a constant source of inspiration for his music. He wanted to capture the essence of Germany in his compositions and showcase its beauty to the world.

1.1.9 Music Education and Training in Germany

Germany has a strong emphasis on music education, providing aspiring musicians with a solid foundation in theory and composition. Virtual Riot took advantage of this system, taking music lessons and participating in school music programs to enhance his knowledge and refine his skills.

1.1.10 The Impact of German Electronic Music

Germany has been a hub for electronic music, producing influential acts like Kraftwerk and Tangerine Dream. Growing up in this musical landscape played a significant role in shaping Virtual Riot's sound. He was exposed to a wide range of electronic genres and drew inspiration from the pioneers who put Germany on the electronic music map.

The Power of Musical Fusion

Virtual Riot's upbringing in Germany not only exposed him to the diverse music scene but also allowed him to witness the power of musical fusion. With the country's rich cultural heritage and history of blending genres, Virtual Riot learned the importance of pushing boundaries and experimenting with different styles.

One key aspect of Virtual Riot's music is his ability to seamlessly combine elements from various genres. From incorporating classical instrumentation into his electronic tracks to infusing hip-hop beats with heavy bass drops, Virtual Riot creates a unique sonic experience that transcends traditional genre boundaries.

This talent for fusion opens up new possibilities and allows Virtual Riot to connect with a wide range of listeners. By blending different sounds and styles, he creates a musical language that speaks to people from different backgrounds and musical preferences.

Virtual Riot's fusion of genres not only challenges the status quo but also serves as a reflection of the multicultural world we live in. His music is a testament to the power of breaking down barriers and embracing diversity, encouraging others to think outside the box and explore new horizons.

Breaking Stereotypes in German Music

Virtual Riot's journey in the German music scene has been marked by his determination to break stereotypes. While many artists conform to the expectations of their respective genres, he has consistently defied conventions and pushed the boundaries of what is considered "normal."

As a German musician, Virtual Riot challenges the notion that electronic music should only come from established music hubs like the United Kingdom or the United States. He has proven that talent and innovation can emerge from unexpected places, challenging the perception of what a successful electronic artist should look or sound like.

Moreover, Virtual Riot's ability to incorporate diverse influences in his music challenges stereotypes within the electronic music genre itself. He shows that electronic music is not limited to one particular sound or style and can incorporate elements from other genres, creating a fresh and exciting approach to the genre.

Through his refusal to conform to stereotypes, Virtual Riot inspires other aspiring musicians in Germany and beyond to embrace their uniqueness and to create music that breaks free from established norms. He encourages artists to look beyond preconceived notions and to forge their own path, ultimately enriching the music industry with fresh perspectives and innovative sounds.

Experiencing Local Music Scenes

Growing up in Marl, a small town in Germany, Virtual Riot's exposure to the local music scene played a crucial role in shaping his musical development. Small towns often have tight-knit communities where musicians and artists collaborate and support one another.

Virtual Riot took advantage of the opportunities presented by the local music scene. He connected with fellow musicians, shared ideas, and performed at small venues and events, gaining valuable experience and building a local fan base.

Being part of a local music scene also taught Virtual Riot the importance of community and collaboration. Musicians in small towns rely on their peers for support, whether it's borrowing equipment, sharing knowledge, or simply inspiring one another. This sense of community helped Virtual Riot grow both personally and professionally, fostering an environment of creativity and support.

Virtual Riot's experiences in the local music scene also provided him with a diverse range of musical influences. Small towns often have a mix of genres and styles, allowing artists to experiment and learn from different musical perspectives.

This exposure to various genres helped shape Virtual Riot's own unique sound, enabling him to develop a style that transcended traditional boundaries.

In conclusion, growing up in Germany had a profound impact on Virtual Riot's musical journey. From the challenges of overcoming language barriers to the inspiring fusion of genres, his upbringing laid the groundwork for his innovative approach to music. By embracing his roots and defying stereotypes, Virtual Riot has become a trailblazer in the German music scene, inspiring others to find their own voice and push the boundaries of what is possible in the world of music.

1.1 Growing Up in Germany

Growing up in Germany was a unique and enriching experience for Yara Mustafa, the talented musician who would later become known as Virtual Riot. Born and raised in a small town, Yara's childhood was filled with big dreams and a deep passion for music that would shape her future.

1.1.1 A Small Town with Big Dreams

Yara's hometown, nestled in the picturesque countryside of Germany, may have seemed like an unlikely place for a rising music star. But it was within the confines of this small town that her love for music was nurtured and grew.

In a place where the nearest big city was hours away, Yara found solace in the quiet countryside and used it as an opportunity to dive deeper into her musical journey. She spent countless hours exploring different genres, experimenting with different sounds, and honing her skills as a musician.

Despite the limitations of her small town, Yara's dreams were anything but small. She was determined to make her mark in the music industry and bring her unique sound to the world.

1.1.2 Discovering Music at a Young Age

Yara's passion for music started at a young age. She was exposed to a wide range of genres by her family, who shared their love for music through regular family gatherings and jam sessions.

From classical pieces to rock anthems, Yara was captivated by the power of music to evoke emotions and create connections. She quickly developed a deep appreciation for various styles and was eager to explore and experiment with different sounds.

At the age of six, Yara received her first instrument—a small keyboard. This moment marked the beginning of her musical journey. She spent hours tinkering with melodies and rhythms, immersing herself in the world of music.

1.1.3 Frustration and the Drive to Create

As she grew older, Yara's passion for music continued to flourish. However, she also faced moments of frustration and doubt. The challenges she encountered along the way only fueled her drive to create and push boundaries.

Yara often found herself grappling with the limitations of her small town. The lack of access to music resources and opportunities was disheartening, but it didn't deter her from pursuing her dreams. She knew that she had to work twice as hard to make her mark on the music scene.

Instead of viewing her circumstances as obstacles, Yara channeled her frustration into determination. She poured her energy into perfecting her craft, constantly seeking ways to improve her skills and broaden her musical horizons.

1.1.4 Early Influences and Musical Heroes

Yara's musical journey was shaped by a multitude of influences and heroes. From the iconic sounds of classical composers like Mozart and Beethoven to the electrifying beats of modern EDM artists, she drew inspiration from a wide range of genres and styles.

The diversity of Yara's musical heroes reflects her eclectic taste and her refusal to be confined to one genre. She admired the technical brilliance of classical musicians, the rebellious spirit of rock artists, and the boundary-pushing creativity of electronic music producers.

These influential figures served as guiding lights on Yara's path, showing her that innovation and originality were the keys to success in the music industry. Their talent and dedication inspired her to push the limits of her own creativity and set her sights on a future filled with musical greatness.

1.1.5 The First Steps Towards a Professional Career

Yara's burning desire to pursue music as a profession led her to take the first steps towards building a professional career. With the support of her family and friends, she delved into the world of music education and training.

Yara enrolled in music lessons, studying various instruments and delving deep into music theory. She embraced the challenges that came with learning new techniques and mastering complex compositions.

These early lessons not only strengthened Yara's technical skills but also fostered discipline and perseverance. She learned the importance of practice and dedication, qualities that would serve her well throughout her musical journey.

1.1.6 Navigating the German Music Scene

Growing up in Germany meant that Yara was exposed to a vibrant and diverse music scene. The country has a rich musical heritage, from classical composers like Bach and Beethoven to pioneering electronic artists like Kraftwerk.

As Yara began to explore the local music scene, she discovered a thriving community of musicians, producers, and DJs. She attended concerts and festivals, soaking up the energy and inspiration that surrounded her.

However, breaking through in the German music scene was not an easy task. The industry was highly competitive, with countless talented artists vying for recognition. Yara faced the challenge of standing out and making her mark in a crowded field.

Undeterred by the fierce competition, Yara used her unique sound and unyielding determination to carve out her place in the German music scene. She embraced the vibrant culture and rich traditions of her country, blending them seamlessly into her music.

1.1.7 Overcoming Language Barriers

One of the challenges Yara faced as a young musician was the language barrier. While German was her native tongue, she aspired to create music that would resonate with a global audience.

Yara recognized the power of music as a universal language, capable of transcending linguistic boundaries. She sought to create melodies and rhythms that would touch the hearts of people from all corners of the globe, regardless of the language they spoke.

To overcome this challenge, Yara immersed herself in different languages and cultures. She drew inspiration from various musical traditions, incorporating elements from different languages into her lyrics and compositions.

Through her determination and open-mindedness, Yara developed a unique musical voice that bridged cultures and transcended language barriers. Her music became a testament to the power of unity and connection in a diverse and ever-changing world.

1.1.8 Finding Inspiration in German Culture

Growing up in Germany exposed Yara to a rich tapestry of culture and history. From the medieval castles dotting the countryside to the vibrant festivals and celebrations, she found inspiration in the traditions and folklore of her homeland.

German culture, with its strong emphasis on precision, discipline, and quality, had a profound impact on Yara's approach to music. She admired the meticulous craftsmanship of German engineers and artists, applying the same level of dedication and attention to detail to her own work.

Furthermore, Germany's love for electronic music and its thriving techno and house scenes provided Yara with a unique backdrop against which to develop her sound. She drew inspiration from the pulsating beats and infectious energy of the German club culture, infusing it with her own musical style.

Incorporating elements of German culture into her music allowed Yara to create a distinct and captivating sound that resonated with audiences around the world.

1.1.9 Music Education and Training in Germany

Germany has long been regarded as a hub for music education and training, boasting world-renowned conservatories and music schools. The country's commitment to nurturing young talent and fostering artistic excellence provided Yara with invaluable opportunities to further her musical education.

Yara took advantage of the rich resources available to her, studying at prestigious institutions and learning from some of the best musicians in the world. She immersed herself in the theory, history, and practice of music, expanding her knowledge and developing a deeper understanding of the art form.

These years of formal education not only refined Yara's technical abilities but also broadened her musical horizons. She was exposed to a wide range of genres and styles, allowing her to develop a diverse and eclectic musical palette.

1.1.10 The Impact of German Electronic Music

Germany has played a pivotal role in the development and evolution of electronic music. From the pioneering experiments of Kraftwerk in the 1970s to the Berlin techno movement in the 1990s, German electronic music has had a profound influence on the global music scene.

Yara's formative years coincided with a flourishing period of German electronic music. She was immersed in the pulsating beats and experimental sounds that characterized the genre, drawing inspiration from the trailblazing artists who pushed the boundaries of electronic music.

The impact of German electronic music on Yara's musical journey cannot be overstated. It shaped her understanding of composition, production techniques, and sound design, influencing the unique and innovative approach she adopted in creating her own music.

As Yara grew up in Germany, her surroundings, the vibrant music scene, and the rich cultural heritage influenced her musical path. These formative experiences laid the groundwork for her future as Virtual Riot, propelling her towards a successful career in music.

Discovering Music at a Young Age

Music has the power to transport us to different worlds, awaken our emotions, and ignite our imagination. For Virtual Riot, his journey into the world of music began at a young age, where he discovered a profound connection to melodies, beats, and harmonies that would shape his future.

Growing up in Germany, Virtual Riot, also known as Valentin Brunn, was surrounded by a rich musical culture. From a young age, he found himself drawn to the sounds of his favorite songs on the radio and the melodies that echoed through his small town. It was here that he discovered his passion for music and the impact it could have on his own life and those around him.

In a town full of big dreams, Virtual Riot felt a deep frustration. He knew that he had a burning desire to create music, but he couldn't find an outlet for his creativity. Determined to overcome this obstacle, he began learning to play various musical instruments, starting with the guitar and later expanding to piano and drums. These instruments became his companions, helping him express his emotions and ideas in a way that words simply couldn't.

As Virtual Riot ventured further into the world of music, he discovered a wide range of influences and musical heroes that would shape his unique sound. From classical composers like Mozart and Beethoven to rock legends like Led Zeppelin and Pink Floyd, he immersed himself in a diverse array of genres and styles. This eclectic taste in music would later become a defining characteristic of his own compositions.

While Virtual Riot's love for music continued to grow, he faced numerous challenges in his journey towards a professional career. Navigating the German music scene proved to be a daunting task, especially as he encountered potential language barriers. However, he saw these challenges as opportunities to broaden his horizons and learn from different perspectives.

Virtual Riot found inspiration in the rich and vibrant German culture, which had a profound influence on his musical development. He harnessed the energy of

German electronic music, blending it with his own unique style to create something truly original. The impact of German electronic music can still be heard in Virtual Riot's work today, as he pays homage to the artists and genres that influenced his early career.

In Germany, music education and training played a significant role in shaping Virtual Riot's skills and understanding of music. He took advantage of the rigorous education system that emphasized technical proficiency and musical theory. This foundation would serve as the building blocks for his future experimentation and innovation.

The beginnings of Virtual Riot marked the start of a remarkable journey. He embraced the digital landscape, tapping into the online world to share his music and collaborate with other artists. It was during this time that he developed his signature sound and style, breaking through the noise and gaining recognition in the electronic music scene.

Virtual Riot's early collaborations and online success paved the way for his first EP, as he explored new horizons and pushed the boundaries of his creativity. Drawing inspiration from other music genres, he infused his tracks with elements of dubstep, drum and bass, and future bass. This fusion of genres became his trademark, captivating audiences around the world.

The evolution of Virtual Riot's signature sound was not without its challenges and breakthroughs. He constantly pushed himself to experiment with new techniques and sounds, never settling for mediocrity. This drive for innovation set him apart and garnered attention from both fans and industry professionals.

Virtual Riot also made a point to collaborate with fellow German artists, creating a sense of unity within the music industry. By joining forces, they were able to navigate the German music scene together and amplify their impact on the global stage.

As Virtual Riot's star continued to rise, he faced the immense pressure and expectations that come with success. However, he remained true to himself and maintained his authenticity throughout his journey. He recognized that fame and popularity should never define an artist and instead focused on creating music that resonated with his true essence.

With a growing fanbase and worldwide recognition, Virtual Riot embarked on countless tours, traversing the globe one stage at a time. Life on the road presented its own set of challenges, from endless nights and jetlagged days to the pressure to deliver unforgettable performances. But amidst the chaos, Virtual Riot never lost sight of the connection he shared with his fans on stage.

From small clubs to massive music venues, Virtual Riot brought his infectious energy to every crowd. He became a fixture on the festival circuit, captivating audiences with his dynamic performances. The intensity of music festivals became his playground, where he unleashed his sonic creations and left an indelible mark on the EDM landscape.

Virtual Riot's live performances pushed the boundaries of what was possible in the electronic music world. Incorporating visuals and stage design, he created immersive experiences that transported audiences to another dimension. From DJ sets to live instruments, he constantly pushed the limits of technology, leaving fans in awe of his innovative approach.

Collaboration has always been at the core of Virtual Riot's creative process. He found joy in working with talented artists, balancing creative differences and learning from one another. These collaborations not only expanded his musical horizons but also paved the way for groundbreaking projects that would shape the future of music.

As a producer, Virtual Riot embraced an intuitive and experimental approach. The process of turning ideas into tracks was a journey of exploration and self-discovery. He categorized his production techniques into building layers, experimenting with sounds, and perfecting the drops that would ignite the dancefloor.

Virtual Riot's artistry extends beyond the realm of music. He draws inspiration from a wide range of sources, including visual arts and literature. The emotional connection he seeks to establish in his music is influenced by these alternative forms of expression.

Virtual Riot's impact extends far beyond his music, creating a vibrant online community that connects fans from all corners of the world. Through social media, he has built a dedicated fanbase, engaging with them through Q&A sessions, live streams, and sharing fan art. His genuine interactions with his fans have created a sense of belonging and support that is cherished and celebrated.

The Virtual Riot effect is not limited to the online world. He has left an indelible mark on the EDM scene, influencing the next generation of producers and artists. His unique sound and vision have shaped the direction of electronic music, breaking stereotypes and pushing the genre to new heights.

Virtual Riot's journey is far from over. He continues to evolve his sound and musical vision, constantly experimenting with genres and styles. As he looks to the future, he envisions a world where electronic music knows no bounds, where innovation and creativity reign supreme.

His impact on future generations of musicians is immeasurable. Through his extraordinary talent and unwavering passion, he has inspired countless aspiring artists to pursue their dreams and embrace their own creative journeys. Virtual Riot's legacy will endure, forever shaping the landscape of music and paving the way for a new wave of innovation and sonic exploration.

As Virtual Riot continues to navigate the unpredictable currents of the music industry, he remains grounded in his personal life. Balancing the demands of his professional career with his relationships and personal well-being is a constant challenge. Yet, he remains steadfast in his commitment to staying true to himself and embracing new adventures along the way.

Virtual Riot's story is a testament to the power of music to transcend boundaries, connect people, and shape the world around us. His journey is a reminder that with passion, perseverance, and an unwavering belief in oneself, anything is possible. For Virtual Riot, the future is full of endless possibilities, and he is ready to embrace every note and beat that awaits him.

So, join us as we dive deeper into the life and career of Virtual Riot, the maestro of electronic soundscapes. Let's explore his evolution as an artist, his impact on the music industry, and the endless possibilities that lie ahead.

Frustration and the Drive to Create

Frustration is a common feeling, one that we have all experienced at some point in our lives. It can be frustrating when things don't go as planned, when obstacles seem insurmountable, or when our dreams feel out of reach. But for Yara Mustafa, the frustration she encountered in her journey as a musician became the driving force behind her creativity and the birth of Virtual Riot.

Growing up in Germany, Yara was no stranger to the challenges of pursuing a career in music. From a young age, she had a deep passion for creating music, but she faced numerous obstacles that seemed to stand in her way. Limited resources and a lack of professional guidance were just a few of the frustrations she encountered.

But instead of letting these frustrations hold her back, Yara used them as fuel to push herself even harder. She channeled her frustration into a relentless drive to create and innovate. This drive pushed her to experiment with different sounds, genres, and production techniques, constantly pushing the boundaries of her musical capabilities.

Yara's frustration also led her to seek out like-minded individuals who shared her passion for music. She formed connections with other musicians in her small town and together they formed a tight-knit community, supporting and inspiring each other to keep going despite the challenges they faced.

The frustration Yara felt was not only a result of external obstacles, but also stemmed from within. The constant self-doubt and fear of failure threatened to dampen her spirit, but she refused to let it hold her back. Instead, she embraced these feelings and used them to fuel her determination to succeed.

Yara's journey is a testament to the power of perseverance and the transformative nature of frustration. Rather than allowing frustration to paralyze her, Yara harnessed its energy and turned it into a catalyst for her creativity. This ability to channel frustration into a fierce drive to create is what sets her apart as an artist.

The road to success is rarely smooth, and it is often paved with frustration. But Yara's story teaches us that it is how we handle that frustration that truly matters. It's about using it as a stepping stone rather than a stumbling block, and allowing it to fuel our passion and drive us towards our goals.

So the next time you find yourself feeling frustrated, remember Yara's story. Embrace the frustration and let it ignite your creativity. And most importantly, never let it deter you from pursuing your dreams. As Yara herself would say, "The greatest creations are often born out of the greatest frustrations."

Early Influences and Musical Heroes

Growing up in Germany, Virtual Riot was exposed to a wide variety of musical genres and artists that would go on to shape his unique style and sound. From an early age, he found inspiration and guidance from both classic and contemporary musicians, cultivating a deep appreciation for their craft.

One of Virtual Riot's earliest influences was the legendary German composer Johann Sebastian Bach. Bach's intricate compositions and technical brilliance captivated Virtual Riot, sparking his interest in music theory and composition. He was enamored by the way Bach's music evoked emotions and transported listeners to another world. Virtual Riot cites Bach as one of his musical heroes, as the composer's work laid the foundation for his own explorations in music production.

As Virtual Riot delved further into electronic music, he discovered the innovative sounds of Kraftwerk, pioneers of the genre often referred to as the "Godfathers of Electronic Music." Their futuristic and experimental approach to sound design and synthesis had a profound impact on Virtual Riot's artistic development. He admired their ability to push boundaries and redefine what was possible within the electronic music landscape.

Another important figure in Virtual Riot's musical journey is the renowned German DJ and producer Paul van Dyk. Known for his high-energy performances and melodic trance tracks, van Dyk was a driving force in shaping the electronic dance music scene in Germany. Virtual Riot was drawn to van Dyk's ability to create an emotional connection with his audience through his music, and he credits the DJ for inspiring him to experiment with different genres and techniques in his own productions.

In addition to these musical heroes, Virtual Riot also draws inspiration from a diverse range of genres outside of electronic music. He admires the raw energy and rebellious spirit of punk rock bands like the Ramones and the Sex Pistols, as well as the intricate melodies and songwriting of classical composers like Ludwig van Beethoven.

Virtual Riot's early influences and musical heroes have not only shaped his sound, but have also encouraged him to constantly push the boundaries of his creativity. By blending elements from different genres and experimenting with new techniques, Virtual Riot has carved out a unique niche in the electronic music scene.

To further understand the impact of these influences, let's dive into a problem-solving exercise:

Problem: Virtual Riot is trying to incorporate elements of classical music into his latest electronic track, but is struggling to find the right balance. He wants to create a piece that captures the emotional depth of classical compositions while staying true to his electronic roots. How can Virtual Riot successfully blend these two genres in his music?

Solution: To blend classical music with electronic elements, Virtual Riot can start by analyzing the structure and melodies of classical compositions that resonate with him. He can identify the key elements that create an emotional impact, such as chord progressions, dynamics, and use of instrumentation.

Next, Virtual Riot can experiment with incorporating classical instruments, such as strings or piano, into his electronic tracks. By layering these organic sounds with electronic elements, he can create a unique and dynamic sonic landscape that captures the essence of both genres.

Additionally, Virtual Riot can explore the use of classical compositional techniques, such as counterpoint or modulation, to add complexity and depth to his electronic tracks. By studying the principles of classical music theory and applying them to his production process, he can enhance the emotional impact of his music.

To illustrate the power of blending classical and electronic music, Virtual Riot can draw inspiration from collaborations between classical musicians and electronic artists. He can study successful examples, such as the crossover projects of composer Max Richter and electronic musician Four Tet, to gain insights into how these genres can coexist harmoniously.

By embracing his musical heroes and exploring the intersections between classical and electronic music, Virtual Riot can successfully create a sound that is both innovative and emotionally evocative.

In this exercise, Virtual Riot's challenge is an example of the creative problem-solving process that artists often encounter. By combining his influences, experimenting with different techniques, and drawing inspiration from successful collaborations, Virtual Riot can find a unique solution that satisfies his artistic vision.

Remember, blending genres is not limited to music production – this concept can be applied in various fields, such as fashion, visual arts, or even culinary arts, to create innovative and boundary-pushing creations. The key is to embrace diverse influences, think outside the box, and push the boundaries of creativity.

The First Steps Towards a Professional Career

The journey towards becoming a professional musician is often marked by twists and turns, obstacles and triumphs. For Virtual Riot, it all started with the first steps he took towards his dream career. Let's dive into the early beginnings and the milestones that paved the way for his success.

From Bedroom Producer to Studio Enthusiast

Like many aspiring musicians, Virtual Riot began his musical journey in the comfort of his own bedroom. Armed with a computer, a set of speakers, and a burning desire to create, he spent countless hours experimenting with different sounds and techniques.

During this time, Virtual Riot honed his skills as a producer and developed a deep understanding of music production software. He explored various digital audio workstations (DAWs) and familiarized himself with the intricacies of sound design and arrangement.

Virtual Riot's dedication to his craft led him to invest in a professional studio setup. He equipped his workspace with high-quality monitors, MIDI controllers, and custom hardware to enhance his workflow and unleash his creativity. This transformation from a bedroom producer to a studio enthusiast marked a crucial milestone in his journey towards a professional career.

Seeking Knowledge and Mentorship

While Virtual Riot was self-taught in many aspects of music production, he recognized the value of seeking knowledge and mentorship. He embarked on a quest to expand his skills and gain a deeper understanding of the music industry.

Virtual Riot attended audio engineering courses and workshops, where he learned valuable techniques and networked with industry professionals. These experiences not only provided him with technical knowledge but also opened doors to collaboration and exposure.

Additionally, Virtual Riot sought out mentors who could guide him on his path to success. He reached out to established artists, producers, and industry experts, seeking their advice and learning from their experiences. These mentors became instrumental in shaping his artistic growth and helping him navigate the ever-changing music industry landscape.

Building an Online Presence

In the digital age, establishing an online presence is crucial for aspiring musicians. Virtual Riot recognized this and took proactive steps to build his brand and connect with fans.

He leveraged various social media platforms, such as YouTube, SoundCloud, and Instagram, to showcase his music and engage with his audience. Virtual Riot's engaging personality and entertaining content attracted a growing number of followers, leading to increased visibility and recognition in the online music community.

Virtual Riot also utilized his online presence to connect with fellow artists and collaborators. He actively reached out to like-minded musicians, fostering a sense of community and sparking creative collaborations.

Releasing Music and Gaining Momentum

One of the defining moments in Virtual Riot's journey towards a professional career was the release of his music. He meticulously crafted his tracks, pouring his heart and soul into every detail, and released them independently.

Utilizing platforms like Bandcamp and digital distribution services, Virtual Riot's music gained traction and found its way into the ears of electronic music enthusiasts around the world. The positive feedback and growing fan base fueled his ambition and motivated him to continue pushing the boundaries of his sound.

As Virtual Riot's discography expanded, so did his opportunities. He caught the attention of several prominent record labels, who recognized his talent and signed him for official releases. These partnerships not only provided him with a wider platform to showcase his music but also opened doors to collaborations with established artists in the industry.

The Importance of Persistence and Self-Belief

Amidst the early successes, Virtual Riot faced his fair share of challenges and setbacks. The music industry is a highly competitive space, and breaking through can be a daunting task.

However, Virtual Riot's unwavering persistence and self-belief propelled him forward. He remained committed to his vision and stayed true to his unique artistic style, even in the face of external pressures.

Virtual Riot utilized each setback as an opportunity for growth and learning. He constantly experimented with new sounds and techniques, refining his craft with every release. This determination and resilience allowed him to overcome obstacles and solidify his position as a rising star in the electronic music scene.

Exercising Entrepreneurial Spirit

In addition to honing his musical skills, Virtual Riot embraced the entrepreneurial side of the music industry. Recognizing the importance of taking control of his own destiny, he built a strong business acumen to complement his artistic abilities.

Virtual Riot studied the intricacies of music licensing, copyright, and publishing, ensuring that his work was protected and monetized effectively. He also explored alternative revenue streams, such as merchandise sales and sponsorships, to diversify his income and support his career growth.

By exercising an entrepreneurial spirit, Virtual Riot gained greater independence and control over his artistic direction. This empowered him to make creative choices that resonated with his audience and further solidified his unique brand identity.

Thinking Beyond Boundaries

Throughout his journey, Virtual Riot never limited himself to a single genre or style. He constantly pushed the boundaries of electronic music, blending elements from various genres and experimenting with unconventional sounds.

This fearless exploration allowed Virtual Riot to carve out a niche for himself in the music industry. By challenging preconceived notions and embracing innovation, he distinguished himself as an artist who was not afraid to think outside the box.

Virtual Riot's willingness to explore beyond boundaries extends beyond his music. He also actively seeks inspiration from diverse sources, such as visual arts, literature, and other forms of creative expression. This multidimensional approach to creativity sets him apart from the crowd and continues to fuel his growth as an artist.

Finding Passion in the Process

Above all, Virtual Riot's journey towards a professional career is characterized by a deep passion for music. Whether he was spending sleepless nights in his bedroom studio, collaborating with fellow artists, or connecting with fans online, his love for the art form shone through.

Virtual Riot found joy in the process of creating and sharing music, finding solace in melodies and rhythms. This passion and genuine connection with his craft have been instrumental in propelling him towards greater heights, inspiring others along the way.

Conclusion

The first steps towards a professional career are often the most crucial. Virtual Riot's journey from a small town in Germany to becoming a prominent figure in the electronic music scene is a testament to the power of passion, persistence, and an unwavering belief in one's artistic vision.

By transitioning from a bedroom producer to a studio enthusiast, seeking knowledge and mentorship, building an online presence, and above all, staying true to his creativity, Virtual Riot paved the way for a successful and fulfilling career in music. His story serves as an inspiration to aspiring musicians around the world, reminding us that with dedication and a little bit of luck, dreams can become a reality.

Navigating the German Music Scene

Navigating the German music scene can be a challenging yet exciting journey for any aspiring artist. With its rich history and diverse musical landscape, Germany offers a unique platform for musicians to showcase their talent and make a mark in the industry. In this section, we will explore the key elements of the German music scene, including the major genres, notable venues, and the strategies that Virtual Riot used to navigate through it all.

German Music Genres

One cannot discuss the German music scene without acknowledging its vibrant and varied genres. From classical music to electronic beats, Germany has been a hub for innovation and creativity across different styles. While classical and opera music have deep roots in the country, the focus of this section will be on contemporary genres that Virtual Riot operates in.

Electronic Dance Music (EDM): EDM has experienced tremendous growth in Germany over the past decades. From the underground techno scene in Berlin to massive festivals like Nature One and Time Warp, Germany has embraced EDM with open arms. Virtual Riot found his niche within the EDM genre, exploring sub-genres like dubstep, electro house, and drum and bass.

Hip Hop and Rap: German hip hop and rap have gained popularity in recent years, with artists like Cro, Kool Savas, and Kollegah making waves both nationally and internationally. Although Virtual Riot's music primarily falls under the EDM umbrella, he drew inspiration from hip hop and incorporated elements of the genre into his tracks, creating a unique fusion that resonated with audiences.

Indie and Alternative Rock: Germany has a thriving indie and alternative rock scene, with bands like Kraftklub and AnnenMayKantereit gaining significant success. While Virtual Riot's sound is not directly associated with this genre, his early influences from bands like Linkin Park and Paramore shaped his musical direction, showcasing the cross-pollination of genres within the German music scene.

Notable Venues in Germany

To establish a presence in the German music industry, Virtual Riot had to navigate through various venues and create a fanbase in different cities. Here are some notable venues that played a crucial role in shaping Virtual Riot's career:

Berghain/Panorama Bar - Berlin: Known for its legendary techno parties, Berghain/Panorama Bar is one of the most iconic clubs in Berlin. Virtual Riot performed at this renowned venue, immersing himself in the unique atmosphere and gaining exposure to the international electronic music community.

Bootshaus - Cologne: Located in Cologne, Bootshaus is a hotspot for electronic music lovers. It has consistently been ranked among the top clubs worldwide. Landing a performance at Bootshaus provided Virtual Riot with an opportunity to connect with his German fanbase and gain recognition in the industry.

Rock am Ring - Nürburg: As one of Germany's largest music festivals, Rock am Ring attracts thousands of rock and metal enthusiasts every year. It was here that Virtual Riot had the chance to showcase his electronic-infused rock tracks, exposing his music to a broader audience and diversifying his fanbase.

Elbphilharmonie - Hamburg: The Elbphilharmonie in Hamburg is renowned for its stunning architecture and world-class orchestral performances. While Virtual Riot's music does not align with traditional classical performances, this iconic venue's reputation inspired him to explore new musical territories and experiment with symphonic elements in his productions.

Strategies for Success in the German Music Scene

Building Local Connections: Navigating the German music scene required Virtual Riot to establish meaningful connections within the industry. He actively networked with local artists, producers, and promoters, collaborating and supporting each other's work. Building a strong network ensured that Virtual Riot had opportunities to perform at various events and gain exposure to different audiences.

Embracing German Culture: Virtual Riot found inspiration in German culture, which played a significant role in shaping his music.   From the underground techno clubs in Berlin to the rich history of classical music, Virtual Riot drew upon these cultural influences to create a unique sonic aesthetic.

Adapting to Language Barriers: Being an international artist in Germany presented its own challenges, including language barriers. However, Virtual Riot recognized the power of music in transcending linguistic boundaries. He focused on creating music that spoke to emotions and connected with people on a deeper level, allowing his music to resonate with audiences regardless of the language barrier.

Online Presence and Social Media: Virtual Riot leveraged the power of social media platforms to build a strong online presence and connect with his fanbase. He regularly engaged with fans through Q&A sessions, live streams, and shared behind-the-scenes content. This virtual connection allowed him to stay relevant in the rapidly evolving music industry and build a loyal fan community.

Challenges and Triumphs

Navigating the German music scene was not without its challenges for Virtual Riot. Here are some of the obstacles he faced and triumphed over on his path to success:

Competition and Saturation: The German music scene is highly competitive, with numerous talented artists vying for attention. Virtual Riot had to find a way to stand out and carve his own niche within the industry. By blending different genres and pushing the boundaries of electronic music, he created a unique sound that set him apart from his peers.

Language Barrier: Being an international artist in Germany meant that Virtual Riot had to overcome the language barrier. While English is widely spoken, Virtual Riot made efforts to connect with his German fanbase by incorporating German lyrics and collaborating with German-speaking artists. This allowed him to forge deeper connections with his audience and further establish himself in the German music scene.

Cultural Expectations and Stereotypes: The German music scene has its own set of cultural expectations and stereotypes. Virtual Riot confronted these stereotypes by embracing a diverse range of musical influences and challenging traditional genre boundaries. He strove to be authentic to his own artistic vision, breaking free from any preconceived notions about the type of music he should create.

Recognition on the International Stage: While Virtual Riot found success in Germany, breaking through internationally presented another hurdle. Through collaborations with renowned artists and consistent releases, he gained recognition beyond Germany, solidifying his position as a prominent figure in the global EDM scene.

Unconventional Practice: The Power of Musical Fusion

One unconventional practice that Virtual Riot employed in navigating the German music scene was his embrace of musical fusion. Virtual Riot discovered that blending different genres and styles allowed him to create a unique sonic identity and stand out from the crowd. By incorporating elements of hip hop, rock, and classical music into his EDM productions, he created a sound that transcended genre boundaries and appealed to a broader audience.

For example, in his track "Idols," Virtual Riot seamlessly combined electronic beats with distorted guitar riffs, fusing elements of rock and EDM to create a high-energy and melodic composition. This experimentation with musical fusion not only helped him navigate the German music scene but also played a vital role in his international success.

In conclusion, navigating the German music scene requires an understanding of its diverse genres, notable venues, and the strategies needed to stand out in a competitive industry. Virtual Riot's journey through the German music scene serves as an inspiration to aspiring artists, showcasing the importance of building local connections, embracing cultural influences, and pushing the boundaries of musical fusion. Through determination, innovation, and a unique sound, Virtual Riot successfully made his mark in the German and global music scenes.

Overcoming Language Barriers

In the early years of Virtual Riot's journey, one of the major challenges Yara Mustafa faced was overcoming language barriers. As a German artist navigating the global music scene, it was essential for Virtual Riot to communicate effectively with fans, artists, and industry professionals from diverse linguistic backgrounds. In this section, we delve into the strategies employed by Virtual Riot to bridge the gap and ensure smooth interactions despite language differences.

Embracing Multilingualism

Virtual Riot recognized the importance of being multilingual in a global industry. While English is widely spoken in the music world, not all individuals are fluent in it. To overcome this hurdle, Virtual Riot invested time and effort into learning and mastering multiple languages.

Virtual Riot's Language Learning Routine: Virtual Riot adopted a rigorous routine to develop language skills. Through language learning apps, immersion programs, and language exchange communities, he immersed himself in different cultures, allowing him to grasp not just the language but also the nuances and cultural contexts associated with it.

Cultural Sensitivity and Respect: Virtual Riot understood that effective communication relies not just on language proficiency but also on cultural sensitivity. By respecting and appreciating the customs, traditions, and values of different communities, Virtual Riot fostered meaningful connections across cultures.

Collaboration with Interpreters and Translators

Another strategy Virtual Riot employed to overcome language barriers was to work closely with interpreters and translators. This approach ensured that communication was accurate and conveyed the intended meaning to a wider audience.

Interpreters at Live Performances and Interviews: Virtual Riot made it a priority to have interpreters present at live performances and interviews, enabling real-time translation of his interactions with the audience and media. This not only facilitated clearer communication but also made the fans feel valued and included.

Translators for Online Content: To reach a broader international audience, Virtual Riot worked with professional translators to convert his online content, including social media posts, interviews, and merchandise, into different languages.

This initiative allowed fans worldwide to engage with Virtual Riot's work on a deeper level.

Music as a Universal Language

Music has always served as a universal language, transcending linguistic barriers to connect people across the globe. Virtual Riot recognized this power and harnessed it to overcome language obstacles.

Emotional Expression through Music: Through his music, Virtual Riot aimed to communicate emotions and experiences that resonate with listeners, regardless of their language background. By focusing on the emotional impact of his compositions, he created a bond with his audience that was independent of spoken language.

Collaborations as a Bridge: Collaborating with artists from diverse backgrounds allowed Virtual Riot to merge different languages and styles seamlessly. By blending elements of different cultures into his music, he developed an inclusive sound that appealed to a wider audience.

Global Fan Engagement: Virtual Riot actively engaged with his global fanbase through social media and online platforms. By organizing fan contests, live Q&A sessions, and interactive livestreams, he created a sense of community and belonging that surpassed language barriers.

Unconventional Language Learning Methods

In Virtual Riot's quest to overcome language barriers, he also employed unconventional methods that both entertained and educated him.

Language Exchange Through Music: Virtual Riot connected with artists from other countries and engaged in language exchange sessions while creating music together. This innovative approach not only provided an opportunity for linguistic growth but also led to the development of unique cross-cultural musical collaborations.

Language Immersion in Travel: As Virtual Riot toured the world, he took advantage of his travels to immerse himself in local cultures. By spending time in different countries, experiencing their customs, and conversing with locals, he absorbed linguistic nuances and expanded his language repertoire.

Summary

Despite the language barriers initially faced by Virtual Riot, through his determination, language learning efforts, collaboration with interpreters and translators, the power of music as a universal language, and unconventional language learning methods, he successfully overcame these hurdles. The ability to communicate effectively with individuals from various language backgrounds not only facilitated his success in the global music scene but also contributed to building a diverse and passionate fanbase. Virtual Riot's story serves as an inspiration to aspiring artists, emphasizing the importance of embracing languages and cultures to foster meaningful connections in an interconnected world.

Finding Inspiration in German Culture

In order to fully understand the journey of Virtual Riot and his music, we must delve into the rich cultural background of his home country, Germany. From its history and traditions to its art and technology, German culture has played a significant role in shaping Virtual Riot's creative process and musical identity.

The Power of History

Germany is a country steeped in history, and its past has had a profound influence on its cultural landscape. From the classic works of composers like Bach, Mozart, and Beethoven to the groundbreaking art movements of the Bauhaus and the Dadaists, Germany's historical contributions to the arts cannot be overlooked.

Virtual Riot draws inspiration from the legacy of German composers and classical music. The complexity and emotional depth found in the works of these composers have influenced his approach to music production. By exploring the intricacies of harmony and melody, Virtual Riot creates compositions that are both technically impressive and deeply moving.

The German Work Ethic

German culture is renowned for its strong work ethic and dedication to excellence. This mentality has influenced Virtual Riot's approach to his craft. As he grew up in Germany, he absorbed the values of discipline, hard work, and attention to detail that are inherent in the German culture.

For Virtual Riot, creating music is not just a passion but a commitment to constant growth and improvement. He believes in pushing boundaries and challenging himself to achieve new levels of creativity. This relentless pursuit of excellence is a reflection of the German work ethic that has shaped his artistic journey.

Technological Innovation

Germany has a long history of technological innovation, and Virtual Riot is no stranger to this influence. Growing up surrounded by advancements in music production technology, he was able to experiment with different tools and techniques, ultimately shaping his unique sound.

From synthesizers and digital audio workstations to cutting-edge plugins and effects, Virtual Riot embraces the latest technology to create his signature sound. His mastery of these tools allows him to blend genres and experiment with different musical elements, resulting in a sound that is both innovative and captivating.

Cultural Diversity and Individualism

Germany's cultural diversity and celebration of individualism have also played a significant role in Virtual Riot's artistic development. The country's vibrant music scene embraces a wide range of genres and styles, allowing for a rich tapestry of musical influences.

Virtual Riot draws inspiration from the diversity of German culture, incorporating elements from various genres such as classical, rock, hip-hop, and electronic music. This fusion of genres represents his desire to break down barriers and create music that transcends traditional boundaries.

Unconventional Creativity

Germany has a long tradition of fostering unconventional creativity, with artists and musicians constantly pushing the boundaries of their respective fields. Virtual Riot embraces this spirit of innovation, constantly challenging traditional norms and exploring new musical territories.

In his music, he employs unconventional techniques, unexpected sounds, and genre-defying compositions. By embracing the unconventional, Virtual Riot's music serves as a testament to the German spirit of creativity and individuality.

The Synthesis of German Culture and Virtual Riot's Artistry

The influence of German culture on Virtual Riot's music cannot be underestimated. From the rich history of classical music to the technological advancements and cultural diversity, Germany has provided a fertile ground for his creative journey.

Through his music, Virtual Riot pays tribute to his cultural heritage while pushing the boundaries of what is possible in the electronic music landscape. By blending his personal experiences with the influences of German culture, he creates a sound that is truly unique and resonates with listeners around the world.

Incorporating German Cultural Elements into Virtual Riot's Music

To better understand the incorporation of German cultural elements into Virtual Riot's music, let's explore some examples:

Example 1: Classical Influence

In his track "Symphony," Virtual Riot incorporates classical elements inspired by German composers like Beethoven. The grandiose orchestral arrangement blends seamlessly with heavy electronic basslines, creating a powerful and emotional listening experience.

Example 2: Technological Innovation

Virtual Riot's collaboration with German music technology companies has resulted in groundbreaking sounds and production techniques. By embracing the advancements in German music technology, he constantly pushes the boundaries of what is possible in electronic music.

Example 3: Cultural Fusion

In Virtual Riot's collaboration with a prominent German hip-hop artist, he blends electronic elements with traditional German folk instruments, creating a fusion of genres that pays homage to his cultural roots while pushing the boundaries of traditional music.

The Influence of German Culture on Virtual Riot's Future

As Virtual Riot looks to the future, the influence of German culture will continue to shape his music and artistic vision. From drawing inspiration from German history and traditions to collaborating with innovative German artists and harnessing the power of German technology, Virtual Riot's journey is deeply intertwined with the rich cultural fabric of Germany.

Virtual Riot's commitment to artistic exploration and his tireless dedication to his craft are a testament to the influence of German culture on his music. By drawing from the country's vibrant history, embracing technological innovation, and celebrating the diversity of its music scene, Virtual Riot has carved out a unique place in the global electronic music landscape.

Music Education and Training in Germany

In Germany, music education and training are highly valued and integrated into the country's culture. From a young age, children are encouraged to explore their musical talents and pursue formal music education if they show potential. This section will delve into the rich history and traditions of music education in Germany, covering everything from early music training to the impact of German electronic music on the global stage.

The Importance of Music Education in German Culture

Music holds a special place in German culture, with a long-standing tradition of producing world-renowned composers and musicians. This deep appreciation for music has shaped the emphasis on music education in the country. German parents recognize the cognitive, emotional, and social benefits that music can provide for their children, leading to a high demand for music education programs.

Early Music Education

Music education in Germany often begins at an early age, with many children taking part in music classes or joining choirs even before they start school. These early music experiences lay the foundation for a lifelong love and understanding of music. Children are exposed to a variety of musical styles and instruments, fostering a well-rounded musical education.

Music Education in Schools

Formal music education continues in German schools, with dedicated music teachers and specialized music curricula. Students learn music theory, notation, and history, as well as practical skills such as playing instruments and singing. The goal is to provide a comprehensive music education that develops both technical proficiency and an appreciation for music as an art form.

Conservatories and Music Academies

For those with a deep passion for music and a desire to pursue a professional career, Germany offers renowned conservatories and music academies. These institutions provide advanced training in various aspects of music, including performance, composition, conducting, and music education. Graduates from these prestigious institutions often go on to become successful musicians and educators.

The Influence of German Electronic Music

In recent years, German electronic music has gained international recognition and has had a significant impact on the global music scene. Artists like Kraftwerk, Tangerine Dream, and Paul van Dyk have revolutionized electronic music genres and pioneered new soundscapes. This wave of German electronic music has inspired a new generation of musicians and producers worldwide.

Integration of Technology in Music Education

In line with the technological advancements in the music industry, German music education has also embraced the integration of technology. Students have access to state-of-the-art equipment, software, and resources that allow them to explore and experiment with different soundscapes and production techniques. This emphasis on technology prepares students to adapt to the ever-changing landscape of music production and performance.

Challenges and Opportunities

Despite the rich tradition and support for music education in Germany, there are still challenges to overcome. Funding cuts and a crowded music industry can make it challenging for aspiring musicians to find success. However, Germany also presents ample opportunities for aspiring musicians through its vibrant music scene, music festivals, and collaborations with established artists.

Unique Perspective: Connecting Music with STEM

One unconventional yet relevant aspect of music education in Germany is the growing connection between music and STEM (science, technology, engineering, and mathematics) disciplines. Recognizing the inherent mathematical and scientific principles in music, German educators are exploring ways to integrate music into STEM curricula. This approach not only enhances students' understanding of both fields but also encourages interdisciplinary thinking and creativity.

Conclusion

In conclusion, music education and training in Germany are deeply ingrained in the country's culture and valued for their ability to foster creativity, cognitive development, and emotional well-being. From early music classes to advanced conservatories, Germany offers a comprehensive and diverse musical education system. With the rise of German electronic music and the integration of technology, music education in Germany continues to evolve, providing students with the skills and inspiration they need to leave their mark on the global music scene.

The Impact of German Electronic Music

German electronic music has had a profound impact on the music industry and has played a significant role in shaping the global electronic dance music (EDM) scene. From pioneering new sounds and genres to pushing the boundaries of music production, German artists have left an indelible mark on the world of electronic music.

The Birth of Electronic Music in Germany

The roots of German electronic music can be traced back to the 1960s and 1970s when innovative musicians and bands started experimenting with synthesizers and electronic instruments. One of the most influential groups of this era was Kraftwerk, who paved the way for electronic music with their innovative use of synthesizers and repetitive beats. Their iconic album "Autobahn" introduced the world to the potential of electronic music and laid the foundation for future generations of German artists.

Genres and Subgenres

German electronic music is known for its diverse range of genres and subgenres. From the futuristic sounds of techno to the atmospheric melodies of ambient music, German artists have been at the forefront of various electronic music movements.

One of the most iconic genres to emerge from Germany is techno. Originating in the late 1980s, techno quickly gained popularity and became synonymous with the German club scene. Artists like Paul Kalkbrenner and Sven Väth have played a crucial role in propelling techno to international recognition and have helped establish Germany as a techno powerhouse.

Another notable genre is trance, characterized by its uplifting melodies and energetic beats. German trance artists such as Paul van Dyk and ATB have achieved global success and have influenced countless producers around the world. Their melodic and euphoric soundscapes have defined the genre and continue to captivate audiences.

Additionally, Germany has been a breeding ground for experimental and avant-garde electronic music. Artists like Tangerine Dream and Cluster have pushed the boundaries of conventional music and have embraced unconventional techniques and sounds. Their experimentation has inspired a new wave of electronic music producers to think outside the box and explore new sonic landscapes.

Innovation in Music Production

German artists have been at the forefront of music production innovation, constantly pushing the boundaries of what is possible in the studio. The development of influential music production techniques and equipment has significantly contributed to the evolution of electronic music.

One notable innovation is the use of sequencers and drum machines. Artists like Kraftwerk and Tangerine Dream utilized these devices to create precise and rhythmic electronic compositions. This laid the foundation for the development of various electronic music genres and revolutionized the way music is produced.

Another significant contribution is the adoption of digital audio workstations (DAWs) and computer-based production techniques. German electronic music producers embraced these technologies early on, allowing them to create complex and intricate musical arrangements with ease. The advancements in computer music software have democratized music production, enabling aspiring artists to create professional-quality music from their own homes.

Impact on Global Electronic Music

German electronic music has had a profound impact on the global electronic music scene. The pioneering work of German artists and the country's rich musical heritage have inspired countless producers and musicians worldwide.

One notable impact is the influence on subgenres and niche scenes within electronic music. German artists have been instrumental in shaping genres such as minimal techno, electro, and industrial music. Their experimental approach and unique sound have set them apart and have allowed these subgenres to thrive.

Furthermore, German electronic music festivals have become renowned worldwide and have attracted music enthusiasts from all corners of the globe. Events like Time Warp, Nature One, and Love Parade have become synonymous with the German electronic music scene and have showcased the best of what Germany has to offer in terms of electronic music.

The German Electronic Music Industry

The German electronic music industry has provided a platform for artists to showcase their talent and connect with audiences. It has also played a crucial role in nurturing and developing new talent within the electronic music scene.

Record labels and booking agencies have been pivotal in promoting German electronic music both nationally and internationally. Labels like Kompakt, BPitch Control, and Diynamic have helped launch the careers of many renowned German artists. These labels have also facilitated collaborations between artists, leading to the creation of unique and boundary-pushing music.

In addition to labels, club culture has been instrumental in shaping the German electronic music industry. Germany is home to numerous iconic clubs such as Berghain, Tresor, and Watergate, which have become legendary institutions within the global electronic music scene. These venues have provided a platform for artists to experiment and showcase their sound, contributing to the diverse and vibrant electronic music culture in Germany.

Conclusion

German electronic music has left an indelible mark on the global music landscape. Through their innovative sound, pioneering spirit, and commitment to pushing boundaries, German artists have shaped electronic music and influenced generations of producers and musicians. The impact of German electronic music can be felt in different genres, production techniques, and the overall culture surrounding electronic music. As the German electronic music scene continues to evolve, it will undoubtedly inspire future artists and shape the future of electronic music.

The Beginnings of Virtual Riot

The Name Game: How Virtual Riot Came to Be

In the world of music, a name can be a powerful tool. It is the first impression that an artist makes on their listeners, and it can create intrigue, curiosity, and even a sense of identity. For Virtual Riot, the German music producer and DJ, choosing a name was not a decision to be taken lightly. It was a process that involved self-reflection, experimentation, and a touch of serendipity.

Virtual Riot, born Christian Valentin Brunn, had a passion for music from a young age. Growing up in Germany, he was surrounded by the rich electronic music scene that the country is known for. Influenced by artists like Skrillex, Noisia, and Porter Robinson, Virtual Riot found himself drawn to the sound of bass music and dubstep.

As a budding musician, Virtual Riot experimented with different musical styles and genres, seeking to find his own unique sound. He spent countless hours locked away in his bedroom studio, honing his skills and exploring the possibilities of electronic music production. It was during one of these late-night sessions that the idea for his stage name came to him.

Virtual Riot had always been fascinated by the concept of virtual reality – the idea of creating immersive digital experiences that transport people to another world. He saw parallels between the virtual landscapes created in virtual reality and the sonic landscapes he was crafting in his music. Both aimed to take the listener on a journey, blurring the lines between reality and imagination.

One night, as he was playing around with different words and ideas, Virtual Riot stumbled upon the word "riot." The word captured the energy and intensity of his music, reflecting the chaotic and exhilarating experience that his listeners would have during his performances. It was the perfect complement to the virtual aspect of his name, creating a name that was both memorable and evocative.

With the name Virtual Riot chosen, the artist began to build his brand around it. He designed a logo that combined futuristic elements with a sense of rebellion, capturing the essence of his music. He started performing at local venues and clubs, showcasing his unique sound and captivating audiences with his high-energy performances.

Soon, Virtual Riot's name started to gain recognition in the EDM scene. His online presence grew as he shared his music on platforms like SoundCloud and YouTube, connecting with fans from around the world. Collaborations with other artists further solidified his place in the industry, establishing him as a name to watch.

Today, Virtual Riot continues to push the boundaries of electronic music, exploring new genres and styles while staying true to his signature sound. His name has become synonymous with innovation and artistic prowess, inspiring a new generation of musicians to embrace their creativity and think outside the box.

The story behind Virtual Riot's name serves as a reminder that the path to success is often filled with unexpected twists and turns. It is a testament to the power of taking risks and embracing one's unique identity. And it is a testament to the fact that sometimes, the best things in life come from a combination of thoughtful deliberation and a touch of spontaneity.

So, the next time you hear the name Virtual Riot, remember the name game that led to its creation. Remember the artist who dared to imagine a world where music and technology intersected in the most electrifying way. And remember that sometimes, a name can be the starting point of something truly extraordinary.

Finding His Sound and Style

Virtual Riot's journey towards finding his distinctive sound and style was a process filled with experimentation, exploration, and self-discovery. As an artist hailing from Germany, he was influenced by the rich electronic music scene of his homeland, but he also looked beyond boundaries to create something unique.

At the beginning of his musical career, Virtual Riot delved into various genres and styles, trying to find his own voice in the vast sea of electronic music. He drew inspiration from his favorite artists, from classical composers to cutting-edge electronic producers, and everything in between. This melting pot of influences helped shape Virtual Riot's initial sound, which encompassed elements of dubstep, drum and bass, and electronica.

However, Virtual Riot's urge to stand out from the crowd pushed him to explore beyond the familiar. He began experimenting with unconventional sounds, blending disparate genres and pushing the boundaries of musical norms. This relentless pursuit of innovation allowed him to carve a niche for himself in the electronic music scene.

One of the key factors in Virtual Riot's evolution as an artist was his willingness to collaborate with other musicians. Recognizing the value of learning from different perspectives, he actively sought out collaborations that would challenge him and expose him to new musical ideas. These collaborations not only broadened his creative horizons but also helped shape his sound and style.

Virtual Riot's approach to collaboration was deeply rooted in open-mindedness and mutual respect. He believed that each artist brought something unique to the table, and through the exchange of ideas and experimentation, they could create something truly extraordinary. This collaborative mindset allowed Virtual Riot to fuse his own musical identity with the styles and influences of others, resulting in a sound that defied categorization.

In addition to collaborations, Virtual Riot's relentless pursuit of perfection led him to constantly refine and redefine his sound. He experimented with different production techniques, delving into the intricacies of sound design and mixing, to create a sonic experience that was both captivating and immersive. This attention to detail and commitment to craftsmanship became the hallmark of Virtual Riot's production style.

Virtual Riot also drew inspiration from unconventional sources outside the realm of music. He found beauty and inspiration in visual arts, literature, and even everyday life experiences. This multidisciplinary approach allowed him to infuse his music with a distinct narrative and emotional depth. By seeking inspiration beyond the confines of his own genre, Virtual Riot was able to create music that resonated with listeners on a profound level.

The culmination of Virtual Riot's exploration and experimentation was the emergence of his signature sound and style. It was a marriage of heavy basslines, intricate melodies, and a seamless blend of genres, all infused with a touch of his own unique personality. Virtual Riot's sound became instantly recognizable, capturing the hearts of fans around the world and solidifying his place in the electronic music landscape.

Virtual Riot's journey towards finding his sound and style serves as a testament to the power of artistic exploration, collaboration, and authenticity. By embracing the unknown, stepping outside of his comfort zone, and drawing inspiration from various sources, he was able to create something truly groundbreaking. His story serves as an inspiration for aspiring artists, reminding them that the path to success lies in embracing one's own unique voice and relentlessly pursuing creative excellence. So, for all the emerging artists out there, find your sound, embrace your style, and let the world witness your artistic evolution.

Early Collaborations and Online Success

In the early days of his music career, Virtual Riot wasn't afraid to collaborate with other artists. He understood the power of working together and saw it as an opportunity to learn and grow as a musician. This approach not only helped him to refine his own sound but also paved the way for his success in the online world.

The Importance of Collaboration

Collaborating with other artists is an essential part of the music industry. It allows musicians to bring different perspectives and skills to the table, resulting in unique and innovative creations. For Virtual Riot, collaborations provided the chance to experiment with new ideas and styles, ultimately shaping his own artistic vision.

One of the key benefits of collaboration is the opportunity to learn from fellow musicians. By working with others, Virtual Riot gained valuable insights and techniques that he might not have discovered on his own. These experiences helped him to broaden his musical horizons and push the boundaries of his sound.

Online Success

While Virtual Riot's early collaborations were crucial to his development as an artist, it was the online world that truly catapulted him to success. With the rise of social media platforms and music-sharing websites, Virtual Riot was able to reach a global audience like never before.

Platforms like SoundCloud and YouTube became essential tools in Virtual Riot's journey. He strategically used these platforms to share his music, gain exposure, and connect with fans. By leveraging the power of the internet, he was able to showcase his talent to a massive online community, leading to a rapid increase in his fanbase.

Navigating the Online Landscape

Navigating the online landscape can be challenging, especially for an emerging artist. Virtual Riot faced his fair share of obstacles along the way, including standing out amongst the flood of content and dealing with criticism.

To overcome these hurdles, Virtual Riot focused on creating high-quality and authentic music. He understood that in a sea of online noise, originality was key. By staying true to himself and his unique artistic vision, he was able to carve out a niche for himself in the EDM community.

Additionally, Virtual Riot engaged with his growing fanbase through social media, live streams, and Q&A sessions. This personal connection allowed him to build a loyal community of supporters who not only enjoyed his music but also felt a genuine connection to him as an artist.

Evolving Sound and Collaborations

As Virtual Riot gained more recognition in the online world, his collaborations with other artists became more prominent. He started working with established names in the EDM scene, such as Skrillex and Zedd, further solidifying his position as a rising star.

These collaborations not only exposed Virtual Riot to larger audiences but also allowed him to experiment with different genres and styles. He embraced the opportunity to blend his own unique sound with the diverse artistic perspectives of his collaborators, resulting in groundbreaking and unconventional music.

Online Success as a Launchpad

The online success Virtual Riot achieved served as a launchpad for his career. It allowed him to gain the attention of record labels, promoters, and festival organizers. As a result, he began receiving invitations to perform at major EDM events, further expanding his reach and influence.

Virtual Riot's ability to navigate the online landscape and build a strong presence also opened doors for him in the music industry. He was approached by various record labels and secured deals that helped him to further develop his sound and advance his career.

Learning from Online Success

Virtual Riot's early collaborations and online success taught him valuable lessons about the power of collaboration and the potential of the internet. These experiences shaped his artistic journey and continue to influence his approach to music-making.

He recognized the importance of staying true to his own unique style while remaining open to collaboration and exploration. Virtual Riot's success story serves as an inspiration for aspiring musicians who dream of making their mark in the online world. By embracing collaboration and leveraging the power of the internet, artists can achieve success and connect with music lovers on a global scale.

Key Takeaways

- Collaborating with other artists provides opportunities for growth and learning, allowing musicians to bring different perspectives and skills to the table.

- The online world can serve as a launching pad for success, allowing artists to reach a global audience and gain exposure like never before.

+ Navigating the online landscape requires originality, authenticity, and personal engagement with fans to stand out and build a loyal community.

+ Collaborations with established artists can lead to new sonic experiments and breakthroughs in music creation.

+ Online success can open doors in the music industry, leading to opportunities for live performances, record deals, and further growth as an artist.

Gaining Recognition in the EDM Scene

Virtual Riot's journey in the world of electronic dance music (EDM) was not an easy one. It took determination, talent, and a lot of hard work to gain recognition in a scene that was already bursting with established artists and rising stars. In this section, we explore the challenges Virtual Riot faced and how he managed to carve out his own path in the EDM scene.

Standing Out in a Crowded Field

When Virtual Riot first entered the EDM scene, he quickly realized that he needed to find ways to stand out from the crowd. With so many different genres and styles of music being produced, it was essential for him to find his unique sound and style that would separate him from the competition.

One of the key strategies Virtual Riot employed was experimentation. He constantly explored new sounds and genres, pushing the boundaries of electronic music. This allowed him to create a distinct and recognizable sound that set him apart from other artists. By combining elements from different genres, he was able to produce tracks that were fresh, innovative, and highly engaging.

> **Problem**
>
> Experimentation and pushing boundaries are essential for artists to stand out in the music industry. How can Virtual Riot continue to innovate and explore new sounds while maintaining his signature style? Provide one example of a genre or style he could incorporate into his music to keep pushing the boundaries.

Building an Online Presence

In the digital age, having a strong online presence is crucial for artists to gain recognition. Virtual Riot understood this and dedicated time and effort to build his online presence. He leveraged social media platforms, such as Twitter and Instagram, to connect with fans and share his music.

Engaging with fans was an important aspect of Virtual Riot's online strategy. He regularly interacted with fans through Q&A sessions, live streams, and fan remix contests. This not only helped him to connect with his audience but also allowed him to showcase his personality and build a loyal fanbase.

> **Problem**
>
> Building a strong online presence requires consistent engagement with fans. What are some creative ways Virtual Riot could use social media to interact with his fans and foster a strong fan community? Provide one example of a unique social media campaign idea.

Collaborations and Networking

Collaborations played a significant role in Virtual Riot's journey to gaining recognition in the EDM scene. He understood the value of working with other artists who shared his vision and brought complementary skills to the table. By collaborating with established and up-and-coming artists, he was able to gain exposure to new audiences and tap into their networks.

Virtual Riot's collaborations were not limited to just music production. He also worked with visual artists, designers, and videographers, creating stunning visuals and music videos that complemented his tracks. This allowed him to enhance the overall experience for his audience and create a cohesive brand.

> **Problem**
>
> Collaborations can be a powerful tool for artists to expand their reach. Identify one artist, either within or outside the EDM scene, whom Virtual Riot could collaborate with to further elevate his music and brand. Explain why this collaboration would be beneficial for both artists involved.

Live Performances and the Power of Stage Presence

Gaining recognition in the EDM scene goes beyond producing great music; it also involves delivering unforgettable live performances. Virtual Riot understood the importance of stage presence and putting on a show that left a lasting impression on the audience.

He invested significant effort into stage design and incorporating visuals into his performances. By creating immersive experiences for the audience, he captivated their attention and elevated the overall impact of his music. Virtual Riot also mastered the art of reading the crowd, adapting his sets to create an energetic and engaging atmosphere.

> **Problem**
>
> Mastering the art of live performances is crucial for an artist's success. Suggest one unconventional element or technology that Virtual Riot could incorporate into his live shows to further enhance his stage presence and create a unique experience for the audience.

In conclusion, gaining recognition in the EDM scene required Virtual Riot to stand out from the crowd, build an online presence, collaborate with other artists, and deliver exceptional live performances. By taking on these challenges head-on and constantly striving for innovation, Virtual Riot managed to establish himself as a respected and influential artist in the EDM world. As we continue on this journey through his life and music, we will discover how Virtual Riot's rise in popularity led him to explore new horizons and make a lasting impact on the music industry.

The First EP: Exploring New Horizons

The journey of Virtual Riot truly took off with the release of his first EP, aptly titled "Exploring New Horizons". This EP marked a turning point in his career, propelling him into the spotlight and solidifying his unique sound and style. In this section, we will delve into the creation, reception, and impact of this groundbreaking EP.

The Creative Process

Creating the "Exploring New Horizons" EP was a labor of love for Virtual Riot. He dedicated countless hours to experimenting with different sounds, melodies, and production techniques. As a self-taught musician, he relied heavily on his instinct and creativity to bring his ideas to life.

One of the defining aspects of Virtual Riot's creative process is his willingness to step outside the boundaries of traditional EDM. He sought inspiration from a wide range of musical genres, incorporating elements of rock, hip-hop, and even classical music into his tracks. This fearless approach allowed him to create a unique and distinct sound that stood out in the EDM landscape.

In addition to his musical influences, Virtual Riot also drew inspiration from his personal experiences and emotions. Each track on the EP tells a story, reflecting his journey as an artist and his constant pursuit of new horizons. This personal touch added depth and authenticity to the music, resonating with listeners on a deeper level.

Tracklist and Themes

The "Exploring New Horizons" EP consisted of six tracks, each offering a glimpse into the sonic world Virtual Riot was crafting. Let's take a closer look at some of the standout tracks and the themes they explored:

1. "Euphoria": This opening track set the tone for the entire EP, immersing listeners in a wave of euphoric energy. With its uplifting melodies and pulsating beats, the track served as a statement of Virtual Riot's determination to push the boundaries of EDM.

2. "Lost in Reality": This track delved into the theme of escapism, capturing the feeling of being lost in a dream-like world. Through its ethereal soundscape and intricate production, Virtual Riot created a sonic journey that transported listeners to another realm.

3. "Breaking Barriers": As the title suggests, this track was a testament to Virtual Riot's desire to break free from the constraints of genre expectations. Blending elements of dubstep, trap, and future bass, he challenged the status quo and redefined what EDM could be.

4. "Rhythm of the Night": This high-energy track paid homage to Virtual Riot's love for the 90s dance music scene. With its catchy hooks and infectious grooves, it became an instant crowd-pleaser and solidified his reputation as a master of blending nostalgia with modern sounds.

Each track on the EP showcased Virtual Riot's versatility as a producer, with no two songs sounding alike. This diversity kept listeners engaged and eager to see what he would explore next.

Reception and Impact

Upon its release, "Exploring New Horizons" received widespread acclaim from fans and critics alike. It quickly gained traction in the EDM community, propelling Virtual Riot into the spotlight as an artist to watch. The EP also garnered attention from industry heavyweights, leading to collaborations and opportunities that further elevated his career.

One of the reasons for the EP's success was its ability to resonate with a wide range of listeners. The unique blend of genres and emotional depth touched the hearts of fans, forging a strong connection between Virtual Riot and his audience. This connection translated into a dedicated fanbase that supported him throughout his journey.

The impact of "Exploring New Horizons" extended beyond Virtual Riot's individual success. It inspired a new wave of producers to experiment with different sounds and genres, encouraging them to push the boundaries of EDM and explore uncharted territories. The EP served as a catalyst for innovation in the electronic music scene, leaving a lasting imprint on the industry.

Lessons and Inspirations

The creation and success of the "Exploring New Horizons" EP taught Virtual Riot valuable lessons that shaped his career. From this experience, he realized the importance of staying true to his artistic vision, even when faced with the pressure to conform to industry norms. He learned that taking risks and embracing his unique style could lead to immense growth and recognition.

Furthermore, the EP served as a constant reminder to Virtual Riot of the power of music to evoke emotions and create connections. It reinforced his belief in the universal language of music and motivated him to continue pushing boundaries and exploring new sonic landscapes.

Conclusion

The release of "Exploring New Horizons" was a defining moment in Virtual Riot's career. With its diverse sound, personal touch, and boundary-pushing approach, the EP captured the hearts of listeners and cemented his place in the EDM landscape. It served as a launchpad for his future successes, setting the stage for his continued evolution as an artist. As Virtual Riot prepared to embark on his next musical exploration, he carried the lessons and inspirations from this EP with him, ensuring that his future endeavors would be just as groundbreaking.

Virtual Riot's Influences from Other Music Genres

Virtual Riot, known for his groundbreaking electronic music, draws inspiration from a wide range of music genres. His unique sound and style are a result of his exploration and experimentation with different musical influences. In this section, we will delve into the genres that have had a significant impact on Virtual Riot's music.

Hip-Hop: The Beat that Moves Virtual Riot

One of the genres that has greatly influenced Virtual Riot's music is hip-hop. Virtual Riot is fascinated with the rhythmic elements and catchy beats found in hip-hop tracks. He recognizes the importance of a strong groove in captivating listeners and keeping them engaged.

To incorporate hip-hop elements into his music, Virtual Riot often integrates intricate drum patterns and clever sampling techniques. He manipulates drum sounds to create punchy and infectious beats, giving his tracks a distinct hip-hop feel. This fusion of electronic and hip-hop elements adds depth and complexity to his music, making it stand out in the electronic music scene.

Metal: The Raw Power in Virtual Riot's Sound

Another genre that has left a lasting impression on Virtual Riot is metal. He is drawn to the intense energy and raw power that metal music embodies. Virtual Riot finds inspiration in the heavy guitar riffs, aggressive vocals, and complex song structures commonly found in metal.

Incorporating metal influences into his tracks, Virtual Riot infuses his music with heavier and grittier sounds. He introduces distorted basslines and incorporates guitar-like melodies, adding a rebellious edge to his electronic compositions. This unique combination of metal and electronic elements gives Virtual Riot's music a distinct and powerful sound that resonates with his audience.

Classical Music: The Art of Storytelling

Classical music has had a profound impact on Virtual Riot's music-making process. He admires the way classical composers tell stories and evoke emotions through their compositions. Virtual Riot seeks to apply the same level of artistry and emotion to his own electronic tracks.

Drawing from classical music, Virtual Riot incorporates beautiful melodies, intricate harmonies, and dynamic shifts into his compositions. He strives to create a sense of narrative and progression in his music, taking listeners on a journey through different moods and emotions. By combining classical elements with electronic production techniques, Virtual Riot creates a unique blend that transcends genres and captivates his audience.

Dubstep: A Genre Revolutionized

Dubstep, a genre known for its heavy basslines and wobbling synths, has been a significant influence on Virtual Riot's music. He was captivated by the groundbreaking sounds and production techniques that emerged from the dubstep scene.

Virtual Riot draws inspiration from the unique sound design and powerful drops that define dubstep. He harnesses the aggressive energy and innovative soundscapes of the genre, infusing them into his own tracks. Virtual Riot pushes the boundaries of dubstep, combining it with other genres and incorporating his own distinctive style to create a fresh and exciting sonic experience.

Jazz: The Spirit of Improvisation

Jazz music has also played a role in shaping Virtual Riot's music. He appreciates the spirit of improvisation and the freedom that jazz musicians embrace in their performances. Virtual Riot seeks to capture that same sense of spontaneity and creativity in his own electronic compositions.

Incorporating jazz influences, Virtual Riot experiments with unconventional chord progressions, unexpected melodies, and unique rhythms. He injects elements of improvisation into his tracks, allowing room for creativity and organic expression. This fusion of jazz and electronic music adds a touch of sophistication and unpredictability to Virtual Riot's sound.

Unconventional Genres: Breaking Barriers

Aside from mainstream genres, Virtual Riot is not afraid to explore unconventional and niche genres. He believes that innovation lies in breaking barriers and thinking outside the box. By delving into diverse genres like funk, reggae, and even video game soundtracks, Virtual Riot takes inspiration from unique sonic palettes and musical concepts.

Virtual Riot incorporates elements from these unconventional genres into his tracks, injecting his signature style and giving his music a distinctive edge. By pushing the boundaries of genre classification, he continues to challenge and surprise his audience, creating music that defies expectations.

Expanding Musical Horizons

Virtual Riot's influences from other music genres have allowed him to create a unique sound that transcends traditional boundaries. By incorporating elements from hip-hop, metal, classical music, dubstep, jazz, and exploring unconventional genres, Virtual Riot has developed a style that is rich, complex, and constantly evolving.

His ability to draw inspiration from various genres demonstrates his open-mindedness and willingness to explore new sonic territories. Virtual Riot's music serves as a testament to the power of blending diverse influences and pushing the boundaries of electronic music.

As aspiring musicians and producers, we can learn from Virtual Riot's approach and embrace the diversity of musical genres. By incorporating different influences into our own compositions, we can develop our unique style and contribute to the evolution of music. Let Virtual Riot's eclectic influences inspire you to embrace experimentation, break genre conventions, and create music that is a true reflection of your artistic vision.

The Evolution of Virtual Riot's Signature Sound

The evolution of Virtual Riot's signature sound is a journey rooted in passion, experimentation, and a relentless pursuit of sonic innovation. From his humble beginnings in a small town in Germany to becoming a prominent name in the EDM scene, Virtual Riot has continually pushed the boundaries of electronic music, carving out a unique sonic landscape that sets him apart.

Virtual Riot's sound can be described as a fusion of various electronic music genres, combining elements of dubstep, trap, drum and bass, and future bass. What sets his sound apart is the meticulous attention to detail, complex sound design, and a keen sense of melody. Each track is a sonic adventure, filled with intricate layers, pulsating basslines, and euphoric melodies that captivate the listener's imagination.

The journey towards finding his signature sound started at a young age. Virtual Riot discovered his love for music early on, experimenting with various instruments and recording techniques. It was during these formative years that he began to understand the power of sound and its ability to evoke emotions. This understanding fueled his desire to create music that could resonate with listeners on a profound level.

As Virtual Riot delved deeper into his musical journey, he found inspiration in a wide array of genres and artists. From classical composers like Beethoven to electronic music pioneers like Skrillex, he absorbed the essence of each, forging a unique sonic identity that is unmistakably his own. This eclectic mix of influences laid the foundation for his diverse and dynamic sound.

The evolution of Virtual Riot's signature sound can be attributed to his relentless experimentation and willingness to push the boundaries of what is possible within the EDM genre. He constantly challenges himself to explore new sonic territories, seeking inspiration from unexpected sources and implementing unconventional techniques.

One of the defining aspects of Virtual Riot's sound is his exceptional sound design skills. He meticulously crafts each sound, painstakingly shaping and layering them to create a rich and immersive sonic experience. His keen attention to detail is evident in the intricate textures and complex arrangements that define his tracks. Whether it's the aggressive growls of a bassline or the ethereal beauty of a melodic synth, each sound element has a purpose and contributes to the overall sonic narrative.

Virtual Riot's signature sound is also characterized by his ability to seamlessly blend different genres, creating a sonic amalgamation that defies categorization. He effortlessly intertwines the aggressive energy of dubstep with the infectious hooks of pop music, creating a hybrid sound that appeals to a wide range of listeners. This ability to combine disparate elements is a testament to Virtual Riot's versatility as a producer and his commitment to pushing the boundaries of genre conventions.

In addition to his musical prowess, Virtual Riot's signature sound is also shaped by his approach to storytelling through music. Each track is a narrative journey, taking the listener on an emotional rollercoaster. From euphoric highs to introspective intros, his music weaves a captivating tale that resonates with audiences worldwide. It is this ability to evoke emotions and create a connection with the listener that sets Virtual Riot's sound apart.

The evolution of Virtual Riot's signature sound is an ongoing process, as he continues to evolve as an artist and explore new creative horizons. His commitment to pushing the boundaries of electronic music and his relentless pursuit of sonic innovation ensure that his sound will continue to captivate and inspire listeners for years to come.

The Virtual Riot Sound: Elements and Techniques

To truly understand the evolution of Virtual Riot's signature sound, it's essential to explore the key elements and techniques that define his music. From complex sound design to innovative production techniques, his approach to music-making is a masterclass in sonic creativity.

One of the defining elements of Virtual Riot's sound is his expert use of sound design. He approaches every sound with meticulous attention to detail, carefully crafting and sculpting each element to fit within the sonic landscape of the track. Whether it's a high-energy bassline or a lush and atmospheric pad, each sound is carefully tailored to create a specific emotional impact.

Virtual Riot draws on a wide range of synthesis techniques to achieve his distinct sound. From subtractive synthesis to frequency modulation (FM) synthesis, he employs various methods to create unique and experimental soundscapes. His sound design process often involves layering multiple sounds together, combining different waveforms and textures to create rich and dynamic timbres.

In addition to sound design, Virtual Riot's use of effects plays a crucial role in shaping his signature sound. He employs a wide range of effects, including distortion, reverb, delay, and modulation, to add depth and character to his tracks. These effects are used not only to enhance individual sounds but also to shape the overall sonic landscape, creating a sense of space and movement within the music.

Virtual Riot also embraces unconventional production techniques to achieve his desired sound. He is known for his intricate and meticulous arrangement, meticulously layering multiple elements together to create a dense and immersive sonic experience. This attention to detail extends to his use of automation, where he carefully modulates various parameters over time to add movement and complexity to his tracks.

Another key aspect of Virtual Riot's signature sound is his innovative approach to rhythm and percussion. He experiments with unconventional rhythms, blending elements from different genres to create a unique and infectious groove. His percussion tracks are intricately programmed and heavily processed, adding depth and energy to his music.

Virtual Riot's music is also characterized by his expert use of melodic elements. Whether it's a catchy vocal hook, a euphoric synth lead, or a haunting piano melody, his melodies are carefully crafted to evoke emotion and captivate the listener. He uses various compositional techniques to create memorable and impactful melodies, incorporating elements from classical music, pop, and beyond.

Beyond the technical aspects of his music, Virtual Riot's signature sound is also shaped by his overarching artistic vision. He approaches each track with a clear concept and narrative in mind, seeking to evoke specific emotions and tell a story through his music. This attention to detail and artistic intentionality give his tracks a depth and resonance that go beyond the surface-level appeal.

In conclusion, the evolution of Virtual Riot's signature sound is a testament to his unwavering commitment to innovation and artistic expression. His mastery of sound design, utilization of effects and production techniques, as well as his unique approach to rhythm and melody, have solidified his position as one of the most distinguished artists in the electronic music scene. As he continues to push boundaries and explore new sonic territories, Virtual Riot's signature sound will undoubtedly leave an indelible mark on the future of electronic music.

Challenges and Breakthroughs in the Early Years

In the early years of Virtual Riot's career, there were numerous challenges and breakthroughs that shaped his journey as a musician. These challenges tested his resilience and determination while providing opportunities for growth and creativity. Let's delve into some of the key challenges and the breakthroughs that marked this pivotal period in Virtual Riot's life.

Navigating an Ever-Changing Music Landscape

One of the significant challenges Virtual Riot encountered in the early years was navigating the rapidly evolving music landscape. As a young artist, he faced the task of finding his own unique sound while keeping up with changing trends and market demands. This required constant experimentation, staying open to new ideas, and pushing the boundaries of traditional genre conventions.

To overcome this challenge, Virtual Riot embraced a fearless attitude towards music production. He continuously explored different genres, blending elements from various styles, and fusing unconventional sounds to create his signature sound. By embracing experimentation and staying true to his creativity, he was able to overcome the challenge of finding his place in the ever-changing music landscape.

Establishing a Strong Presence in a Saturated Market

Another significant challenge for Virtual Riot in the early years was establishing a strong presence in a highly saturated music market. With numerous emerging artists and established musicians vying for attention, it was crucial for Virtual Riot to stand out and capture the audience's interest.

To breakthrough in this competitive landscape, Virtual Riot worked relentlessly to refine his craft and develop a unique musical identity. He dedicated countless hours to honing his production skills, experimenting with different sounds, and perfecting his live performances. By consistently delivering high-quality music and engaging performances, Virtual Riot was able to distinguish himself from his peers and gain recognition among a discerning audience.

Overcoming Financial Limitations

Like many aspiring musicians, Virtual Riot faced financial limitations that posed a significant challenge in the early years. Producing music, promoting his work, and pursuing opportunities for growth required financial resources that he did not always have readily available.

To overcome this challenge, Virtual Riot took a DIY approach to his career. He leveraged online platforms and social media to promote his music, connect with fans, and secure performance opportunities. Through strategic self-promotion and building a dedicated fanbase, Virtual Riot was able to generate income and reinvest it into his music career. This resourcefulness and determination allowed him to overcome financial limitations and continue his journey towards success.

Nurturing Relationships and Collaborations

Building relationships and collaborations in the music industry can be a challenging task. Virtual Riot faced the obstacle of establishing connections and finding artists who shared his vision and values. Collaborations not only provide opportunities for growth and learning but also broaden an artist's reach and audience.

To overcome this challenge, Virtual Riot actively sought out like-minded artists and producers who complemented his musical style. By fostering genuine connections and working closely with these collaborators, he was able to create impactful music and expand his creative horizons. Virtual Riot's collaborations proved to be instrumental in his breakthrough, allowing him to tap into new ideas, styles, and perspectives.

Pushing Through Self-Doubt and Creative Blocks

Evolving as an artist often comes with moments of self-doubt and creative blocks. Virtual Riot was no exception as he faced periods of uncertainty and struggled to push forward in his musical journey.

To overcome these challenges, Virtual Riot embraced resilience and developed strategies to overcome creative blocks. He prioritized self-care, allowing himself time to rest and recharge when faced with creative exhaustion. Additionally, he sought inspiration from various sources outside of music, such as visual arts and literature, to ignite new ideas and break through creative barriers.

Virtual Riot's breakthrough came when he realized that creativity is a journey, and setbacks are a natural part of the process. By embracing his own unique path and persevering through self-doubt, Virtual Riot was able to unleash his full creative potential.

Breakthrough: Gaining Recognition in the EDM Scene

Despite the challenges he faced early on, Virtual Riot experienced a breakthrough in gaining recognition in the EDM scene. Through his dedication, perseverance, and unique musical approach, he captured the attention of industry influencers and a growing fanbase.

Virtual Riot's breakthrough came when his music resonated with the audience on a deeper level. His genre-blurring sound and emotionally charged tracks struck a chord with listeners, setting him apart from other artists in the scene. This breakthrough not only solidified his place in the music industry but also fueled his drive for further success and artistic exploration.

In conclusion, the early years of Virtual Riot's career were packed with challenges and breakthroughs that shaped his journey as a musician. Navigating an ever-changing music landscape, establishing a strong presence in a saturated market, overcoming financial limitations, nurturing relationships and collaborations, and pushing through self-doubt were key challenges that he successfully conquered. Through resilience, experimentation, resourcefulness, and perseverance, Virtual Riot emerged as a force to be reckoned with in the EDM scene, paving the way for further growth and success.

Virtual Riot's Collaborations with German Artists

Virtual Riot is no stranger to collaboration, and his partnerships with German artists have played a significant role in shaping his musical journey. Through his unique style and innovative approach to music production, Virtual Riot has collaborated with some of the most talented and influential artists in Germany. In this section, we will explore Virtual Riot's collaborations with German artists, the creative process behind these partnerships, and the impact they have had on his music.

Finding the Right Artists to Collaborate With

Collaborations are an essential part of Virtual Riot's creative process. He believes in the power of combining different musical styles and ideas to create something truly unique and compelling. When it comes to collaborating with German artists, Virtual Riot looks for artists who share a similar vision and passion for pushing boundaries in electronic music.

Virtual Riot is known for his versatile production style, seamlessly blending elements from genres such as dubstep, drum and bass, and future bass. When searching for German collaborators, he seeks artists who can complement his sound while bringing their own unique perspective to the table.

Balancing Creative Differences and Personalities

Collaborations can be a delicate balancing act, especially when it comes to creative differences and personalities. Virtual Riot believes that effective collaboration requires open communication, mutual respect, and a willingness to compromise. When working with German artists, Virtual Riot embraces the diversity of ideas and perspectives they bring to the table.

There are times when creative differences arise, but Virtual Riot sees these moments as learning opportunities. He believes that the best collaborations come from a healthy exchange of ideas and a willingness to find common ground. By embracing the unique qualities of his German collaborators, Virtual Riot creates a space where everyone's contributions are valued.

Learning from Each Other: The Collaborative Process

The collaborative process is a chance for artists to learn from each other and expand their musical horizons. Virtual Riot takes this opportunity to immerse himself in the world of his German collaborators, learning about their influences, techniques, and musical backgrounds.

By understanding each artist's strengths and preferences, Virtual Riot can seamlessly integrate his own style with theirs. This process involves experimentation, exploration, and a willingness to step outside of his comfort zone. Through this exchange of ideas, Virtual Riot and his German collaborators push each other to new creative heights.

The Highs and Lows of Collaborative Projects

Collaborative projects can be an exhilarating rollercoaster ride, filled with highs and lows. Virtual Riot acknowledges that not every collaboration will be a smooth journey from start to finish. Challenges and disagreements can arise, but he views them as necessary steps in the creative process.

Virtual Riot believes that the most successful collaborations are those that overcome obstacles and find innovative solutions together. These challenges, although demanding, can lead to breakthrough moments and result in something truly extraordinary.

Virtual Riot's Favorite Collaborations

Throughout his career, Virtual Riot has had the opportunity to collaborate with several talented German artists. One of his favorite collaborations was with German DJ and producer, Zedd. Together, they created a track that combined their respective styles and pushed the boundaries of electronic music.

Another notable collaboration was with German singer and songwriter, Kim Petras. Their project resulted in a unique blend of Virtual Riot's hard-hitting production and Kim's distinctive vocal style, creating a powerful and captivating sound.

Virtual Riot's Collaborative Wishlist

Virtual Riot has an ever-growing list of artists he dreams of collaborating with in the future. One German artist he hopes to work with is German electronic music duo, Digitalism. Their fusion of electronic and rock influences intrigues Virtual Riot, and he envisions an exciting collaboration that combines their unique styles.

Additionally, Virtual Riot expresses a desire to collaborate with German rapper Cro. He believes that the combination of Cro's melodic rap and his own production would create a fresh and dynamic sound, appealing to a wide audience.

Virtual Riot's Perspective on Collaboration in the Music Industry

Virtual Riot views collaboration as an opportunity for growth and exploration. He believes that working with other artists not only enhances his own creativity but also contributes to the overall advancement of the music industry.

According to Virtual Riot, collaboration is an essential element of keeping the music scene vibrant and exciting. It allows artists to pool their talents, push boundaries, and create something that resonates with listeners on a deeper level. In his view, collaboration is not about competition but rather a celebration of the diverse talents that exist within the German music industry.

Virtual Riot's Advice for Successful Collaborations

Based on his experience, Virtual Riot offers advice for artists seeking successful collaborations. He emphasizes the importance of clear communication, respect for each other's ideas, and a shared vision.

Virtual Riot also encourages artists to be open-minded and receptive to different perspectives. He believes that the most groundbreaking collaborations often emerge from unexpected places, and it's crucial to stay open to new ideas and approaches.

Virtual Riot's Collaborations Outside of the EDM Scene

While Virtual Riot is primarily known for his work in the EDM scene, he is not limited to collaborating within this genre. He actively seeks collaborations outside of EDM to explore new musical territories and expand his artistic horizons.

For instance, Virtual Riot has collaborated with German classical pianist, Alice Sara Ott, on a project that blends electronic production with classical piano melodies. This unique fusion showcases Virtual Riot's versatility and willingness to experiment with different genres.

Virtual Riot's Impact on Collaborative Music Production

Virtual Riot's collaborations with German artists have had a significant impact on the music industry. Not only have these partnerships produced innovative and genre-defying tracks, but they have also inspired a new generation of musicians to think outside the box.

Virtual Riot's approach to collaboration, characterized by open-mindedness and a willingness to merge diverse styles, has become a blueprint for successful collaborations in the music industry. His ability to seamlessly integrate different artistic perspectives has paved the way for other artists to push boundaries and create groundbreaking music.

In conclusion, Virtual Riot's collaborations with German artists have been instrumental in shaping his musical journey. Through open communication, creative exploration, and a commitment to pushing boundaries, Virtual Riot has created a space where unique ideas can flourish. His collaborations transcend genres, resulting in innovative and captivating tracks that inspire and influence the music industry as a whole. Whether it's teaming up with German DJs, producers, or even classical musicians, Virtual Riot's collaborations continue to redefine the possibilities of electronic music.

Navigating the German Music Industry

The German music industry is a unique and dynamic landscape that has produced some of the most influential and successful artists in the world. For Virtual Riot, navigating this industry has been both challenging and rewarding, filled with opportunities and obstacles. In this section, we will explore the intricacies of the German music industry and how Virtual Riot has carved his path within it.

Understanding the German Music Scene

To navigate the German music industry, it is essential to have a deep understanding of the local music scene. Germany is known for its diverse and vibrant music culture, with a rich history of classical music, opera, and traditional folk music. However, it is the electronic music scene that has gained significant prominence in recent years.

Virtual Riot recognized the importance of immersing himself in the German music scene from an early age. Growing up in Germany provided him with a unique advantage in understanding the local tastes, preferences, and trends. He delved into the underground music culture and attended local shows to get a firsthand experience of the German music scene.

Building Connections and Collaborations

Navigating the German music industry often requires building strong connections and collaborations with both artists and industry professionals. Virtual Riot strategically sought out opportunities to collaborate with German artists to not only expand his network but also gain credibility within the industry.

Collaborations allowed Virtual Riot to tap into the creative energy and unique perspectives of his peers, creating a synergy that propelled his music career forward. By working with established German artists, he was able to bridge the gap between the underground music scene and the mainstream industry.

Independence vs. Record Labels

One of the significant decisions that artists face in the music industry is whether to pursue their career independently or sign with a record label. Virtual Riot chose to maintain his independence initially, releasing his music through online platforms and establishing a strong online presence.

However, as his popularity grew, Virtual Riot recognized the potential benefits of signing with a record label. He carefully evaluated various offers from both German and international labels, weighing the advantages of increased exposure, promotion, and financial support against the potential loss of artistic control.

Eventually, Virtual Riot decided to sign with a German record label that aligned with his artistic vision and allowed him to maintain a significant degree of creative freedom. This decision proved crucial in securing his place within the German music industry while retaining his unique sound and style.

Industry Challenges and Overcoming Barriers

Like any industry, the German music industry comes with its fair share of challenges. For Virtual Riot, one of the primary hurdles was overcoming language barriers. As an English-speaking artist in a predominantly German-speaking industry, Virtual Riot had to navigate the complexities of communication and ensure that his music resonated with a broader audience.

He actively sought out opportunities to collaborate with German artists, which not only helped him connect with the local audience but also allowed him to improve his fluency in the German language. Through perseverance and dedication, Virtual Riot was able to bridge the language gap and establish himself as an artist with a global appeal.

Embracing German Music Education

Germany has long been renowned for its exceptional music education system. From specialized music schools to conservatories, the country provides aspiring artists with numerous opportunities for formal training and education. Virtual Riot recognized the value of music education and embraced it as a way to refine his skills and expand his musical knowledge.

He enrolled in music classes at a young age, honing his skills in music theory, composition, and various instruments. This formal education provided him with a solid foundation and a comprehensive understanding of music, equipping him with the tools necessary to create innovative and technically proficient tracks.

Storytelling and the German Music Tradition

German culture and music have a rich tradition of storytelling. From classical music compositions to contemporary electronic tracks, German artists have excelled in weaving narratives and evoking emotions through their music. Virtual Riot drew inspiration from this storytelling tradition, incorporating elements of narrative structure and thematic exploration into his compositions.

By embracing the storytelling aspects of German music, Virtual Riot was able to create immersive and captivating tracks that resonated deeply with his audience. His ability to convey emotions and tell a story through his music set him apart in the German music industry and helped him build a dedicated fanbase.

The Future of the German Music Industry

The German music industry is constantly evolving, and Virtual Riot remains at the forefront of this transformation. As technology advances and new music genres emerge, Virtual Riot continues to push boundaries and explore new sonic territories.

Looking ahead, Virtual Riot envisions a German music industry that embraces innovation, fosters diverse talent, and maintains a strong connection with its rich musical heritage. He believes that by staying true to their unique artistic visions and embracing change, German artists can continue to make a significant impact on the global music stage.

Industry Insights: Overcoming Challenges

Navigating the German music industry can be a daunting task for aspiring artists. However, Virtual Riot's journey offers valuable insights into overcoming challenges and achieving success:

+ Embrace the local music scene: Immerse yourself in the local music culture to gain a deep understanding of the market and its trends.

+ Build strong connections: Collaborate with artists and industry professionals to expand your network and gain credibility within the industry.

+ Consider independence vs. record labels: Evaluate the benefits and drawbacks of signing with a record label, considering factors such as artistic control and financial support.

+ Overcome language barriers: If language poses a challenge, actively work on improving your fluency and seek out opportunities to collaborate with artists who can bridge the communication gap.

+ Embrace music education: Music education can provide a solid foundation and enhance your technical skills, enabling you to create innovative and captivating compositions.

+ Embrace storytelling: Draw inspiration from the storytelling tradition in German music to create immersive and emotionally resonant tracks.

+ Stay adaptable and innovative: Embrace technological advancements, explore new genres, and push boundaries to stay relevant and thrive in an evolving industry.

As Virtual Riot's success in the German music industry continues to grow, his journey serves as a source of inspiration for aspiring artists who seek to navigate their own paths in this dynamic and competitive landscape.

The Rise of Virtual Riot

Hitting the Festival Circuit

Hitting the festival circuit was a pivotal moment in Virtual Riot's career. It was a stepping stone that catapulted him into the realm of stardom and introduced his unique sound to a broader audience. In this section, we will explore the exhilarating journey of Virtual Riot as he navigated through the electrifying world of music festivals.

The Thrill of the Stage

Stepping onto the festival stage was a rush unlike any other for Virtual Riot. The sheer magnitude of the crowd, the pulsating energy in the air, and the anticipation of performing his music live created an electric atmosphere that fueled his passion. The festival circuit provided Virtual Riot with a platform to connect with fans on a more profound level, allowing him to showcase his talent and share his music with thousands of people.

Collaborating with Big Names

Collaborations played a significant role in Virtual Riot's ascent in the festival scene. Joining forces with big names in the industry not only gave him the opportunity to work with established artists but also exposed his music to a wider audience. These collaborations allowed Virtual Riot to push the boundaries of his sound and explore new musical territories, enhancing his reputation as an innovative and versatile artist.

Breaking Through the Mainstream

Through his electrifying performances at festivals, Virtual Riot made a profound impact on the mainstream music scene. His ability to seamlessly blend different genres and captivate audiences with his high-energy sets set him apart from the crowd. Virtual Riot's fresh approach to electronic music breathed new life into the scene, captivating fans and opening doors for other artists to experiment and break free from traditional EDM norms.

Evolution of Virtual Riot's Sound

The festival circuit played a pivotal role in shaping Virtual Riot's signature sound. Performing in front of diverse crowds allowed him to gauge their reactions and understand what resonated with them. This valuable feedback influenced his music production process and inspired him to constantly evolve and innovate. Virtual Riot's sound became synonymous with heavy basslines, intricate melodies, and infectious energy, setting him apart from his peers.

Dealing with Success and Maintaining Authenticity

As Virtual Riot's star continued to rise on the festival circuit, he faced the challenge of balancing his newfound success with staying true to his artistic vision. The pressure to conform to mainstream expectations and commercial demands threatened his authenticity. However, Virtual Riot remained steadfast, staying true to his creative instincts and refusing to compromise on his unique sound. This unwavering commitment to his artistic integrity endeared him even more to his fans, who appreciated his genuine approach to music.

Virtual Riot's Impact on the German Music Scene

Virtual Riot's success on the festival circuit had a profound impact on the German music scene. As one of the pioneers of innovative electronic music, virtually Riot served as an inspiration for a new generation of German artists. His distinct style and fearlessness in pushing boundaries opened the doors for others to explore their creativity and contribute to the evolution of the German music scene.

Virtual Riot's Influence on German Electronic Music

Virtual Riot's influence on German electronic music cannot be overstated. Through his powerful and captivating festival performances, he redefined what it meant to be an electronic artist in Germany. His unique sound and energetic stage presence inspired countless aspiring musicians to experiment with different genres and techniques. Virtual Riot's impact continues to be felt in the German electronic music landscape, leaving a lasting legacy for future generations.

Virtual Riot's Role in the Global EDM Movement

As Virtual Riot's popularity grew on the festival circuit, so did his influence in the global EDM movement. His electrifying performances and innovative sound caught the attention of music enthusiasts worldwide. Virtual Riot's ability to create a bridge between different genres and captivate audiences transcended geographical boundaries, making him a key player in the global EDM scene.

Virtual Riot's Perspective on Fame and Popularity

Throughout his journey on the festival circuit, Virtual Riot maintained a grounded perspective on fame and popularity. He embraced his success humbly, remaining grateful for the support of his fans and the opportunities that came his way. Despite the pressures of the industry, Virtual Riot's focus remained on creating music that resonated with his audience and staying true to his artistic vision.

Virtual Riot's Global Fanbase and Worldwide Tours

The festival circuit acted as a catalyst for Virtual Riot's fanbase, which expanded exponentially as he toured around the world. His ability to connect with fans through his exhilarating live performances translated into a loyal following. Virtual Riot embarked on worldwide tours, selling out venues and spreading his unique sound to fans in different corners of the globe. His global fanbase became a testament to the universal appeal of his music.

In conclusion, the festival circuit was a transformative experience for Virtual Riot. It provided him with the platform to showcase his talent, collaborate with esteemed artists, and make an indelible impact on the music scene. Through his electrifying performances, Virtual Riot broke through the barriers of the mainstream, maintained his authenticity, and left an enduring mark in the world of electronic music. The festival circuit was a crucial chapter in Virtual Riot's journey, propelling him towards a future filled with unlimited possibilities and artistic evolution.

Collaborating with Big Names in the Industry

Collaborations are an essential part of the music industry, and for Virtual Riot, working with big names in the industry has played a crucial role in his career. These collaborations have allowed Virtual Riot to expand his reach, experiment with different genres, and gain recognition from a broader audience. In this section, we will explore Virtual Riot's experiences collaborating with some of the industry's biggest names and the impact it has had on his music and career.

The Power of Collaboration

Collaborating with established artists can open doors for emerging musicians, and Virtual Riot understands the power of these partnerships. By teaming up with big names in the industry, he has had the opportunity to tap into their expertise, creativity, and fan base, resulting in unique and exciting musical projects. These collaborations have also allowed Virtual Riot to learn from others in the industry and push the boundaries of his own musical style.

Finding the Right Artists to Collaborate With

Choosing the right artists to collaborate with is essential for any successful project. For Virtual Riot, it is important to find artists who share a similar vision and complement his own musical style. He looks for artists who bring something new and different to the table, as well as those who are open to experimentation and pushing creative boundaries. Virtual Riot believes that collaborations should be a mutually beneficial partnership, where both artists are able to learn and grow from the experience.

Balancing Creative Differences and Personalities

Collaborating with big names in the industry often means working with artists who have their own unique creative vision and style. Balancing creative differences and personalities can be a challenge, but it is a critical part of the collaboration process. Virtual Riot approaches these challenges with an open and flexible mindset, embracing the opportunity to learn from others and expand his musical horizons. He believes that the best collaborations are born from a combination of diverse perspectives and talents.

The Collaborative Process

The collaborative process varies from project to project, but it generally involves a combination of brainstorming, sharing ideas, and experimentation. Virtual Riot emphasizes the importance of open and honest communication throughout the process, allowing all parties involved to have a voice and contribute to the final product. He values the input and expertise of his collaborators, while also bringing his own unique style and ideas to the table.

The Highs and Lows of Collaborative Projects

Collaborative projects can be incredibly rewarding but also come with their fair share of challenges. Virtual Riot acknowledges that not every collaboration will be smooth sailing, and there will inevitably be highs and lows along the way. However, he believes that these challenges are an integral part of the creative process and can ultimately lead to exciting and unexpected outcomes. Virtual Riot embraces both the triumphs and the struggles, recognizing that they contribute to his growth as an artist.

Virtual Riot's Favorite Collaborations

Over the course of his career, Virtual Riot has had the privilege of working with many talented artists. Some of his favorite collaborations include tracks with prominent EDM producers such as Excision, Skrillex, and Zedd. These collaborations have allowed Virtual Riot to experiment with different subgenres of electronic music, blending his own unique style with the signature sound of his collaborators. These tracks have received widespread recognition and have helped Virtual Riot establish himself as a versatile and influential artist in the industry.

Virtual Riot's Collaborative Wishlist

As an artist always looking to push the boundaries of his sound, Virtual Riot has a collaborative wishlist filled with names of artists he dreams of working with. Some of the artists on his list include Daft Punk, Flume, and Porter Robinson. Virtual Riot admires these artists for their innovative approach to music production and believes that a collaboration with any of them would result in something truly groundbreaking.

Virtual Riot's Perspective on Collaboration in the Music Industry

Virtual Riot views collaboration as a cornerstone of the music industry, emphasizing its ability to foster creativity, inspire growth, and create something truly unique. He believes that collaboration is not just limited to working with other musicians, but extends to other creative fields as well. Virtual Riot encourages artists to step outside their comfort zones, seek out new collaborations, and explore the possibilities that arise through the power of teamwork.

Virtual Riot's Advice for Successful Collaborations

Based on his own experiences, Virtual Riot has some valuable advice for artists looking to embark on collaborative projects. He emphasizes the importance of open and honest communication, finding common ground, and embracing the creative process. Virtual Riot also encourages artists to be open to new ideas and perspectives, as collaboration often leads to unexpected and exciting outcomes. Above all, he believes that successful collaborations require mutual respect, trust, and a shared passion for creating outstanding music.

Virtual Riot's Collaborations Outside of the EDM Scene

While Virtual Riot is primarily known for his contributions to the electronic music scene, he has also ventured into collaborations outside of the EDM genre. He has worked with hip-hop artists, pop singers, and even classical musicians, showcasing his versatility as a producer and embracing the opportunity to explore different musical styles. These collaborations have allowed Virtual Riot to reach new audiences and challenge himself creatively.

Virtual Riot's Impact on Collaborative Music Production

Virtual Riot's collaborations have had a significant impact on the landscape of collaborative music production. His willingness to experiment with different genres and work with artists from diverse musical backgrounds has inspired other musicians to think outside the box and push the boundaries of their own sound. Virtual Riot's unique approach to collaboration has helped redefine the collaborative process in the music industry, emphasizing the power of teamwork and mutual creativity.

In summary, collaborating with big names in the industry has played a crucial role in Virtual Riot's career. These collaborations have allowed him to expand his reach, experiment with different genres, and gain recognition from a broader audience. By embracing the challenges and opportunities that come with collaboration, Virtual Riot has been able to create unique and exciting projects that have left a lasting impact on the music industry.

Breaking Through the Mainstream

Breaking through the mainstream in the music industry can be an elusive goal for many artists, but Virtual Riot managed to accomplish just that. With his unique blend of electronic music, Virtual Riot captured the attention of both fans and industry professionals, propelling him into the spotlight. In this section, we will explore the challenges he faced, the strategies he employed, and the impact it had on his career.

The Struggle Against Conformity

When Virtual Riot first burst onto the scene, he found himself immersed in a sea of artists vying for attention. The mainstream music industry tends to favor a certain sound and style, making it difficult for artists with unique visions to break through.

Conformity often becomes the norm, as artists attempt to fit into the mold that is expected of them.

Virtual Riot, however, was determined not to succumb to the pressure to conform. He embraced his individuality and pushed the boundaries of his genre. By experimenting with different sounds, fusing different genres, and incorporating fresh elements into his music, he created a distinct and recognizable style that set him apart from the crowd.

Embracing Innovation and Unconventional Approaches

One of the keys to Virtual Riot's success in breaking through the mainstream was his willingness to embrace innovation and explore unconventional approaches. He wasn't afraid to take risks and think outside the box, constantly pushing the limits of what was considered the norm in electronic music.

For example, Virtual Riot was one of the first artists in his genre to actively incorporate live instruments into his performances. By blending electronic elements with live guitar and drums, he created a one-of-a-kind experience for his audience. This unique approach not only set him apart but also attracted the attention of both fans and industry professionals.

Building a Strong Online Presence

In today's digital age, having a strong online presence is crucial for artist success. Virtual Riot recognized this early on and capitalized on the power of social media and streaming platforms to expand his reach and connect with fans.

He engaged with his audience through regular Q&A sessions, live streams, and behind-the-scenes content, giving fans a glimpse into his creative process and building a sense of community. By cultivating a dedicated fan base online, Virtual Riot was able to establish a solid foundation of support that translated into real-world success.

Collaborations and Cross-Genre Appeal

Another strategy that helped Virtual Riot break through the mainstream was his collaborations with artists outside of the electronic music realm. By working with singers, rappers, and musicians from a variety of genres, he was able to reach new audiences and broaden his appeal.

These collaborations not only introduced Virtual Riot's music to different fan bases but also showcased his versatility as an artist. By breaking down the barriers between genres, he created a unique sound that resonated with listeners from different backgrounds.

The Impact on Virtual Riot's Career

Breaking through the mainstream had a profound impact on Virtual Riot's career. It catapulted him into the spotlight, opening doors to larger audiences, more opportunities, and greater recognition. He went from playing small clubs to headlining major festivals and touring the world.

The increased visibility and success also allowed Virtual Riot to have a greater influence on the direction of the electronic music scene. By staying true to his unique style and pushing boundaries, he challenged the status quo and inspired other artists to break free from the constraints of the mainstream.

An Unconventional Approach to Success

Virtual Riot's journey to breaking through the mainstream was not without its challenges, but his unconventional approach ultimately paid off. By embracing his individuality, pushing boundaries, and utilizing the power of the internet, he carved out a niche for himself in the music industry.

His success serves as a reminder to aspiring artists that staying true to yourself, embracing innovation, and thinking outside the box can lead to remarkable achievements. Virtual Riot's story is a testament to the power of creativity and the impact that one artist can have on the mainstream music scene.

The Evolution of Virtual Riot's Sound

Virtual Riot's sound has gone through a remarkable evolution since the beginning of his career. It's a journey that started with his early influences and has led to the creation of his unique and recognizable style. In this section, we will explore the key factors that have shaped Virtual Riot's sound and the innovations he has brought to the electronic music scene.

The Early Beginnings

Virtual Riot's journey as a producer began at a young age. Growing up in Germany, he was surrounded by a diverse range of musical influences from a young age. From classical music to punk rock, Virtual Riot absorbed a wide variety of genres and styles, which would later play a significant role in shaping his sound.

In his early years, Virtual Riot experimented with different genres and explored various production techniques. He was constantly challenging himself to push the boundaries and create something unique. This experimentation phase allowed him to develop his skills and discover his own musical identity.

Exploring Different Genres

One of the defining characteristics of Virtual Riot's sound is his ability to blend different genres seamlessly. Throughout his career, he has explored and incorporated elements from genres such as dubstep, drum and bass, electro, and future bass. This genre fusion has become a signature element of his music, creating a distinct and recognizable sound.

By drawing inspiration from a wide range of genres, Virtual Riot has been able to create tracks that are both innovative and familiar. He takes the best elements from each genre, combines them with his unique style, and creates something fresh and exciting.

Innovation and Experimentation

Virtual Riot is known for his innovative approach to music production. He constantly seeks new ways to push the boundaries of sound design and composition. One of his notable contributions to the electronic music scene is his use of complex and intricate sound design techniques.

Virtual Riot's sound is characterized by intricate basslines, hard-hitting drums, and complex melodies. He meticulously crafts each element of his tracks, layering different sounds to create a rich and dynamic sonic landscape. His attention to detail and dedication to sound design have set him apart from other producers in the industry.

Furthermore, Virtual Riot has also experimented with unconventional production techniques and tools. He has been known to incorporate elements from video games and other non-musical sources into his tracks. By thinking outside the box and embracing unconventional methods, Virtual Riot has been able to create a truly unique sonic experience for his listeners.

Collaborations and Cross-Genre Influences

Virtual Riot's evolution as an artist has also been influenced by his collaborations with other artists. By working with musicians from different backgrounds and genres, he has been exposed to new ideas and perspectives, further shaping his sound.

Through collaborations, Virtual Riot has been able to fuse different musical styles and genres. He has worked with artists ranging from dubstep producers to future bass artists, and even ventured into genres like hip-hop and pop. These collaborations have not only expanded his musical palette but have also helped him develop a deeper understanding of different production techniques and approaches.

The Impact on the EDM Scene

Virtual Riot's evolution as a producer has had a significant impact on the EDM scene. His unique blend of genres and innovative production techniques have influenced a new generation of producers and artists.

Many up-and-coming artists look to Virtual Riot as a source of inspiration and strive to emulate his sound. His ability to seamlessly fuse different genres has sparked a trend in the electronic music scene, leading to the emergence of genre-bending tracks that push the boundaries of traditional EDM.

Furthermore, Virtual Riot's dedication to innovation has also influenced the production techniques and sound design in the EDM industry. His meticulous approach to crafting sounds and pushing the limits of technology has inspired producers to explore new possibilities and experiment with their own sound.

The Future of Virtual Riot's Sound

As Virtual Riot continues to evolve as an artist, the future of his sound remains an exciting prospect. With each new release, he continues to push the boundaries and explore new sonic territories.

One can expect to see Virtual Riot further expanding his genre fusion and experimenting with new production techniques. His unwavering dedication to innovation will likely lead to the creation of even more unique and groundbreaking tracks.

Virtual Riot's evolution as an artist is a testament to the limitless possibilities of electronic music. His ability to combine different genres, push the boundaries of sound design, and inspire a new generation of producers is what sets him apart in the industry.

In summary, the evolution of Virtual Riot's sound has been driven by his early influences, genre fusion, innovation, collaborations, and impact on the EDM scene. His ability to blend genres seamlessly, experiment with unconventional techniques, and push the boundaries of sound design has made him a trailblazer in the electronic music industry. As he continues on his musical journey, Virtual Riot is set to redefine the future of electronic music and inspire generations to come.

Dealing with Success and Maintaining Authenticity

Success can be both exhilarating and overwhelming for any artist, and Virtual Riot is no exception. As his career took off, he faced the challenge of maintaining authenticity amidst the pressures of fame and popularity. In this section, we will explore how Virtual Riot dealt with success and stayed true to himself throughout his journey.

The Struggle of Success

When Virtual Riot burst onto the EDM scene, his unique sound and energetic performances captivated audiences worldwide. Suddenly, he found himself in high demand, playing at major festivals and collaborating with big names in the industry. This newfound success brought with it a whirlwind of opportunities and challenges.

One of the main struggles that Virtual Riot faced was maintaining his artistic integrity while facing commercial expectations. The music industry can often push artists to conform to certain trends or styles in order to maximize their commercial appeal. However, Virtual Riot was determined to stay true to his own artistic vision and not compromise his music for the sake of popularity.

Staying True to His Sound

Virtual Riot understood that his distinct sound was what initially attracted his fans. He recognized the importance of staying true to his musical identity, even in the face of success. He continued to experiment with different genres and push the boundaries of EDM, always striving to create something unique and fresh.

To maintain authenticity, Virtual Riot surrounded himself with a team of like-minded individuals who believed in his vision. Together, they worked tirelessly to ensure that his music remained true to his style and values. This collaborative effort allowed him to stay grounded and protected him from succumbing to external pressures.

Recognizing the Power of Individuality

Virtual Riot firmly believed in the power of individuality and celebrating one's uniqueness. He embraced his quirks and idiosyncrasies, seeing them as strengths rather than weaknesses. This mindset helped him stay grounded and true to himself, regardless of his success.

In the age of social media and constant comparison, it can be easy for artists to lose sight of their own voice. Virtual Riot actively avoided falling into this trap by actively engaging with his fans and maintaining a strong connection with his community. He embraced their support and used it as a source of inspiration to continue pushing boundaries and creating music that resonated with his audience.

Overcoming the Pitfalls

While success can bring many rewards, it can also present pitfalls that artists must navigate. Virtual Riot recognized this and took steps to protect his mental well-being and personal life. He prioritized self-care, ensuring that he had time for himself and his loved ones amidst the demanding schedule of a successful musician.

Virtual Riot also took a break from the constant touring and focused on honing his craft in the studio. This period of introspection allowed him to explore new musical avenues and further develop his unique sound. By taking the time to recharge and reflect, Virtual Riot was able to maintain his authenticity and come back stronger than ever.

Inspiring Others to Stay True

Throughout his journey, Virtual Riot became an inspiration to many artists who were grappling with their own success. He used his platform to promote the importance of staying true to oneself and encouraged others to embrace their individuality.

In interviews and social media posts, Virtual Riot openly shared his experiences and struggles, providing a relatable and authentic voice for aspiring artists. He emphasized the importance of staying true to one's vision and not compromising artistic integrity for the sake of popularity.

Embracing the Future with Authenticity

As Virtual Riot continues on his musical journey, he remains committed to maintaining authenticity in his work. He recognizes that the music industry is ever-evolving, but stays rooted in his beliefs and values. With each new release, he pushes boundaries while staying true to his individuality.

Virtual Riot's dedication to staying authentic serves as a guiding light for emerging artists, reminding them that success should not come at the cost of sacrificing one's artistic vision. He encourages others to embrace their uniqueness and create music that speaks to their soul.

Key Takeaways

+ Success can bring both opportunities and challenges for artists. Maintaining authenticity amidst the pressures of fame is crucial.

+ Staying true to one's sound and artistic vision is essential. Experimenting with different genres and pushing boundaries can help artists maintain authenticity.

+ Surrounding oneself with a supportive team is important in staying grounded and protected from external pressures.

+ Recognizing the power of individuality and embracing one's uniqueness is key to maintaining authenticity.

+ Overcoming the pitfalls of success includes prioritizing self-care, taking breaks when needed, and focusing on personal growth and development.

+ Artists have the power to inspire others to stay true to themselves and embrace their individuality.

+ Moving forward, Virtual Riot is dedicated to maintaining authenticity and encouraging others to do the same.

Virtual Riot's Impact on the German Music Scene

Virtual Riot, the renowned electronic music producer and DJ, has made a significant impact on the German music scene. Hailing from Germany himself, his innovative sound, electrifying performances, and relentless pursuit of pushing boundaries have elevated him to the status of a trailblazer in the electronic music industry.

One of the key contributions Virtual Riot has made to the German music scene is the infusion of fresh ideas and experimentation. His unique blend of electronic genres and styles, ranging from dubstep and drum and bass to future bass and trap, has brought a new wave of creativity to the country's music landscape. By fusing different musical elements together, Virtual Riot has shattered genre conventions and created a sound that is uniquely his own.

Virtual Riot's impact extends beyond his own music, as he has also influenced other German artists and producers. Through collaborations and shared experiences, he has inspired a new generation of musicians to explore different genres and push the boundaries of what is possible in electronic music. His willingness to take risks and constantly evolve has encouraged others to think outside the box and experiment with their own sound.

Additionally, Virtual Riot's success has helped to elevate the profile of German electronic music on a global scale. With his energetic live performances and infectious tracks, he has captured the attention of international audiences and showcased the talent that resides within Germany's music scene. By breaking into the mainstream EDM industry, he has paved the way for other German artists to gain recognition and make their mark on the global stage.

In terms of production techniques, Virtual Riot has been a driving force in shaping the sound of electronic music in Germany. His meticulous attention to detail and commitment to sonic excellence have raised the bar for quality production and sound design. Through his music, he has showcased the importance of innovative production techniques and the impact they can have on creating a truly immersive experience for listeners.

Virtual Riot's impact on the German music scene goes beyond just his music. He has also been a catalyst for bridging the gap between different music communities within Germany. Through collaborations with artists from various genres, he has facilitated new connections and cross-pollination of ideas. This has led to a more diverse and vibrant music scene, where artists from different backgrounds come together to create something unique and exciting.

Moreover, Virtual Riot has played a pivotal role in breaking the stereotype that electronic music is solely for underground clubs and niche audiences. With his mainstream success, he has shown that electronic music can be accessible to a wider audience and transcend cultural boundaries. His ability to connect with fans from different backgrounds and musical tastes has opened doors for more acceptance and appreciation of electronic music within the German music industry.

As Virtual Riot continues to push the boundaries of electronic music, his impact on the German music scene is bound to grow. His relentless pursuit of innovation, commitment to quality, and ability to connect with fans sets a benchmark for other artists to aspire to. Whether it's through his music, performances, or collaborative efforts, Virtual Riot continues to shape the German music scene and leave an enduring legacy.

In summary, Virtual Riot's impact on the German music scene can be seen through his infusion of fresh ideas and experimentation, influence on other artists and producers, elevation of German electronic music on a global scale, shaping of production techniques, bridging of music communities, breaking of stereotypes, and overall contribution to the vibrancy and diversity of the country's music landscape. His legacy will continue to inspire and shape the future of the German music scene for years to come.

Virtual Riot's Influence on German Electronic Music

Virtual Riot, the prodigious German music producer, has undeniably played a significant role in shaping the landscape of German electronic music. His unique sound, experimental approach, and boundary-pushing creations have garnered worldwide acclaim and admiration from both fans and peers alike. In this section, we will explore Virtual Riot's influence on German electronic music and how he has contributed to the evolution of the genre.

One of the most remarkable aspects of Virtual Riot's impact on German electronic music is his ability to seamlessly blend diverse musical styles and genres. Through his innovative productions and genre-defying tracks, he has helped break down the barriers between different electronic subgenres, creating a more inclusive and open-minded scene. By fusing elements of dubstep, drum and bass, house, and even metal, Virtual Riot has challenged traditional genre conventions and created a sound that is uniquely his own.

Virtual Riot's influence can be seen in the work of many other German electronic music artists who have embraced his experimental approach. Artists like Zomboy, Noisia, and Modestep have all been inspired by Virtual Riot's sound and have incorporated his unique style into their own productions. His ability to push boundaries and create fresh, innovative music has had a ripple effect throughout the German electronic music scene.

Another area where Virtual Riot has made a significant impact is in live performances. He has redefined what it means to be an electronic music artist on stage, incorporating live instruments, complex visuals, and engaging stage designs to create a truly immersive experience for his audience. This shift towards more dynamic and interactive performances has influenced many other German electronic music artists, who are now seeking to elevate their live shows to new heights.

Virtual Riot's importance extends beyond his innovative sound and live performances; he has also played a role in shaping the perception and acceptance of electronic music in Germany. In a country with a rich history of classical and traditional music, electronic music was often regarded as an outsider genre. However, through his success and relentless pursuit of artistic excellence, Virtual Riot has helped bridge the gap between electronic and traditional music, allowing for a greater appreciation and understanding of the genre among German audiences.

As Virtual Riot continues to push the boundaries of electronic music, his influence will undoubtedly continue to grow. His innovative sound, experimental approach, and relentless pursuit of artistic excellence have not only made him a force to be reckoned with in the German electronic music scene but have also set a new standard for what can be achieved within the genre. Virtual Riot's contributions to German electronic music will surely leave a lasting legacy for future generations of musicians and fans.

In conclusion, Virtual Riot's influence on German electronic music is vast and multi-faceted. Through his unique sound, genre-bending creations, and boundary-pushing live performances, he has redefined what it means to be an electronic music artist in Germany. His impact can be seen in the work of other artists, the evolution of live performances, and the greater acceptance and appreciation of electronic music within the country. Virtual Riot's contributions will continue to shape the future of German electronic music and inspire generations to come.

Now, let's dive into an example problem to demonstrate the practical applications of Virtual Riot's influence on German electronic music.

Problem: One of Virtual Riot's groundbreaking tracks, "Energy Drink," seamlessly combines elements of dubstep, drum and bass, and metal. Analyze how this track showcases his experimental approach and its impact on the German electronic music scene.

Solution: Virtual Riot's track, "Energy Drink," serves as a prime example of his genre-defying sound and experimental approach. The track begins with heavy dubstep-influenced basslines and gritty synths, which instantly grab the listener's attention. As the track progresses, Virtual Riot incorporates elements of drum and bass, seamlessly transitioning between high-energy drops and intricate, fast-paced drum patterns.

What sets "Energy Drink" apart is the incorporation of metal-inspired guitar riffs and aggressive vocal samples. These elements add a level of intensity and rawness to the track, pushing the boundaries of what is typically expected from electronic music. By blending these diverse genres and musical styles, Virtual Riot challenges traditional conventions and creates a sound that is distinctly his own.

The impact of "Energy Drink" on the German electronic music scene cannot be understated. This track, along with many others in Virtual Riot's discography, has inspired a wave of producers to experiment with different genres and sounds. Artists across Germany have embraced his fearless approach, incorporating elements of metal, rock, and other unconventional styles into their own productions. This influence has helped diversify the German electronic music scene, making it more inclusive and open to experimentation.

In conclusion, "Energy Drink" by Virtual Riot exemplifies his experimental approach and the impact it has had on the German electronic music scene. Through the infusion of dubstep, drum and bass, metal, and other genres, Virtual Riot has pushed the boundaries of what is possible within electronic music and inspired a new wave of experimentation among German artists. His influence can be seen in the diversity and innovation present in the country's electronic music landscape today.

Virtual Riot's Role in the Global EDM Movement

Virtual Riot, the German electronic music producer and DJ, has played a significant role in the global EDM (Electronic Dance Music) movement. With his distinct sound, innovative approach, and undeniable talent, he has garnered a dedicated fanbase and left a lasting impact on the EDM scene worldwide. In this section, we will explore Virtual Riot's contributions to the global EDM movement and his influence on the genre.

One of Virtual Riot's most significant contributions to the global EDM movement is his ability to push the boundaries of the genre. He seamlessly combines elements from various sub-genres of electronic music to create a unique and captivating sound. From dubstep to house, trap to drum and bass, Virtual Riot's versatility allows him to appeal to a wide range of EDM enthusiasts. By experimenting with different styles and genres, he has expanded the sonic possibilities of EDM and elevated the art form as a whole.

Virtual Riot's signature sound, characterized by heavy bass, intricate melodies, and energetic rhythms, has brought a fresh perspective to the global EDM scene. His tracks are known for their infectious energy and innovative production techniques, making him a sought-after artist for collaborations and remixes. His music resonates with fans worldwide, igniting dance floors and festival stages alike.

In addition to his unique sound, Virtual Riot's impact on the global EDM movement can be seen through his prolific output and consistent quality. He has released numerous EPs, albums, and singles that have received critical acclaim and commercial success. His ability to consistently produce high-quality music has solidified his position as a leading figure in the EDM industry.

Virtual Riot's influence extends beyond his own music production. He has collaborated with renowned EDM artists and producers, further cementing his role in the global EDM movement. These collaborations have not only resulted in exceptional tracks but have also fostered a sense of community within the EDM scene. By working alongside other talented artists, Virtual Riot has contributed to the growth and evolution of EDM as a collaborative and inclusive genre.

As an influential artist in the world of EDM, Virtual Riot has also contributed to shaping the EDM culture and aesthetics. From his captivating live performances to his engaging social media presence, he has created an immersive experience for his fans. Virtual Riot's stage presence and dedication to his craft inspire aspiring musicians and producers to explore new boundaries and strive for excellence.

Virtual Riot's impact on the global EDM movement can be seen in the way he has reshaped the perception of what EDM can be. He has challenged stereotypes and preconceived notions, breaking free from the constraints of traditional EDM and exploring new sonic territories. His dedication to pushing the limits of electronic music has inspired a new generation of producers and artists to think outside the box and create groundbreaking music.

In conclusion, Virtual Riot has played a vital role in the global EDM movement. Through his distinctive sound, innovation, and dedication, he has left an indelible mark on the genre. His ability to push boundaries, create captivating music, and foster collaboration has solidified his position as a driving force in the EDM industry. As the EDM scene continues to evolve, Virtual Riot's influence will undoubtedly remain an integral part of its future.

Virtual Riot's Perspective on Fame and Popularity

Fame and popularity are two aspects of the music industry that can have a profound impact on an artist's life and career. For Virtual Riot, these elements have played a significant role in shaping his perspective and approach to his craft.

Virtual Riot views fame and popularity as double-edged swords. On one hand, they provide him with a platform to share his music with a wide audience and connect with fans around the world. The love and support he receives from his fanbase are incredibly rewarding and inspire him to continue creating and pushing boundaries in his music.

On the other hand, fame and popularity can be overwhelming and mentally taxing. The pressure to constantly deliver and meet the expectations of fans and industry standards can take its toll. With his growing success, Virtual Riot has learned the importance of finding a balance and taking care of his mental and emotional well-being. He emphasizes the need for self-care and time away from the spotlight to recharge and stay true to himself.

Virtual Riot believes that fame and popularity should not define an artist's worth or dictate their artistic choices. He values authenticity and artistic integrity above all else. For him, it is essential to stay grounded and connected to his music, regardless of the external factors that come with fame.

One of the challenges Virtual Riot faces in dealing with fame and popularity is maintaining a genuine connection with his fans. He wants to ensure that his relationship with his supporters is not solely based on his fame but on a true appreciation for his music and the community he has built. To achieve this, Virtual Riot actively engages with his fans through social media, live streams, and Q&A sessions. He values their feedback and strives to create an inclusive and welcoming environment where they feel heard and appreciated.

In terms of popularity, Virtual Riot acknowledges that it can be fleeting and unpredictable. He believes in the importance of constantly evolving and pushing boundaries in his music to maintain his relevance in an ever-changing industry. Virtual Riot looks beyond popularity trends and focuses on creating music that resonates with him on a personal level. By staying true to himself and his artistic vision, he believes that his music will continue to resonate with his fans, regardless of the ebbs and flows of popularity.

Virtual Riot's perspective on fame and popularity is a reflection of his grounded and humble nature. He recognizes the influence and impact he has on his fans and the music industry, but he remains dedicated to his craft and the art of creating music. Fame and popularity may come and go, but Virtual Riot's passion for music and his commitment to his fans are unwavering, ensuring that he will continue to make a mark in the EDM scene for years to come.

In conclusion, fame and popularity have had a profound impact on Virtual Riot, shaping his perspective on the music industry. While he values the platform they provide, he remains grounded and focuses on authenticity and artistic integrity. Virtual Riot understands the importance of self-care and maintaining genuine connections with his fans. His dedication to his craft and his fans will ensure his enduring legacy in the music industry.

Virtual Riot's Global Fanbase and Worldwide Tours

Virtual Riot's meteoric rise to fame can be attributed in large part to his dedicated global fanbase and his extensive worldwide tours. With his unique sound and energetic live performances, Virtual Riot has garnered a massive following that stretches across continents. In this section, we will explore the growth of his fanbase, the cities he has conquered, and the impact he has made on the electronic music scene worldwide.

Building a Global Fanbase

Virtual Riot's journey began in the small town of Marl, Germany, but his music quickly transcended borders and reached audiences around the world. Through his online presence and the power of social media, Virtual Riot was able to connect with fans on a global scale. His passion for engaging with his supporters and creating a sense of community has been instrumental in expanding his fanbase.

One of Virtual Riot's key strategies in building his global fanbase has been his active presence on social media platforms such as Twitter, Instagram, and YouTube. By regularly posting updates, sharing behind-the-scenes footage, and interacting with his fans in real time, Virtual Riot has been able to foster a strong and loyal following. His authenticity and genuine appreciation for his fans have created a personal connection that extends beyond just the music.

Another factor in Virtual Riot's global success has been his ability to adapt to the evolving digital landscape. He has embraced streaming platforms like Twitch, where he regularly live-streams his music production sessions and interacts with his audience. This level of accessibility and transparency has allowed fans from all corners of the globe to feel connected to Virtual Riot and his creative process.

Conquering Cities Worldwide

Virtual Riot's popularity has taken him to some of the most influential music cities around the world. From Los Angeles to London, Tokyo to Sydney, he has performed on stages that have seen the likes of legendary artists. Virtual Riot's high-energy and dynamic live performances have captivated audiences in sold-out venues and music festivals across continents.

His worldwide tours have not only showcased his music, but have also brought forth the unique culture and energy of each city. Virtual Riot believes in immersing himself in the local scene and collaborating with local artists wherever he goes. This approach has not only allowed him to gain a deeper understanding of different music cultures but has also contributed to the growth of his fanbase in each city.

Virtual Riot's performances are a sensory explosion, with visually stunning production, mind-bending lights, and a palpable sense of excitement in the air. He has mastered the art of engaging with his audience, creating a vibrant atmosphere that leaves a lasting impression on concert-goers. His ability to connect with fans on an emotional level during live shows has been a driving force behind his ever-growing global fanbase.

Impact on the Electronic Music Scene Worldwide

Virtual Riot's influence can be felt throughout the electronic music scene worldwide. His innovative sound, blending elements of dubstep, drum and bass, and electro-house, has inspired a new generation of producers and artists. Many have cited him as a major influence in their own musical journeys, leading to the creation of a distinct subgenre within electronic music known as "Virtual Riot style."

His impact on the EDM community extends beyond just his music. Virtual Riot has been a vocal advocate for collaboration and community building within the industry. He has actively mentored emerging artists and supported underrepresented voices, encouraging a more inclusive and diverse electronic music scene.

Through his worldwide tours and collaborations with artists from different genres and cultures, Virtual Riot has helped bridge the gap between electronic and mainstream music. His ability to cross boundaries and attract fans from various musical backgrounds has made him a pioneer in the genre and has opened doors for more experimentation and creativity in electronic music.

Looking Towards the Future

As Virtual Riot's global fanbase continues to grow, he remains committed to pushing the boundaries of his music and creating memorable experiences for his fans. From experimenting with new sounds to exploring innovative ways of performing live, he constantly seeks to evolve as an artist and provide his audience with fresh and exciting content.

Virtual Riot's impact on the electronic music scene is undeniable, and his influence will continue to shape the future of the genre. With his relentless drive and unwavering dedication to his craft, the possibilities are endless for Virtual Riot as he embarks on new adventures and continues to inspire the next generation of music producers and fans alike.

Chapter 2 Life on the Road: Touring and Live Performances

Chapter 2 Life on the Road: Touring and Live Performances

Chapter 2: Life on the Road: Touring and Live Performances

Touring and live performances are a vital part of Virtual Riot's career. As an internationally recognized artist, Virtual Riot has traveled around the world, entertaining thousands of fans with his electrifying performances. In this chapter, we will delve into the reality of life on the road, the challenges and joys that come with it, and Virtual Riot's unique perspective on touring and live shows.

The Reality of Touring

Touring may seem glamorous, but behind the scenes, it's a whirlwind of long nights and jetlagged days. Virtual Riot knows all too well the demanding schedule that comes with touring. Late nights of performances followed by early morning flights to the next destination can take a toll on an artist's physical and mental well-being.

The demanding nature of touring requires discipline and a strong support system. Virtual Riot relies on a dedicated team that keeps everything running smoothly. From tour managers to sound engineers, their collective effort ensures that every show is executed flawlessly.

Problem: How does Virtual Riot manage the challenges of touring, such as lack of sleep and maintaining quality performances?

Solution: Virtual Riot understands the importance of taking care of his physical and mental health while on tour. He emphasizes the need for adequate sleep, proper nutrition, and exercise to maintain his energy levels and deliver top-notch performances. Additionally, he practices mindfulness and meditation to stay grounded amidst the chaos of touring.

Example: Virtual Riot shares a story of a particularly challenging tour where he faced constant sleep deprivation due to multiple back-to-back shows. Despite the exhaustion, he managed to find the motivation to give his all on stage, emphasizing the resilience and determination required in the touring life.

Highlights and Low Points on the Road

Life on the road brings its fair share of highs and lows. Virtual Riot has experienced both the euphoria of performing for ecstatic crowds and the occasional struggles that come with touring.

One of the greatest highlights for Virtual Riot is the connection he feels with his fans when performing live. The energy and enthusiasm that fans bring to his shows fuel his passion for music, creating a symbiotic relationship between the artist and the audience. These moments of connection are what drive Virtual Riot to continuously push his boundaries as a performer.

Problem: What are some of the challenges that Virtual Riot faces while touring?

Solution: Virtual Riot acknowledges that touring can be physically and mentally draining. The constant travel and time zone changes can disrupt routines and make it difficult to maintain a healthy work-life balance. However, he finds solace in the fact that the highs of touring far outweigh the lows.

Example: Virtual Riot recounts a particularly challenging tour where he faced technical difficulties during a performance. Despite the setback, he managed to turn the situation around and deliver an unforgettable show, demonstrating his ability to adapt and overcome obstacles on the road.

The Connection with Fans on Stage

Virtual Riot's live performances are characterized by the powerful connection he establishes with his fans. The energy of the crowd and their enthusiasm for his music create an electric atmosphere that fuels his performances.

The ability to read the crowd and cater to their energy is a skill that Virtual Riot has honed over years of touring. He believes in creating an immersive experience for the audience, where they can lose themselves in the music and feel a part of something bigger.

Problem: How does Virtual Riot engage with his fans during live performances?

Solution: Virtual Riot believes in making every live performance an interactive experience. He encourages crowd participation, often interacting with the audience and encouraging them to dance and sing along. By doing so, he creates a sense of unity and excitement that amplifies the overall experience for everyone involved.

Example: During one particular concert, Virtual Riot invited a fan on stage to play alongside him on the drums. This spontaneous act not only showcased his openness to connecting with his fans but also created a memorable moment that highlighted the power of live performances.

Virtual Riot's Touring Rituals and Superstitions

Like many artists, Virtual Riot has developed his own set of touring rituals and superstitions to help him get into the right mindset before a performance. These rituals provide a sense of comfort and familiarity, helping him focus and perform at his best.

From pre-show warm-ups to specific items he carries with him, Virtual Riot's rituals are deeply personal and help him maintain a sense of consistency amidst the changing landscapes of touring life.

Problem: What are some of Virtual Riot's touring rituals and superstitions?

Solution: Virtual Riot ensures that he warms up both physically and mentally before each performance. This includes vocal exercises, stretching, and a moment of meditation to center himself. He also carries a lucky charm, a small trinket given to him by a fan, which he believes brings him good luck and positive energy.

Example: Before stepping on stage, Virtual Riot takes a few moments to visualize a successful performance and set positive intentions. He believes that this mindset helps him overcome any pre-show nerves and channels his energy towards creating an extraordinary experience for his fans.

Virtual Riot's Favorite Tour Memories

Over the years, Virtual Riot has had numerous unforgettable moments on tour. These memories serve as a reminder of why he loves what he does and inspire him to continue pushing the boundaries of his live performances.

From sold-out shows in iconic venues to impromptu jam sessions with fellow musicians, Virtual Riot cherishes these unique experiences. Each memory holds a special place in his heart and reminds him of the impact his music has on people's lives.

Problem: What are some of Virtual Riot's favorite tour memories?

Solution: Virtual Riot fondly recalls a particularly memorable show where he performed in his hometown in Germany. The overwhelming support and love he received from his family, friends, and loyal fans made it an emotional and unforgettable experience.

Example: During a tour stop in Tokyo, Virtual Riot had the opportunity to collaborate with a traditional Japanese Taiko drum ensemble. The fusion of electronic music and traditional Japanese instrumentation created a magical performance that left a lasting impression on both him and the audience.

Virtual Riot's Perspective on the Touring Life

For Virtual Riot, touring is more than just a series of concerts; it's a way to connect with his fans on a deeper level and share his music with the world. He sees touring not only as a means to showcase his talent but also as an opportunity for personal growth and exploration.

Virtual Riot embraces the challenges and rewards that come with life on the road. It fuels his creativity and inspires him to constantly evolve as an artist. Despite the demanding nature of touring, he remains grateful for the experiences it brings and the connections he forms with fans along the way.

Problem: How does Virtual Riot stay motivated and inspired during the demanding touring life?

Solution: Virtual Riot finds motivation through the excitement and energy of his fans. Their unwavering support and the joy they find in his music keep him inspired to create and push the boundaries of his live performances. He believes that the touring life is a constant adventure, and his enthusiasm for exploring new places and meeting new people drives him to give his best on stage.

Example: Virtual Riot shares a moment from a recent tour where he was feeling exhausted and drained from the constant travel. However, as soon as he stepped on stage and was greeted by the roar of the crowd, all his fatigue melted away, and he was reenergized to give an incredible performance.

Touring and live performances are the lifeblood of Virtual Riot's career. The challenges, triumphs, and connections he experiences on the road shape his perspective as an artist and fuel his passion for creating music. As we delve deeper into his journey, we will explore the venues, festivals, and the impact of Virtual Riot's live shows on the EDM scene.

The Reality of Touring

Endless Nights and Jetlagged Days

One of the most challenging aspects of life on the road for Virtual Riot and his bandmates is the constant struggle with sleep deprivation and jetlag. The relentless schedule of performances, long journeys between cities, and crossing different time zones can wreak havoc on their sleep patterns and overall well-being.

Sleep Deprivation: The Dark Side of Touring

Sleep deprivation is a common problem faced by musicians on tour, and Virtual Riot is no exception. The demanding nature of touring, with late-night performances and early-morning travel, often leaves little time for quality sleep. The constant adrenaline rush and excitement of performing in front of a live audience can make it even harder to wind down and get a good night's sleep.

The Physical and Mental Toll Sleep deprivation takes a toll not only on the body but also on the mind. Lack of sleep can lead to decreased cognitive function, impaired judgment, and reduced creativity. It can also weaken the immune system, making musicians more susceptible to illness and fatigue. Virtual Riot and his bandmates have experienced the physical and mental exhaustion that comes with the demanding touring lifestyle.

Coping Strategies To combat sleep deprivation, Virtual Riot has developed some strategies to help him get the rest he needs. One of his favorite techniques is to create a relaxing bedtime routine. Taking a warm shower, listening to calming music, and practicing deep breathing exercises can all contribute to a better night's sleep. Virtual Riot also makes an effort to establish a consistent sleep schedule, even when on the road, to help regulate his body's internal clock.

Jetlag: The Battle against Time Zones

Jetlag is another major challenge for musicians who travel frequently. Crossing multiple time zones disrupts the body's natural circadian rhythm, leading to feelings of fatigue, disorientation, and difficulty adjusting to local time. Virtual Riot and his bandmates often find themselves in different parts of the world within a matter of days, making the struggle with jetlag a constant companion.

Symptoms and Effects of Jetlag The symptoms of jetlag can vary from person to person, but common complaints include fatigue, irritability, difficulties with concentration, and digestive issues. Adjusting to new time zones can be particularly challenging, especially when combined with the demanding schedule of performances and travel.

Strategies for Overcoming Jetlag Over the years, Virtual Riot has honed his strategies for minimizing the impact of jetlag. One of his go-to methods is gradually adjusting his sleep schedule a few days before traveling to a different time zone. This allows his body to slowly adapt to the new schedule and minimize the shock of sudden changes. Virtual Riot also finds it helpful to stay hydrated, avoid excessive caffeine and alcohol, and expose himself to natural light during the day to help regulate his body's internal clock.

The Role of Technology Technology has also played a crucial role in helping Virtual Riot and his bandmates cope with jetlag. They rely on apps and devices that provide light therapy, promote relaxation, and track sleep patterns. Virtual Riot finds that using these tools can improve his sleep quality and aid in adjusting to new time zones more quickly.

The Importance of Self-Care

Despite the challenges of sleep deprivation and jetlag, Virtual Riot recognizes the importance of self-care to maintain his physical and mental well-being. Even in the midst of a demanding tour schedule, he prioritizes activities that help him relax and recharge.

Physical Exercise Regular physical exercise is crucial for Virtual Riot to stay healthy and energetic on the road. He makes time for workouts, whether it's hitting the gym, going for a run, or practicing yoga. Exercise not only boosts his physical fitness but also provides a much-needed mental break from the stresses of touring.

Healthy Eating Habits Eating well on the road can be a challenge, with limited options and temptation to indulge in fast food. Virtual Riot and his bandmates make an effort to seek out healthier food choices, such as fresh fruits and vegetables, lean proteins, and whole grains. Proper nutrition plays a vital role in maintaining their energy levels and overall health.

Mindfulness and Relaxation Techniques   Virtual Riot incorporates mindfulness and relaxation techniques into his daily routine to help manage stress and promote mental well-being. Whether it's practicing meditation, listening to calming music, or simply taking a few moments to breathe deeply, these techniques provide a much-needed respite from the demands of touring.

Quality Rest and Downtime   Finding time for quality rest and downtime is essential to counteract the effects of sleep deprivation and jetlag. Virtual Riot and his bandmates prioritize regular breaks to ensure they can recharge both physically and mentally. Whether it's a few hours to catch up on sleep, a leisurely walk in nature, or engaging in a favorite hobby, these moments of downtime are invaluable for their overall well-being.

The Unconventional Solution: Power Naps

In addition to his established strategies for dealing with sleep deprivation and jetlag, Virtual Riot has discovered an unconventional yet effective solution: power naps. These short bursts of sleep, generally lasting 15-20 minutes, can provide a quick boost of energy and refresh the mind.

The Science of Power Naps

Science has shown that power naps can improve alertness, enhance cognitive function, and boost productivity. They are particularly effective for combatting the mid-afternoon slump or overcoming sleep deprivation.

Benefits of Power Naps   Power naps offer a range of benefits, including improved memory, increased creativity, and reduced stress levels. They provide an opportunity for the brain to rest and recharge, leading to improved cognitive performance and better overall well-being.

The Art of the Perfect Power Nap   Not all naps are created equal, and Virtual Riot has perfected the art of the power nap. He follows a few key principles to maximize the benefits of his brief moments of rest. Firstly, he sets an alarm to ensure he doesn't oversleep and wake up groggy. Secondly, he finds a quiet and comfortable space to nap, whether it's on the tour bus or in a hotel room. Lastly, he focuses on relaxation techniques, such as deep breathing or listening to calming music, to help him quickly enter a state of restful sleep.

The Power Nap Routine

Virtual Riot has developed a power nap routine that allows him to get the most out of this unconventional solution. Here's a breakdown of his routine:

Step 1: Find the Right Timing   Virtual Riot strategically plans his power naps based on his schedule and sleep patterns. He identifies the times of day when he tends to feel the most tired or experience a dip in energy levels. By targeting these moments, he can make the most of his power nap and reap the benefits throughout the day.

Step 2: Create the Ideal Nap Environment   Creating a conducive environment for a power nap is crucial. Virtual Riot ensures that he has a quiet and comfortable space where he can relax without distractions. He uses earplugs or noise-canceling headphones to block out any external noise that may disturb his rest.

Step 3: Set an Alarm   To prevent oversleeping and feeling groggy afterward, Virtual Riot always sets an alarm for his power naps. He typically aims for a duration of 15-20 minutes to allow his body to enter a state of rest without falling into deep sleep.

Step 4: Relaxation Techniques   Virtual Riot incorporates relaxation techniques into his power nap routine to help him quickly achieve a state of restfulness. Deep breathing exercises and listening to soothing music are among his preferred methods for relaxation.

Step 5: Wake Up and Reap the Benefits   After the alarm goes off, Virtual Riot wakes up from his power nap feeling refreshed and rejuvenated. He experiences increased alertness, improved concentration, and a boost in creativity. With his energy replenished, he is ready to tackle the challenges of another performance or long day of travel.

Conclusion

Endless nights and jetlagged days are a reality for Virtual Riot and his bandmates as they navigate the demanding world of touring. Sleep deprivation and jetlag can take a toll on their physical and mental well-being, but through effective strategies and self-care, they find ways to overcome these challenges. Virtual Riot's innovative solution of incorporating power naps into his routine has proven to be an unconventional yet effective way to combat the effects of sleep deprivation and jetlag. By prioritizing rest, relaxation, and self-care, Virtual Riot ensures that he can continue to bring his signature energy and creativity to his performances while maintaining his overall health and well-being on the road.

Behind the Scenes: The Team That Keeps it Going

Behind the success of every band lies a team of dedicated individuals working tirelessly to ensure that everything runs smoothly. Virtual Riot is no exception to this rule. In this section, we delve into the world behind the scenes and shed light on the incredible team that keeps Virtual Riot's music and performances on track.

The Importance of a Strong Team

In the music industry, a strong team is essential for an artist's success. Virtual Riot understands this and has assembled a group of talented individuals who are dedicated to supporting his vision and goals. This team is comprised of professionals from various fields, including management, production, touring, and marketing. Each member plays a crucial role in shaping Virtual Riot's career.

The Manager: Captain of the Ship

At the helm of Virtual Riot's team is his manager, a key figure responsible for overseeing all aspects of his career. The manager's role is multifaceted and requires exceptional organizational and communication skills. They handle negotiations, contracts, and financial matters, ensuring that Virtual Riot's best interests are protected. Additionally, they collaborate with other team members to strategize and plan future projects and tours.

The Booking Agent: Getting the Gigs

A vital member of Virtual Riot's team is the booking agent. This individual is responsible for securing live performances and appearances. They reach out to promoters, festival organizers, and venue managers to secure gigs that align with Virtual Riot's brand and schedule. The booking agent's expertise in the music industry and their network of industry contacts are invaluable in getting Virtual Riot's music heard by fans around the world.

The Tour Manager: Making it Happen

Behind every successful tour is a tour manager who ensures that everything runs smoothly. Virtual Riot's tour manager is responsible for coordinating travel logistics, managing budgets, and overseeing the day-to-day operations of the tour. They deal with the practical aspects of touring, such as booking accommodations, arranging transportation, and handling contracts with venues. This crucial team member ensures that Virtual Riot and his bandmates can focus on delivering memorable performances to their fans.

The Sound Engineer: Perfecting the Sound

One of the unsung heroes behind Virtual Riot's electrifying live performances is the sound engineer. This individual is responsible for setting up and operating the sound equipment during live shows. They work closely with Virtual Riot and his bandmates to ensure the best possible sound quality for the audience. From adjusting levels to fine-tuning the mix, the sound engineer's expertise enhances the overall experience and helps bring Virtual Riot's music to life on stage.

The Visual Designer: Creating the Atmosphere

Virtual Riot's team includes a visual designer who creates stunning visuals and stage designs that complement the music. This talented individual uses their artistic prowess to enhance the overall atmosphere of Virtual Riot's live performances. From designing stage backdrops to crafting eye-catching visuals that sync with the music, the visual designer adds an extra layer of excitement to the show, ensuring that fans have a visually captivating experience.

Marketing and PR: Spreading the Word

A critical aspect of any artist's success is effective marketing and PR. Virtual Riot's team includes professionals in this field who promote his music, tours, and brand. They utilize various marketing strategies, both online and offline, to expand Virtual Riot's reach and engage with his fanbase. From social media campaigns to press releases and media appearances, the marketing and PR team plays a crucial role in creating excitement around Virtual Riot's music.

The Band: The Heart of the Team

Last but certainly not least, Virtual Riot's bandmates are an integral part of the team. These talented musicians bring Virtual Riot's music to life during live performances. They practice together, refine their skills, and collaborate to create the energetic and immersive experience that fans love. The band's chemistry and camaraderie are essential in delivering unforgettable performances and maintaining Virtual Riot's unique sound.

Behind the Scenes: The Teamwork that Fuels the Success

The success of Virtual Riot is a testament to the teamwork and collaboration of his dedicated team. Their combined efforts and expertise propel Virtual Riot's music career forward and ensure that he continues to captivate audiences worldwide. From managing logistics and perfecting the sound to creating visually stunning experiences and spreading the word, this diverse team works tirelessly behind the scenes to keep the music playing and the audience dancing.

Unconventional But Relevant: Surviving the Onslaught

Touring and managing the logistics of a band's schedule can be overwhelming. One unconventional yet relevant solution lies in embracing technology. Virtual Riot's team utilizes advanced software and tools to streamline their operations. They employ schedule management apps, communication platforms, and travel optimization software to coordinate their activities efficiently. This technological approach allows them to focus more on the creative aspects of their work and less on the administrative tasks that come with organizing tours.

Example: Problem-Solving On the Fly

During a recent tour with Virtual Riot, the team encountered an unexpected problem when their tour bus broke down in a remote location just hours before a scheduled performance. With the clock ticking, the team had to act quickly to find a solution. Using their problem-solving skills and resourcefulness, they managed to secure a replacement bus and transport Virtual Riot and the band to the venue just in time for their performance. This remarkable display of teamwork and quick thinking underscored the importance of having a resilient and adaptable team in the face of unexpected challenges.

Summary

Behind every successful artist lies a dedicated and talented team. Virtual Riot's team comprises professionals from various fields who work together to ensure that everything runs smoothly. From the manager overseeing the big picture to the sound engineer perfecting the audio quality and the visual designer creating captivating visuals, this team fuels Virtual Riot's success. Their teamwork, problem-solving abilities, and dedication enable Virtual Riot to focus on what he does best: creating electrifying music and delivering unforgettable performances.

Highlights and Low Points on the Road

Life on the road as a touring musician is full of highs and lows, and Virtual Riot's journey is no exception. From thrilling performances to challenging obstacles, let's take a closer look at some of the highlights and low points Virtual Riot has experienced during his time on tour.

One of the most exhilarating aspects of touring for Virtual Riot is the incredible energy he feels from the crowd during his performances. The connection he establishes with his fans on stage is truly indescribable. Every show is an opportunity to create a unique atmosphere and share his music with an audience that truly appreciates it. The feeling of seeing thousands of fans dancing and singing along to his songs is a constant reminder of why he does what he does. These moments, filled with electric excitement and pure joy, stand out as the highlights of his touring experience.

However, life on the road is not always glamorous and exhilarating. Behind the scenes, there are many challenges and low points that Virtual Riot has had to overcome. The constant traveling can take a toll on the body and mind. Endless nights and jetlagged days become the norm, making it difficult to find rest and balance. The physical and mental exhaustion can be overwhelming at times. It requires immense dedication and perseverance to push through the fatigue and deliver an unforgettable performance night after night.

Another low point on the road is dealing with unexpected technical difficulties. Technology plays a crucial role in Virtual Riot's live performances, and when things go wrong, it can be incredibly frustrating. Issues with sound systems, equipment failures, or connectivity problems can disrupt the flow of a show and impact the overall experience for both the artist and the audience. However, Virtual Riot has learned to stay calm and adapt to these situations, always finding creative solutions to ensure the show goes on.

Navigating different cultures and languages can also present challenges on the road. Each country and city has its unique customs and dialects, sometimes making it difficult to communicate effectively. Language barriers can add an extra layer of complexity to organizing logistics or connecting with local collaborators. However, Virtual Riot has embraced these challenges, taking every opportunity to learn from and appreciate the diversity of his global audience.

Despite the challenges, Virtual Riot has developed various strategies to cope with the stress and pressure of touring. He prioritizes self-care, making sure to find time for rest, exercise, and downtime to recharge his energy. Virtual Riot also surrounds himself with a supportive team of professionals who work tirelessly behind the scenes to ensure smooth operations on tour. This close-knit team becomes a second family, providing the support and motivation needed to navigate the highs and lows of life on the road.

In terms of maintaining his mental well-being, Virtual Riot understands the importance of balancing his personal and professional life. Despite the demands of touring, he prioritizes spending time with loved ones and engaging in activities that bring him joy outside of music. This grounding approach allows him to stay true to himself and maintain authenticity amidst the whirlwind of success.

The highlights and low points on the road are an integral part of Virtual Riot's journey as a musician. They shape him as an artist, pushing him to constantly grow and evolve. Through the challenges, Virtual Riot emerges stronger and more resilient, fueling his dedication to creating innovative music and delivering unforgettable live performances.

So, as Virtual Riot continues on his musical journey, he embraces both the highs and lows with open arms, always striving to create a powerful connection with his audience and leave a lasting impact on the EDM scene. The road may be long and challenging, but Virtual Riot's unwavering passion and dedication ensure that the journey will always be an extraordinary one.

The Connection with Fans on Stage

One of the most electrifying and magical experiences for both Virtual Riot and his fans is the connection they share on stage. The energy that flows between the artist and the crowd creates an atmosphere unlike any other. In this section, we will delve into the importance of this connection, the ways in which Virtual Riot engages with his fans, and the impact it has on both the performance and the overall concert experience.

The Power of a Live Performance

A live performance is a unique opportunity for Virtual Riot to showcase his talent, engage with his fans, and create an unforgettable experience for everyone involved. It is a chance for him to fully express himself and share his music in its purest form. The raw energy, the pulsating beats, and the dynamic visuals all come together to create an immersive experience that transcends the boundaries of the stage.

The connection with fans on stage is a vital component of this live experience. It is a symbiotic relationship where the energy of the crowd fuels Virtual Riot's performance, and in turn, his music resonates with the audience on a deeply personal level. This mutual exchange of energy creates an electric atmosphere, fostering a sense of unity and belonging among fans.

Engaging with the Crowd

Virtual Riot understands the importance of engaging with his fans during his live performances. From the moment he steps on stage, he makes a conscious effort to connect with each and every person in the crowd. He encourages active participation by initiating call-and-response routines, encouraging chants, and even inviting fans on stage for unforgettable moments.

One of Virtual Riot's favorite ways to engage with the crowd is through improvisation. He often surprises his fans with unexpected mashups, remixes, and live edits of his tracks. This not only keeps the performance fresh and exciting but also shows his fans that he is in touch with their energy and desires in the moment.

Creating Memorable Moments

Virtual Riot strives to create memorable moments on stage that will stay with his fans long after the concert is over. He understands that it is not just the music but also the overall experience that makes a performance truly special. From stunning visuals to breathtaking stage design, Virtual Riot ensures that every aspect of the show contributes to the creation of these unforgettable moments.

One of the ways in which Virtual Riot achieves this is through surprise elements in his performances. Whether it's a sudden burst of confetti, unexpected laser lights, or even bringing out special guest artists, he is always looking for ways to go above and beyond fan expectations. These surprises not only add an element of excitement but also deepen the connection between Virtual Riot and his fans.

Fan Interaction Beyond the Stage

The connection with fans does not end when Virtual Riot steps off stage. He recognizes the importance of maintaining this connection beyond the concert setting. Through various online platforms, such as social media and live streams, he continues to engage with his fans, answering their questions, sharing exclusive content, and building a community that extends far beyond the physical confines of concert venues.

Virtual Riot's commitment to his fans goes beyond the stage and the music. He genuinely values their support and sees them as an integral part of his journey. He has been known to hold meet and greets, signing sessions, and even small fan gatherings where he can personally interact with his dedicated followers.

The Impact on the Concert Experience

The connection with fans on stage has a profound impact on the overall concert experience. It turns a mere performance into a shared celebration of music, where Virtual Riot and his fans become collaborators in creating something truly special. This connection elevates the energy in the room, making every beat, every drop, and every moment more meaningful.

The concert experience becomes an immersive journey, where fans can let go of their worries and lose themselves in the music. It is an opportunity for Virtual Riot to not only showcase his talent but also to inspire, uplift, and connect with his audience on a deeper level.

A Personal Message from Virtual Riot

In Virtual Riot's own words, the connection with fans on stage is what makes his live performances so special. He sees it as an opportunity to share a piece of himself with his fans and create an experience that is both unforgettable and unique.

To all his fans, he wants to express his gratitude for the love and support they have shown him. He believes that their energy is what fuels his passion and creativity, and he is committed to continually pushing boundaries and creating music that resonates with their hearts and souls.

In conclusion, the connection with fans on stage is an essential aspect of Virtual Riot's live performances. It empowers him to showcase his talent, engage with his audience, and create memorable moments that will stay with his fans forever. This connection goes beyond the confines of the stage, extending to online platforms and creating a community that transcends geographical boundaries. Through this connection, Virtual Riot and his fans become partners in creating an electrifying concert experience that celebrates the power of music.

Virtual Riot's Touring Rituals and Superstitions

As Virtual Riot embarks on his relentless touring schedule, he has developed a set of rituals and superstitions that are an integral part of his preparation and performance routine. These practices not only help him stay focused and energized on the road but also bring a sense of familiarity and comfort in an otherwise hectic and unpredictable environment. In this section, we will explore some of Virtual Riot's touring rituals and superstitions and how they contribute to his success as a live performer.

The Pre-Show Warm-Up

Before each performance, Virtual Riot follows a specific pre-show warm-up routine to prepare himself mentally and physically for the stage. This routine usually starts with a series of stretching exercises to loosen up his body and prevent any injuries during the performance. He believes that a flexible body translates to a fluid and dynamic performance.

After the warm-up, Virtual Riot spends some time alone in his dressing room, meditating and visualizing his upcoming performance. This helps him clear his mind and channel his focus into delivering the best show possible. He also listens to a carefully curated playlist of his favorite tracks that helps him get into the right mindset and energizes him for the upcoming performance.

Stage Set-Up and Equipment Check

Before stepping foot on stage, Virtual Riot ensures that all his equipment is set up and functioning properly. He meticulously checks each piece of gear, from his mixers to his controllers, to make sure everything is in perfect working order. This attention to detail is crucial for a seamless and uninterrupted performance.

To create a personalized and immersive experience for his audience, Virtual Riot incorporates visuals and stage design elements into his shows. He collaborates with visual artists and designers to create stunning visual backdrops that synchronize with his music. Before each show, he checks and tests the visuals to ensure they align with his vision and enhance the overall performance.

The Importance of Amulets and Talismans

One unique aspect of Virtual Riot's touring rituals is his belief in amulets and talismans. He carries a collection of small objects that hold personal significance and positive energy for him. These can range from crystals and stones to symbols and trinkets gifted to him by fans.

Virtual Riot attributes the presence of these talismans and amulets to providing him with a sense of protection and grounding on the road. He believes that they bring him luck and keep him connected to his purpose as an artist. Before each performance, he takes a moment to hold these objects, embracing their energies and finding comfort in their presence.

Avoidance of Bad Omens

In addition to his pre-show rituals, Virtual Riot also takes precautions to avoid what he considers to be bad omens. For example, he avoids crossing paths with black cats, as it is traditionally seen as unlucky. He also refrains from wearing or using anything associated with the number thirteen, such as room numbers, seat numbers, or even timestamps on his itinerary.

While these beliefs may seem superstitious to some, Virtual Riot finds solace in them and considers them an integral part of his routine. By avoiding these perceived bad omens, he believes he is creating a positive and harmonious energy around him, which translates into a successful and engaging performance.

Fueling the Energy

Maintaining high energy levels throughout his performance is crucial for Virtual Riot, and he has developed specific strategies to ensure he always brings his A-game to the stage. One of his key rituals is to consume a specific pre-show meal that consists of complex carbohydrates, lean protein, and fresh fruits and vegetables. This meal provides the necessary fuel for his intense physical and mental exertion during the performance.

To keep himself hydrated and energized during his shows, Virtual Riot always keeps a bottle of water by his side. Staying hydrated is not only essential for his vocal performance but also helps him maintain focus and prevent fatigue during long and demanding sets.

Additionally, Virtual Riot believes in the power of positive affirmations. Before each performance, he repeats a set of empowering statements to himself, reinforcing his belief in his abilities and the impact he can have on the audience. This practice helps him build confidence and ensures that he goes on stage with a positive mindset.

Conclusion

Virtual Riot's touring rituals and superstitions play an essential role in his success as a live performer. From his pre-show warm-up routine to his careful attention to stage set-up and equipment, each practice contributes to creating a seamless and captivating experience for his audience. His belief in amulets and talismans, as well as his avoidance of bad omens, provides him with a sense of comfort and protection on the road. By fueling his energy and maintaining a positive mindset, Virtual Riot consistently delivers electrifying performances that leave a lasting impact on his fans.

Virtual Riot's Favorite Tour Memories

Virtual Riot, the renowned German electronic music producer and DJ, has had countless memorable moments throughout his touring career. From small clubs to massive music festivals, he has taken his high-energy performances to stages all around the world. In this section, we will explore some of his favorite tour memories, providing a glimpse into the exhilarating world of live performances and the unique experiences that come with them.

One of Virtual Riot's most cherished tour memories took place during a performance at the iconic Ultra Music Festival in Miami. The crowd was buzzing with anticipation as he took the stage, and the atmosphere was electric. As he dropped one of his signature bass-heavy tracks, the entire audience erupted into a frenzy. The energy in the air was palpable, and Virtual Riot couldn't help but get caught up in the moment. He recalls feeling an indescribable connection with the crowd, as if their collective enthusiasm was fueling his performance. This unforgettable experience solidified his love for performing on the festival circuit.

Another cherished memory for Virtual Riot occurred during a tour stop in Tokyo, Japan. The city's vibrant nightlife and rich music culture left a lasting impression on him. The crowd's energy was infectious, and he found himself feeding off their enthusiasm throughout the entire set. The audience's reaction to his music was overwhelming, and he was blown away by the fact that people from all corners of the globe could come together and connect through music. This experience not only highlighted the universality of music but also reinforced Virtual Riot's commitment to his craft.

While headlining a tour in his home country of Germany, Virtual Riot had the opportunity to perform at a historic venue in Berlin. The venue was packed with fans who had been eagerly awaiting his arrival. The moment he stepped on stage, he was overwhelmed by the sheer sense of pride and joy emanating from the crowd. It was a powerful reminder of how far he had come from his humble beginnings in a small town in Germany. This particular tour memory left a profound impact on Virtual Riot, motivating him to continue pushing the boundaries of his music and inspiring others to pursue their own dreams.

In addition to these large-scale performances, Virtual Riot also has fond memories of intimate club shows. One such memory occurred during a show at a legendary underground venue in London. The small, dimly lit space created an intimate atmosphere that allowed him to connect with the audience on a deeper level. He vividly remembers the energy in the room as he played his set, with every person in the crowd dancing and vibing to the music. This intimate setting provided a unique opportunity for Virtual Riot to interact with fans, exchange stories, and share his love for electronic music.

Virtual Riot's favorite tour memories extend beyond the performances themselves. He often recalls the moments spent with his bandmates and the behind-the-scenes camaraderie that accompanies life on the road. Late-night jam sessions in hotel rooms, impromptu meet-ups with fellow artists, and exploring new cities together have all contributed to the vibrant tapestry of his touring experiences. These moments of connection and friendship serve as a constant source of inspiration for Virtual Riot, reminding him of the power of music to bring people together.

In conclusion, Virtual Riot's favorite tour memories encapsulate the essence of his journey as an artist. From electrifying festivals to intimate club shows, each performance has had a unique impact on him. These memories, along with the moments shared with his bandmates and the connections forged with fans, have shaped his perspective on music and driven his passion for creating unforgettable live experiences. Virtual Riot continues to embark on new adventures, eagerly awaiting the opportunity to create even more cherished tour memories in the future.

Virtual Riot's Cope with Touring Stress and Pressure

Touring can be an exhilarating experience for any musician, but it can also come with its fair share of stress and pressure. Virtual Riot, like many artists, has had to develop coping mechanisms to navigate the challenges that come with life on the road. In this section, we will explore how he manages touring stress and pressure and maintains a healthy mindset.

The Reality of Touring

Touring may seem glamorous from the outside, but the reality is often far from it. Endless nights, jetlag, and the constant rush from one city to another can take a toll on even the most resilient individuals. Virtual Riot understands this reality and has found ways to cope with the physical and mental demands of touring.

Embracing Self-Care

One of the key ways Virtual Riot copes with touring stress is by prioritizing self-care. He recognizes the importance of maintaining a healthy body and mind while on the road. This includes getting enough rest, eating well, and exercising regularly. Virtual Riot understands that taking care of his physical health is essential in sustaining the energy required for his performances.

Staying Connected with Loved Ones

Touring often means being away from family and friends for extended periods. Virtual Riot acknowledges the emotional strain that this can have and makes a conscious effort to stay connected with his loved ones. He utilizes video calls, social media, and even brings family members and close friends on tour whenever possible. By doing so, he maintains a support system that helps him cope with the pressures of touring.

Mindfulness and Meditation

To manage the mental stress of touring, Virtual Riot incorporates mindfulness and meditation into his daily routine. These practices allow him to stay present and grounded amidst the chaos of touring. Whether it's finding a quiet moment backstage or practicing mindfulness exercises on the tour bus, Virtual Riot understands the importance of taking time for himself to reset and refocus.

Journaling and Reflecting

Touring can be a whirlwind of experiences and emotions, making it easy to lose sight of personal growth and reflection. To combat this, Virtual Riot maintains a journal where he documents his thoughts and experiences on tour. Journaling allows him to process his feelings, reflect on his journey, and maintain a sense of gratitude for the opportunities he has been given.

Support Network

Virtual Riot recognizes the importance of building a strong support network while on tour. He surrounds himself with a team of professionals who understand the unique challenges of the music industry and provide guidance and support. This network includes tour managers, personal assistants, and close friends who help him navigate the stresses and pressures of touring.

Maintaining Hobbies and Passions

Beyond music, Virtual Riot recognizes the importance of maintaining hobbies and passions while on tour. Whether it's reading, playing video games, or exploring local attractions, he finds joy and relaxation in activities outside of music. These hobbies provide a much-needed escape from the demands of touring and help him maintain a balanced mindset.

Staying Positive and Grateful

Most importantly, Virtual Riot maintains a positive and grateful mindset throughout his touring journey. He understands that the stresses and pressures he faces are part of the process and chooses to focus on the positive aspects of his career. By practicing gratitude and reminding himself of the opportunities he has been given, Virtual Riot is able to overcome the challenges of touring with a positive outlook.

Conclusion

Touring can be both a thrilling and demanding experience for musicians like Virtual Riot. By embracing self-care, staying connected with loved ones, practicing mindfulness, journaling, building a support network, maintaining hobbies, and cultivating a positive mindset, he effectively copes with the stress and pressure that come with life on the road. Through his experiences, Virtual Riot inspires others to prioritize their well-being and find healthy ways to navigate the challenges of touring.

Virtual Riot's Transformation Onstage

Virtual Riot is not just a musician, he is a performer. When he steps onto the stage, he undergoes a transformative experience that takes his music to a whole new level. The atmosphere changes, the energy intensifies, and Virtual Riot becomes a larger-than-life presence.

One of the key aspects of Virtual Riot's transformation onstage is his ability to engage with the audience. He knows how to read the crowd and feed off their energy, creating a symbiotic relationship between himself and his fans. This connection is essential for Virtual Riot, as he believes that music is meant to be shared and experienced together.

To enhance this connection, Virtual Riot incorporates various visual elements into his performances. He understands the importance of creating a visually captivating show that complements his music. From mesmerizing light displays to immersive stage designs, Virtual Riot aims to create a multi-sensory experience that transports his audience to another dimension.

But it's not just the visuals that transform Virtual Riot onstage. He also uses his body language and stage presence to captivate his audience. With every beat, he moves with purpose, commanding the stage and commanding attention. His energy is contagious, and it spreads throughout the crowd, creating a collective experience that is truly unique.

In addition to his physical transformation, Virtual Riot also pushes the boundaries of technology in his live performances. He constantly seeks innovative ways to blend traditional instruments with electronic music, creating a seamless fusion of sound. Whether it's playing the guitar or controlling a synthesizer, Virtual Riot demonstrates his versatility as a musician while pushing the limits of what is possible in a live setting.

Virtual Riot's transformation onstage is not just about the spectacle. It is an opportunity for him to express himself fully and authentically. Through his music, his performance, and his connection with the audience, he is able to transcend the boundaries of time and space, transporting everyone in the room to a place where anything is possible.

But perhaps the most remarkable aspect of Virtual Riot's transformation onstage is his ability to maintain his genuine self throughout. Despite the lights, the sound, and the overwhelming energy, Virtual Riot never loses sight of who he is as an artist.

He stays true to his creative vision, and his transformation is an extension of his authentic self.

In conclusion, Virtual Riot's transformation onstage is a sight to behold. From the moment he steps onto the stage, he commands attention and creates an immersive experience for his audience. Through visuals, body language, technology, and his genuine passion for music, Virtual Riot takes his performances to a whole new level, leaving a lasting impact on all who witness his transformative presence. So, if you ever have the chance to see Virtual Riot live, prepare yourself for an unforgettable experience that will leave you in awe of his onstage transformation.

Virtual Riot's Relationship with Bandmates on the Road

Being on the road can be exciting, but it can also be challenging, especially when you're traveling and performing with a group of bandmates. For Virtual Riot, the relationship with his bandmates is a crucial part of his success and enjoyment on tour. In this section, we will explore the dynamics of Virtual Riot's relationship with his bandmates and how they navigate the ups and downs of life on the road together.

Building a Strong Foundation

The foundation of any successful relationship is built on trust, respect, and communication. For Virtual Riot and his bandmates, this is no exception. Before hitting the road, they spend ample time getting to know each other, both on a personal and professional level. They understand the importance of establishing clear expectations, goals, and boundaries from the start.

Shared Experiences and Vulnerability

Life on tour can be intense, and Virtual Riot and his bandmates experience a range of emotions together. From the highs of electrifying performances to the lows of exhaustion and homesickness, they go through it all as a team. This shared experience creates a bond that goes beyond words and allows them to be vulnerable with each other.

Problem 1: One night, after a particularly challenging performance, tensions arise between Virtual Riot and one of his bandmates. They have a difference of opinion on an aspect of the show, which leads to a heated argument. As a result, the atmosphere becomes tense, and it starts to impact their overall dynamics on tour. How can Virtual Riot and his bandmate resolve this conflict and rebuild their relationship?

Solution 1: Virtual Riot recognizes the importance of addressing the issue promptly. He invites his bandmate for a one-on-one conversation in a neutral and calm setting. He starts by expressing his appreciation for their input and acknowledges their shared goal of putting on the best show possible. Virtual Riot openly shares his perspective and acknowledges his bandmate's point of view. Together, they brainstorm solutions, focusing on finding a compromise that benefits both parties. Through open and honest communication, they are able to resolve the conflict and strengthen their relationship.

Support and Encouragement

Life on tour can be physically and mentally exhausting, and everyone needs support from their bandmates. Virtual Riot and his bandmates understand the importance of encouraging and lifting each other up during difficult times. They celebrate each other's successes and offer a helping hand when someone is feeling overwhelmed.

Problem 2: One of Virtual Riot's bandmates is feeling burnout from the constant touring schedule. They're finding it difficult to balance work and personal life, and it's starting to affect their overall performance. How can Virtual Riot and the rest of the band offer support and encouragement to help their bandmate through this challenging period?

Solution 2: Virtual Riot and the rest of the band have an open and honest conversation with their struggling bandmate. They express their concerns and reassure them that they are there to provide support. They collectively come up with solutions to alleviate the burnout, such as adjusting the schedule to allow for more downtime or implementing self-care practices on the road. Moreover, they organize team-building activities and create an environment where they can unwind and de-stress together. By fostering a supportive atmosphere, they help their bandmate navigate the challenges and regain their motivation.

Resolving Conflicts and Maintaining Harmony

Conflicts are inevitable when spending a significant amount of time together on the road, but Virtual Riot and his bandmates work hard to address and resolve them in a healthy manner. They prioritize open communication and active listening, allowing each member to express their opinions and concerns without judgment. They understand the importance of finding common ground and maintaining a harmonious atmosphere.

Problem 3: During a long tour, Virtual Riot and one of his bandmates find themselves constantly clashing over minor issues. The tension between them is starting to affect the overall morale of the group. How can Virtual Riot and his bandmate resolve their conflicts and restore the harmony within the band?

Solution 3: Virtual Riot initiates a group meeting to address the underlying issues and promote open dialogue. The bandmates are encouraged to voice their concerns and frustrations, using "I" statements instead of accusatory language. Virtual Riot emphasizes the importance of active listening and encourages each member to find common ground. Through compromise and empathy, they identify solutions that work for everyone involved. Moreover, they establish a system for regular check-ins to address any emerging conflicts promptly. This open and ongoing communication helps resolve the conflicts and rebuild the harmony within the band.

Celebrating Successes and Milestones

Another important aspect of Virtual Riot's relationship with his bandmates is celebrating successes and milestones together. They understand the significance of acknowledging and appreciating each other's achievements, whether it's a successful show, a new collaboration, or personal growth. These celebrations not only boost morale but also strengthen their bond as a team.

Problem 4: Virtual Riot and his bandmates have just wrapped up a highly successful international tour, marked by sold-out shows and positive reviews. How can they celebrate their achievements and strengthen their bond as a team?

Solution 4: Virtual Riot organizes a special band celebration to commemorate the successful tour. They gather in a relaxed setting to reflect on their journey, share memorable moments, and express their gratitude for each other's contributions. They create a highlight reel of the tour, incorporating backstage footage and messages from fans. Each band member takes turns giving heartfelt speeches, expressing their appreciation for the collective effort that made the tour such a success. They conclude the celebration by raising a toast to their achievements and the exciting future ahead.

Unconventional Yet Relevant Insight

Being on the road can be a rollercoaster of emotions, and the relationships among bandmates can be tested. However, Virtual Riot and his bandmates embrace the challenges as opportunities for growth and strengthening their bonds. They recognize that conflicts are natural, and resolving them requires open communication and a willingness to listen and understand each other's perspectives. By prioritizing their relationships and supporting each other through highs and lows, they build a strong foundation for long-term success.

Example: During a particularly grueling tour, Virtual Riot and his bandmates decide to partake in a team-building activity that involves collaborating with a local charity. They spend a day volunteering at a community center, interacting with underprivileged youth and helping with various projects. This experience not only brings them closer together but also provides a fresh perspective on their own challenges. They realize the importance of gratitude and find renewed motivation in making a positive impact beyond their music.

In conclusion, Virtual Riot's relationship with his bandmates is built on trust, respect, and open communication. They navigate the challenges of life on the road by supporting and understanding each other. By celebrating successes, resolving conflicts maturely, and embracing unconventional team-building experiences, they cultivate a bond that strengthens their music and propels them forward on their journey.

Virtual Riot's Perspective on the Touring Life

Touring life can be both exhilarating and exhausting for any artist, and Virtual Riot is no exception. As he has risen to become a prominent figure in the electronic dance music (EDM) scene, he has experienced the ups and downs of life on the road. In this section, we will delve into Virtual Riot's perspective on touring and explore the unique insights he brings to the table.

The Reality of Touring

Touring may seem like a glamorous adventure, but Virtual Riot provides a candid look behind the scenes to reveal the realities of this demanding lifestyle. He acknowledges the endless nights and jetlagged days that come with traveling from one city to another. The constant movement can take a toll on both physical and mental well-being, but Virtual Riot approaches it with a determined spirit.

Behind the Scenes: The Team That Keeps it Going

While Virtual Riot is the face of the act, he recognizes that touring is a team effort. Behind the scenes, there is a dedicated group of professionals who work tirelessly to ensure smooth operations. From tour managers to sound engineers, there is a network of individuals who play crucial roles in making each show a success. Virtual Riot holds immense gratitude for his team, as they contribute significantly to his touring experience.

Highlights and Low Points on the Road

Touring is a rollercoaster ride, filled with highs and lows. Virtual Riot highlights the incredible moments on stage where he feels the energy of the crowd and witnesses the power of music to bring people together. These moments make all the challenges worthwhile.

However, he also acknowledges the low points that inevitably come with the touring life. From missing family and friends to grappling with homesickness, Virtual Riot opens up about the emotional toll that being on the road can have. Nevertheless, he finds strength in the support of his fans, who constantly remind him of the impact his music has on their lives.

The Connection with Fans on Stage

One of the most rewarding aspects of touring for Virtual Riot is the connection he establishes with his fans. They are the reason he continues to push through the demanding schedule and grueling performances. The energy in the room, the shared love for music, and the unity that comes from a collective experience are what make live shows so special for him.

Virtual Riot's Touring Rituals and Superstitions

Like many musicians, Virtual Riot has developed his own rituals and superstitions to help him stay focused and centered before each performance. These might include specific warm-up routines, meditation practices, or even wearing a lucky charm. While these rituals may seem trivial to some, they provide him with a sense of comfort and confidence as he takes the stage.

Virtual Riot's Favorite Tour Memories

Throughout his touring career, Virtual Riot has accumulated countless unforgettable memories. Whether it's an extraordinary crowd reaction, a breathtaking venue, or a surprise encounter with a fellow artist, these moments stay etched in his mind. Some of his favorite memories include impromptu collaborations with other musicians, which add a unique element of spontaneity to his shows.

Virtual Riot's Coping with Touring Stress and Pressure

The demanding nature of touring can bring forth high levels of stress and pressure. Virtual Riot has developed his own coping mechanisms to navigate these challenges. He emphasizes the importance of taking care of his physical and mental well-being, including regular exercise, healthy eating, and setting aside time for self-care activities. These practices enable him to maintain balance and cope with the pressures of touring.

Virtual Riot's Transformation Onstage

When Virtual Riot steps onto the stage, he undergoes a remarkable transformation. The shy and reserved person offstage is replaced by a confident and animated performer. This transformation is a testament to his passion for music and his desire to provide an unforgettable experience for his audience.

Virtual Riot's Relationship with Bandmates on the Road

Touring often involves spending an extended amount of time with fellow bandmates. Virtual Riot values the relationships he builds with his bandmates and considers them an essential support system on the road. They share not only the highs and lows of touring but also the joy of creating music together. This camaraderie contributes to the overall touring experience and helps foster a sense of unity within the band.

Virtual Riot's Perspective on the Touring Life

In Virtual Riot's view, the touring life is a bittersweet journey that comes with its own set of challenges and rewards. While it may involve sacrifices and demanding schedules, the opportunity to share his passion for music with audiences around the world is a dream come true. He believes that the experiences gained on tour, both personally and professionally, have shaped him into the artist he is today. Virtual Riot remains grateful for the unwavering support of his fans, who inspire him to continue pushing boundaries and evolving his musical craft.

As Virtual Riot continues to embark on new adventures and create groundbreaking music, his perspective on the touring life will undoubtedly continue to evolve. While he appreciates the opportunity to connect with fans and showcase his talent, he also recognizes the need for self-care and balance to sustain a long and fulfilling career in the music industry.

In conclusion, Virtual Riot's perspective on the touring life is a testament to the complex nature of being a musician on the road. From the realities of constant travel to the extraordinary moments on stage, he offers a raw and honest account of the joys and challenges that come with a life dedicated to music. Virtual Riot's insights serve as both an inspiration and a reminder to aspiring artists that the journey is not always glamorous, but it is undoubtedly worth pursuing wholeheartedly.

Exploring Different Venues and Music Festivals

Small Clubs to Massive Music Venues

In the early days of Virtual Riot's career, he started performing in small clubs in his hometown of Germany. These intimate venues provided him with an opportunity to connect with a smaller but dedicated group of fans who were passionate about electronic music. The atmosphere in these clubs was electric, with the crowd pulsating to the beats and melodies of Virtual Riot's music.

At these small club shows, Virtual Riot honed his skills as a performer, learning how to read the crowd and tailor his sets to create an unforgettable experience. He experimented with different mixes, tempos, and transitions to keep the energy high and the crowd engaged. These shows were a testing ground for Virtual Riot, allowing him to experiment with new sounds and gauge the audience's response.

As Virtual Riot's popularity grew, so did the size of the venues he performed in. He soon found himself playing at local music festivals and larger music venues across Germany. These massive music venues brought with them a whole new level of energy and excitement. The crowds were larger, the production values were higher, and the experience was on a whole different scale.

Virtual Riot embraced the challenge of performing in these larger venues, pushing himself to deliver a show that was even more immersive and captivating. He worked closely with his team to create visually stunning stage designs and incorporate high-tech lighting and special effects. This attention to detail elevated his performances, creating a mesmerizing and unforgettable experience for the audience.

The transition from small clubs to massive music venues also meant adapting his performance style. Virtual Riot started incorporating live instruments into his sets, bringing a unique and dynamic element to his performances. Whether it was playing the guitar, drums, or keyboards, his live instrumentation added an extra layer of excitement and authenticity to his shows.

One of Virtual Riot's favorite memories from this period was performing at a renowned music festival in Germany. The energy in the crowd was palpable as thousands of fans came together to celebrate their love for electronic music. The synergy between Virtual Riot and the audience was electric, with everyone united by a shared passion for the music.

Virtual Riot continues to evolve his live performances, pushing the boundaries of what is possible in a live show. He embraces new technologies and incorporates them into his performances, creating a truly immersive experience for the audience.

From holographic displays to interactive visuals, Virtual Riot aims to transport his fans to another world, where music becomes an all-encompassing experience.

In conclusion, Virtual Riot's journey from performing in small clubs to massive music venues has been a testament to his dedication and talent. He has not only entertained thousands of fans but has also inspired a new generation of musicians and performers. His ability to connect with the audience and create unforgettable experiences sets him apart in the electronic music industry. As he continues to grow and evolve as an artist, Virtual Riot's live performances will undoubtedly leave a lasting impact on the music scene.

The Intensity of Music Festivals

Music festivals are a cultural phenomenon that have taken the world by storm. These events bring together thousands of music lovers for a multi-day celebration of live performances, immersive experiences, and a sense of community. In this section, we will explore the intensity of music festivals, from the overwhelming energy of the crowd to the electrifying performances on stage.

The Power of the Crowd

One of the defining characteristics of music festivals is the incredible energy generated by the crowd. When thousands of people come together with a shared passion for music, the atmosphere becomes electric. The synergy between the performers and the audience creates a feedback loop of excitement, where the energy in the crowd fuels the artists on stage, and in turn, their performances fuel the energy of the crowd.

However, the intensity of the crowd can also be overwhelming. The sheer number of people, combined with the adrenaline-fueled atmosphere, can lead to chaotic moments. It is crucial for festival-goers to be aware of their surroundings and to practice good crowd etiquette. This includes respecting personal space, helping others in need, and being mindful of the impact of their actions on those around them.

Unforgettable Performances

Music festivals offer a unique platform for artists to showcase their talent and connect with a massive audience. The performances at music festivals are often larger-than-life, with artists pulling out all the stops to deliver an unforgettable show. From stunning visuals and mesmerizing light displays to intricate stage designs and pyrotechnics, these performances go beyond the boundaries of what is possible in a typical concert setting.

For festival-goers, witnessing these extraordinary performances can be a life-changing experience. The energy and passion that artists bring to the stage are contagious, and being part of a crowd that sings and dances along to every song creates a sense of unity and belonging.

A Playground of Creativity

Music festivals are not only about the music; they also provide a platform for creativity and self-expression. The festival grounds are transformed into immersive worlds, with whimsical art installations, vibrant costumes, and interactive experiences at every turn. From large-scale sculptures to captivating performances by street artists, the festival environment becomes a playground for exploring and celebrating creativity.

Attending a music festival allows individuals to step out of their comfort zones and embrace their own creativity. Many festival-goers use the opportunity to dress up in unique outfits, experimenting with bold fashion choices and accessories. It is a time to let go of inhibitions and to fully immerse oneself in the spirit of the festival.

The Challenges of Festival Culture

While music festivals are undoubtedly thrilling, they also present challenges that can test the endurance of both attendees and performers. The physical demands of spending long hours on your feet, navigating large crowds, and enduring unpredictable weather conditions can take a toll on even the most enthusiastic festival-goers.

For artists, playing at multiple festivals within a short period means constant travel, late-night performances, and little time for rest. The pressure to deliver memorable shows and the constant need to be "on" can lead to physical and mental exhaustion. It is essential for both attendees and performers to prioritize self-care and take breaks when needed to ensure a safe and enjoyable experience.

Navigating the Festival Landscape

With the rising popularity of music festivals, there is a wide array of options to choose from. Each festival has its own unique vibe, lineup, and location, catering to different musical tastes and preferences. Navigating the festival landscape requires research, planning, and sometimes tough decisions on which events to attend.

For festival-goers, it is crucial to be well-prepared and informed. This includes knowing the festival's rules and regulations, understanding the layout of the grounds, and planning ahead for essentials such as food, water, and shelter. It is also essential to familiarize oneself with the lineup and schedule to maximize the festival experience and ensure that you don't miss out on your favorite artists.

A New Chapter in Music History

Music festivals have become an integral part of contemporary music culture. They have paved the way for new forms of artistic expression, pushing the boundaries of what is possible in live performances and creating lasting memories for both artists and fans. The intensity of music festivals lies not only in the physical and emotional experiences they offer but also in the impact they have on the music industry as a whole.

As the popularity of music festivals continues to grow, it is an exciting time to be part of this cultural phenomenon. Whether you are an avid festival-goer or an aspiring artist, the intensity of music festivals serves as a reminder of the power of music to bring people together and create unforgettable moments.

Exercises

1. Think of a memorable live performance you have experienced, either at a music festival or a concert. Reflect on the energy of the crowd and how it enhanced your enjoyment of the show. What elements made the performance stand out for you?

2. Research an upcoming music festival that interests you. Consider factors such as the lineup, location, and atmosphere. Write a short paragraph describing why you would like to attend this festival and what you hope to experience.

3. Imagine you are an artist performing at a music festival. Brainstorm ideas for a visually stunning stage design that reflects your music and artistic vision. Consider elements such as lighting, props, and special effects. Sketch a rough diagram of your ideal stage setup.

4. Reflect on the challenges of attending a music festival, such as dealing with large crowds, unpredictable weather, and potential fatigue. Write a list of practical tips and tricks to help festival-goers have an enjoyable and safe experience.

5. Conduct research on the environmental impact of music festivals. Explore initiatives that some festivals have implemented to reduce their carbon footprint and promote sustainability. Write a short essay discussing the importance of eco-consciousness in the festival industry and propose innovative ideas for future festivals to consider.

Resources

- "The Festival Book" by Natasha Dow Schüll - "Music/Culture: The Politics of Genre" by Gina Arnold - "Live at the Fillmore East and West: Getting Backstage and Personal with Rock's Greatest Legends" by John Glatt - "The Thirty-Year Honeymoon" by Amy Rigby - "The Music Festival Guide: For Music Lovers and Musicians" by Taylor Donohue

Unforgettable Performances and Memorable Moments

When it comes to Virtual Riot's live performances, there is one thing you can always count on: an unforgettable experience that will stay with you long after the show is over. Virtual Riot is known for pushing boundaries and creating unique and engaging performances that leave a lasting impact on the audience. In this section, we will explore some of the most memorable moments from Virtual Riot's live shows and music festivals.

One of the defining features of Virtual Riot's performances is the energy he brings to the stage. Whether he's performing in a small club or a massive music venue, Virtual Riot knows how to captivate the crowd and keep them dancing all night long. His sets are a rollercoaster of emotions, filled with hard-hitting drops, melodic interludes, and unexpected twists and turns.

One unforgettable performance took place at the Electric Daisy Carnival (EDC) in Las Vegas. The crowd was buzzing with anticipation as Virtual Riot took the stage. As the first notes of his hit track "Energy Drink" filled the air, the crowd erupted into cheers and began jumping and dancing in unison. The energy in the air was palpable, and Virtual Riot fed off the crowd's enthusiasm, delivering a high-octane performance that left everyone breathless.

But it's not just the big music festivals where Virtual Riot shines. He also knows how to create magical moments in intimate settings. During a show at a small club in Berlin, Virtual Riot surprised the audience by bringing out a live drummer to accompany his set. The combination of electronic beats and live percussion created a unique and immersive experience that had the crowd cheering for more.

Another memorable moment from Virtual Riot's live performances was during a show in London. As the night wore on and the crowd's energy began to wane, Virtual Riot pulled out all the stops to reenergize the crowd. He invited a group of breakdancers onto the stage and started beatboxing, creating a spontaneous and electrifying moment that had everyone on their feet. The combination of live music, dance, and beatboxing created an unforgettable performance that left a lasting impression on everyone in attendance.

Virtual Riot is also known for his visually stunning stage productions. During his performances, he incorporates captivating visuals and stage design that transport the audience to another world. One such moment was during a show in Los Angeles, where Virtual Riot used a holographic projector to create an immersive 3D visual experience. As the crowd looked on in awe, Virtual Riot seamlessly blended music and visuals to create a truly mesmerizing performance.

But it's not just the grand gestures that make Virtual Riot's live performances unforgettable. Sometimes, the most memorable moments are the small details that show his connection with the audience. During a show in his hometown of Marl, Germany, Virtual Riot took a moment to step away from the DJ booth and dance with the crowd. The genuine joy on his face as he interacted with his fans created a sense of intimacy and camaraderie that made the night truly special.

In conclusion, Virtual Riot's live performances are a testament to his talent and dedication as an artist. From explosive music festivals to intimate club shows, Virtual Riot knows how to create unforgettable moments that leave a lasting impact on the audience. Through his energy, stage presence, and unique creative vision, Virtual Riot continues to push the boundaries of live performance and inspire a new generation of music enthusiasts.

Chapter 2. Life on the Road: Touring and Live Performances

2.3.4 Bringing the Energy to Every Crowd

Bringing the energy to every crowd is a key aspect of Virtual Riot's live performances. With a captivating stage presence and a deep understanding of his audience, Virtual Riot has perfected the art of connecting with the crowd and creating an unforgettable experience for his fans.

Understanding the Crowd Dynamics

One of the first steps in bringing the energy to every crowd is understanding the dynamics of the audience. Virtual Riot recognizes that each crowd is unique, with their own preferences and energy levels. He takes the time to analyze the atmosphere and adapt his set accordingly, ensuring that the crowd remains engaged and energized throughout the performance.

Virtual Riot pays close attention to the demographic of the audience, the venue size, and the overall mood of the event. By gauging the crowd's reaction to different tracks and beats, he is able to make real-time adjustments to his setlist, keeping the energy levels high and the audience excited.

Creating Memorable Moments

Virtual Riot believes that live performances should be about creating memorable moments that will stay with the audience long after the show is over. He goes beyond just playing his tracks and focuses on delivering a complete experience that will leave a lasting impression.

One way Virtual Riot achieves this is by incorporating unexpected elements into his performances. From surprise guest appearances to unique visual effects, he constantly seeks ways to surprise and delight his audience. By creating these unforgettable moments, Virtual Riot ensures that every crowd he performs for feels a sense of excitement and anticipation.

Building a Connection with the Crowd

Bringing the energy to every crowd is not just about the music, but also about building a connection with the audience. Virtual Riot understands the importance of engaging with his fans on a personal level and creating a sense of community during his live performances.

He regularly interacts with the crowd, encouraging them to sing along, jump, and dance. By actively involving his fans in the performance, Virtual Riot creates a collective experience that amplifies the energy in the room. He takes the time to acknowledge the audience, show his appreciation for their support, and make them feel like an integral part of the show.

Reading the Crowd's Energy

To truly bring the energy to every crowd, Virtual Riot relies on his ability to read and respond to the audience's energy levels. He pays attention to their reactions, body language, and enthusiasm, allowing him to gauge the tempo and intensity needed to keep the crowd engaged.

When the energy in the room dips, Virtual Riot knows how to elevate it by introducing a new track, a surprising drop, or even interacting with the crowd directly. He understands that the energy of the crowd is a two-way street, and by feeding off their energy, he is able to take his performance to new heights.

Maintaining Consistency and Authenticity

Lastly, bringing the energy to every crowd requires consistency and authenticity. Virtual Riot stays true to his unique sound and style while adapting it to fit the energy of each performance. He believes that being true to himself and his music is what sets him apart and allows him to connect with his audience on a deeper level.

By staying authentic, Virtual Riot brings a genuine passion to his live performances, creating an electric atmosphere that resonates with the crowd. He believes that the key to bringing the energy to every crowd is to stay true to himself and his music, and let that authenticity shine through in every aspect of the performance.

Chapter Summary

In this chapter, we explored how Virtual Riot brings the energy to every crowd during his live performances. Understanding the crowd dynamics, creating memorable moments, building a connection with the crowd, reading their energy, and maintaining consistency and authenticity are all important aspects of Virtual Riot's approach to live performances. By considering these factors, Virtual Riot ensures that each audience has a unique and unforgettable experience, leaving them energized and wanting more.

+ **Ear Protection:** Protecting his hearing is a top priority for Virtual Riot. He always carries high-quality earplugs to shield his ears from the loud music and maintain his long-term hearing health.

+ **Positive Mindset:** Virtual Riot believes that maintaining a positive mindset is crucial for a successful festival experience. He embraces the unpredictable nature of festivals and approaches each performance with an open and optimistic mindset.

+ **Exploring the Festival Grounds:** In his downtime, Virtual Riot loves to explore the festival grounds, discover new artists, and connect with fellow musicians and fans. He believes that immersing himself in the festival experience beyond his own performance provides new perspectives and endless inspiration.

Advice for Emerging Artists

For emerging artists dreaming of performing at festivals, Virtual Riot offers some valuable advice based on his own experiences and journey:

+ **Stay True to Yourself:** Authenticity is key. Virtual Riot encourages artists to stay true to their own unique sound and style, rather than conforming to trends or trying to please others. Embracing individuality is what sets artists apart.

+ **Consistency and Persistence:** Building a career takes time, effort, and persistence. Virtual Riot advises emerging artists to focus on creating quality music consistently and persevering despite any challenges they may encounter along the way.

+ **Live Performances Matter:** Virtual Riot emphasizes the importance of honing live performance skills. Engaging and connecting with the audience is just as significant as producing great music. Practice and refine your stage presence to leave a lasting impression.

+ **Network and Collaborate:** Building connections within the music industry is crucial for growth. Virtual Riot encourages emerging artists to network with other artists, industry professionals, and fans. Collaboration can open doors to new opportunities and help expand one's reach.

- **Embrace Online Platforms:** Utilize social media and music streaming platforms to showcase your music and connect with fans. Virtual Riot emphasizes the power of online platforms in reaching a broader audience and gaining recognition.

Virtual Riot's Legacy in the Festival World

As Virtual Riot's influence continues to grow in the festival world, his unique perspective and innovative approach to music production and performance leave a lasting impact on the EDM scene. Through his energetic and captivating live shows, he aims to create an unforgettable festival experience for his audience, inspiring them to delve deeper into the world of electronic music.

Virtual Riot's perspective on festival culture serves as a reminder of the power of music to bring people together, foster a sense of belonging, and create lifelong memories. His unwavering passion for festivals and commitment to his craft make him an influential force in shaping the future of EDM festivals and the music industry as a whole.

In the next chapter, we will explore the thrilling life on the road, as we dive into Virtual Riot's experiences, challenges, and triumphs during touring and live performances. Stay tuned for an in-depth look at the exhilarating world behind the scenes!

Virtual Riot's Festival Must-Haves

When it comes to music festivals, Virtual Riot knows a thing or two about what it takes to have an incredible experience. From small local shows to massive international events, Virtual Riot has seen it all and knows exactly what items are essential for a successful and enjoyable festival journey.

The Festival Survival Kit

To ensure a smooth and worry-free festival experience, Virtual Riot always packs a festival survival kit. This kit includes all the necessary essentials for staying comfortable and prepared throughout the event. Here are some of Virtual Riot's must-haves:

- **Comfortable Footwear:** A good pair of shoes is crucial for surviving long hours of dancing and walking between stages. Virtual Riot opts for comfortable sneakers or boots that provide support and cushioning.

- **Hydration Pack:** Staying hydrated is key during a music festival. Virtual Riot always carries a hydration pack filled with water to ensure he can stay refreshed and avoid dehydration.

- **Sun Protection:** Music festivals often take place outdoors, exposing attendees to the sun's rays. Virtual Riot never forgets to pack sunscreen, a hat, and sunglasses to protect himself from the sun's harmful UV rays.

- **Earplugs:** Music festivals can be loud, and protecting your hearing is essential. Virtual Riot always brings a pair of high-quality earplugs to enjoy the music while minimizing the risk of hearing damage.

- **Portable Charger:** With all the photos, videos, and social media sharing happening at festivals, a portable charger is a must. Virtual Riot ensures his devices always have enough juice to capture the moments that matter.

- **Wet Wipes and Hand Sanitizer:** Keeping clean and germ-free can be a challenge at crowded festivals. Virtual Riot carries wet wipes and hand sanitizer to freshen up and maintain good hygiene throughout the event.

The Fashion Statement

Music festivals are not only about the music but also about expressing oneself through fashion. Virtual Riot loves to stand out in the crowd and always brings a few key fashion items to make a statement. Here are some of Virtual Riot's festival fashion must-haves:

- **Statement Accessories:** Virtual Riot loves to accessorize his festival outfits with eye-catching items such as colorful bandanas, funky sunglasses, and unique hats. These accessories add a touch of personality and flair to his overall look.

- **Bright and Colorful Clothing:** Festivals are the perfect opportunity to embrace vibrant colors and bold patterns. Virtual Riot makes sure to pack a variety of colorful clothing items like tie-dye shirts, neon shorts, and vibrant leggings to match the energetic festival vibes.

- **Durable Backpack or Fanny Pack:** Carrying personal belongings conveniently and securely is essential at festivals. Virtual Riot prefers a durable backpack or fanny pack that can hold his essentials while keeping his hands free to dance and enjoy the music.

- **Comfy and Breathable Fabrics:** Long hours spent dancing and moving around call for comfortable and breathable fabrics. Virtual Riot chooses lightweight materials like cotton and linen that allow his skin to breathe and keep him cool throughout the festival.

- **Statement Sneakers:** Comfort and style go hand in hand for Virtual Riot. He always brings a pair of statement sneakers that not only provide the necessary support for long hours on his feet but also add an extra flair to his festival outfits.

The Unconventional Extras

In addition to the essentials and fashion items, Virtual Riot loves to bring some unconventional extras to enhance his festival experience. These extras not only add to the fun but also create memorable moments. Here are some of Virtual Riot's favorite unconventional festival must-haves:

- **Glow Sticks and LED Accessories:** Adding a touch of glow and spark to his festival experience, Virtual Riot always brings glow sticks and LED accessories. They create an enchanting visual spectacle and make him an instant hit among fellow festival-goers.

- **Inflatable Lounger:** When it's time to take a break and relax, Virtual Riot loves to kick back on an inflatable lounger. It provides a comfortable spot to rest and enjoy the festival ambiance while making him the envy of other attendees.

- **Portable Bluetooth Speaker:** Virtual Riot enjoys having impromptu jam sessions with fellow festival-goers. He carries a portable Bluetooth speaker to share his favorite tunes with others, creating an instant party wherever he goes.

- **Costume Accessories:** To up the fun factor and embrace the festival spirit, Virtual Riot often packs costume accessories like wigs, masks, and face paint. These playful items not only add to his enjoyment but also encourage interaction with other festival attendees.

- **Kandi Bracelets:** Kandi bracelets have become a festival tradition, and Virtual Riot is fully on board. He makes and trades kandi bracelets with other attendees as a way to connect and spread positive vibes within the festival community.

Whether it's the festival survival kit essentials, fashion items to make a statement, or the unconventional extras that create unforgettable memories, Virtual Riot knows how to make the most of his festival experience. By following his festival must-haves, you too can be prepared to rock out and have a fantastic time at your next music festival adventure. Remember to always stay safe, hydrated, and true to yourself amidst the festival madness.

Virtual Riot's Advice for Emerging Artists at Festivals

Being an emerging artist in the music industry can be both exciting and challenging. It's a journey filled with ups and downs, but if you're passionate about your music and willing to work hard, you can achieve great things. As someone who has experienced the festival circuit firsthand, Virtual Riot has some valuable advice to offer to emerging artists looking to make their mark at festivals. Here are some insights and tips from Virtual Riot himself:

1. Be Authentic and True to Yourself

One of the most important pieces of advice Virtual Riot gives to emerging artists is to stay true to themselves and their unique sound. In a world where trends come and go, it's crucial to carve out your own musical identity. Don't try to imitate other artists or chase after what's popular at the moment. Embrace your individuality and let your music reflect who you truly are as an artist. Authenticity will set you apart from the crowd and help you build a loyal fanbase.

2. Put on a Memorable Performance

At festivals, you have the opportunity to showcase your talent and leave a lasting impression on the audience. Virtual Riot advises emerging artists to focus not only on their music but also on delivering a captivating live performance. Engage with the crowd, bring energy to the stage, and create a memorable experience for everyone present. Experiment with different ways to make your set unique, whether it's through visuals, stage design, or incorporating live instruments. Push the boundaries and offer something that stands out in the minds of festival-goers.

3. Collaborate and Network

Collaborations can be powerful tools for emerging artists, allowing you to expand your reach and expose your music to new audiences. Virtual Riot encourages artists to seek out collaborations with other like-minded individuals, both within and outside the EDM scene. Collaborating with artists from different genres can bring fresh perspectives and inspire new creative directions. Additionally, networking with industry professionals, DJs, and other artists at festivals can open doors to new opportunities and help you establish valuable connections.

4. Embrace the Festival Culture

Festivals are more than just a platform to perform. They are vibrant communities that bring together music lovers from all walks of life. Virtual Riot advises emerging artists to fully immerse themselves in the festival culture. Attend other artists' sets, explore different stages, and engage in conversations with other festival-goers. Embracing the festival experience allows you to connect with your audience on a deeper level and gain a better understanding of what drives people's passion for music.

5. Be Prepared and Professional

Preparation is key to success at festivals. Virtual Riot stresses the importance of being well-prepared and professional in every aspect of your performance. Practice your set meticulously and ensure that everything goes smoothly on stage. Arrive early, communicate effectively with the festival organizers, and be respectful of other artists' time slots. Attention to detail and a professional approach will not only enhance your reputation but also increase the likelihood of future festival invitations.

6. Stay Grounded and Learn from Every Experience

As an emerging artist, it's important to stay grounded and maintain a humble attitude. Virtual Riot advises against letting success get to your head and to embrace each opportunity as a chance to learn and grow. Whether you perform at a small club or a massive festival, there's always something to be gained from the experience. Take the time to reflect on your performances, identify areas for improvement, and use each gig as a stepping stone towards your ultimate musical goals.

7. Take Care of Yourself

Last but certainly not least, Virtual Riot emphasizes the importance of self-care. The festival circuit can be exhausting, with long nights and jetlagged days. It's crucial to prioritize your physical and mental well-being. Get enough sleep, eat healthily, and stay hydrated. Take breaks when needed and find time to recharge. Remember that your artistic journey is a marathon, not a sprint, so taking care of yourself is essential for longevity in the industry.

In conclusion, Virtual Riot's advice for emerging artists at festivals revolves around authenticity, putting on a memorable performance, seeking collaborations and networking, embracing festival culture, being prepared and professional, staying grounded, and taking care of oneself. By following these tips, emerging artists can navigate the festival circuit with confidence and make a lasting impact on both the industry and their audience. Keep pushing boundaries, stay true to yourself, and let your music shine on the stages of festivals around the world. Good luck!

Virtual Riot's Role in Shaping Festival Lineups

Virtual Riot, the renowned German music producer, has played a significant role in shaping festival lineups around the world. With his unique blend of electronic dance music (EDM) genres and innovative soundscapes, he has captivated audiences and left a lasting impact on the global EDM scene. In this section, we will explore the ways in which Virtual Riot has influenced the selection and diversification of artists at music festivals.

Embracing Diversity and Genre Fusion

Virtual Riot holds a strong belief in the power of musical diversity and genre fusion. He has always been open to collaborating with artists from various backgrounds, genres, and styles. Through his collaborations with musicians spanning hip-hop, rock, and pop genres, he has broken down barriers and pushed the boundaries of EDM.

Virtual Riot's commitment to musical diversity is mirrored in his impact on festival lineups. By showcasing a unique mix of artists from different genres, he has encouraged festival organizers to embrace a wider range of musical styles. As a result, festivals that previously focused on specific genres have now started to incorporate a more eclectic mix, catering to a broader audience and creating a vibrant and inclusive musical experience.

Spotlighting Emerging Artists

One of Virtual Riot's notable contributions to festival lineups is his keen eye for talent and his dedication to supporting emerging artists. He recognizes the importance of providing opportunities for up-and-coming musicians to gain exposure and showcase their skills on a larger stage.

Virtual Riot actively seeks out collaborations with emerging artists, introducing them to his vast audience and helping them gain recognition within the EDM community. By including these talented newcomers in his performances and recommending them for festival lineups, he has played a significant role in showcasing their potential and jump-starting their careers.

The impact of Virtual Riot's support for emerging artists goes beyond individual success stories. It has inspired festival organizers to prioritize the inclusion of promising new talent in their lineups, creating a more dynamic and inclusive environment for artists of all levels of experience.

Promoting Diversity and Inclusion

Virtual Riot is a strong advocate for diversity and inclusion, both in the music industry and society as a whole. He firmly believes that everyone should have a voice and equal opportunities within the EDM scene.

In his collaborations and performances, Virtual Riot actively seeks out artists from underrepresented groups and provides a platform for them to share their unique perspectives. By including a diverse range of artists in festival lineups, he encourages inclusivity and challenges traditional norms within the EDM community.

Virtual Riot's commitment to diversity and inclusion has sparked conversations and driven positive change within the music festival circuit. Organizers are now more intentional about creating lineups that reflect the diversity of their audiences, fostering an environment where different cultures, backgrounds, and identities can thrive.

Elevating the EDM Experience

Virtual Riot's influence on festival lineups is not limited to his selection of artists. He has also revolutionized the live EDM experience through his innovative performances and stage production.

By pushing the limits of technology and incorporating captivating visuals, Virtual Riot has elevated the EDM experience for festival-goers. His performances are immersive and engaging, creating an atmosphere where the audience can fully immerse themselves in the music.

This focus on transforming the live performance has had a ripple effect on festival organizers. They are now more discerning in their selection of artists, considering not only their musical prowess but also their ability to put on a visually dynamic show. The result is a greater emphasis on stage production and visually stunning performances, enhancing the overall festival experience for attendees.

Creating Unforgettable Moments

Virtual Riot is known for his ability to create unforgettable moments on stage. With his dynamic energy and connection to the crowd, he leaves a lasting impact on festival audiences worldwide.

By consistently delivering powerful and inspiring performances, Virtual Riot has influenced festival lineups to prioritize artists who can deliver that same level of connection and engagement. Organizers now seek out artists who can create meaningful and memorable experiences for festival-goers, ensuring that every moment spent at the event is impactful and unforgettable.

Virtual Riot's role in shaping festival lineups goes beyond his own performances. His ability to create these unforgettable moments has set a new standard for live EDM shows and has influenced the overall programming decisions of festivals around the world.

Example: Electric Land Festival

To illustrate Virtual Riot's impact on festival lineups, let's take a closer look at the Electric Land Festival. Before Virtual Riot's rise to prominence, Electric Land focused primarily on mainstream EDM acts, showcasing artists from a narrow range of sub-genres.

However, after seeing Virtual Riot's dynamic performances and experiencing the diversity and energy he brought to the stage, the festival organizers decided to make some changes. They sought out artists from various genres and backgrounds, incorporating hip-hop, alternative rock, and experimental electronic acts into their lineup. This shift allowed Electric Land to attract a broader audience and create a unique festival experience unlike anything seen before.

Notably, Virtual Riot himself headlined the festival, sharing the main stage with musicians whose styles ranged from trap to indie pop. The resulting lineup received widespread acclaim, with attendees praising the festival's commitment to diversity and innovative programming.

The success of Electric Land Festival's revised lineup highlighted the influence that Virtual Riot and his unique musical style had on shaping the festival's direction. It inspired other festivals to follow suit, embracing a more diverse and inclusive approach to their programming.

Conclusion

Virtual Riot's contribution to shaping festival lineups cannot be overstated. Through his commitment to diversity, promotion of emerging artists, and dedication to creating unforgettable experiences, he has left an indelible mark on the global EDM scene. Festival organizers around the world now recognize the importance of embracing diversity, promoting emerging talent, and creating captivating experiences for their attendees. Virtual Riot's impact on festival lineups continues to inspire positive change and shape the future of the music festival circuit.

Virtual Riot's Influence on Festival Crowd Energy

Festival crowds are known for their electrifying energy and passion for music. They come together from all corners of the world to celebrate their favorite artists and immerse themselves in an atmosphere of pure joy and excitement. Virtual Riot, with his unique blend of electronic music genres and innovative sound design, has had a profound influence on the energy and vibes of festival crowds around the globe.

One of the key ways Virtual Riot has impacted festival crowd energy is through his ability to create powerful and infectious drops in his tracks. A drop is the climactic part of a song where all the elements come together in a burst of energy, driving the crowd into a frenzy. Virtual Riot has mastered the art of crafting drops that are both sonically impressive and emotionally impactful, leaving the crowd begging for more.

Take, for example, his track "Energy Drink." The buildup is filled with anticipation, with tension building as each layer is added. When the drop finally hits, it's like a sonic explosion, releasing an immense amount of energy onto the crowd. The combination of heavy bass, melodic elements, and expertly crafted sound design creates a euphoric experience that resonates with festival-goers and fuels their energy throughout the performance.

Another aspect of Virtual Riot's influence on festival crowd energy is his ability to seamlessly blend different genres and styles within his sets. He effortlessly transitions from hard-hitting dubstep to melodic future bass, creating a dynamic and diverse musical journey for the crowd. This versatility keeps the audience engaged and on their toes, as they never know what sonic experience Virtual Riot will deliver next. The element of surprise and the constant evolution of his sound keeps the energy levels high and ensures that the crowd is always in the moment, fully immersed in the music.

Virtual Riot's impact on festival crowd energy extends beyond just his own performances. As an influential figure in the EDM scene, his unique sound and innovative approach to music production have inspired and influenced other artists. Many up-and-coming producers and DJs have taken cues from Virtual Riot's style, incorporating elements of his sound into their own productions. This ripple effect has led to a broader transformation in festival crowd energy, as more artists explore experimental and genre-blending approaches to their music.

In addition to his musical contributions, Virtual Riot also understands the importance of engaging with the audience and creating a sense of community within the festival space. His on-stage presence and interactions with the crowd contribute to the overall energy and atmosphere of the performance. Whether it's through his contagious dance moves, his lively stage presence, or his genuine enthusiasm for the music, Virtual Riot connects with the audience on a personal level, elevating the collective energy of the crowd.

Virtual Riot's influence on festival crowd energy can also be attributed to his commitment to pushing the boundaries of technology in his live performances. He is known for incorporating cutting-edge visuals, stage designs, and lighting effects into his shows, creating a multisensory experience that enhances the overall impact of his music. These immersive visual elements add an extra layer of excitement to the performance and amplify the energy of the crowd.

To further illustrate the impact of Virtual Riot on festival crowd energy, let's consider a real-world example. At the Electric Daisy Carnival (EDC), one of the largest EDM festivals in the world, Virtual Riot performed on the main stage. His set was a captivating display of his signature sound, combining heavy bass drops, intricate melodies, and breathtaking visuals. The crowd's energy levels soared as they danced in unison, feeding off the energy created by Virtual Riot. The moment was electric and created a lasting memory for all in attendance.

In conclusion, Virtual Riot's influence on festival crowd energy is undeniable. Through his powerful drops, genre-blending style, engagement with the audience, use of innovative technology, and overall commitment to pushing the boundaries of electronic music, he has transformed the festival experience for countless fans. His impact is not only felt during his own performances but also in the broader EDM scene, inspiring a new wave of creativity and energy among both established and emerging artists. Virtual Riot's legacy in shaping the energy and vibes of festival crowds will continue to reverberate for years to come, leaving an indelible mark on the music industry.

Pushing Boundaries with Live Performances

Incorporating Visuals and Stage Design

When Virtual Riot takes the stage, it's not just about the music. The visual experience is equally important, and the incorporation of visuals and stage design plays a crucial role in creating an immersive atmosphere for the audience. In this section, we will explore how Virtual Riot incorporates visuals and stage design into his live performances, highlighting the importance of unique and engaging visuals.

Creating a Visual Narrative

Incorporating visuals and stage design is not just about adding flashy lights or random images. Virtual Riot takes a thoughtful and intentional approach in creating a visual narrative that complements his music.

One aspect of creating this visual narrative is through the use of synchronized visuals that are triggered in real-time with the music. This requires careful coordination between Virtual Riot and his visual team to ensure the visuals align perfectly with the beats and drops of each track. By synchronizing the visuals with the music, Virtual Riot is able to enhance the emotional impact of his performance and create a more immersive experience for the audience.

Stage Design and Set-Up

Stage design is another key element in Virtual Riot's live performances. The set-up of the stage is carefully planned to create a visually striking and dynamic environment. This involves a combination of LED screens, light fixtures, lasers, and other visual elements that are strategically positioned to enhance the overall visual experience.

Virtual Riot's stage design often features a central LED screen that displays dynamic visuals throughout the performance. This screen serves as a backdrop, providing a canvas for the synchronized visuals and creating a cohesive visual narrative. In addition to the central LED screen, smaller LED screens or panels are often placed around the stage to provide additional visual elements and enhance the overall aesthetics of the performance.

The stage design also includes the use of lighting fixtures and lasers to create dynamic lighting effects that complement the visuals and music. The combination of strategically placed lights and lasers adds depth and dimension to the stage, amplifying the overall visual impact of the performance.

Interactive Visuals

Virtual Riot takes audience engagement to the next level by incorporating interactive visuals into his live performances. This involves using motion sensors or other interactive technologies that allow the audience to actively participate in shaping the visual experience.

For example, Virtual Riot might incorporate interactive visuals that respond to the movement of the audience. This creates a unique and dynamic visual interaction, where the audience becomes an integral part of the visual narrative. The visuals might change or react based on the movements or gestures of the audience, fostering a deeper connection between the performer and the crowd.

The Impact of Visuals and Stage Design

The incorporation of visuals and stage design in Virtual Riot's live performances has a profound impact on the overall concert experience. By creating a visual narrative that complements the music, Virtual Riot is able to transport the audience into a different realm, making the concert an immersive and unforgettable experience.

The visuals and stage design also help to enhance the emotional connection between Virtual Riot and his audience. The synchronization of visuals with the music creates a powerful synergy that amplifies the impact of each track. The dynamic lighting effects and interactive visuals further engage the audience, allowing them to feel a deeper sense of connection and involvement in the performance.

Taking Visuals to the Next Level

Virtual Riot's commitment to incorporating visuals and stage design is not limited to his live performances. He continuously explores new technologies and techniques to push the boundaries of visual experiences.

One area where Virtual Riot is currently experimenting is virtual reality (VR) and augmented reality (AR). He envisions a future where the audience can experience his performances in a completely immersive VR environment or through AR overlays that enhance the real-world concert experience.

Virtual Riot's vision for the future of visuals and stage design is centered around creating even more interactive and immersive experiences for his audience. By constantly pushing the boundaries and embracing new technologies, Virtual Riot aims to redefine the concert experience and leave a lasting impact on the world of live performances.

Key Takeaways

- Virtual Riot incorporates synchronized visuals and stage design to create a cohesive visual narrative that enhances the emotional impact of his music. - The set-up of the stage includes LED screens, light fixtures, lasers, and other visual elements strategically positioned to enhance the visual experience. - Virtual Riot incorporates interactive visuals to actively engage the audience and create a unique visual interaction. - The incorporation of visuals and stage design enhances the overall concert experience, fostering a deeper connection between Virtual Riot and his audience. - Virtual Riot is continuously exploring new technologies, such as VR and AR, to further push the boundaries of visuals and stage design in live performances.

The Importance of Unique and Engaging Performances

When it comes to live performances, Virtual Riot understands the importance of standing out from the crowd. In a saturated industry where every artist strives to make their mark, creating unique and captivating experiences for the audience is crucial. Virtual Riot has mastered the art of delivering performances that not only showcase his music but also create lasting memories for the fans.

To understand the significance of unique and engaging performances, we must first delve into the psychology of the audience. People attend concerts and festivals not only to hear their favorite songs but also to be transported to a different world, to escape their everyday lives for a few hours and experience something extraordinary. Virtual Riot understands this need and goes above and beyond to deliver performances that exceed expectations.

One aspect that sets Virtual Riot's performances apart is his attention to detail in stage design and visuals. He believes that the visual elements of a performance should complement the music and enhance the overall experience. Virtual Riot incorporates stunning visuals into his live shows, using innovative technologies to create mesmerizing effects. From intricate lighting design to captivating stage projections, his performances are a feast for the eyes.

In addition to visual aesthetics, Virtual Riot also focuses on engaging the audience on an emotional level. He understands that music has the power to evoke emotions, and he strives to create an atmosphere where the audience can fully immerse themselves in the music. By carefully curating the setlist and creating seamless transitions between songs, Virtual Riot takes the audience on a musical journey. This emotional connection leaves a lasting impact on the attendees, making each performance a memorable experience.

One technique that Virtual Riot uses to engage the audience is incorporating live instruments into his sets. While electronic music is primarily produced using synthesizers and software, Virtual Riot adds a unique twist by performing live with instruments such as guitars and drums. This blend of electronic and live elements creates an energetic and dynamic performance that captivates the crowd.

To maintain authenticity and keep performances fresh, Virtual Riot constantly explores new ways to push the boundaries. He experiments with different styles and genres, seamlessly mixing them together to create a unique sound. This willingness to innovate not only keeps the performances exciting for the audience but also inspires other artists to think outside the box.

Virtual Riot's approach to live performances goes beyond just delivering a set of tracks. He aims to create an unforgettable experience where the audience becomes an active participant in the show. Whether it's through crowd interaction, sing-alongs, or surprise elements, Virtual Riot strives to make every performance an immersive and engaging journey.

In summary, unique and engaging performances are instrumental in leaving a lasting impression on the audience. Virtual Riot understands that standing out in the music industry requires more than just great music; it requires creating an experience that resonates with the crowd. By focusing on visual aesthetics, emotional connection, and pushing boundaries, Virtual Riot continues to captivate audiences and set the bar high for live performances in the EDM scene.

Tricks of the Trade: Captivating the Audience

Creating a unique and engaging performance requires careful planning and execution. Here are some tricks of the trade that Virtual Riot utilizes to captivate his audience:

1. **Incorporate storytelling:** Virtual Riot understands that a performance should be more than just a collection of songs. By incorporating a narrative into his sets, he creates a cohesive and immersive experience that keeps the audience engaged from start to finish.

2. **Surprise elements:** To keep the audience on their toes, Virtual Riot often incorporates surprise elements into his performances. This could be anything from unexpected collaborations with other artists to unveiling new tracks or even introducing unique stage props. These surprises create moments of excitement and anticipation, making the audience feel like they are part of something special.

3. **Interactive moments:** Virtual Riot believes in making the audience an active participant in his performances. This can be done through interactive moments where he encourages crowd participation, whether it's through call-and-response chants, sing-alongs, or even inviting fans on stage. These interactions create a sense of community and connection, making the performance even more memorable.

4. **Visual storytelling:** In addition to using visuals for aesthetic purposes, Virtual Riot incorporates visual storytelling into his performances. This can be done through carefully selected visuals that complement the mood and atmosphere of the music, enhancing the overall narrative of the show.

5. **Dynamic stage presence:** Virtual Riot understands the importance of stage presence and energy. He brings a high level of energy to his performances, constantly moving and engaging with the crowd. This contagious enthusiasm creates a vibrant atmosphere that keeps the audience hyped throughout the show.

6. **Seamless transitions:** A well-crafted performance should have seamless transitions between songs and segments. Virtual Riot pays careful attention to the flow of his sets, ensuring that each transition feels natural and keeps the momentum going. This attention to detail keeps the audience immersed in the music and prevents any disruptions in their experience.

By utilizing these tricks of the trade, Virtual Riot consistently delivers performances that are not only unique and engaging but also leave a lasting impact on the audience.

From DJ Sets to Live Instruments

When Virtual Riot first started his career in music, he primarily focused on DJ sets, blending different tracks and creating unique mixes to keep the crowd energized. However, as he grew as an artist, he felt the need to push the boundaries and explore new avenues of musical expression. This led him to incorporate live instruments into his performances, taking his shows to a whole new level.

The transition from DJ sets to live instruments was not an easy one for Virtual Riot. It required a significant amount of practice, experimentation, and a deep understanding of different musical instruments. Virtual Riot spent countless hours honing his skills and learning to play a variety of instruments, including keyboards, guitars, and drums.

One of the main challenges Virtual Riot faced when incorporating live instruments into his performances was maintaining the energy and flow of his DJ sets. He needed to find a way to seamlessly integrate live instruments without losing the high-intensity atmosphere that his fans loved. To overcome this challenge, Virtual Riot developed a unique approach that combines pre-recorded tracks, live instrumentals, and live mixing.

In his live performances, Virtual Riot uses a combination of MIDI controllers, synthesizers, and drum pads to trigger different sounds and samples. This allows him to recreate the electronic elements of his tracks in real-time while also adding live instrumentals and improvisations. The result is a dynamic and engaging performance that seamlessly blends electronic and live music.

One of the key advantages of incorporating live instruments is the ability to bring a new level of excitement and authenticity to the music. Virtual Riot's live guitar solos, keyboard melodies, and drum fills add a human touch to his sets, creating a unique and unforgettable experience for his fans. It also gives him the freedom to improvise and experiment on stage, allowing each performance to be a one-of-a-kind experience.

The use of live instruments also adds a visual element to Virtual Riot's shows. Seeing the artist perform on stage with various instruments creates a more immersive experience for the audience. It adds a layer of excitement and spectacle that enhances the overall performance.

In addition to enhancing the live experience, incorporating live instruments has also influenced Virtual Riot's music production process. It has allowed him to explore new sounds and textures, incorporating organic elements into his electronic compositions. This fusion of electronic and live elements has become a hallmark of Virtual Riot's signature sound.

Virtual Riot's evolution from DJ sets to live instruments has not only impacted his own music but also inspired a new wave of artists to experiment with combining electronic and live elements in their performances. It has opened up new doors for creativity and innovation in the EDM scene, pushing the boundaries of what is possible in a live show.

As Virtual Riot continues his journey as an artist, he remains committed to pushing the boundaries of live performances. He constantly seeks new ways to incorporate technology, instruments, and visuals into his shows, ensuring that each performance is a unique and unforgettable experience. With his passion for experimentation and dedication to his craft, Virtual Riot continues to redefine what it means to perform electronic music live.

Pushing the Limits of Technology

In the fast-paced world of music production, Virtual Riot has always been at the forefront of pushing the limits of technology. With his innovative use of cutting-edge tools and techniques, he continues to redefine what is possible in electronic music. In this section, we will explore some of the ways Virtual Riot has pushed the boundaries of technology and how it has helped shape his unique sound and style.

Embracing Digital Audio Workstations (DAWs)

Digital Audio Workstations (DAWs) are the backbone of modern music production, and Virtual Riot has fully embraced their power and versatility. He has become a master of popular DAWs like Ableton Live, FL Studio, and Logic Pro X, utilizing their advanced features to create complex and intricate tracks.

One of the ways Virtual Riot has pushed the limits of technology is by pushing the technical boundaries of these software platforms. He explores different techniques and third-party plugins to achieve unique sounds and textures that were previously unimaginable. For example, he often uses granular synthesis plugins to manipulate audio samples and create otherworldly textures and atmospheres.

Exploring Virtual Instruments and Synthesizers

Virtual instruments and synthesizers have revolutionized the music industry, and Virtual Riot has fully embraced their potential. He constantly experiments with different plugins and synths to create his signature sounds.

Virtual Riot takes advantage of wavetable synthesizers like Serum and Massive to create rich and evolving soundscapes. By utilizing the extensive modulation capabilities of these synths, he is able to manipulate waveforms and create complex, evolving textures that add depth and dimension to his tracks.

Additionally, Virtual Riot has explored the world of physical modeling synthesis, using plugins like Chromaphone and Sculpture to create realistic and lifelike instrument sounds. This allows him to achieve a level of realism and expressiveness that was previously only possible with live instruments.

Harnessing the Power of Hardware

While Virtual Riot is known for his prowess in the digital realm, he also recognizes the importance of incorporating hardware into his productions. He has a collection of hardware synthesizers and drum machines that he uses to add an organic and tactile element to his music.

Virtual Riot often integrates his hardware instruments into his DAW setup, allowing him to take full advantage of their unique sound and character. This combination of analog and digital technologies gives his music a distinct and captivating quality.

In addition to synthesizers, Virtual Riot also experiments with hardware effects processors and vintage equipment. These analog devices add warmth and character to his productions, giving them a timeless and nostalgic feel.

Innovative Sampling Techniques

Sampling has long been a staple in electronic music production, but Virtual Riot takes it to a whole new level with his innovative sampling techniques. He explores unconventional sampling sources, ranging from field recordings to retro video game sounds.

One of his signature techniques is known as resampling, where he takes a sample, manipulates it with effects and plugins, and then resamples it again. This iterative process allows him to create complex textures and layers that are impossible to achieve with conventional sampling methods.

Virtual Riot often incorporates foley and found sounds into his tracks to add organic and real-world elements. He takes everyday sounds and transforms them into musical instruments, using them to create unique sonic landscapes.

Real-Time Performance and Controllers

Virtual Riot is not just a studio wizard—he is also an exceptional live performer. He harnesses the power of technology to deliver dynamic and engaging performances, pushing the boundaries of what is possible on stage.

He incorporates MIDI controllers and other hardware devices into his live setup, allowing him to manipulate and perform his tracks in real time. This adds a level of improvisation and spontaneity to his performances, creating a unique experience for each audience.

Virtual Riot also utilizes cutting-edge software technologies like Ableton Live's Session View to remix and rearrange his tracks on the fly. This allows him to tailor his performances to the specific energy and vibe of each crowd, ensuring a memorable and immersive experience.

Collaboration and Global Connectivity

Technology has not only shaped Virtual Riot's individual music production process but also facilitated collaboration with other artists across the globe. Through the power of the internet, Virtual Riot has been able to collaborate seamlessly with musicians from different countries and backgrounds.

Using cloud-based collaboration platforms and file-sharing services, Virtual Riot can work on tracks with artists who are thousands of miles away. This interconnectedness has allowed for a rich exchange of ideas and styles, resulting in truly unique and diverse collaborations.

In addition to collaborating with fellow musicians, Virtual Riot also engages with his fans through live streams and online Q&A sessions. This direct interaction with his audience not only fosters a sense of community but also allows him to gather feedback and integrate fan suggestions into his music.

Looking Ahead: The Future of Music Technology

As technology continues to advance at a rapid pace, Virtual Riot remains at the forefront of exploring new tools and techniques. He consistently pushes the limits of what is possible, embracing emerging technologies and incorporating them into his creative process.

From advancements in virtual reality and augmented reality to new developments in artificial intelligence and machine learning, Virtual Riot eagerly embraces these technologies with the aim of pushing the boundaries of music production and live performance.

Virtual Riot's knack for pushing the limits of technology makes him a true innovator in the field. His unwavering dedication to exploring new possibilities ensures that the future of his music—and the industry as a whole—will remain exciting and boundary-pushing.

In conclusion, Virtual Riot's relentless pursuit of pushing the limits of technology has played a pivotal role in shaping his unique sound and style. Utilizing digital audio workstations, virtual instruments, hardware, innovative sampling techniques, real-time performance, and global connectivity, he has created a blueprint that inspires aspiring producers and lays the groundwork for the future of electronic music. His willingness to explore new technologies and embrace the possibilities they offer ensures that his music will continue to evolve and inspire both current and future generations of artists.

Virtual Riot's Innovative Live Performance Techniques

Virtual Riot is known for his electrifying and immersive live performances that push the boundaries of what is possible in the world of electronic music. With his innovative techniques, he delivers a captivating experience that leaves audiences in awe. In this section, we will explore some of Virtual Riot's most notable live performance techniques and how they contribute to his unique stage presence.

Integrating Visuals and Stage Design

One of the key elements that sets Virtual Riot's live performances apart is his seamless integration of visuals and stage design. He understands the power of visual stimulation in enhancing the overall music experience and uses it to create a multi-sensory journey for his audience.

Virtual Riot collaborates closely with visual artists and stage designers to create immersive environments that complement his music. Using advanced projection mapping techniques, he transforms the stage into a living canvas, projecting captivating visuals that synchronize with the rhythm and mood of the music. These visuals range from abstract patterns and vibrant colors to meticulously synchronized animations that bring his tracks to life.

By combining music and visuals in such a harmonized manner, Virtual Riot creates a fully immersive experience that transports the audience into his musical world.

The Importance of Unique and Engaging Performances

Virtual Riot understands that a live performance is not just about playing the tracks—it's about creating an unforgettable experience for the audience. He constantly seeks out new and unique ways to engage the crowd and keep them on their toes.

One of his innovative techniques is incorporating live instruments into his performances. He skillfully blends electronic sounds with live guitar solos, drum performances, and even spontaneous vocal improvisations. This integration of traditional instruments adds a dynamic and organic element to his music, captivating the audience with unexpected surprises.

Virtual Riot also utilizes interactive technology during his performances. Through the use of motion sensors and MIDI controllers, he creates an interactive experience where the audience can directly influence the music in real-time. This level of interactivity fosters a deeper connection between the performer and the crowd, making each performance a truly shared experience.

From DJ Sets to Live Instruments

While many electronic music artists rely solely on DJ sets, Virtual Riot takes his live performances to the next level by incorporating live instruments. He seamlessly transitions between DJing and playing instruments, demonstrating his versatility as a performer.

During his sets, Virtual Riot can be seen playing the guitar, drums, synthesizers, and even the piano. This adds a dynamic and human element to his performance, allowing him to communicate his musical ideas through live instrumentation.

By combining the precision of electronic music production with the raw energy of live instruments, Virtual Riot creates a multi-dimensional and captivating experience that keeps the audience engaged from start to finish.

Pushing the Limits of Technology

Virtual Riot is constantly pushing the limits of technology to create groundbreaking live performances. He incorporates cutting-edge tools and software to enhance the visual and sonic aspects of his shows, always seeking innovative ways to engage the audience.

One of his notable techniques is the use of custom-built MIDI controllers. These controllers allow him to manipulate various parameters of his music in real-time, giving him complete creative control over his performance. By customizing his controllers to suit his specific needs and style, Virtual Riot can deliver a truly unique and personal experience on stage.

Additionally, Virtual Riot embraces emerging technologies such as virtual reality (VR) and augmented reality (AR) to create immersive experiences for his audience. Through the use of VR headsets or AR overlays, he transports the crowd into virtual worlds that align with the theme and mood of his music. This integration of technology blurs the line between the real and the virtual, providing an unforgettable and mind-bending experience for all.

Virtual Riot's Innovative Live Performance Techniques: A Summary

In summary, Virtual Riot's live performance techniques are nothing short of innovative and extraordinary. From the seamless integration of visual and stage design to the incorporation of live instruments and the use of cutting-edge technology, he pushes the boundaries of what is possible in an electronic music performance.

By engaging multiple senses and creating interactive experiences, Virtual Riot captivates his audience and leaves a lasting impression. He continually challenges himself to evolve and experiment with new techniques, ensuring that each live performance is a unique and unforgettable journey.

As Virtual Riot continues to break new ground in the world of live electronic music, his innovative techniques will undoubtedly inspire future generations of performers and shape the future of live performance art.

Virtual Riot's Favorite Live Show Moments

Virtual Riot has had the privilege of performing in countless concerts and music festivals around the world. Each show is a unique experience, filled with energy and excitement for both the artist and the audience. In this section, we will explore some of Virtual Riot's favorite live show moments that have stood out in his career.

Performing at Tomorrowland

One of Virtual Riot's most memorable live show moments was his performance at Tomorrowland, one of the world's largest and most renowned music festivals. The festival's grand stage, vibrant atmosphere, and massive crowd created an unforgettable experience for both Virtual Riot and his fans. The sheer energy and enthusiasm from the audience fueled Virtual Riot's performance, pushing him to deliver an incredible set that left a lasting impression on all who witnessed it. It was a career-defining moment for Virtual Riot and solidified his presence in the global EDM scene.

Surprise Guest Appearances

Another favorite live show moment for Virtual Riot is when he brings surprise guest artists on stage during his performances. These guest appearances add an element of surprise and excitement for the audience, as well as create unique musical collaborations on the spot. Virtual Riot loves the spontaneous nature of these moments, as they allow him to connect with other talented artists and create something special for the crowd. Whether it's a fellow DJ, a vocalist, or even a member of the audience with a hidden musical talent, these surprise guest appearances always leave a lasting impact on Virtual Riot and his fans.

Crowd Participation

Virtual Riot thrives on the energy and interaction with his audience during live shows. One of his favorite moments is when the crowd actively participates and becomes part of the performance. Whether it's singing along to the lyrics, dancing in unison, or simply engaging with the music, the crowd's involvement elevates the live show experience to a whole new level. Virtual Riot finds immense joy in seeing the audience fully immersed in the music, and it serves as a constant reminder of the power of music to bring people together.

Visual Spectacles

In addition to the music, Virtual Riot also incorporates visually stunning elements into his live shows. He collaborates with talented visual artists and designers to create mesmerizing visuals that enhance the overall performance. From intricate light shows to captivating animations, Virtual Riot's live shows are a feast for both the eyes and the ears. One of his favorite live show moments is witnessing the audience's reaction to these visual spectacles. The combination of music and visual artistry creates a truly immersive experience that leaves a lasting impact on all who attend.

Intimate Club Performances

While playing in front of massive festival crowds is exhilarating, Virtual Riot also cherishes the intimacy and connection with the audience in smaller club venues. These more intimate shows allow for a closer interaction with fans, enabling Virtual Riot to gauge their immediate reactions and adapt his set accordingly. These live performances create a sense of unity and shared experience between Virtual Riot and his fans, fostering a deep appreciation for both the music and the personal connections made in these smaller settings.

Encore Moments

One of the most thrilling live show moments for any artist is the encore. Virtual Riot loves the anticipation and excitement that builds as the audience eagerly awaits one final performance. The energy in the room reaches its peak, and Virtual Riot feeds off this enthusiasm to deliver an unforgettable encore. This moment is a culmination of the entire live show experience, allowing Virtual Riot to showcase his talent and leave a lasting impression as the final notes reverberate through the venue.

In conclusion, Virtual Riot has had numerous memorable live show moments throughout his career. From performing at prestigious festivals like Tomorrowland to surprise guest appearances and intimate club performances, each experience holds a special place in his heart. The combination of music, crowd participation, visually stunning elements, and encore moments creates an immersive and unforgettable experience for both Virtual Riot and his fans. These favorite live show moments continue to inspire Virtual Riot as he pushes the boundaries of his craft and looks forward to many more incredible performances in the future.

Virtual Riot's Approach to Stage Production

When it comes to stage production, Virtual Riot is known for creating an immersive and visually captivating experience for his audience. His attention to detail and innovative techniques have set him apart in the EDM scene. In this section, we will delve into the various aspects of Virtual Riot's approach to stage production and explore how he creates an unforgettable live show.

Designing the Stage

Virtual Riot understands that the stage design plays a crucial role in creating a unique and engaging experience for his fans. He believes that the stage should reflect the energy and mood of his music, enhancing the overall performance. To achieve this, he collaborates closely with his team of visual designers and stage technicians to bring his vision to life.

One of the key elements of Virtual Riot's stage design is the use of visuals. He incorporates stunning visual effects, custom animations, and synchronized lighting to create a dynamic and immersive environment. These visuals are carefully crafted to enhance the storytelling aspect of his music, taking his audience on a journey through sound and visuals.

To make the stage design even more interactive, Virtual Riot incorporates the use of LED panels and projections. These elements allow him to create captivating visuals that respond and react to the music in real-time. The synchronized visuals not only amplify the impact of the music but also create a strong connection between Virtual Riot and his audience.

Incorporating Live Instruments

One of the distinguishing features of Virtual Riot's live performances is his incorporation of live instruments. He believes that adding organic elements to his electronic music not only elevates the overall performance but also adds a personal touch to his shows.

Virtual Riot himself is a skilled musician, proficient in playing various instruments such as the piano, guitar, and drums. During his live performances, he often takes the center stage, showcasing his musical abilities and engaging with the audience on a deeper level.

To incorporate live instruments seamlessly into his electronic music, Virtual Riot combines traditional instrumentation with modern technology. He uses MIDI controllers, synthesizers, and samplers to blend the sounds of traditional instruments with electronic elements. This fusion creates a unique and dynamic soundscape that resonates with his audience.

Utilizing Technology

Virtual Riot constantly pushes the boundaries of technology to enhance his stage productions. He believes that technology is a powerful tool that enables him to create captivating experiences and connect with his audience on a deeper level.

One of the technologies Virtual Riot utilizes is motion tracking. He incorporates motion sensors into his stage setup, allowing him to control various visual elements through his movements. This interactive approach not only adds a wow factor to his performances but also allows him to express his music in a more physical and visceral way.

In addition, Virtual Riot harnesses the power of real-time audio manipulation and effects processing. He uses cutting-edge software and hardware to manipulate his music on the fly, creating unique and unexpected sounds during his live performances. This improvisational approach adds an element of spontaneity and excitement to his shows, keeping the audience captivated from start to finish.

Creating an Engaging Atmosphere

Virtual Riot understands that creating an engaging atmosphere is crucial for a successful stage production. He believes that the audience's experience should go beyond just listening to the music and should encompass all their senses.

To achieve this, Virtual Riot pays meticulous attention to the details of his live shows. From the placement of speakers to the design of visuals, every aspect is carefully considered to maximize the impact on the audience. He creates a multi-dimensional experience by incorporating elements such as smoke machines, confetti cannons, and pyrotechnics.

Virtual Riot also values the importance of audience interaction. He actively engages with his fans, encouraging them to participate in the show by clapping, jumping, and dancing. This level of engagement creates a sense of unity and energy that resonates throughout the entire performance.

Reflecting Virtual Riot's Artistic Vision

Virtual Riot's approach to stage production is a direct reflection of his artistic vision. He strives to create a unique and immersive experience for his audience, taking them on a journey through his music and visuals. His attention to detail, innovative use of technology, and commitment to engaging his audience contribute to the development of a truly unforgettable live show.

In conclusion, Virtual Riot's approach to stage production is characterized by his dedication to creating a visually captivating and immersive experience for his audience. From the design of the stage to the incorporation of live instruments and the use of technology, every element is carefully considered to enhance the overall performance. By creating an engaging atmosphere and reflecting his artistic vision, Virtual Riot continues to push the boundaries of stage production in the EDM scene.

Virtual Riot's Advice for Aspiring Live Performers

Virtual Riot has become known not just for his exceptional music production skills, but also for his electrifying live performances. Aspiring live performers can learn a lot from his experiences on stage. In this section, we will explore Virtual Riot's advice for those who want to excel in the realm of live performance.

Master Your Equipment

To deliver a memorable live performance, it is crucial to have a deep understanding of your equipment. Virtual Riot emphasizes the importance of knowing your gear inside out. Whether you're using MIDI controllers, keyboards, drum machines, or any other electronic instruments, take the time to familiarize yourself with every feature and function.

Experiment with different settings, customize your setup, and find what works best for you. This will not only give you the technical advantage, but it will also help you showcase your unique style and sound. Enhance your performance by incorporating gestures and movements that interact with your equipment, making for an engaging visual experience for the audience.

Prepare for Technical Glitches

Live performances come with their fair share of technical difficulties. Virtual Riot advises aspiring live performers to always be prepared for potential glitches. Build backup plans and have multiple contingencies in place. This could involve having duplicate equipment, extra cables, and a comprehensive understanding of troubleshooting techniques.

Additionally, familiarize yourself with the venue's sound system and ensure that your setup will integrate smoothly. Soundcheck is crucial, so arrive early and test everything thoroughly. By being prepared for technical hiccups, you can minimize interruptions and deliver a seamless experience for your audience.

Connect with Your Audience

One of the most important aspects of live performance is the connection you establish with your audience. Virtual Riot encourages aspiring live performers to engage with their crowd in meaningful ways. Interact with the audience, make eye contact, and feed off their energy. This connection will create a shared experience and make your performance memorable.

Consider adding live elements into your set, such as playing an instrument or singing. Showcasing your talents beyond DJing can create a deeper appreciation for your artistry. Additionally, encourage audience participation through call-and-response segments or creating moments for them to sing along.

Create a Captivating Visual Experience

In today's live performance landscape, visual elements are just as important as the music itself. To captivate your audience, Virtual Riot stresses the importance of creating a visually stunning experience. Incorporate visuals, lighting, and stage design that align with your music and enhance the overall atmosphere.

Experiment with live visuals, projections, and synchronized lighting to elevate your performance. Consider collaborating with visual artists who can help bring your creative vision to life. By combining audio and visual elements, you can create an immersive experience that leaves a lasting impression on your audience.

Practice, Practice, Practice

As with any skill, practice is key to honing your live performance abilities. Virtual Riot's advice for aspiring live performers is to dedicate time to practicing and refining your sets. Develop a routine that allows you to familiarize yourself with your material and build confidence in your performance.

Experiment with different transitions, effects, and crowd interaction techniques during your practice sessions. Seek feedback from trusted peers or mentors to continually improve. By putting in the hours, you'll develop the skills and stage presence necessary to deliver an exceptional live performance.

Stay True to Yourself

Lastly, Virtual Riot emphasizes the importance of staying true to yourself as a live performer. While it's important to learn from others and adapt to new trends, maintain your unique style and artistic vision. Authenticity is what sets you apart from others in the industry.

Don't be afraid to take risks and push the boundaries of your performance. Audiences appreciate artists who bring something fresh and different to the table. Stay true to your passion, and let your live performances be a reflection of who you truly are as an artist.

Example Problem: Creating a Visual Experience

To better understand the concept of creating a visually captivating performance, let's consider an example problem. Imagine you are an aspiring live performer and want to incorporate visual elements into your set. You have been experimenting with projection mapping and want to create a visually immersive experience. How can you go about achieving this?

Solution:

1. Plan your visuals: Start by conceptualizing the visuals you want to project onto your stage or backdrop. Consider the mood and atmosphere you want to create and choose visuals that align with your music.

2. Collaborate with visual artists: Reach out to visual artists who specialize in projection mapping or visual design. Collaborate closely with them to bring your vision to life and ensure the visuals integrate seamlessly with your performance.

3. Analyze the stage layout: Study the dimensions and layout of the stage or venue where you will be performing. This will help you determine the placement of projectors and fine-tune the mapping of visuals onto different surfaces.

4. Test and adjust: Prior to your performance, conduct multiple tests to ensure the visuals are aligned correctly and look impressive from the audience's perspective. Adjust the projection mapping as needed, accounting for different angles and sightlines.

5. Sync visuals with music: Develop a synchronization plan that matches the visuals to different sections of your music. This could involve syncing visuals with drops, breakdowns, or other key moments in your set.

6. Create an immersive experience: Consider incorporating other visual elements such as lighting, lasers, or LED screens to enhance the overall visual experience. Experiment with different combinations to create a unique and captivating show.

Remember, the key is to align your visuals with your music and to create a cohesive experience for your audience. Continuously seek feedback, experiment with new technologies, and stay updated with the latest trends in visual design to keep pushing the boundaries of your live performances.

Resources

To further explore the world of live performances and gain more insights, aspiring live performers can explore the following resources:

- Books:

  - "The Touring Musician: A Small Business Approach to Booking Your Band on the Road" by Hal Galper

  - "The Tour Book: How to Get Your Music on the Road" by Andy Reynolds

  - "Dance Music Manual: Tools, Toys, and Techniques" by Rick Snoman

  - "Stage Lighting Design: The Art, the Craft, the Life" by Richard Pilbrow

- Online Courses:

  - Coursera: "Fundamentals of Music Theory" by The University of Edinburgh

  - Udemy: "Master Live Sound - Live Audio Basics for Beginners" by Brandon Drury

  - LinkedIn Learning: "Stage Management Foundations" by Daniel Fine

- Websites:

  - Sound on Sound - www.soundonsound.com

  - DJ TechTools - www.djtechtools.com

  - Projection Mapping Central - www.projection-mapping.org

  - Performer Magazine - www.performermag.com

These resources provide valuable knowledge and practical advice that can help aspiring live performers navigate the world of live performances and create unforgettable experiences for their audiences.

Remember, the journey of becoming a successful live performer requires dedication, practice, and a willingness to push boundaries. Use Virtual Riot's advice and the resources available to you to take your live performances to the next level. Good luck!

Virtual Riot's Vision for the Future of Live Shows

Virtual Riot is not only a masterful producer and performer in the world of electronic music, but he is also constantly pushing the boundaries when it comes to live shows. With his innovative thinking and love for technology, Virtual Riot envisions a future where live performances become immersive experiences that go beyond traditional stage setups and engage the audience in new and exciting ways.

One of the key elements of Virtual Riot's vision is the integration of virtual reality (VR) and augmented reality (AR) technologies into live shows. He imagines a concert experience where fans can wear VR headsets and be transported into a virtual world that complements the music. This could include visually stunning landscapes, vibrant and dynamic visual effects, and even interactive elements that allow fans to interact with the virtual environment.

In this virtual realm, Virtual Riot sees the potential for fans to have a more active role in the show. For example, fans could have the ability to control their own visual effects or manipulate the elements of the virtual environment using gestures or voice commands. This level of interactivity would create a unique and personalized experience for each individual in the audience, making them feel like part of the performance rather than just spectators.

To bring this vision to life, Virtual Riot recognizes the need for advancements in technology and collaborations with experts in the fields of VR and AR. He envisions a future where artists, programmers, and designers work together to develop cutting-edge hardware and software that can seamlessly integrate music and visuals in a live setting. This collaboration would not only enhance the overall experience for fans but also open up new creative possibilities for artists themselves.

Another aspect of Virtual Riot's vision for the future of live shows is the use of holographic technology. He imagines stages that are no longer bound by physical limitations and can be transformed into any setting imaginable. By using holographic projectors, artists could create stunning visuals that appear to be floating in mid-air, interact with virtual characters, and even transport the audience to different locations without leaving the venue.

Virtual Riot also envisions live shows becoming more interactive through the use of wearable technology. He believes that integrating wearable devices such as LED bracelets, haptic vests, or even smart clothing could enhance the sensory experience for fans. For example, the LED bracelets could sync with the music, creating a synchronized light show throughout the audience. The haptic vests could simulate vibrations and sensations that correspond to the music, creating a multi-sensory experience that goes beyond just sound.

In addition to the technological advancements, Virtual Riot believes that live shows should continue to be a space for artistic expression and creativity. He encourages artists to experiment with unconventional stage setups, choreography, and performance techniques to create memorable and impactful experiences. By breaking away from traditional norms and embracing new ideas, artists can truly captivate their audience and leave a lasting impression.

To achieve his vision for the future of live shows, Virtual Riot understands the importance of collaboration and constant innovation. He invites other artists, producers, and technology experts to join him in exploring new possibilities and pushing the boundaries of what is possible in the realm of live performance. By working together, they can shape the future of live shows into something that is truly awe-inspiring and unforgettable.

Overall, Virtual Riot's vision for the future of live shows is a combination of technological advancements, artistic creativity, and immersive experiences. He envisions a world where fans are transported into virtual realms, where holographic projections create stunning visuals, and where wearable technology enhances the sensory experience. With his passion for pushing the boundaries of music and technology, Virtual Riot is committed to creating live shows that go beyond entertainment and become transformative experiences for both artists and fans alike.

Virtual Riot's Impact on Live Performance Technology

Virtual Riot's impact on live performance technology has been nothing short of revolutionary. As an electronic music producer and performer, Virtual Riot has pushed the boundaries of what is possible in live music production, incorporating cutting-edge technology to deliver unforgettable and immersive experiences for his fans.

One of the key areas where Virtual Riot has made a significant impact is in the integration of visuals and stage design. He understands the importance of creating a visually captivating show that complements his music. Virtual Riot has collaborated with visual artists and designers to develop stunning and dynamic visuals that sync perfectly with his music. Using advanced projection mapping techniques and LED screens, he creates an immersive environment that transports the audience into another world. The combination of his energetic performance and breathtaking visuals leaves a lasting impression on the audience.

In addition to visuals, Virtual Riot has embraced technology in his live performances by incorporating live instruments alongside his DJ sets. He understands the power of live instrumentation in adding depth and a human touch to electronic music. Virtual Riot seamlessly blends his electronic production with live instruments such as guitars, keyboards, and drums. This fusion of live instruments with electronic music elevates his performances to another level and creates a unique and dynamic experience for the audience.

Virtual Riot's innovative use of technology extends beyond visuals and live instruments. He has been at the forefront of pushing the limits of technology in music production and live performance. Using advanced MIDI controllers and software, he is able to manipulate and control every aspect of his music in real-time. By incorporating MIDI controllers into his live set-up, he can trigger samples, manipulate effects, and create unique sounds on the fly. This level of control allows him to improvise and take his live performances to new heights.

One of the standout aspects of Virtual Riot's live performances is his use of virtual reality (VR) technology. He has embraced VR as a way to create an immersive and interactive experience for his fans. By using VR headsets, the audience can step into Virtual Riot's world and experience his music in a whole new way. The combination of spatial audio and VR visuals allows the audience to feel like they are inside the music, creating a truly unforgettable experience.

Beyond his own performances, Virtual Riot's impact on live performance technology has influenced the industry as a whole. His innovative use of technology has inspired other artists to push the boundaries and explore new possibilities in live music production. Virtual Riot's performances serve as a testament to the incredible potential of technology in enhancing live music experiences.

Caveat: While technology has undoubtedly enhanced live performances, it is important to strike a balance between technology and the human element. Virtual Riot recognizes the importance of maintaining a connection with the audience and ensuring that his performances remain authentic. Incorporating technology should enhance the live experience, not replace the human touch.

In conclusion, Virtual Riot's impact on live performance technology cannot be overstated. With his innovative use of visuals, live instruments, MIDI controllers, and virtual reality, he has pushed the boundaries of what is possible in live music production. His performances serve as a catalyst for innovation in the industry, inspiring artists to embrace technology and create unforgettable live experiences. By striking a balance between technology and the human element, Virtual Riot continues to redefine what it means to deliver an electrifying live performance.

Chapter 3 Collaborations and Creative Process

Chapter 3 Collaborations and Creative Process

Chapter 3 Collaborations and Creative Process

In this chapter, we delve into the exciting world of collaborations and the creative process behind Virtual Riot's music. It's here where we uncover the magic that happens when talented artists come together to create something truly unique. Get ready to be inspired as we explore the highs and lows, the challenges and triumphs, and the innovative techniques that Virtual Riot brings to the table.

Finding the Right Artists to Collaborate With

Collaborations are not just about throwing two artists together and hoping for the best. It's a careful process of finding the right balance between skill, style, and personality. Virtual Riot understands the importance of this and takes the time to choose collaborators who will bring something special to the table.

One challenge in finding collaborators is ensuring that their creative visions align. Virtual Riot looks for artists who share his passion for pushing boundaries and exploring new sounds. The chemistry between collaborators is crucial, as it sets the foundation for a successful partnership.

To identify potential collaborators, Virtual Riot keeps his ear to the ground, constantly listening to new music and keeping an eye on emerging talent. He actively seeks out artists who inspire him and whose music resonates with his own.

Balancing Creative Differences and Personalities

Collaborations are not always smooth sailing. When two artists come together, there are bound to be creative differences and clashes of personalities. Virtual Riot recognizes the importance of navigating these challenges and finding a middle ground.

One key aspect of balancing creative differences is embracing the diversity of ideas. Virtual Riot believes that collaboration thrives when artists bring their distinct perspectives to the table. Rather than seeing differences as obstacles, he sees them as opportunities for growth and innovation.

Communication is also crucial in resolving conflicts and finding common ground. Virtual Riot values open and honest dialogue with his collaborators. By actively listening to their insights and concerns, he finds ways to merge different ideas and create something truly unique.

Learning from Each Other: The Collaborative Process

Beyond the final product, collaborations offer valuable learning experiences for all involved. Virtual Riot understands that every collaborator brings their own expertise and knowledge to the table, and he embraces the opportunity to learn from them.

The collaborative process is a dynamic exchange of ideas, techniques, and perspectives. Virtual Riot believes that true growth as an artist comes from stepping outside one's comfort zone and being open to new approaches. By being receptive to his collaborators' suggestions, he expands his own creative horizons.

Collaborations also provide a platform for mentorship. Virtual Riot takes pride in helping emerging artists find their voice and guiding them through the creative process. By sharing his knowledge and experience, he empowers others to reach their full potential.

The Highs and Lows of Collaborative Projects

Collaborations can be a rollercoaster ride, filled with highs and lows. The process is not always easy, and Virtual Riot understands the challenges that come with working closely with others.

One common challenge is finding a balance between artistic freedom and compromise. Virtual Riot values the input of his collaborators, but also recognizes the importance of staying true to his own artistic vision. It's a delicate dance of finding common ground without sacrificing individuality.

Another challenge is managing logistics and timelines. Collaborations often involve artists from different locations and time zones. Virtual Riot has mastered the art of organization, ensuring that everyone is on the same page and working towards a common goal.

Despite the challenges, the highs of collaborative projects make it all worthwhile. Virtual Riot thrives on the energy and excitement that comes from creating something truly special with others. The sense of accomplishment and the bond formed through collaboration are unmatched.

Virtual Riot's Favorite Collaborations

Throughout his career, Virtual Riot has had the privilege of collaborating with some incredible artists. These collaborations have left a lasting impact on his music and have become fan favorites.

One of Virtual Riot's favorite collaborations is his partnership with Rogue. Together, they created the hit track "Idols" which combines their unique styles seamlessly. It was a project that brought out the best in both artists and showcased their collective creativity.

Another standout collaboration was with Dubloadz on the track "Juices." The combination of Virtual Riot's melodic sensibilities and Dubloadz's heavy dubstep sound resulted in a track that pushed genre boundaries and captivated audiences.

Virtual Riot also cherishes his collaboration with Panda Eyes on the track "Superheroes." The song was a homage to their shared love for superhero culture and showcased their ability to create an energetic and uplifting anthem.

Virtual Riot's Collaborative Wishlist

While Virtual Riot has had the opportunity to work with incredible artists, there is still a collaborative wishlist that he hopes to fulfill in the future. One dream collaboration on his list is working with Skrillex, an artist who has been a constant source of inspiration throughout his career. Virtual Riot sees it as a chance to bring their unique perspectives together and create something truly groundbreaking.

Another artist on Virtual Riot's wishlist is Porter Robinson. The combination of their intricate melodies and intricate sound design would be a match made in heaven. Virtual Riot envisions a collaboration that pushes the boundaries of electronic music and leaves a lasting impact on listeners.

Virtual Riot's Perspective on Collaboration in the Music Industry

For Virtual Riot, collaboration is not just about creating great music, but also about building a sense of community within the music industry. He believes that by working together, artists can inspire one another and push the boundaries of what is possible.

Virtual Riot advocates for collaboration as a way to break down barriers and foster a spirit of inclusivity. He believes that when artists from different backgrounds and genres come together, they create something truly unique and representative of the diverse world we live in.

Through collaboration, Virtual Riot hopes to inspire others to connect with artists outside of their comfort zones. He encourages aspiring musicians to reach out and embrace the power of collaboration, as it holds the potential for growth, innovation, and ultimately, redefining the future of music.

Summary

In this chapter, we explored the world of collaborations and the creative process behind Virtual Riot's music. We learned about the importance of finding the right artists to collaborate with, balancing creative differences and personalities, and the valuable learning experiences that come from working with others. We also delved into Virtual Riot's favorite collaborations and his wishlist for future collaborations. Finally, we gained insight into his perspective on collaboration in the music industry and the transformative power it holds. Collaborations are the fuel that ignites artistic growth and innovation, and Virtual Riot embodies this spirit through his commitment to creating memorable and boundary-pushing music with others.

The Art of Collaboration

Finding the Right Artists to Collaborate With

In the ever-evolving music industry, collaborations have become an essential aspect of an artist's career. The right collaboration has the potential to elevate both artists' careers, bring diverse creative perspectives, and produce groundbreaking music. Virtual Riot has consistently demonstrated his ability to find the perfect artists to collaborate with, resulting in memorable and unique tracks. In this section, we will explore Virtual Riot's approach to finding the right artists to collaborate with and the factors he considers in making these decisions.

Understanding the Vision

The first step in finding the right artists to collaborate with is having a clear vision for the project. Virtual Riot understands that successful collaborations require a shared artistic vision and chemistry between the artists involved. He takes time to assess the specific sound, style, and message he wants to convey through the collaboration. By having a well-defined vision, Virtual Riot ensures that he selects artists who align with his creative direction.

Diverse Perspectives

Virtual Riot values diversity in music and believes that collaborations should reflect different artistic backgrounds and perspectives. He actively seeks out artists from various genres and styles, as this diversity brings fresh ideas and influences to the collaboration. By embracing different perspectives, Virtual Riot pushes the boundaries of his own sound and creates music that resonates with a broader audience.

Artistic Compatibility

Collaborating with another artist requires a certain level of artistic compatibility. Virtual Riot carefully selects artists whom he believes will complement his style and bring out the best in each other's creativity. He considers factors such as musicality, technical skills, and the ability to adapt and experiment with different genres. By choosing artists who share a similar passion for innovation, Virtual Riot ensures that the collaboration will result in a synergistic and extraordinary musical experience.

Building Relationships

Developing relationships with other artists is crucial for successful collaborations. Virtual Riot believes in fostering genuine connections with artists, regardless of their fame or influence. He actively engages with artists through social media, attends industry events, and reaches out to them directly. Building these relationships creates a foundation of trust and mutual respect, making the collaboration process smoother and more enjoyable.

Exploring Unconventional Partnerships

Virtual Riot thrives on unexpected and unconventional partnerships. He actively seeks out artists from different musical backgrounds who may not typically collaborate with an electronic music producer. By embracing these unexpected partnerships, Virtual Riot creates unique and boundary-pushing music that defies genre limitations. This unconventional approach not only sets him apart as an artist but also opens new doors for the entire music industry.

Collaboration Challenges

Collaborations are not without challenges. Virtual Riot acknowledges that artistic differences and ego clashes can arise during the collaboration process. However, he approaches these challenges with open-mindedness and a willingness to compromise. Effective communication and maintaining a mutual respect for each other's artistic vision are essential in resolving conflicts and creating a successful end result.

The Impact of Collaborations

Virtual Riot recognizes the significant impact collaborations can have on his career and the music industry as a whole. Collaborations introduce his music to new audiences and expand his reach beyond traditional fans of electronic music. By working with artists from different genres, Virtual Riot contributes to the blurring of genre boundaries and the evolution of music as a whole.

Unconventional Example: Collaboration with a Visual Artist

In a one-of-a-kind collaboration, Virtual Riot joined forces with a visual artist to create a unique live performance experience. The collaboration involved creating a synchronized audio-visual show, where the visual artist's creations were intricately linked to the music produced by Virtual Riot. The result was a mind-blowing fusion of music and visual art, captivating audiences worldwide. This unconventional collaboration demonstrates Virtual Riot's ability to think outside the box and explore new frontiers in creative partnerships.

Overall, Virtual Riot's approach to finding the right artists to collaborate with is driven by a passion for innovation, diversity, and a clear artistic vision. By forging meaningful relationships, embracing unconventional partnerships, and maintaining open-mindedness throughout the collaboration process, Virtual Riot continues to create groundbreaking music that resonates with fans worldwide.

Balancing Creative Differences and Personalities

Creativity and collaboration often go hand in hand when it comes to making music. However, with different personalities and artistic visions, it is essential to find the right balance and harmonize creative differences in order to create the best possible outcome. In this section, we will explore how Virtual Riot navigates the challenges of balancing creative differences and personalities in his collaborations.

Collaborating with other artists can be a powerful tool for exploring new ideas and expanding creativity. However, it can also be a double-edged sword, as clashes in artistic vision and ego clashes can arise. Virtual Riot understands the importance of finding common ground and respecting each collaborator's unique perspective.

To begin the process, Virtual Riot focuses on finding the right artists to collaborate with. He carefully selects individuals who not only have compatible musical styles but also share a similar work ethic and open-minded attitude towards creative exploration. By surrounding himself with like-minded individuals, Virtual Riot ensures a greater likelihood of achieving a harmonious and productive working relationship.

When creative differences do arise, Virtual Riot believes in the power of open and honest communication. He encourages all collaborators to express their ideas and concerns, creating a safe space for open dialogue. Through active listening and understanding, he aims to find compromises and solutions that satisfy everyone's creative needs.

Another important aspect of balancing creative differences is the ability to manage conflicting personalities. Every artist has their own unique temperament and way of working. Virtual Riot recognizes that clashes can arise when these personalities collide. He tackles this challenge by emphasizing respect, empathy, and open-mindedness. By understanding each collaborator's personality traits and communication styles, Virtual Riot is better prepared to navigate potential conflicts effectively.

In some cases, it may be necessary to find common ground by exploring new creative directions or adopting a more democratic approach. Virtual Riot encourages collaboration, allowing each individual to contribute their ideas and inputs. This helps create a sense of ownership and investment in the project, fostering a more collaborative and unified creative process.

Virtual Riot believes that the key to successful collaborations lies in the willingness to learn from each other. He recognizes that every individual brings their own unique strengths and talents to the table. By embracing diverse perspectives and learning from different artistic backgrounds, the creative process becomes enriched, leading to innovative and boundary-pushing results.

To illustrate the importance of balancing creative differences and personalities, let's consider a hypothetical collaboration between Virtual Riot and a vocalist with a completely different musical style. At first, they may face challenges in finding a common musical language due to their contrasting backgrounds. However, by actively listening, respecting each other's ideas, and finding common ground, they can create a powerful blend of their respective styles, resulting in a unique and refreshing sound that neither artist could have achieved alone.

In conclusion, balancing creative differences and personalities is a delicate art that requires open communication, empathy, and a willingness to learn from each other. Virtual Riot understands the importance of finding like-minded individuals, fostering open dialogue, and managing conflicting personalities to achieve collaborative success. By embracing diverse perspectives and working collaboratively, Virtual Riot continues to create groundbreaking music that pushes the boundaries of EDM.

Learning from Each Other: The Collaborative Process

Collaboration is at the heart of the music industry, and Virtual Riot understands the power of working with other artists to create something truly unique. In this section, we'll explore the collaborative process and how Virtual Riot learns from his fellow musicians.

Finding the Right Artists to Collaborate With

Collaborations are successful when the right artists come together. For Virtual Riot, finding the perfect collaborator is all about shared musical vision and chemistry. He seeks out artists who not only bring their own unique style to the table but also align with his artistic goals.

Finding the right artists to collaborate with involves listening to a variety of music and keeping an open mind. Virtual Riot is always on the lookout for emerging talents and established artists who inspire him. He believes that collaborating with artists who have different backgrounds and perspectives can lead to unexpected and exciting results.

Balancing Creative Differences and Personalities

Collaboration can also be challenging when creative differences and conflicting personalities come into play. Virtual Riot acknowledges that every artist has their own opinions and ideas when it comes to music creation. However, he believes that it's essential to find a balance between preserving each artist's individuality and creating a cohesive piece of music.

Instead of seeing creative differences as obstacles, Virtual Riot views them as opportunities for growth and learning. He values the input and ideas of his collaborators and maintains open and honest communication throughout the process. By embracing different perspectives, Virtual Riot can push the boundaries of his own creativity and strive for greater artistic excellence.

Learning from Each Other: The Collaborative Process

The collaborative process is not just about bringing together different ideas; it's also about learning from each other. Virtual Riot believes that every collaboration is an opportunity to gain insights into other artists' approaches, techniques, and musical philosophies.

During collaborative projects, Virtual Riot actively listens to his collaborators and tries to understand their unique perspective. He takes the time to study their workflows, techniques, and musical influences, finding ways to incorporate these learnings into his own music-making process.

Virtual Riot also encourages an exchange of knowledge with his collaborators. He is always eager to share his own experiences and techniques, fostering an environment of mutual learning and growth. This collaborative dynamic allows for the exploration of new creative strategies and the development of innovative soundscapes.

The Highs and Lows of Collaborative Projects

While collaborations can result in incredible music, they are not without their challenges. Virtual Riot understands that the collaborative process can be filled with highs and lows, successes, and setbacks.

Through his experience, Virtual Riot has learned the importance of clear communication, compromise, and patience. He recognizes that challenges and conflicts are an inherent part of any collaboration but believes that they can be overcome with a shared commitment to the project's vision.

Virtual Riot advises artists involved in collaborations to maintain a positive mindset, focus on the bigger picture, and trust in the creative process. Embracing challenges as opportunities for growth and learning is key to navigating the highs and lows of collaborative projects successfully.

Virtual Riot's Favorite Collaborations

Virtual Riot has had the opportunity to collaborate with a diverse range of artists throughout his career. Some of his favorite collaborations have been with musicians who share his passion for blending genres and pushing the boundaries of electronic music.

One notable collaboration was with Dubstep artist Excision on the track "Throwin' Elbows." The combination of Virtual Riot's intricate sound design and Excision's heavy-hitting drops created a track that resonated with fans from both artists' fan bases.

Another memorable collaboration was with songwriter and vocalist Carrie Skipper on the track "In My Head." Virtual Riot appreciated her strong lyrical storytelling and melodic sensibilities, which added a new dimension to his music.

Overall, Virtual Riot cherishes collaborations that allow him to step out of his comfort zone and explore new sonic territories. These collaborations not only result in exceptional music but also open up possibilities for future artistic endeavors.

Virtual Riot's Collaborative Wishlist

Virtual Riot has an extensive list of dream collaborators he hopes to work with in the future. Some artists on his collaborative wishlist include breakthrough EDM producer Rezz, genre-defying experimental artist Flying Lotus, and legendary songwriter and producer Pharrell Williams.

He is also interested in cross-genre collaborations that merge electronic music with other musical genres such as hip-hop, rock, and classical. Virtual Riot believes that these collaborations have the potential to break down barriers and reach new audiences.

Virtual Riot's collaborative wishlist is a testament to his dedication to continuous growth and exploration as an artist. He is constantly seeking out new experiences and challenging himself to create music that pushes the boundaries.

Virtual Riot's Perspective on Collaboration in the Music Industry

For Virtual Riot, collaboration is not just about combining different musical ideas; it's about creating something greater than the sum of its parts. He believes that collaboration is crucial in a constantly evolving music industry, as it allows artists to learn from each other and expand their creative horizons.

Virtual Riot embraces collaboration as a way to connect with fellow artists and to inspire and be inspired. He sees it as a collaborative journey that requires mutual respect, open-mindedness, and a shared passion for music.

In the highly competitive music industry, Virtual Riot believes that collaboration can lead to unique opportunities for all artists involved. By working together, artists can support each other's growth and contribute to the overall advancement of their respective genres and the music industry as a whole.

In summary, Virtual Riot views collaboration as not only a means of creating music but also as a transformative and educational experience. By finding the right collaborators, balancing creative differences, and learning from each other, artists can push the boundaries of creativity and create music that resonates with audiences worldwide.

...

The Highs and Lows of Collaborative Projects

Collaborative projects in the music industry can be both exhilarating and challenging. They often involve bringing together artists with different backgrounds, creative visions, and personal styles. In this section, we will explore the highs and lows that can come with collaborative projects and how artists like Virtual Riot navigate these experiences.

The Highs of Collaborative Projects

Collaborative projects offer a range of benefits that can elevate an artist's work and create unique and memorable musical experiences. Some of the highs of collaborative projects include:

Expanding Creative Horizons: Collaborative projects provide an opportunity for artists to step outside their comfort zones and explore new genres, styles, and techniques. Working with other musicians can expose them to fresh perspectives and ideas, sparking their creativity and pushing them to experiment and grow.

Sharing the Workload: Collaborations allow artists to share the workload involved in creating music. The process of producing a track can be time-consuming and mentally taxing, but with collaborators, the burden is divided. This not only lightens the load but also brings diverse skill sets to the table, enhancing the overall quality of the project.

Learning from Each Other: Collaborating with artists who have different strengths and experiences can be a valuable learning opportunity. Each collaborator brings their own unique techniques, knowledge, and musical influences to the project, allowing for skill-sharing and creative cross-pollination.

Building a Stronger Network: Collaborative projects foster connections and relationships within the music industry. By working with other artists, Virtual Riot not only expands his own network but also benefits from the networks of his collaborators. This can open doors to new opportunities, such as introductions to industry professionals, exposure to new audiences, and access to bigger platforms.

Creating a Fusion of Styles: When artists with distinct musical styles come together, the result can be a fusion of sounds that captivates listeners. Collaborations allow for the blending of different genres, influences, and sonic palettes, creating a unique sonic landscape that stands out in the industry.

The Lows of Collaborative Projects

While collaborative projects have many benefits, they also come with their fair share of challenges. It's important to acknowledge and address these lows to ensure productive and harmonious collaborations. Some of the lows of collaborative projects include:

Creative Differences: Collaborations bring together artists with their own artistic visions and preferences. Creative differences can arise, leading to conflicts over musical decisions, production techniques, or even the direction of the project. Resolving these differences requires open communication, compromise, and a shared understanding of the project's goals.

Balancing Egos: Each collaborator brings their own unique talents and accomplishments to the table, and it's essential to balance egos in order to create a harmonious working environment. The focus should always remain on creating the best possible music and not getting caught up in individual status or self-importance.

Logistical Challenges: Collaborative projects often involve coordinating schedules, managing different time zones, and finding ways to work together remotely. This can be a logistical challenge, especially when dealing with multiple collaborators or artists who are constantly on the road. Effective communication and strong project management skills are crucial in overcoming these hurdles.

Differing Work Ethic: Each artist has their own work ethic and level of commitment to the project. It can be frustrating when collaborators do not put in equal effort or fail to meet deadlines. Transparent expectations and clear project plans can help mitigate these challenges and ensure that everyone is on the same page.

Financial Considerations: Collaborative projects may involve financial aspects such as sharing royalties, expenses, or revenue from performances. Determining how to distribute financial resources can sometimes be a sensitive topic and requires open discussions and fair agreements.

Navigating the Collaborative Journey

With the potential for both highs and lows in collaborative projects, it is important for artists like Virtual Riot to approach these endeavors with a strategic mindset and a commitment to open communication. Here are some tips for navigating the collaborative journey:

Establishing Clear Roles and Expectations: Before diving into a collaborative project, it is essential to establish clear roles, responsibilities, and expectations for each collaborator. This includes defining individual contributions, decision-making processes, and project milestones. Regular check-ins can ensure that everyone remains aligned and on track.

Open and Honest Communication: Effective communication is paramount in collaborative projects. It is crucial to create a safe and respectful environment where all collaborators feel comfortable expressing their ideas, concerns, and creative visions. Regular meetings, brainstorming sessions, and feedback loops allow everyone to stay connected and engaged throughout the project.

Flexibility and Compromise: Collaborations often require compromise and flexibility. Artists may need to let go of their initial ideas or make adjustments to accommodate the creative direction of the project. Finding the right balance between honoring individual artistic visions and working towards a cohesive end result is key.

Resolving Conflicts Professionally: Conflicts are common in collaborative projects, but they should be addressed professionally and with respect.

Constructive dialogue, active listening, and a willingness to find common ground can help resolve conflicts and prevent any negative impact on the project or the relationships involved.

Celebrating Successes Together: When collaborative projects come to fruition, it's important to celebrate the achievements together as a team. Recognizing and acknowledging the hard work, dedication, and creativity of each collaborator strengthens the bond and encourages future collaborations.

Navigating the highs and lows of collaborative projects is an essential part of an artist's journey. By embracing the benefits and challenges, Virtual Riot continues to create exciting and innovative music through collaborative endeavors. Every collaboration brings its unique set of highs and lows, but with the right approach and mindset, artists can create extraordinary musical experiences that resonate with audiences around the world.

Virtual Riot's Favorite Collaborations

Collaborations have always been an essential aspect of Virtual Riot's music career. Throughout the years, he has worked with numerous talented artists across different genres, pushing the boundaries of electronic music and delivering unique and captivating tracks. In this section, we will explore some of Virtual Riot's favorite collaborations, highlighting the creative process, the impact of each collaboration, and the magic that happens when artists come together to create something special.

Zedd x Virtual Riot: "Lions in the Wild"

One of Virtual Riot's most memorable collaborations was with the renowned electronic music producer Zedd. Together, they created the track "Lions in the Wild," which was released in 2016. This collaboration showcased Virtual Riot's versatility as an artist and his ability to adapt to different EDM subgenres.

The creative process behind this collaboration was an exciting journey. Both Virtual Riot and Zedd brought their unique styles and approaches to the table, merging their talents to create a powerful and energetic track. The combination of Virtual Riot's signature heavy basslines and Zedd's melodic sensibilities resulted in a track that perfectly balanced energy and emotion.

"Lions in the Wild" was well-received by fans and critics alike, becoming a hit in the electronic music scene. Its success solidified Virtual Riot's position as a prominent figure in the EDM industry and opened doors to more exciting collaboration opportunities.

Virtual Riot x Dubloadz: "Juices"

When Virtual Riot collaborated with Dubloadz on the track "Juices," it was a match made in heaven for bass music enthusiasts. Released in 2017, this collaboration showcased the blending of their unique production styles, resulting in a track that was both heavy and highly energetic.

The creative process for "Juices" was an intense and passionate collaboration. Virtual Riot and Dubloadz combined their expertise in sound design and production to create a hard-hitting track that sent shockwaves through the dubstep community. The track's intricate basslines and mind-bending drops captivated listeners and solidified both Virtual Riot and Dubloadz as masters of their craft.

The impact of "Juices" was immense, with the track becoming a staple in bass music sets around the world. It showcased the power of collaboration in the electronic music scene, bringing together two talented artists and creating something that was greater than the sum of its parts.

Virtual Riot x Panda Eyes: "Superheroes"

Virtual Riot's collaboration with Panda Eyes on the track "Superheroes" highlighted their shared love for energetic and melodic dubstep. Released in 2018, this track captivated listeners with its infectious energy and catchy melodies.

The creative process behind "Superheroes" was a true testament to the synergy between Virtual Riot and Panda Eyes. Both artists brought their unique musical ideas to the table, resulting in a track that seamlessly blended Virtual Riot's heavy bass elements with Panda Eyes' melodic prowess. The result was a sonic adventure that took listeners on a journey through a world of superpowers and epic battles.

"Superheroes" quickly became a fan favorite, solidifying Virtual Riot and Panda Eyes as a dynamic duo in the dubstep scene. The track's combination of hard-hitting drops and beautiful melodies resonated with audiences worldwide, showcasing the power of collaboration in creating something truly remarkable.

Virtual Riot x Dirtyphonics: "Beat Dem Up"

The collaboration between Virtual Riot and Dirtyphonics on the track "Beat Dem Up" pushed the boundaries of heavy bass music. Released in 2019, this track was a powerful fusion of Virtual Riot's intricate sound design and Dirtyphonics' aggressive soundscapes.

The creative process behind "Beat Dem Up" was an intense and exhilarating experience for both Virtual Riot and Dirtyphonics. They combined their expertise in crafting hard-hitting drops and driving rhythms to create a track that was relentless in its energy. The result was a sonic assault that left listeners craving more.

"Beat Dem Up" was praised for its originality and innovative production techniques. The track's raw power and unique approach to bass music showcased the limitless possibilities of collaboration in electronic music.

In conclusion, Virtual Riot's favorite collaborations have been a testament to the power of teamwork and creative synergy. From working with renowned producers like Zedd and Dirtyphonics to collaborating with fellow bass music enthusiasts like Dubloadz and Panda Eyes, Virtual Riot has consistently pushed the boundaries of electronic music through his collaborative projects. These collaborations have not only produced incredible tracks but have also inspired future generations of music producers to explore new territories and challenge the norms of the industry. The magic that happens when artists come together is undeniable, and Virtual Riot's favorite collaborations are a testament to the power of unity in creating exceptional music.

Virtual Riot's Collaborative Wishlist

Collaboration is the lifeblood of the music industry. It allows artists to pool their creativity and skills to create something truly unique. Virtual Riot understands the power of collaboration and has always been open to working with other artists. In this section, we explore Virtual Riot's collaborative wishlist - the artists he dreams of working with and the kind of music he envisions creating together.

Dream Collaborators

Virtual Riot has a long list of dream collaborators who he hopes to work with in the future. One name that stands out is Skrillex, a pioneer of electronic dance music. Virtual Riot admires Skrillex's ability to push the boundaries of the genre and create groundbreaking sounds. He envisions a collaboration that combines Skrillex's hard-hitting drops with his own melodic and experimental style.

Another artist that Virtual Riot hopes to collaborate with is Billie Eilish. He is fascinated by her unique approach to music and her ability to tell stories through her lyrics. Virtual Riot believes that their collaboration could result in a genre-bending track that blends elements of electronic music with Billie's haunting vocals.

Virtual Riot also dreams of collaborating with a legendary rock band like Radiohead. He is inspired by their eclectic sound and innovative approach to music. Virtual Riot envisions a collaboration that fuses their atmospheric rock with his electronic production to create a truly genre-defying masterpiece.

Genre Exploration

Virtual Riot is not confined to one particular genre and his collaborative wishlist reflects his desire to explore different musical styles. One genre that he is eager to delve into is hip-hop. He believes that combining his electronic production with the raw energy of hip-hop could result in a fresh and dynamic sound. Virtual Riot envisions collaborating with artists like Kendrick Lamar or Tyler, the Creator to create a track that seamlessly blends their rap skills with his unique production style.

In addition to hip-hop, Virtual Riot is also interested in pushing the boundaries of pop music. He admires artists like Taylor Swift and Ariana Grande for their ability to create catchy and infectious pop songs. Virtual Riot envisions collaborating with these artists to create a pop track that combines their irresistible hooks with his innovative production techniques.

Experimental Projects

Virtual Riot's collaborative wishlist also includes some unconventional and experimental projects. He is particularly interested in working with symphony orchestras to create orchestral-electronic hybrids. Virtual Riot believes that combining the grandeur of a symphony orchestra with his electronic production could result in a truly epic and cinematic experience.

Additionally, Virtual Riot hopes to collaborate with visual artists to create immersive audio-visual experiences. He envisions working with cutting-edge projection mapping artists to create mind-bending visuals that interact with and enhance his music.

The Power of Collaboration

Virtual Riot recognizes that collaborations are not just about creating great music; they are also about personal growth and learning. He believes that collaborating with artists from different backgrounds and disciplines can lead to new perspectives and fresh ideas. Virtual Riot sees collaboration as a way to challenge himself and push the boundaries of his own creativity.

In conclusion, Virtual Riot's collaborative wishlist is a testament to his open-mindedness and willingness to explore new possibilities. Whether it's working with his musical heroes, experimenting with different genres, or embarking on unconventional projects, Virtual Riot is excited about the power of collaboration and the endless opportunities it brings.

Virtual Riot's Perspective on Collaboration in the Music Industry

Virtual Riot, known for his innovative sound and boundary-pushing tracks, has gained significant recognition in the electronic music industry. His unique approach to music production and collaborations has cemented his position as a game-changer in the industry. In this section, we will explore Virtual Riot's perspective on collaboration and how it shapes the music industry.

Collaboration is a vital aspect of any creative process, and for Virtual Riot, it is no exception. He believes that collaborating with other artists not only expands his creative horizons but also brings fresh ideas and diverse perspectives to his music. According to Virtual Riot, collaboration is all about finding the right artists to work with—those who share a similar vision and bring unique contributions to the table.

Finding the right collaborators requires careful consideration. Virtual Riot values creative differences and believes that they can lead to truly exceptional results. When working with other artists, he embraces their distinct styles and personalities, viewing them as opportunities to learn from each other. These collaborations often push the boundaries of electronic music, resulting in tracks that blend diverse genres and defy traditional categorization.

However, Virtual Riot also acknowledges that the collaborative process isn't always smooth sailing. Balancing creative differences and finding common ground can be challenging. Yet, he believes that these struggles are necessary for growth and development as an artist. Through compromise and open communication, he navigates these challenges, ultimately creating music that transcends individual styles and reflects the collective energy of the collaboration.

One of Virtual Riot's favorite aspects of collaboration is the learning experience it provides. Each collaboration brings new insights and techniques that he can incorporate into his own work. He believes that this cross-pollination of ideas helps to push the industry forward, sparking creativity and inspiring future collaborations.

Virtual Riot's collaborations extend beyond the electronic dance music (EDM) scene. He actively seeks partnerships with artists from various genres, believing that diversity leads to innovation. By crossing musical boundaries and experimenting with different styles, Virtual Riot aims to challenge preconceived notions of what electronic music can be.

Virtual Riot's perspective on collaboration extends beyond the creative process. He sees it as a means to foster a sense of community in the music industry. By working together, artists can support and uplift one another, ultimately strengthening the industry as a whole. Virtual Riot has been known to champion emerging artists, providing mentorship and guidance to help them navigate their own artistic journeys.

For Virtual Riot, collaboration is not limited to creating music but also extends to building connections with fans. He actively engages with his fanbase through Q&A sessions and live streams, fostering a sense of community and inclusion. This direct interaction allows fans to feel a part of the creative process, creating a symbiotic relationship between artist and audience.

In addition to collaborations with other artists, Virtual Riot emphasizes the importance of collaboration within teams working behind the scenes. From managers to sound engineers, each person plays a crucial role in bringing his music to life. By fostering a collaborative and supportive environment, Virtual Riot ensures that his live performances and studio productions are nothing short of exceptional.

In conclusion, Virtual Riot's perspective on collaboration in the music industry emphasizes the value of diverse perspectives and shared creativity. Through collaboration, he pushes the boundaries of electronic music, creating tracks that defy genres and elevate the industry as a whole. Collaboration, both with other artists and with fans, forms the foundation of a strong and vibrant music community. It is through these collaborations that Virtual Riot continues to leave an indelible mark on the music industry, inspiring future generations of musicians and pushing the boundaries of what is possible in electronic music.

Virtual Riot's Advice for Successful Collaborations

Collaborations in the music industry can be a tricky business. It's not just about finding artists whose skills complement each other, but also about navigating different personalities and creative differences. Virtual Riot has had his fair share of successful collaborations throughout his career, so let's dive into his advice for making collaborations work:

Finding the Right Artists to Collaborate With

Virtual Riot emphasizes the importance of finding the right artists to collaborate with. He believes that the key to a successful collaboration is finding someone who shares a similar artistic vision and has a genuine passion for music. It's not just about fame or popularity; it's about finding a genuine connection with the artist you're working with.

When looking for partners to collaborate with, Virtual Riot suggests stepping outside of your comfort zone and exploring different genres and styles. Sometimes the most unexpected collaborations can lead to the most fruitful and innovative results. So don't be afraid to think outside the box and experiment with new musical territories.

Balancing Creative Differences and Personalities

Collaborations inevitably bring together different creative visions, and Virtual Riot acknowledges the challenges that come with merging these distinct styles. He advises artists to approach collaborations with an open mind and a willingness to compromise.

Virtual Riot believes that the key to balancing creative differences lies in effective communication and mutual respect. Listen to each other's ideas and be open to constructive feedback. Finding a middle ground between your creative visions can lead to unique and exciting artistic expressions.

Understanding each other's personalities is also crucial in maintaining a harmonious collaboration. Virtual Riot suggests taking the time to get to know your collaborator and build a personal connection. By understanding each other's strengths, weaknesses, and preferences, you can create a supportive and productive working environment.

Learning from Each Other: The Collaborative Process

Collaborations are not just about combining talents; they're also about learning from each other. Virtual Riot encourages artists to view collaborations as opportunities for growth and expansion. Each collaborator brings their unique perspectives and skills to the table, and by embracing this diversity, you can push your creative boundaries.

During the collaborative process, Virtual Riot advises being open to new ideas and approaches. Don't be afraid to experiment and explore unfamiliar territories. By stepping out of your comfort zone, you can discover new techniques and refine your own artistic style.

The Highs and Lows of Collaborative Projects

Collaborations come with their highs and lows, and Virtual Riot acknowledges the challenges that arise during the process. He believes that it's essential to embrace both the successes and the failures and learn from each experience.

Not every collaboration will result in a groundbreaking hit, and that's okay. Virtual Riot encourages artists to view every collaboration as a valuable learning opportunity. Even if a project doesn't meet your expectations, you can gain insights and grow as an artist.

Virtual Riot's Favorite Collaborations

Throughout his career, Virtual Riot has had the privilege of collaborating with many talented artists. Some of his favorite collaborations include working with Dubstep artist Excision, American DJ and record producer FuntCase, and German Drum and Bass duo Noisia.

These collaborations allowed Virtual Riot to explore new genres and styles while combining his unique sound with other artists' signatures. By working together, they created tracks that became fan favorites, showcased their individual talents, and pushed the boundaries of electronic music.

Virtual Riot's Collaborative Wishlist

Virtual Riot has a wishlist of artists he dreams of collaborating with. He admires the creative approaches of artists like Flume, Porter Robinson, and Skrillex, whose music constantly challenges the norms of electronic music. Collaborating with these artists would allow him to explore new sonic landscapes and push his own creative boundaries even further.

Virtual Riot's Perspective on Collaboration in the Music Industry

For Virtual Riot, collaboration is not just about creating music; it's about building a strong community within the music industry. He believes that collaborating with other artists is a way to foster camaraderie, support, and inspiration.

Virtual Riot encourages artists to reach out to each other, attend music events and networking opportunities, and be open to new collaborations. By building a network of like-minded artists, you can create a supportive community where you can learn from and grow together.

Virtual Riot's Advice for Successful Collaborations

Based on his own experiences, Virtual Riot offers the following advice for successful collaborations:

- Find artists whose artistic vision aligns with yours, regardless of their popularity or fame.

- Embrace creative differences and find a balance between your artistic styles.

- Communicate openly and be open to compromise and feedback.

- View collaborations as opportunities for growth and learning from one another.

- Embrace both the successes and failures of collaborative projects, and learn from each experience.

- Build personal connections with your collaborators to create a supportive and productive working environment.

- Step out of your comfort zone and explore new genres and styles together.

- Collaborate with a diverse range of artists to push your creative boundaries.

- Build a strong community within the music industry through networking and supporting other artists.

By following these pieces of advice, artists can increase their chances of having successful collaborations that not only produce great music but also foster personal and artistic growth. Collaboration is an opportunity to explore new horizons, learn from others, and leave a lasting impact on the music industry.

Virtual Riot's Collaborations Outside of the EDM Scene

Virtual Riot, known for his incredible talent in the electronic dance music (EDM) scene, has not limited himself to collaborating only within his genre. He has also ventured into collaborating with artists and musicians from various other music styles, bringing his signature sound and production skills to create unique and exciting cross-genre collaborations.

One notable collaboration outside of the EDM scene for Virtual Riot was with a renowned hip-hop artist. In this collaboration, he combined his expertise in electronic production with the artist's lyrical prowess to create a track that seamlessly blended elements of EDM and hip-hop. The result was a fresh and energetic sound that captivated audiences from both genres.

Another surprising collaboration for Virtual Riot was with a prominent jazz musician. Together, they explored the fusion of electronic beats and improvisational jazz melodies, pushing the boundaries of each genre and creating an entirely new sonic experience. The combination of Virtual Riot's precise and intricate production techniques with the jazz musician's virtuosity resulted in a captivating and innovative collaboration.

Virtual Riot also collaborated with a classical composer, merging electronic sounds with orchestral arrangements. By incorporating elements of orchestral instrumentation and complex harmonies into his electronic productions, he created a breathtaking and awe-inspiring composition that bridged the gap between the worlds of electronic music and classical music.

In addition to these cross-genre collaborations, Virtual Riot has also worked with folk musicians to bring a unique twist to traditional folk songs. By infusing electronic elements into the acoustic instrumentation and folk melodies, he breathed new life into these timeless songs, appealing to both traditional folk music enthusiasts and electronic music fans.

Virtual Riot's collaborations outside of the EDM scene showcase his versatility as a producer and his willingness to explore new musical territories. These collaborations have not only widened his artistic horizons but have also introduced his unique style and sound to audiences who may not typically gravitate towards EDM.

It is worth noting that these collaborations have not only benefited Virtual Riot as an artist but have also made a significant impact on the artists he has collaborated with. By bringing his production expertise and fresh perspective to these projects, he has helped to expand the boundaries of their respective genres and create music that is truly groundbreaking.

Through these collaborations, Virtual Riot has proven that artistic exploration and genre-blending can lead to exciting and innovative musical experiences. By venturing beyond the EDM scene and collaborating with artists from diverse genres, he continues to push the limits of his own creativity and inspire others to do the same.

In conclusion, Virtual Riot's collaborations outside of the EDM scene have showcased his ability to seamlessly merge electronic music with various other genres. These cross-genre collaborations have resulted in groundbreaking and innovative music, expanding the boundaries of different musical styles and captivating audiences across genres. Virtual Riot's willingness to explore new territories and push the limits of his own creativity highlights his versatility as an artist and his dedication to creating unique and exciting musical experiences.

Virtual Riot's Impact on Collaborative Music Production

Collaboration is a key aspect of the music industry, and Virtual Riot has made a significant impact on the world of collaborative music production. Through his innovative approach and unique vision, Virtual Riot has elevated the art of collaboration, pushing boundaries and inspiring a new generation of musicians. In this section, we will explore the various ways in which Virtual Riot has influenced collaborative music production.

Building Bridges: Connecting Artists

One of Virtual Riot's greatest contributions to collaborative music production is his ability to bring together artists from different backgrounds and genres. He has a natural talent for recognizing the potential in others and fostering creative partnerships. Whether it's working with vocalists, instrumentalists, or fellow producers, Virtual Riot creates a collaborative space where diverse talents can coexist and thrive.

Virtual Riot's impact on collaborative music production can be seen through his collaborations with artists such as Muzzy, Dubloadz, and Barely Alive. By combining their unique styles and strengths, they have created groundbreaking tracks that have resonated with audiences worldwide. Through these collaborations, Virtual Riot has not only elevated his own music but has also provided a platform for other artists to showcase their talents.

Breaking Barriers: Blurring Genre Lines

Virtual Riot's impact on collaborative music production can also be seen in his ability to break down genre barriers. He is known for his genre-bending approach, seamlessly blending elements of dubstep, drum and bass, house, and more. This versatility allows him to collaborate with artists from a wide range of genres, resulting in innovative and boundary-pushing tracks.

Through his collaborations, Virtual Riot has demonstrated that music knows no boundaries. He has shown that artists can come together, combining their unique styles and influences, to create something truly extraordinary. By pushing the limits of genre conventions, Virtual Riot has inspired a new wave of collaborative music production, encouraging artists to think outside the box and experiment with different sounds.

The Power of Synergy: Enhancing Creativity

Collaborative music production is not just about combining individual talents; it is about harnessing the power of synergy. Virtual Riot understands this concept deeply and knows that the whole is greater than the sum of its parts. Through his collaborative projects, he has created an environment where ideas flow freely, and creativity is amplified.

Virtual Riot's impact on collaborative music production lies in his ability to cultivate an atmosphere of shared inspiration and exploration. By working closely with other artists, he encourages them to step out of their comfort zones and tap into their full creative potential. This level of collaboration pushes boundaries and allows for the creation of truly groundbreaking music.

Embracing Technology: Digital Collaboration

In an era where technology has become a central part of music production, Virtual Riot has fully embraced digital collaboration. Through online platforms and tools, he has been able to collaborate with artists from around the world, breaking down geographical barriers and expanding the possibilities of collaborative music production.

Virtual Riot's impact on collaborative music production can be seen through his extensive work with producers and artists online. By utilizing platforms such as SoundCloud and social media, he has been able to connect with like-minded individuals and collaborate on projects that would have been otherwise impossible. This digital collaboration has opened up a world of opportunities for artists, allowing them to collaborate with individuals they may have never met otherwise.

The Unconventional Approach: Thinking Outside the Box

In addition to his technical contributions to collaborative music production, Virtual Riot also brings an unconventional approach to the table. He challenges traditional notions of collaboration and encourages artists to think outside the box.

For example, Virtual Riot often incorporates unconventional sounds and samples into his music, which adds a unique flavor to his collaborations. By pushing boundaries and taking risks, he inspires his collaborators to experiment and explore new sonic territories.

Example: Collaborative Innovation

To illustrate Virtual Riot's impact on collaborative music production, let's take a look at his collaboration with fellow producer Muzzy. In their track "Endgame," Virtual Riot and Muzzy combine their respective styles of dubstep and drum and bass to create a high-energy, genre-blurring masterpiece. By merging these distinct genres, they have crafted a track that stands out from the crowd and has garnered widespread acclaim.

This collaboration not only showcases Virtual Riot's ability to bring together artists from different backgrounds but also highlights his knack for pushing genre boundaries. "Endgame" exemplifies the power of collaboration in pushing the limits of creativity and redefining what is possible in music.

Conclusion

Virtual Riot's impact on collaborative music production is undeniable. Through his ability to connect artists, break genre barriers, embrace technology, and think outside the box, he has revolutionized the collaborative process. His innovative approach has inspired countless musicians and shaped the future of collaborative music production. As he continues to push boundaries and explore new horizons, Virtual Riot's impact will undoubtedly be felt for years to come.

Virtual Riot as a Producer

From Ideas to Tracks: The Creative Process

Ever wonder how your favorite Virtual Riot tracks come to life? In this section, we'll dive into the creative process behind Virtual Riot's music production and explore the journey from a simple idea to a fully-realized track.

The Spark of Inspiration

Every track starts with a spark of inspiration. For Virtual Riot, this can come from anywhere and at any time. It could be a melody that pops into his head while taking a shower or a sound that catches his ear while walking down the street. The key is to always stay open to inspiration and be ready to capture those moments when they arise.

Turning Ideas Into Reality

Once the initial idea is sparked, it's time to turn it into a tangible track. Virtual Riot begins by laying down the foundation, establishing the key and tempo of the track. This is the stage where he starts exploring different chord progressions and melodies, experimenting with different combinations until the right vibe is achieved.

Building Layers and Experimenting with Sounds

With the foundation in place, Virtual Riot starts building layers of sound. This is where the track truly comes to life. He meticulously crafts each layer, experimenting with different synthesizers, samples, and effects to create unique and interesting textures. This is also where his expertise as a sound designer shines through, as he carefully selects and tweaks each sound to fit the overall vision of the track.

The Quest for the Perfect Drop

One of the most exciting parts of the creative process is crafting the drop. This is the part of the track that gets the crowd moving and creates those unforgettable moments on the dancefloor. Virtual Riot approaches the drop with meticulous attention to detail, experimenting with different sound design techniques, rhythmic patterns, and dynamics to create a drop that is both powerful and infectious.

Enhancing the Track with Mixing and Mastering

Once the track is fully arranged and all the elements are in place, Virtual Riot moves on to the mixing and mastering stage. This is where he fine-tunes the levels, applies EQ and compression, and adds the final touch of polish to make sure the track sounds great on any system. Virtual Riot's meticulous attention to detail in this stage ensures that his tracks have the impact and clarity needed to stand out in today's music landscape.

Embracing Collaborations and Feedback

Virtual Riot understands the power of collaboration and the value of getting feedback from trusted sources. He is not afraid to reach out to other artists for input or to collaborate on projects. This collaborative mindset allows him to continuously grow and explore new creative possibilities.

Pushing the Boundaries

Innovation and pushing the boundaries of electronic music are key aspects of Virtual Riot's creative process. He is always looking for new ways to incorporate unique sounds, experiment with unconventional techniques, and explore different genres. This commitment to innovation keeps his music fresh and exciting, constantly pushing the limits of what's possible.

Finding Balance

Finding balance is crucial in the creative process. Virtual Riot understands the importance of taking breaks, stepping away from the project, and coming back with fresh ears. This allows him to maintain perspective and prevent creative burnout. It's all about finding the right balance between intense focus and allowing room for creativity to flow naturally.

Staying True to the Vibe

Throughout the entire creative process, Virtual Riot stays true to the vibe and emotion he wants to convey through his music. Whether it's a high-energy banger or a more introspective track, he ensures that every element serves the overall vision and mood of the piece. This commitment to artistic integrity is what sets Virtual Riot apart as a producer.

Practicing and Continuing Education

Virtual Riot's creative process is also fueled by a dedication to continuous learning and improvement. He is constantly exploring new production techniques, experimenting with different tools, and staying up-to-date with the latest trends in music production. This commitment to growth allows him to evolve his sound and stay at the forefront of the electronic music scene.

Unconventional Problem-solving

In the creative process, it's inevitable to encounter roadblocks and challenges. Virtual Riot approaches these obstacles with a unique and unconventional mindset. He embraces these challenges as opportunities for innovation, finding creative solutions that elevate the final product. Whether it's through experimenting with unusual effects or reimagining traditional musical structures, Virtual Riot's unconventional problem-solving creates tracks that leave a lasting impact.

Empowering the Listener

Virtual Riot's ultimate goal in the creative process is to empower the listener. Through his music, he aims to create a space for self-expression, escapism, and connection. He believes that music has the power to transform and uplift, and his creative process is guided by this belief.

Summary

In this section, we explored the creative process behind Virtual Riot's music production. From the initial spark of inspiration to the final mix and master, Virtual Riot takes us on a journey of how ideas are transformed into fully-realized tracks. We learned about the importance of experimentation, collaboration, and pushing boundaries to create unique and impactful music. Virtual Riot's commitment to continuous learning, balance, and staying true to the artistic vision ensures that his tracks stand out in the ever-evolving world of electronic music. Ultimately, his goal is to create music that empowers and connects with the listener, leaving a lasting impact.

Building Layers and Experimenting with Sounds

Building layers and experimenting with sounds are integral processes in the music production journey of Virtual Riot. As a producer, Virtual Riot constantly strives to create unique and captivating tracks by carefully constructing intricate layers of sounds. In this section, we will explore Virtual Riot's approach to building layers and his penchant for sound experimentation. We will delve into his creative process, the role of technology, and his favorite production techniques.

The Creative Process

For Virtual Riot, the creative process is a fluid and ever-evolving journey. It begins with an initial idea or concept that serves as the foundation for the track. This idea could stem from a melody, chord progression, or even a sound texture that captures Virtual Riot's attention. Once the initial spark ignites, he meticulously builds upon it, adding various elements and layers to create depth and complexity in the track.

Virtual Riot understands the importance of balance in layering sounds. Each layer should serve a purpose and contribute to the overall sonic landscape of the track. He carefully selects different sounds from his extensive sample library to create contrast, complementarity, and synergy among the layers.

To maintain a sense of cohesion and excitement throughout the track, Virtual Riot experiments with different combinations of sounds. He explores various tonalities, textures, and rhythmic patterns to find the perfect blend that grabs the listener's attention and keeps them engaged.

Building Layers

Building layers is all about constructing a sonic tapestry that captures the essence of Virtual Riot's vision. Each layer adds a unique element to the track, contributing to its richness and complexity. Here are some techniques Virtual Riot employs when building layers:

- **Melodic Layers:** Virtual Riot often starts with a melodic layer as the foundation of his tracks. This could include catchy synth melodies, harmonious chord progressions, or arpeggiated patterns. These melodic layers create the emotional core of the track and guide the listener through the musical journey.

- **Bass Layers:** Powerful and impactful basslines are a hallmark of Virtual Riot's sound. He carefully constructs bass layers using a combination of synthesized bass sounds, processed samples, and creative effects. These bass layers provide depth, energy, and drive to the track, enhancing the overall impact of the music.

- **Rhythmic Layers:** Virtual Riot pays great attention to the rhythmic elements in his tracks. He incorporates percussive layers, intricate drum patterns, and rhythmic glitches to add complexity and groove. These layers create a solid backbone that keeps the track moving forward and creates a strong foundation for other elements to build upon.

- **Atmospheric Layers:** To immerse the listener in a unique sonic environment, Virtual Riot incorporates atmospheric layers. These layers often consist of ambient pads, ethereal textures, and field recordings. They provide a sense of depth and space within the track, evoking specific moods or atmospheres.

- **Vocal and FX Layers:** Virtual Riot frequently uses vocal samples and vocal chops to add excitement and personality to his tracks. He chops, processes, and manipulates these samples to create unique vocal layers that blend seamlessly with the other elements. Additionally, he adds various sound effects to enhance transitions, build tension, or create interesting sonic moments.

By skillfully layering these different elements, Virtual Riot creates a multidimensional sonic experience that captivates the listener from start to finish.

Experimenting with Sounds

Virtual Riot is known for pushing the boundaries of sound and constantly experimenting with new techniques and ideas. His willingness to step outside traditional norms and explore the unknown has led to the development of his unique sound. Here are some ways he experiments with sounds:

- **Sound Design:** Virtual Riot devotes a significant amount of time to sound design, exploring various synthesis techniques and tools to create his own unique sounds. He often starts with a simple sound and then manipulates it using filters, effects, and modulation to achieve the desired result. This experimentation allows him to craft sounds that stand out and bring a fresh perspective to his tracks.

- **Unconventional Sampling:** Virtual Riot finds inspiration in unconventional sampling, using everyday objects, nature sounds, and even recordings of unexpected events. He believes that these unconventional samples add a touch of novelty and surprise to his music, creating moments of intrigue and excitement for the listener.

- **Genre Fusion:** Virtual Riot loves to experiment with genre fusion, blending elements from different genres to create innovative and genre-bending tracks. He finds inspiration in diverse music styles such as rock, jazz, hip-hop, and classical, and seamlessly integrates them into his electronic productions. This experimentation with genre fusion brings a unique flavor to his sound and sets him apart from others in the EDM scene.

- **Effect Processing:** Virtual Riot is a master of creative effect processing. He explores various plugins and techniques to manipulate sounds, create unusual textures, and transform familiar sounds into something extraordinary. By experimenting with effects such as reverb, delay, distortion, and granular synthesis, he adds depth and character to his tracks.

- **Randomness and Chance:** Virtual Riot embraces randomness and chance in his creative process. He believes that embracing happy accidents and unexpected outcomes can lead to innovative and surprising sonic results. By intentionally introducing elements of randomness in his production, he allows for spontaneous discoveries and embraces the element of surprise.

Virtual Riot's approach to sound experimentation fosters a sense of curiosity and exploration, constantly pushing the boundaries of his creativity and pioneering new sonic territories.

Favorite Production Techniques

Virtual Riot has several favorite production techniques that he frequently utilizes to achieve his desired sound. These techniques not only enhance his tracks but also contribute to his distinct style. Here are a few of his favorites:

+ **Layering and Stacking:** Virtual Riot believes in the power of layering sounds to create a lush and full-bodied mix. He often duplicates and stacks similar or complementary elements, such as synths or drums, and applies subtle variations to each layer to add depth and richness. This technique adds a sense of fullness to the sound while maintaining clarity and separation among the elements.

+ **Parallel Processing:** To achieve a balanced and impactful mix, Virtual Riot extensively uses parallel processing techniques. He creates parallel channels for specific elements like drums or bass and applies different processing chains to each channel. This allows him to control the dynamics, tonal characteristics, and saturation of individual elements while preserving their natural character within the mix.

+ **Creative Automation:** Virtual Riot is a strong advocate for using automation as a creative tool. He automates various parameters within his tracks, such as filter cutoffs, effects parameters, and modulation settings. This dynamic approach to automation creates movement, interest, and a sense of progression throughout the track.

+ **Microsample Manipulation:** Virtual Riot often explores microsample manipulation techniques to add intricate details and unique textures to his tracks. He takes tiny snippets of audio, manipulates them with effects, pitch-shifting, or time-stretching, and weaves them into the fabric of the track. This technique adds an element of surprise and unpredictability to the sound design.

+ **Layered Reverb and Delay:** To create a sense of space and depth, Virtual Riot employs layered reverb and delay effects. He applies different reverbs and delays to specific layers or elements in the mix, tailoring each effect to enhance the particular sound's characteristics. This technique adds a three-dimensional quality to the mix, making it feel more immersive and spacious.

* **Selectively Distorting Harmonics:** Virtual Riot loves to selectively distort specific harmonics within sound sources to add character and impact. By applying distortion plugins or using waveshaping techniques, he can shape the timbre, accentuate certain frequencies, and create harmonic richness. This technique adds vitality and grit to the sound design.

These favorite techniques provide a glimpse into Virtual Riot's production arsenal, highlighting his commitment to crafting meticulously crafted tracks that captivate and inspire listeners.

Unconventional but Relevant: Creating Emotion through Sound

While the technical aspects of building layers and experimenting with sounds are crucial, Virtual Riot also believes in creating emotional connections through the sonic elements. He understands that music has the power to evoke emotions, and he strives to instill his tracks with emotional depth and meaning.

To achieve this, Virtual Riot incorporates unconventional elements into his compositions. He often draws inspiration from personal experiences, memories, and emotions, and translates them into sound. By carefully selecting and designing sounds that resonate with specific emotions, he creates tracks that evoke a range of feelings, from euphoria to nostalgia to introspection.

For example, Virtual Riot might intentionally use certain melodic intervals or harmonic progressions that evoke a sense of longing or melancholy. He might experiment with different tonalities or musical modes to create specific emotional atmospheres. These unconventional approaches enable him to create music that resonates deeply with his audience, forging a genuine connection between the listener and the artist.

Virtual Riot's ability to create emotion through sound demonstrates his artistic depth and commitment to producing music that goes beyond technical proficiency. It is this emotional resonance that makes his music timeless and continues to captivate listeners worldwide.

Exercises

1. Select one of Virtual Riot's tracks and analyze the layers within it. Identify the different elements present in the track (melodic, bass, rhythmic, atmospheric,

vocal, etc.) and describe how they interact with each other to create a cohesive and engaging composition.

2. Experiment with layering different sounds in your own music production. Start with a simple musical idea and gradually add layers to build complexity and depth. Pay attention to the balance between the layers and how they contribute to the overall atmosphere of the track.

3. Choose a familiar sound or instrument and experiment with sound design techniques to create a unique variation of that sound. Apply effects, modulation, or unconventional processing to transform the sound into something fresh and unexpected.

4. Listen to a Virtual Riot track and try to identify specific production techniques he might have used. Focus on aspects like layering, effect processing, automation, and sound manipulation. Analyze how these techniques contribute to the overall sound and impact of the track.

5. Take a sample of everyday sounds (e.g., traffic, rain, footsteps) and incorporate it into your music production. Experiment with unconventional sampling techniques and creative manipulation to transform the sample into something musical and unique.

Resources

+ Virtual Riot's YouTube channel: *youtube.com/virtualriotmusic* - This channel provides valuable insights into Virtual Riot's production techniques, tutorials, and behind-the-scenes content. It's a great resource for aspiring producers looking to learn from his expertise.

+ "The Sound Effects Bible" by Ric Viers - This book offers a comprehensive guide to sound effects creation, manipulation, and processing. It provides a wealth of inspiration and practical techniques that can be applied to sound experimentation in music production.

+ Online communities and forums such as *EDMprod* and *Gearslutz* provide a platform for producers to share knowledge, ask questions, and gain insights into the production techniques used by Virtual Riot and other professionals in the industry.

Remember, building layers and experimenting with sounds is not just about technical proficiency, but also about pushing boundaries, embracing creativity, and creating emotional connections through music. So, don't be afraid to explore new sonic territories and let your imagination run wild!

The Quest for the Perfect Drop

In the fast-paced and ever-evolving world of electronic dance music (EDM), creating the perfect drop is considered the holy grail for producers. The drop is the climactic moment in a song that unleashes an intense burst of energy and gets the crowd jumping. It is the moment that sends shivers down your spine and makes you lose yourself in the music. Producing a drop that elicits this kind of response is no easy feat, and producers like Virtual Riot have made it their mission to master this art form.

Understanding the Anatomy of a Drop

Before delving into the quest for the perfect drop, it's important to understand its anatomy. The drop typically follows a buildup section that gradually increases tension and anticipation. It is characterized by a sudden and powerful release of energy, often accompanied by hard-hitting beats, distorted basslines, and catchy melodies. The drop is where producers can showcase their creativity, technical skills, and unique sound.

Mastering Sound Design and Mixing

One of the key elements in creating a killer drop is sound design. Producers like Virtual Riot spend countless hours experimenting with different synthesizers, effects, and audio processing techniques to create unique and impactful sounds. They dive deep into the world of synthesis, manipulating waveforms, and crafting intricate soundscapes that can take the listener on a sonic journey.

Additionally, the mixing process plays a crucial role in the overall impact of the drop. Properly balancing the levels of each element, shaping the frequency spectrum, and adding depth and width to the mix can make the drop sound powerful and immersive. Virtual Riot meticulously fine-tunes every aspect of the mix to ensure that every element shines through and contributes to the overall impact of the drop.

Rhythm, Groove, and Dynamics

In EDM, the drop is not just about a booming kick drum and heavy bass. It's also about the rhythm, groove, and dynamics that make people want to move. Virtual Riot understands the importance of crafting a drop that has a strong rhythmic foundation and infectious groove. By experimenting with different drum patterns, percussion elements, and syncopation, he creates drops that make it impossible for the audience to resist the urge to dance.

Furthermore, Virtual Riot pays close attention to the dynamics of the drop. By incorporating elements of tension and release, he builds anticipation and keeps the listener engaged. Whether it's through the clever use of silence, unexpected pauses, or explosive sound effects, Virtual Riot knows how to keep the energy levels high and the crowd on their toes.

Emotional Impact and Memorable Melodies

While the drop is often associated with high-energy and intensity, Virtual Riot recognizes the importance of emotional impact and memorable melodies. It's not just about making people jump up and down; it's about creating a moment that resonates with the listener on a deeper level. By infusing his drops with melodic elements and catchy hooks, Virtual Riot adds another layer of complexity and emotional depth.

Virtual Riot draws inspiration from a wide range of musical genres, from classical compositions to contemporary pop hits. This eclectic mix of influences allows him to create drops that are not only sonically interesting but also emotionally captivating. Whether it's a haunting piano melody, a soaring vocal chop, or a nostalgic synth lead, Virtual Riot knows how to create melodies that tug at the heartstrings and elevate the drop to new heights.

Experimentation and Boundary-Pushing

The quest for the perfect drop requires a willingness to push boundaries and explore new territory. Virtual Riot is known for his fearless approach to experimentation, constantly challenging himself to break free from the conventions of the genre. He is always on the lookout for fresh sounds, innovative production techniques, and unconventional song structures that can take his drops to the next level.

In addition to technical experimentation, Virtual Riot also explores the fusion of different musical styles and genres. By blending elements of dubstep, future bass, trap, and more, he creates drops that defy categorization and appeal to a wide range of listeners. This open-mindedness and willingness to think outside the box have earned him a reputation as a trailblazer in the EDM industry.

The Quest Continues

For Virtual Riot, the journey towards the perfect drop is a never-ending one. It's not about reaching a destination but about constant growth, exploration, and evolution as an artist. He knows that there will always be new techniques to learn, new sounds to discover, and new ways to captivate his audience with his drops.

Virtual Riot's relentless pursuit of perfection serves as an inspiration to aspiring producers worldwide. Through his dedication, passion, and innovative spirit, he continues to redefine the boundaries of what is possible in electronic music. The quest for the perfect drop may be elusive, but with Virtual Riot leading the way, it's a journey worth embarking on. So turn up the volume, let the bass drop, and get ready to experience music like never before.

The Role of Technology in Music Production

The world of music production has undergone a revolutionary transformation thanks to advancements in technology. These innovations have significantly influenced the way musicians create, record, and produce their music. In this section, we will explore the crucial role that technology plays in music production, discussing its impact on creativity, sound manipulation, and the overall production process.

The Digital Revolution: From Analog to Digital

To understand the role of technology in music production, we must first acknowledge the crucial shift from analog to digital systems. In the past, music was primarily recorded and manipulated using analog equipment, such as tape machines and analog synthesizers. However, the advent of digital technology has revolutionized the music industry.

Digital recording and production technologies offer numerous benefits over analog systems. First and foremost, digital systems provide higher audio fidelity, allowing artists to capture and reproduce sound with unparalleled accuracy. Additionally, digital formats offer greater flexibility and convenience, with the ability to edit, manipulate, and arrange recordings easily. This newfound flexibility enables musicians to experiment and explore creative possibilities, pushing the boundaries of their artistic vision.

Software-Based Production: Empowering Musicians

One of the most significant advancements in music production technology is the rise of software-based production tools. Digital audio workstations (DAWs) have become an essential part of any modern music producer's toolkit. These software platforms offer a comprehensive set of tools for recording, editing, mixing, and mastering music.

DAWs provide musicians with the ability to create complex arrangements, experiment with different sound textures, and refine their compositions with precise control. The user-friendly interfaces and intuitive workflows of DAWs have made music production more accessible than ever before, empowering musicians of all skill levels to realize their artistic vision.

Moreover, software plugins have expanded the sonic palette available to musicians. These virtual instruments and effects recreate the sounds of classic analog gear and offer an almost limitless range of possibilities. From realistic piano sounds to otherworldly synth textures, musicians can now access a vast array of sounds without the need for expensive hardware.

Automation and Precision Control

Another significant advantage of technology in music production is the ability to automate various aspects of the production process. Automation allows musicians to program changes in parameters, such as volume, panning, and effects, over time. This capability ensures precise control and consistent execution, even with complex arrangements.

Automation also enables musicians to experiment with movement and dynamics in their music. By automating parameters like filter sweeps, modulation effects, or even subtle volume changes, artists can add depth, expressiveness, and a sense of movement to their compositions. This level of precision control would be challenging, if not impossible, to achieve without technology.

Sampling and Sound Manipulation

Technology has revolutionized the way musicians manipulate and shape sound. Sampling, the process of capturing and reusing snippets of existing audio recordings, is a prime example of this transformation. With the advent of digital technology, the process of sampling has become more accessible and efficient.

Sampling allows musicians to incorporate elements from a vast range of sources into their compositions. Whether it's a drum break from a classic funk record or a vocal sample from a jazz standard, the ability to manipulate and repurpose existing recordings opens up a new world of creative possibilities. Advanced sampling software and hardware enable musicians to manipulate and transform these samples, creating unique and innovative soundscapes.

Furthermore, technology has also led to the development of powerful sound manipulation techniques, such as time-stretching, pitch-shifting, and granular synthesis. Musicians can now manipulate audio recordings in ways that were once unimaginable, stretching or compressing time, altering pitch, or dissecting sounds into microscopic grains. These techniques enable artists to transform ordinary sounds into extraordinary sonic experiences, pushing the boundaries of conventional music production.

Collaboration and Remote Recording

Technology has also revolutionized the way musicians collaborate and record music together. In the past, physical proximity was necessary for musicians to work together in the studio. However, advancements in technology have made remote collaboration and recording a reality.

With the advent of high-speed internet connections and cloud-based storage, musicians can now work together seamlessly, regardless of their physical location. Platforms like Splice and Dropbox allow artists to share project files, record tracks remotely, and provide feedback in real-time. This level of collaboration has opened up new opportunities for artists from different parts of the world to work together creatively, fostering unique musical collaborations.

The Importance of Human Artistry

While technology has undoubtedly transformed the music production landscape, it is essential to remember that artistry and human creativity remain at the core of the process. Technology should be seen as a tool that enhances and enables the artist's vision, rather than a substitute for talent and artistry.

Ultimately, the success of music production relies not only on the technology used but also on the artist's ability to harness its potential and infuse their creative ideas. Regardless of the advancements in technology, it is the human touch, emotions, and artistic decisions that shape the final product, making each production unique and genuine.

Key Takeaways

- Technology has played a crucial role in transforming the music production landscape, moving from analog to digital systems.

- Digital recording and production technologies offer higher audio fidelity and greater flexibility, enabling musicians to experiment and explore creative possibilities.

- Software-based production tools, such as digital audio workstations (DAWs) and plugins, empower musicians to create complex arrangements and access a vast range of sounds.

- Automation provides precise control over parameters, adding movement and dynamics to compositions.

- Sampling and sound manipulation techniques allow musicians to repurpose existing audio recordings and manipulate sound in innovative ways.

- Technology enables remote collaboration and recording, fostering unique musical collaborations.

- Despite technological advancements, human artistry and creativity remain essential in the music production process.

Exercise

Imagine you are a music producer working on a new track. Discuss how you would utilize technology in the production process to enhance your creative ideas and push the boundaries of conventional music production. Consider the use of virtual instruments, effects, automation, and sound manipulation techniques.

Virtual Riot's Favorite Production Techniques

In this section, we will delve into the specific production techniques that Virtual Riot, the renowned music producer, holds dear to his heart. These techniques have played a crucial role in shaping his unique sound and have become an integral part of his music-making process.

Layering and Sound Design

One of Virtual Riot's favorite production techniques is layering. He believes that layering different elements together can create a rich and textured sound that captivates listeners. Virtual Riot approaches layering by combining a variety of sounds, such as synths, samples, and real-world recordings, to build a complex sonic landscape.

To achieve effective layering, Virtual Riot emphasizes the importance of sound design. He often starts his process by designing the individual sounds he plans to use in his tracks. By tweaking oscillators, applying effects, and manipulating parameters, he creates unique and dynamic sounds that can cut through the mix and make his tracks stand out.

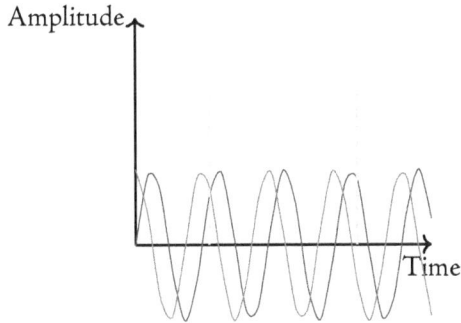

Figure 0.1: Layering different sounds to create a rich and textured sound.

Arrangement and Dynamics

Virtual Riot pays great attention to arrangement and dynamics in his tracks. He believes that the way different elements are structured and the dynamics applied to them can greatly influence the overall impact of a piece of music.

To create a sense of tension and release, Virtual Riot often incorporates techniques such as risers, impacts, and drops into his arrangements. These elements help build anticipation and energy, leading to powerful and memorable moments in his tracks.

In terms of dynamics, Virtual Riot emphasizes the importance of contrast. By carefully controlling the loudness and softness of different sections within a track, he creates a dynamic and engaging listening experience. This can be achieved through techniques like sidechain compression, automation, and volume rides.

Sampling and Vocal Processing

Sampling plays a significant role in Virtual Riot's production process. He often samples various sources, including old records, video games, and other tracks, to create unique and interesting textures in his music. Virtual Riot believes that sampling provides endless creative possibilities and can add a nostalgic or unexpected element to a track.

In addition to sampling, Virtual Riot is known for his skillful vocal processing. He often uses effects like pitch shifting, time stretching, and vocal chopping to manipulate vocal recordings and create interesting vocal textures. This adds depth and character to his tracks, giving them a distinct and recognizable sound.

Mixing and Mastering

Virtual Riot recognizes the importance of a well-balanced mix and master in achieving a professional sound. He pays attention to every element in the mix, ensuring that each sound has its place and contributes to the overall sonic picture.

Virtual Riot employs various techniques during the mixing stage, such as EQing, compression, and reverb, to shape and enhance individual elements. He also emphasizes the importance of using reference tracks to compare and benchmark the quality of his mix against other professional productions.

When it comes to mastering, Virtual Riot believes that less is more. He aims for a transparent and natural-sounding master, avoiding excessive loudness and unnecessary processing. He focuses on maintaining the integrity of the mix while ensuring it translates well across different playback systems.

Key Takeaways

In this section, we explored Virtual Riot's favorite production techniques, including layering and sound design, arrangement and dynamics, sampling and vocal processing, as well as mixing and mastering. These techniques have not only contributed to Virtual Riot's success as a music producer but have also shaped the landscape of electronic music. By experimenting with these techniques and incorporating your own creative twists, you can take your productions to new and exciting heights. So go ahead, have fun, and let your imagination run wild in the studio!

Virtual Riot's Studio Setup and Gear

One of the key aspects of Virtual Riot's success lies in his impeccable studio setup and choice of gear. With the right tools at his disposal, he is able to bring his musical visions to life and create his unique sound. Let's delve into the details of Virtual Riot's studio setup and gear.

The Studio: A Creative Sanctuary

Virtual Riot's studio is more than just a room filled with equipment. It's a creative sanctuary where he can fully immerse himself in the music-making process. The studio is carefully designed to optimize the workflow and inspire creativity. The wall is adorned with posters and artwork that reflects his musical influences, serving as a constant reminder of the power of music.

Hardware and Software

When it comes to hardware, Virtual Riot believes in investing in quality equipment that delivers top-notch sound and durability. His gear includes a combination of analog and digital instruments, ranging from synthesizers to drum machines. Some of his favorite hardware components include:

- **Roland Juno-106 Analog Synthesizer:** Known for its warm and rich sound, the Juno-106 is a staple in Virtual Riot's setup. He often uses it to create lush pads and captivating melodies.

- **Moog Subsequent 37 Analog Synthesizer:** Virtual Riot loves the versatility of the Subsequent 37. Its powerful sound and intuitive interface allow him to experiment with different tones and textures.

- **Native Instruments Maschine:** This hardware/software hybrid combines the best of both worlds. Virtual Riot utilizes Maschine for its intuitive beat-making capabilities, allowing him to create dynamic drum patterns.

- **Akai Professional MPK249 MIDI Controller:** With its responsive keys and extensive control options, the MPK249 is Virtual Riot's go-to MIDI controller. It enables him to add expressive touches and perform intricate melodies.

In addition to hardware, Virtual Riot's studio houses a range of software tools that enhance his production workflow. He utilizes industry-standard software such as Ableton Live, Logic Pro, and Native Instruments Komplete. These programs provide him with a wide array of virtual instruments, effects, and mixing tools, allowing him to shape his tracks exactly as he envisions.

Custom-built Tools

Virtual Riot's innovation extends beyond off-the-shelf gear. He has developed his own custom-built tools that aid in his production process. One notable creation is his MIDI Fighter, a unique controller that he designed to have high responsiveness and a tactile feel. This custom controller allows him to incorporate live performance elements seamlessly into his studio productions.

Creating the Perfect Acoustic Environment

To ensure accurate sound representation, Virtual Riot has paid close attention to the acoustic treatment of his studio. He has installed professional-grade sound diffusers and absorbers, strategically placed to minimize unwanted reflections and resonances. This meticulous attention to detail ensures that the sound heard in his studio is faithful to his creative intentions.

Staying Current with Technology

Driven by his passion for innovation, Virtual Riot constantly keeps up with the latest advancements in technology. He explores cutting-edge gear and software updates, always on the lookout for tools that can push the boundaries of his creativity. By staying at the forefront of technological advancements, he ensures that his music remains fresh and relevant in an ever-evolving landscape.

Virtual Riot's Tips and Tricks

Virtual Riot understands that gear alone does not make a great producer. It's the skill and creativity of the person behind the tools that truly matters. Here are some of his tips and tricks for aspiring producers:

- Experimentation: Don't be afraid to break the rules and try unconventional techniques. Some of the most unique sounds come from pushing the boundaries and thinking outside the box.

- Focus on Music Theory: Regardless of the gear you use, having a solid foundation in music theory will take your productions to the next level. Invest time in understanding chord progressions, melodies, and song structure.

- Practice and Patience: Developing your skills as a producer takes time and effort. Embrace the learning process, be patient with yourself, and practice consistently. Rome wasn't built in a day, and neither are great tracks.

- Trust Your Ears: While gear can enhance your sound, ultimately, your ears should be the final judge. Train your ears to identify what sounds good and trust your instincts in the mixing process.

◆ Collaborate and Learn: Virtual Riot encourages collaboration with other artists. By working with different perspectives and styles, you can learn new techniques and broaden your creative horizons.

In conclusion, Virtual Riot's studio setup and gear play a crucial role in his music-making process. From meticulously chosen hardware and software to custom-built tools, he has crafted an environment that fosters creativity and allows his unique sound to flourish. By pushing the boundaries and staying at the forefront of technology, he continues to shape the future of electronic music. Aspiring producers can learn from his insights and use them as stepping stones on their own musical journeys.

Virtual Riot's Advice for Aspiring Music Producers

Aspiring music producers, listen up! Virtual Riot is here to share some valuable advice to help you navigate the exciting and challenging world of music production. With his years of experience and success in the industry, Virtual Riot has plenty of wisdom to share. So, grab your headphones and let's dive into his top tips and tricks.

1. Embrace your uniqueness

First and foremost, Virtual Riot wants you to remember that your uniqueness is your superpower. In a world full of aspiring producers, it's important to find your own voice and signature style. Don't be afraid to experiment, push boundaries, and think outside the box. The key to standing out and making a lasting impression is to embrace your true self and let your creativity flow.

2. Learn the fundamentals

While creativity is essential, it's equally important to have a solid foundation in music theory and production techniques. Take the time to learn the basics of music theory, such as scales, chords, and harmonies. This knowledge will help you craft melodies and harmonies that are pleasing to the ear.

Additionally, invest time in learning the ins and outs of your music production software. Understand the different effects, synthesis techniques, and mixing tools available to you. Mastering the fundamentals will give you the skills to bring your musical ideas to life.

3. Get hands-on experience

Theory and knowledge are essential, but practical experience is equally valuable. Virtual Riot encourages aspiring producers to get their hands dirty and start creating music. Don't be afraid to start small and work on your own projects. Experiment with different genres, styles, and techniques. The more you practice, the better you'll become.

Collaborating with other musicians and producers is another excellent way to gain experience. Working with different talents exposes you to new ideas and perspectives. It also helps develop your communication and teamwork skills, which are vital in the music industry.

4. Stay organized and disciplined

Producing music requires discipline. Virtual Riot advises aspiring producers to establish schedules and routines to stay organized and focused. Set aside dedicated time for music production, whether it's a few hours a day or a block of time on the weekends. Treat it as a commitment and stick to it.

Keeping your files and projects organized is also crucial. Create a logical folder structure for your samples, project files, and presets. This will save you time and frustration in the long run, allowing you to find what you need quickly and easily.

5. Seek feedback and learn from others

Feedback is a valuable asset for growth and improvement. Virtual Riot encourages aspiring producers to actively seek feedback from trusted sources, such as fellow producers, mentors, or online communities. Constructive criticism can help you identify areas for improvement and refine your skills.

Additionally, don't be afraid to learn from others in the industry. Study the work of successful producers, analyze their tracks, and try to understand their production techniques. Virtual Riot suggests dissecting tracks you admire and experimenting with similar sounds or approaches in your own music. This will help you develop your own style while learning from the best.

6. Keep experimenting and evolving

The music industry is constantly evolving, with new trends and technologies emerging all the time. Virtual Riot advises aspiring producers to stay curious, keep experimenting, and be open to change. Embrace new production techniques, explore different genres, and stay updated with the latest advancements in technology.

Experimentation is the key to innovation, and Virtual Riot encourages you to step out of your comfort zone and push the boundaries. Don't be afraid to break the rules and try unconventional approaches. The more you explore, the more unique and original your sound will be.

Conclusion

Becoming a successful music producer is an exciting journey filled with challenges and opportunities. Virtual Riot's advice for aspiring producers can help you navigate this path with confidence. Embrace your uniqueness, learn the fundamentals, gain practical experience, stay organized, seek feedback, and never stop experimenting.

Virtual Riot's words of wisdom serve as a reminder that success in the music industry comes from a combination of hard work, creativity, and a relentless pursuit of growth and improvement. So, fire up your music production software, follow these tips, and let your passion for music drive you towards your dreams. The world is waiting for your unique sound!

Virtual Riot's Perspective on the Future of Music Production

Virtual Riot, a renowned producer in the electronic dance music (EDM) scene, has always been at the forefront of innovation when it comes to music production. With his unique sound and relentless pursuit of creativity, he is undoubtedly a visionary in the industry. In this section, we will explore Virtual Riot's perspective on the future of music production, including his thoughts on technology, creative process, and the evolving role of producers.

Embracing Technological Advancements

As technology continues to advance at an unprecedented rate, Virtual Riot believes that producers need to fully embrace these advancements and leverage them to push the boundaries of music production. From software and plugins to hardware and virtual reality, there are endless possibilities for creating new and exciting sounds.

One area that Virtual Riot is particularly excited about is the integration of artificial intelligence (AI) in music production. He envisions a future where AI algorithms can assist in the creative process, helping producers generate unique ideas, experiment with new sounds, and even provide real-time feedback and suggestions. However, he emphasizes the importance of maintaining the human touch and creativity, as AI should be seen as a tool rather than a replacement for human expression.

Unlocking Creativity through Collaboration

Virtual Riot strongly believes in the power of collaboration in the music production process. By working with other producers, musicians, and artists from different genres, he believes that new and groundbreaking ideas can emerge. Collaborations not only bring fresh perspectives and diverse influences but also create a space for learning and growth.

In the future of music production, Virtual Riot envisions a global collaborative environment where artists from different parts of the world can seamlessly connect and create music together. With advancements in communication technology, such as virtual reality and real-time collaboration platforms, geographical barriers will become irrelevant, leading to incredible artistic collaborations that transcend borders.

Adapting to Changing Consumption Patterns

With the rapid evolution of music consumption patterns, Virtual Riot emphasizes the need for producers to adapt and evolve their approach. Streaming platforms, social media, and online communities have transformed the way people discover and consume music. To stay relevant, producers must understand these changes and tailor their production strategies accordingly.

Virtual Riot predicts that in the future, producers will need to create music that not only sounds great but also provides an immersive and multi-sensory experience. Visual elements, live performances, and interactive technology will become integral parts of the music production process. Producers will need to think beyond traditional audio formats and embrace new mediums to engage and captivate their audience.

Continued Focus on Quality and Authenticity

While technological advancements offer exciting opportunities, Virtual Riot emphasizes that the focus should always remain on quality and authenticity. As producers gain access to increasingly powerful tools and software, it's crucial to remember that technology is just a means to an end, not the end itself.

Virtual Riot encourages aspiring producers to focus on developing their unique sound and style, rather than relying solely on trends or popular genres. Authenticity and originality are key ingredients for longevity in the music industry. By staying true to their artistic vision and constantly honing their skills, producers can create music that resonates with listeners on a deeper level.

Pushing the Boundaries of Genre

Virtual Riot has always been known for pushing the boundaries of genre and experimenting with different styles. He believes that the future of music production lies in the fusion of genres and the creation of entirely new sonic landscapes.

By blending elements from multiple genres, producers can create refreshing and innovative sounds that defy categorization. Virtual Riot encourages producers to break free from conventional genre constraints and explore uncharted territories. This mindset not only leads to artistic growth but also sparks new trends and influences in the industry.

Unconventional Creative Techniques

In addition to embracing technological advancements and collaboration, Virtual Riot encourages producers to explore unconventional creative techniques. He believes that stepping outside of one's comfort zone and breaking free from traditional production methods can lead to groundbreaking results.

For example, he suggests experimenting with unconventional sound design by manipulating everyday objects and recording unique sounds in unexpected environments. By incorporating these unconventional sounds into their productions, producers can add a distinct layer of originality and vibrancy to their music.

The Importance of Continuous Learning

As music production continues to evolve, Virtual Riot stresses the importance of continuous learning. Producers need to keep up with the latest trends, techniques, and technologies to stay relevant in an ever-changing landscape.

Virtual Riot encourages producers to seek out educational resources, attend workshops, and engage with other producers to expand their knowledge and skills. He believes that a curious and open-minded attitude is essential for artistic growth and the ability to adapt to new challenges.

The Future Looks Promising

In conclusion, Virtual Riot's perspective on the future of music production is one filled with excitement and endless possibilities. With advancements in technology, the increasing importance of collaboration, and a focus on creativity and authenticity, the future of music production is set to be a vibrant and innovative journey.

Producers who embrace these changes, experiment with unconventional techniques, and continuously learn and evolve will be at the forefront of the industry. Virtual Riot's own success and impact serve as a testament to the power of embracing the future and pushing the boundaries of music production.

Virtual Riot's Role in Shaping the Sound of EDM

EDM, short for Electronic Dance Music, has undergone significant evolution over the years, and Virtual Riot has played a pivotal role in shaping its sound. With his innovative approach to music production, unique style, and ability to push boundaries, Virtual Riot has left an indelible mark on the EDM scene.

Experimental Sound Design

One of the key contributions Virtual Riot has made to the sound of EDM is his experimental approach to sound design. He constantly pushes the limits of technology and explores new sonic possibilities, resulting in groundbreaking tracks that captivate listeners. His use of complex synthesis techniques, unconventional samples, and intricate layering creates a rich and dynamic sound palette that is distinctively his own.

Virtual Riot's experimentation with sound extends beyond traditional EDM genres. He draws inspiration from various music styles, incorporating elements of dubstep, drum and bass, glitch hop, and more into his tracks. This fusion of genres not only sets him apart from his peers but also expands the sonic landscape of EDM as a whole.

Melodic Complexity and Emotional Depth

While EDM has often been associated with high-energy beats and catchy hooks, Virtual Riot brings a new level of melodic complexity and emotional depth to the genre. His compositions feature intricate melodies, lush chord progressions, and harmonically rich arrangements that evoke a wide range of emotions.

Virtual Riot's mastery of music theory allows him to create intricate melodies that are both infectious and emotionally resonant. He carefully crafts his tracks, ensuring that each musical element serves a purpose and contributes to the overall emotional journey of the listener. Whether it's a euphoric build-up, a melancholic breakdown, or a powerful drop, Virtual Riot's music engages the listener on a deeper level.

Influence on Production Techniques

Virtual Riot's innovative production techniques have had a significant influence on the broader EDM community. His meticulous attention to detail, impeccable sound engineering skills, and out-of-the-box thinking have inspired countless aspiring producers to push the boundaries of their own music.

One of the techniques Virtual Riot is known for is his use of resampling. He employs this method to create unique and complex sound textures by manipulating and processing existing audio material. This approach not only adds depth and character to his tracks but also encourages other producers to experiment with unconventional methods of sound design.

Furthermore, Virtual Riot's emphasis on quality mixing and mastering has raised the production standards within the EDM industry. His meticulous approach to sonic balance and clarity has inspired producers to prioritize technical excellence in their own work, resulting in higher production values across the genre.

Breaking Genre Stereotypes

In addition to shaping the sound of EDM, Virtual Riot has played a pivotal role in breaking genre stereotypes within the industry. Traditionally, EDM has been associated with a limited range of sounds and clichéd formulas. However, Virtual Riot's willingness to explore new sonic territories and challenge musical conventions has helped redefine the genre.

By blending elements from different genres and exploring unconventional musical approaches, Virtual Riot has shown that EDM can be a platform for artistic experimentation and innovation. He has paved the way for other artists to embrace their unique style and think outside the box, leading to a more diverse and dynamic EDM landscape.

Encouraging Artistic Exploration

Virtual Riot's pioneering spirit and commitment to artistic exploration have not only influenced the sound of EDM but have also inspired a new generation of musicians to think creatively and push their boundaries. His success story serves as a testament to the power of artistic individuality and the importance of staying true to one's vision.

Through his music and public persona, Virtual Riot encourages aspiring artists to experiment, take risks, and pursue their artistic passions. He emphasizes the importance of authenticity and self-expression, urging artists to find their own voice and create music that reflects their unique perspectives.

In conclusion, Virtual Riot's role in shaping the sound of EDM cannot be overstated. His experimental sound design, melodic complexity, influential production techniques, genre-defying approach, and commitment to artistic exploration have left an indelible mark on the genre. As EDM continues to evolve, Virtual Riot's contributions will continue to inspire and shape the future of electronic music.

Virtual Riot's Influence on Music Production Techniques

Virtual Riot is not only known for his incredible talent as a producer but also for his unique and innovative approach to music production techniques. Throughout his career, he has continually pushed the boundaries of what is possible in the electronic music scene, inspiring countless producers and shaping the sound of EDM. In this section, we will explore some of the key ways in which Virtual Riot has influenced music production techniques.

Digital Sound Design

One area where Virtual Riot has had a significant impact is in the realm of digital sound design. He has become known for his ability to create intricate and complex sounds using virtual synthesizers and plugins. His attention to detail and meticulous approach to sound design have set a new standard in the industry.

Virtual Riot's influence can be seen in the rise of virtual instruments and software synthesizers that aim to emulate the unique sounds he has created. Producers around the world are trying to replicate his signature basslines, leads, and effects. The advanced sound design techniques he employs, such as layering multiple sounds and using granular synthesis, have become go-to strategies for producers looking to create cutting-edge electronic music.

Mixing and Mastering Techniques

In addition to his prowess in sound design, Virtual Riot has also left his mark on mixing and mastering techniques. His tracks are known for their crystal-clear mix and powerful, well-balanced sound. As a result, many producers look to his productions as a benchmark for achieving professional-level mixes.

One technique that Virtual Riot has popularized is parallel processing. By using parallel compression, he is able to add depth and power to his tracks while preserving the dynamics of the individual sounds. This technique has become widely adopted by producers and has become an essential tool in the mixing toolbox.

Virtual Riot's approach to mastering is also worth noting. He emphasizes the importance of dynamic range and strives to maintain the natural dynamics of a track while still achieving loudness. This approach has influenced many producers to prioritize the quality of the sound over sheer loudness in their own productions.

Arrangement and Song Structure

Virtual Riot's influence extends beyond the technical aspects of music production to the creative domain of arrangement and song structure. He has a knack for creating dynamic and engaging arrangements that captivate listeners from start to finish. His ability to build tension and release it with powerful drops has become a hallmark of his style.

Many producers study Virtual Riot's tracks to understand how he constructs his arrangements and transitions between different sections of a song. His use of clever melodies, impactful drops, and unexpected twists keeps his music fresh and exciting.

Incorporating Live Instruments

While Virtual Riot is primarily known for his electronic productions, he has also made waves by incorporating live instruments into his music. Whether it's a guitar riff or a piano melody, he has seamlessly blended these organic elements with electronic sounds to create a unique sonic experience.

His use of live instruments has inspired other producers to experiment with combining analog and digital elements in their productions. This fusion of traditional and contemporary sounds has opened up new avenues of creativity and has resulted in a rich and diverse landscape of electronic music.

Adapting to New Technologies

One of Virtual Riot's strengths is his ability to adapt to new technologies and incorporate them into his music production workflow. He is constantly exploring and experimenting with the latest hardware and software tools to push the boundaries of what is possible.

From exploring new synthesis techniques to embracing emerging production software, Virtual Riot's curiosity and openness to new technologies have propelled his music forward. He has embraced advancements in virtual reality and artificial intelligence to create immersive experiences that go beyond traditional music production.

Unconventional Sampling Techniques

Virtual Riot is known for his unconventional approach to sampling, often using unexpected sources to create unique sounds. Whether it's sampling random objects or layering field recordings, he is always looking for new and interesting sonic elements to incorporate into his tracks.

This approach has inspired other producers to think outside the box when it comes to sampling, encouraging them to explore unconventional sources and take risks with their sound design. Virtual Riot's willingness to push the boundaries of what is considered normal has expanded the palette of possibilities for producers worldwide.

In conclusion, Virtual Riot's influence on music production techniques is undeniable. Through his innovative sound design, mixing and mastering techniques, arrangement and song structure choices, incorporation of live instruments, adaptation to new technologies, and unconventional sampling techniques, he has redefined what is possible in the realm of electronic music production. His approach has inspired countless producers and will continue to shape the future of music production.

Musical Influences and Inspirations

Exploring Genres and Pushing Boundaries

In the ever-evolving world of music, artists are constantly seeking new ways to express themselves and push the boundaries of their craft. Virtual Riot is no exception. One of the most exciting aspects of his career has been his willingness to explore different genres and experiment with various styles, creating a unique sound that is both familiar and innovative. In this section, we will delve into Virtual Riot's approach to exploring genres, the impact of his boundary-pushing mindset, and the significance of this exploration in shaping the landscape of electronic dance music (EDM).

Embracing Musical Diversity

Virtual Riot's exploration of genres can be traced back to his early influences and his desire to create music that reflects his diverse musical taste. Growing up in Germany, he was exposed to a wide range of musical genres, from classical and electronic music to rock and hip-hop. This eclectic background laid the foundation for his willingness to experiment and push the boundaries of traditional EDM.

Virtual Riot's approach to exploring genres is rooted in his curiosity and open-mindedness. He recognizes that music is a universal language that transcends boundaries and connects people on a deeper level. By embracing musical diversity, he has been able to infuse his tracks with elements from various styles, creating a fusion that is uniquely his own.

Breaking the Mold

Pushing boundaries is an integral part of Virtual Riot's creative process. He thrives on challenging the status quo and taking risks in his music. By blending genres and experimenting with different sounds, he has been able to create a distinct sound that defies traditional categorization.

One of the ways Virtual Riot breaks the mold is by incorporating unexpected elements into his tracks. Whether it's infusing heavy metal guitar riffs into a dubstep drop or incorporating elements of classical music into a trap beat, he continuously pushes the boundaries of what is possible in EDM. This fearless approach not only keeps his music fresh and exciting but also inspires other artists to think outside the box.

Expanding the EDM Landscape

Virtual Riot's exploration of genres and his boundary-pushing mindset have had a profound impact on the EDM landscape. By defying genre norms and challenging traditional conventions, he has helped expand the boundaries of what is considered EDM.

His willingness to experiment has opened doors for other artists to explore new musical territories and bring fresh ideas to the genre. Virtual Riot's success has shown that there is an audience for music that goes beyond traditional EDM boundaries, encouraging artists to be more daring and innovative in their sound.

Inspiring Creativity

Virtual Riot's exploration of genres and pushing of boundaries serves as an inspiration to emerging artists and producers. His fearlessness in embracing different styles and his ability to seamlessly blend them together has shown that there are no limits when it comes to music.

His approach encourages artists to think outside the box, to challenge themselves creatively, and to embrace the unknown. By pushing the boundaries of what is possible in EDM, Virtual Riot has inspired a new wave of creativity and innovation within the genre.

The Power of Collaboration

Collaboration plays a significant role in Virtual Riot's exploration of genres and pushing of boundaries. Working with artists from different musical backgrounds allows him to combine their unique styles with his own, resulting in groundbreaking tracks that defy genre limitations.

Through collaboration, Virtual Riot has been able to push the boundaries even further, merging genres and creating music that is truly groundbreaking. This open-minded approach to collaboration has not only expanded his own creativity but has also fostered a sense of community within the EDM scene.

Unconventional Problem Solving

Exploring genres and pushing boundaries often presents artists with new challenges and problems to solve. Virtual Riot approaches these obstacles with a creative and unconventional mindset, finding innovative solutions that enhance his music.

For example, when faced with the challenge of blending acoustic instruments with electronic sounds, Virtual Riot developed unique production techniques to seamlessly merge the two worlds. By experimenting with different processing methods and combining unconventional instruments, he was able to create a sound that is both organic and futuristic.

Example: Fusion of Dubstep and Jazz

One notable example of Virtual Riot's genre exploration and boundary pushing is his fusion of dubstep and jazz. In his track "One For All, All For One," he masterfully combines the hard-hitting basslines of dubstep with the complex harmonies and improvisational nature of jazz.

To achieve this fusion, Virtual Riot carefully selected jazz instrumentation, such as the saxophone and trumpet, and incorporated them into the drops of the track. He also drew inspiration from the improvisational nature of jazz, infusing moments of spontaneity and unpredictability into the song structure.

The result is a track that defies traditional genre boundaries and offers a unique listening experience for fans of both dubstep and jazz. This fusion showcases Virtual Riot's ability to think outside the box and highlights the power of exploring genres and pushing boundaries.

Resource: Virtual Riot's Creative Process

For those looking to explore genres and push boundaries in their own music, Virtual Riot offers valuable insights into his creative process. In interviews and tutorials, he shares his production techniques, discusses his favorite tools and plugins, and provides guidance on how to approach genre fusion.

Virtual Riot's openness about his creative process serves as a valuable resource for aspiring producers and artists. By learning from his experiences and incorporating his techniques into their own work, musicians can expand their range and bring fresh ideas to the table.

Exercise: Genre Fusion Experiment

To further encourage exploration of genres and pushing of boundaries, here is a creative exercise for readers: Select two contrasting genres or styles of music and try to fuse them together in a unique and innovative way. Experiment with combining different elements, instrumentation, and production techniques to create a track that defies traditional categorization. Focus on finding a harmonious balance between the two genres while also bringing something new and unexpected to the table. Embrace the spirit of exploration and let your creativity run wild.

Remember, the goal of this exercise is not to conform to any particular set of rules or expectations but to push the boundaries of what is possible in music. Embrace the unknown, draw inspiration from Virtual Riot's genre exploration, and let your imagination guide you on this musical adventure.

Resources

- Virtual Riot's YouTube channel: A valuable resource for tutorials, production techniques, and behind-the-scenes insights into Virtual Riot's creative process.

- Virtual Riot's social media accounts: Follow Virtual Riot on platforms such as Instagram and Twitter to stay updated on his latest projects and get a glimpse into his artistic journey.

- Virtual Riot's collaborations: Explore Virtual Riot's collaborations with artists from various genres to gain inspiration and further explore the possibilities of genre fusion.

- Interviews and podcasts: Seek out interviews and podcasts featuring Virtual Riot, where he discusses his approach to genre exploration and pushing boundaries in more detail.

- Study other artists: Take the time to explore other artists who have successfully fused genres and pushed boundaries in their music. Analyze their techniques, production styles, and the impact they have had on their respective genres.

Remember, the key to successful genre exploration and pushing boundaries is to approach it with an open mind, embrace the unknown, and remember that the possibilities in music are endless.

Mixing Old and New: The Fusion of Styles

In the ever-evolving world of music, artists often find themselves faced with the challenge of creating something fresh and innovative, while still paying homage to the foundations of their craft. For Virtual Riot, this challenge has been embraced and transformed into an art form through the fusion of old and new styles.

Blending Genres: Creating a Musical Tapestry

One of the key aspects of Virtual Riot's unique sound is his ability to seamlessly blend genres together, creating a musical tapestry that is both familiar and groundbreaking. By taking elements from different musical styles, he is able to create something that is truly his own.

To achieve this fusion of styles, Virtual Riot draws from a wide range of influences. From classic rock to hip hop, from jazz to heavy metal, he incorporates elements from various genres into his electronic compositions. By doing so, he is able to bring a fresh perspective to electronic music, infusing it with elements that may seem unexpected or unconventional.

The Evolution of Virtual Riot's Sound: A Journey of Musical Exploration

Virtual Riot's journey of musical exploration starts with a deep appreciation for the classics. He believes in the importance of understanding the roots of music and immersing oneself in the rich history of different genres. This understanding allows him to effectively blend old and new styles, creating something that is steeped in tradition yet cutting-edge.

One way Virtual Riot achieves this fusion is by incorporating classic instruments into his electronic productions. From live guitars to pianos, he brings a human touch to his music, connecting the digital world with the analog. This seamless integration of traditional instruments into electronic compositions is a testament to his creative vision.

Unlocking Creative Potential: Breaking Boundaries

To truly blend old and new styles, Virtual Riot believes in breaking the boundaries of musical genres. By challenging the limits of traditional musical norms, he creates a pathway for innovation and experimentation.

One unconventional practice that Virtual Riot embraces is the use of unconventional and unexpected sounds. He pushes the sonic boundaries of his compositions by incorporating unconventional elements, such as everyday objects or field recordings, into his tracks. By doing so, he adds a layer of uniqueness and unpredictability to his music.

The Impact of Fusion: Inspiring Creativity

Virtual Riot's fusion of old and new styles has not only influenced his own music but has also inspired a new generation of musicians and producers. This blending of genres has opened doors for artists to think outside the box and experiment with their own sound.

By fusing different styles, Virtual Riot challenges the notion of what is considered "normal" in music. He encourages artists to be bold, to think beyond the boundaries of genre, and to create without fear of judgment.

Conclusion: Embracing the Fusion

In the realm of music, the fusion of old and new styles is a constant source of inspiration and creativity. Virtual Riot has masterfully embraced this fusion, weaving together different genres and techniques to create a sound that is uniquely his own.

Through his exploration of musical boundaries and his commitment to blending old and new elements, Virtual Riot has not only left an indelible mark on the electronic music scene but has also redefined what is possible in music.

Aspiring musicians and producers can learn from Virtual Riot's approach, understanding the importance of paying homage to musical traditions while also pushing the boundaries of creativity. By embracing the fusion of old and new, artists can create something truly innovative and timeless.

Finding Inspiration Beyond Music

In the world of music, inspiration can come from a myriad of sources. While many musicians draw inspiration primarily from within the realm of music itself, Virtual Riot takes a different approach. He believes in finding inspiration beyond the borders of his own discipline, exploring various art forms, experiences, and aspects of life that bring fresh ideas and perspectives to his work. This section delves into the diverse sources of inspiration that fuel Virtual Riot's creativity and contribute to his unique musical style.

Exploring Genres and Pushing Boundaries

One of the ways Virtual Riot finds inspiration beyond music is through exploring different genres and pushing the boundaries of traditional musical styles. By venturing into unfamiliar territories, he opens himself up to new sounds, textures, and emotions that can inform his own compositions.

For example, Virtual Riot may draw inspiration from classical music, studying the works of composers such as Beethoven or Mozart. The rich harmonies, intricate melodies, and dramatic compositions of classical music can provide a wealth of creative ideas that can be incorporated into his electronic productions. By blending these classical elements with his signature heavy bass and futuristic sounds, Virtual Riot creates a sound that is both innovative and nostalgic.

Similarly, he may explore genres like jazz, funk, or even world music, immersing himself in the rhythms and melodies of different cultures. These genres offer a treasure trove of inspiration, introducing him to unconventional chord progressions, complex rhythms, and unique instrumentation. By incorporating elements from these genres into his own music, Virtual Riot adds depth and richness to his compositions, making them stand out in the electronic music landscape.

Mixing Old and New: The Fusion of Styles

In addition to exploring different genres, Virtual Riot finds inspiration by blending old and new musical styles. He recognizes that the past can hold great wisdom and beauty, and by revisiting and reimagining older musical elements, he can create something fresh and exciting.

For instance, Virtual Riot may listen to vintage recordings, discovering forgotten gems from the past. He takes inspiration from the production techniques, instrumentation, and arrangements of older recordings, then combines them with modern electronic elements. The result is a fusion of the classic and the contemporary, a sound that pays homage to the past while pushing the boundaries of the present.

In his creativity, Virtual Riot may also experiment with sampling, taking snippets of older songs or iconic melodies and recontextualizing them in his own music. By breathing new life into these familiar sounds, he creates a sense of nostalgia for listeners while delivering a fresh and modern musical experience.

Finding Inspiration Beyond Music

While music is Virtual Riot's primary passion, he also finds inspiration in other art forms, experiences, and aspects of life. He believes that great art exists within a larger cultural context, and by immersing himself in various disciplines, he can expand his creative horizons.

For example, Virtual Riot finds inspiration in visual arts, exploring paintings, sculptures, and other forms of visual expression. The colors, shapes, and textures of artwork can evoke emotions and spark ideas that he translates into sonic landscapes. By studying the works of renowned artists and exploring different art movements, Virtual Riot gains a fresh perspective on composition, arrangement, and storytelling within his music.

Virtual Riot also draws inspiration from literature, diving into novels, poetry, and philosophical texts. The written word can ignite his imagination, igniting new ideas and concepts that he weaves into his music. From the vivid imagery of a prose to the profound insights of a philosophical treatise, literature opens up a world of inspiration that fuels his creative process.

Beyond the realm of art, Virtual Riot finds inspiration in everyday experiences and the world around him. Whether it's a walk in nature, a conversation with a friend, or a journey to a new city, these moments offer a wellspring of inspiration. By staying curious, observant, and open-minded, he discovers hidden connections, stories, and emotions that shape his music.

The Role of Emotional Connection in Music-Making

At the core of Virtual Riot's creative process is the importance of emotional connection. He believes that music should not only be technically impressive but also resonant on an emotional level. To achieve this, he draws inspiration from his own experiences, memories, and emotions, infusing his compositions with personal depth and vulnerability.

For Virtual Riot, finding inspiration beyond music allows him to tap into a wider range of emotions and experiences. By exploring art, literature, and the world around him, he deepens his understanding of the human condition. This understanding allows him to create music that not only captures the listeners' attention but also touches their hearts and souls.

By blending technical prowess with emotional depth, Virtual Riot strives to create a listening experience that is both exciting and meaningful. He brings together the diverse range of inspirations he finds beyond music to craft a sound that is uniquely his own, resonating with his audience on a profound level.

Pushing the Boundaries: An Unconventional Example

To highlight how Virtual Riot's inspiration beyond music translates into his creative process, let's explore an unconventional example: his fascination with architecture. Virtual Riot believes that architecture, like music, has the power to evoke strong emotions and leave a lasting impact on people.

When studying the design of buildings, Virtual Riot focuses on the spatial arrangement, the interplay of light and shadow, and the overall atmosphere created by the architecture. He takes these concepts and translates them into musical elements, creating sonic spaces that mimic the grandeur and beauty of architectural masterpieces.

For example, imagine a large, soaring cathedral with its towering arches and intricate stained glass windows. Virtual Riot would analyze the architectural features of the space and translate them into music by using layered melodies, expansive reverbs, and ethereal synthesizer textures. The composition would aim to capture the immersive and reverent atmosphere of the cathedral, allowing listeners to feel as if they are standing in the presence of something awe-inspiring.

By drawing inspiration from architecture in this way, Virtual Riot brings a fresh perspective to his music, blending the tangible world of buildings with the intangible world of sound. This unconventional approach pushes the boundaries of traditional music production and results in a truly unique and captivating sonic experience.

Exploring Beyond the Borders of Music

In conclusion, Virtual Riot's innovative approach to finding inspiration beyond music sets him apart as a musician. By exploring different genres, blending old and new styles, and seeking inspiration from visual arts, literature, and the world around him, he expands his creative horizons and infuses his music with depth and originality. His ability to connect emotionally with his audience through his compositions is a testament to the power of finding inspiration beyond the borders of one's own discipline. As Virtual Riot continues to push the boundaries of music-making, his journey serves as an inspiration for aspiring musicians to explore the vast and diverse world of creativity that exists beyond their own musical sphere.

The Role of Emotional Connection in Music-Making

Music has the incredible power to evoke emotions and connect with listeners on a deep and personal level. It has the ability to move us, to make us feel joy, sadness, excitement, or even nostalgia. But what is it about music that creates such a strong emotional connection? What is the role of emotions in the process of music-making? In this section, we will explore these questions and delve into the fascinating relationship between emotions and music.

Emotions are an integral part of the human experience, and they greatly influence our perception and reaction to music. When we listen to a song or create music ourselves, we tap into the vast range of emotions that make us human. Whether it's the soaring melodies of a symphony, the energetic beats of a dance track, or the soulful lyrics of a ballad, music has the ability to express and convey emotions in a way that words alone cannot.

The emotional impact of music can be attributed to several key factors. First and foremost, the melody, rhythm, and harmonies in music can directly stimulate our brain's emotional centers. Research has shown that certain musical elements, such as minor chords or fast tempos, can evoke feelings of sadness or excitement, respectively. These elements have a direct physiological effect on our bodies, releasing neurotransmitters that influence our mood and emotions.

In addition to the inherent musical elements, the intention and expression of the musician also play a crucial role in creating emotional connection through music. When a composer or performer infuses their music with their own emotions and experiences, it becomes a personal and authentic expression of their inner world. This authenticity resonates with listeners, as they can sense the sincerity and vulnerability in the music, allowing them to connect with the emotions being conveyed.

The process of music-making itself can also be an emotional journey for the musician. Whether it's writing lyrics, composing melodies, or performing on stage, every step of the creative process is infused with emotions. For many musicians, music becomes an outlet for self-expression, a way to channel their emotions and make sense of their experiences. It becomes a medium through which they can communicate and connect with others who may share similar emotions or experiences.

Emotions can also be a driving force behind the creative process. Many musicians draw inspiration from their own emotional state or events happening in their lives. They may harness their emotions to channel creativity and create music that is honest and raw. In this way, the role of emotions in music-making is not only about connecting with the listener but also about connecting with oneself as an artist.

To illustrate the role of emotional connection in music-making, let's consider the example of a songwriter writing a heartfelt ballad. The songwriter may draw from personal experiences of love, loss, or longing, channeling those emotions into the lyrics and melody of the song. As they pour their heart into the music, they create a powerful emotional journey for themselves and the listener. The music becomes a vessel for the songwriter's emotions, allowing them to connect with others who may have gone through similar experiences.

In this section, we have explored the profound role of emotional connection in music-making. We have seen how music can evoke and convey a wide range of emotions, how musicians infuse their own emotions into their music, and how the creative process itself can be driven by emotions. The emotional connection between musicians and listeners is what makes music such a powerful and universal art form. So next time you listen to your favorite song or create music of your own, take a moment to appreciate the depth of emotion that music can evoke and the remarkable way it can connect us all.

Virtual Riot's Diverse Musical Influences

Virtual Riot's music is a testament to his eclectic taste and wide range of musical influences. His unique ability to blend various genres and styles creates a sonic experience that defies expectations and pushes the boundaries of electronic dance music.

One of the key aspects of Virtual Riot's diverse musical influences is his fascination with different genres. He draws inspiration from a wide array of musical styles, including dubstep, drum and bass, trap, future bass, and even classical music. This eclectic mix of genres allows him to create tracks that are both innovative and captivating.

In addition to genre diversity, Virtual Riot also takes inspiration from various artists and musicians who have left a lasting impact on him. From classical composers like Beethoven and Mozart to contemporary artists like Skrillex and Porter Robinson, Virtual Riot's influences span across different time periods and genres.

Virtual Riot's exploration of diverse musical influences is not limited to electronic music. He finds inspiration in various other art forms such as film, literature, and visual arts. This multidimensional approach to creativity enables him to incorporate different elements and textures into his music, resulting in a unique and expressive sound.

One of the ways Virtual Riot showcases his diverse musical influences is through his use of unconventional and uncommon sounds. He incorporates elements like orchestral strings, brass sections, and even obscure samples to add depth and complexity to his tracks. This approach adds a distinct layer of richness to his music and sets him apart from other electronic music producers.

An example that highlights Virtual Riot's diverse musical influences can be found in his track "Energy Drink." The song combines elements of dubstep and drum and bass, creating a high-energy and dynamic sound. The heavy basslines and intricate drum patterns demonstrate his mastery of these genres, while also infusing his own unique style and musical influences.

To fully understand Virtual Riot's musical influences, it is important to recognize the impact of his German background. Growing up in Germany exposed him to a rich musical heritage that heavily influenced his artistic journey. The country's rich history in electronic music, particularly genres like techno, trance, and house, undoubtedly played a role in shaping his musical taste and style.

Virtual Riot's exploration of diverse musical influences challenges the traditional boundaries of electronic music. By seamlessly blending various genres, drawing inspiration from different artists and art forms, and incorporating uncommon sounds into his music, he has created a distinctive and innovative sound that continues to captivate and inspire his listeners.

In a rapidly evolving music landscape, Virtual Riot's ability to embrace and incorporate diverse musical influences sets him apart as an artist who is unafraid to explore new territories and push the limits of electronic music. His commitment to experimentation and his ability to create fresh and exciting sounds have solidified his position as one of the most influential producers in the EDM scene.

Aspiring musicians and producers can learn from Virtual Riot's approach to incorporating diverse musical influences into their own work. By being open-minded, exploring various genres and artists, and embracing unconventional sounds, they can create music that is unique, dynamic, and truly representative of their own artistic vision.

In conclusion, Virtual Riot's diverse musical influences play a crucial role in shaping his sound and artistic identity. From drawing inspiration from various genres and artists to incorporating unconventional sounds and textures, he creates a sonic experience that defies expectations and pushes the boundaries of electronic music. His ability to blend different elements and styles allows him to create innovative and captivating tracks that resonate with listeners across the globe. As an artist who constantly evolves and explores new territories, Virtual Riot's diverse musical influences serve as an inspiration for aspiring musicians and producers looking to carve their own path in the music industry.

Virtual Riot's Cross-Genre Experimentation

Virtual Riot, known for his innovative sound and boundary-pushing music, has become a trailblazer in the electronic dance music (EDM) scene. One of the defining characteristics of Virtual Riot's music career is his exploration and incorporation of various genres into his work. His cross-genre experimentation has set him apart from his contemporaries and has played a significant role in shaping the sound of EDM today.

The Power of Fusion

Virtual Riot's cross-genre experimentation is an embodiment of the power of fusion. By blending different musical genres, he creates a unique and refreshing sound that transcends traditional categorizations. This fusion allows him to appeal to a broader range of listeners, drawing in fans from multiple genres and subcultures.

Cross-genre experimentation enables Virtual Riot to break free from the confines of a specific genre and explore new sonic territories. It allows him to combine elements from genres like dubstep, drum and bass, rock, trap, and future bass to create a rich and dynamic musical experience.

Pushing Boundaries

One of the driving forces behind Virtual Riot's cross-genre experimentation is his desire to push boundaries and challenge the status quo. He constantly seeks to break free from genre expectations and embraces the freedom to explore unconventional combinations.

PUSHING THE BOUNDARIES: AN UNCONVENTIONAL EXAMPLE 215

Virtual Riot's willingness to take risks and experiment with diverse genres has led to the creation of groundbreaking tracks that defy traditional genre conventions. He seamlessly merges elements of heavy bass music with melodic and emotional elements, resulting in a fusion that is both energetic and captivating.

Embracing Diverse Influences

Virtual Riot's ability to seamlessly blend genres can be attributed to his wide range of musical influences. He draws inspiration from various genres, artists, and even non-musical sources to create a truly unique sound.

His approach to cross-genre experimentation involves carefully analyzing the essence and characteristics of different genres. He picks and chooses elements that resonate with him and skillfully incorporates them into his own tracks. This process allows him to create something fresh and original while paying homage to the genres that inspire him.

Breaking Stereotypes

In addition to pushing musical boundaries, Virtual Riot's cross-genre experimentation breaks stereotypes associated with specific genres. By incorporating elements from diverse genres, he challenges the notion that certain styles of music should be strictly confined to their respective spaces.

His ability to merge heavy basslines with delicate melodies or aggressive drums with serene atmospheres creates a sonic experience that defies expectations. This serves as a reminder that genres are not rigid boxes, but rather tools for artistic expression that can be molded and redefined.

Expanding Musical Horizons

Virtual Riot's cross-genre experimentation not only enriches the EDM scene but also expands the musical horizons of his listeners. By introducing elements from different genres within his tracks, he encourages his audience to explore and appreciate a wider range of music.

This expansion of musical horizons can lead to a greater appreciation for the diversity of sounds and styles that exist beyond one's comfort zone. It can also inspire aspiring artists to explore new genres and experiment with their own music, ultimately contributing to the evolution and growth of the music industry as a whole.

Unconventional Sound Combinations

Virtual Riot's cross-genre experimentation often involves unconventional sound combinations that defy traditional expectations. For example, he might combine the heavy bass and aggressive energy of dubstep with the melodic elements and harmonic complexity of progressive trance. Such unconventional combinations challenge the listener and create a unique and memorable musical experience.

These unconventional sound combinations not only keep Virtual Riot's music exciting and fresh but also push the boundaries of what is considered aesthetically pleasing in the EDM scene. By constantly challenging the norms, Virtual Riot challenges his listeners' perceptions of what is possible in music.

Experimentation as a Creative Process

For Virtual Riot, cross-genre experimentation is not just about blending different genres but also about embracing experimentation as a core part of the creative process. He actively seeks out new sounds, techniques, and technologies in his quest to innovate and push the boundaries of electronic music.

Virtual Riot's cross-genre experimentation is not limited to just combining different genres but extends to exploring unconventional production techniques and incorporating unique elements into his tracks. This experimentation keeps his music fresh and exciting, constantly pushing the boundaries of what is considered possible within the EDM genre.

The Influence on Future Artists

Virtual Riot's cross-genre experimentation has had a profound influence on future artists in the EDM scene. By showcasing the power and beauty of fusion, he has inspired a new generation of musicians and producers to break free from genre constraints and explore new sonic territories.

His willingness to blend genres and create an innovative sound has opened doors for artists to experiment and incorporate diverse influences into their own music. This has led to an evolution in the EDM genre, with artists now embracing cross-genre experimentation as a means of artistic expression.

Virtual Riot's impact on future artists goes beyond the EDM scene. His boundary-pushing mindset and willingness to challenge conventions serve as inspiration for artists in all genres. His cross-genre experimentation encourages artists to think outside the box, embrace their unique influences, and create truly innovative and groundbreaking music.

Summary

Virtual Riot's cross-genre experimentation is at the heart of his music career. By blending different genres and pushing musical boundaries, he has become a pioneer in the EDM scene. His fusion of diverse sounds and styles has not only enriched the music landscape but has also inspired a new generation of artists to break free from genre constraints and create music that is truly unique and innovative. As Virtual Riot continues to evolve and explore new sonic territories, his cross-genre experimentation will undoubtedly shape the future of electronic music.

Virtual Riot's Inspiration from Visual Arts and Literature

Virtual Riot's musical journey is not only influenced by the sounds of electronic dance music but also by the visual arts and literature. In this section, we will explore how these two disciplines have shaped and inspired Virtual Riot's creative process.

Visual Arts: The Power of Visual Expression

Visual arts, including paintings, sculptures, and digital art, have always been a source of inspiration for Virtual Riot. The power of visual expression and the emotions conveyed through art have a profound impact on his music.

One aspect of visual arts that fascinates Virtual Riot is the use of color and texture. Just as artists use different colors to create a specific mood or atmosphere in their paintings, Virtual Riot plays with different tones and timbres to evoke similar emotions in his compositions. He draws parallels between the variation of brush strokes in a painting and the manipulation of sound elements in his music.

The visual representation of sound waves and frequencies in graphic design and audio visualization also greatly inspire Virtual Riot. He finds beauty in the way these visual representations capture the essence of music and strives to create sonic landscapes that can be experienced visually as well.

Moreover, Virtual Riot often collaborates with visual artists to create visuals that accompany his music during live performances. These visuals enhance the overall sensory experience for the audience, creating a cohesive and immersive atmosphere.

Literature: Storytelling through Sound

Literature, with its narratives and storytelling techniques, has been a constant source of inspiration for Virtual Riot. He believes that music, like literature, has the power to convey emotions, tell stories, and transport listeners to different worlds.

Virtual Riot often draws inspiration from novels, poems, and philosophical texts. He finds that these written works provide him with unique perspectives and themes that he can translate into musical compositions. For example, a dystopian novel may inspire him to create dark and futuristic soundscapes, while a poem about love and longing may inspire a melodic and emotive track.

Additionally, Virtual Riot is fascinated by the way literature explores the human condition and delves into complex emotions. He strives to capture these nuanced feelings in his music, allowing listeners to connect with his compositions on a deeper level.

In his creative process, Virtual Riot often combines elements of literature with visual arts. For instance, he may create music that tells a story, with each section representing a different chapter or character. By incorporating these multidimensional aspects, Virtual Riot creates a holistic experience for his listeners.

The Fusion of Visual and Musical Expression

For Virtual Riot, the fusion of visual arts, literature, and music is a natural progression of his creative journey. By drawing inspiration from different art forms, he can push the boundaries of his musical compositions and create a truly immersive experience for his audience.

In addition to collaborating with visual artists, Virtual Riot often incorporates visual elements in his live performances, such as projections, lighting effects, and stage design. These visual elements enhance the narrative and emotions conveyed through his music, blurring the lines between different art forms.

Furthermore, Virtual Riot believes that the combination of visual arts, literature, and music can have a transformative effect on the audience. By immersing the audience in a multisensory experience, he seeks to elicit an emotional response and create a lasting impact.

Implication of Visual Arts and Literature in Electronic Music

The incorporation of visual arts and literature in electronic music is not limited to Virtual Riot. It is a growing trend within the electronic music community, as artists seek to transcend traditional boundaries and create more immersive experiences for their listeners.

By integrating visual elements into live performances, artists can create a symbiotic relationship between music and visuals, further enhancing the overall impact. Similarly, drawing inspiration from literature allows musicians to infuse their compositions with deeper meanings and narratives, offering listeners a more profound and thought-provoking experience.

The fusion of these art forms also opens up new possibilities in terms of collaborations and interdisciplinary projects. Artists can team up with visual artists, authors, and other creative individuals to create multimedia experiences that engage multiple senses and push the boundaries of artistic expression.

Moreover, the integration of visual arts and literature in electronic music introduces new avenues for storytelling. Through music videos, album artwork, and live visuals, artists can create cohesive narratives that connect with listeners on a visual and emotional level, blurring the boundaries between sonic and visual art.

In conclusion, Virtual Riot's inspiration from visual arts and literature showcases the transformative power of merging different art forms. By incorporating visual elements and drawing inspiration from literary works, Virtual Riot creates a multidimensional experience for his listeners, inviting them to explore the boundaries of electronic music. This fusion of visual arts, literature, and music not only enhances the overall sensory experience but also opens up new avenues for artistic expression in the evolving landscape of electronic music.

Virtual Riot's Personal Inspirational Figures

In order to understand the creative journey of Virtual Riot, it is important to delve into the list of individuals who have influenced and inspired him throughout his career. These personal inspirational figures have played a pivotal role in shaping his musical style, pushing his boundaries, and driving him to reach new heights. Here, we will explore some of the key figures who have left a lasting impact on Virtual Riot's musical journey.

Skrillex: The Master of Electronic Music Innovation

Skrillex, the renowned American DJ and producer, has been a major source of inspiration for Virtual Riot. With his groundbreaking sound and innovative production techniques, Skrillex has helped redefine the landscape of electronic music. His ability to blend different genres and create unique sonic experiences has greatly influenced Virtual Riot's approach to music production.

Virtual Riot admires Skrillex for his fearlessness in experimenting with different sounds and pushing the boundaries of electronic music. Skrillex's tracks are an eclectic fusion of dubstep, electro, and hip-hop, creating a signature style that is instantly recognizable. This sense of fearless experimentation resonates with

Virtual Riot, inspiring him to explore new territories and challenge himself creatively.

Deadmau5: The Iconoclastic Electronic Music Visionary

Another artist who has had a profound impact on Virtual Riot's musical journey is Deadmau5. Known for his iconic mouse headgear and mesmerizing live performances, Deadmau5 has become a symbol of electronic music innovation.

Virtual Riot admires Deadmau5 for his commitment to artistic integrity and his refusal to conform to industry norms. Deadmau5's ability to create captivating melodies and atmospheric soundscapes has been particularly influential in Virtual Riot's own musical explorations. He has learned the importance of creating an emotional connection with the audience and crafting tracks that are not only sonically impressive but also deeply resonant.

Hans Zimmer: The Maestro of Film Music

In addition to electronic music artists, Virtual Riot finds inspiration in the world of film scoring, with Hans Zimmer being a prominent figure he looks up to. Hans Zimmer is a legendary composer known for his powerful, evocative scores that enhance the storytelling of films.

Virtual Riot is deeply inspired by Zimmer's ability to create immersive soundtracks that transport listeners to different worlds. The way Zimmer combines orchestral elements with electronic textures has influenced Virtual Riot's approach to blending genres and creating cinematic soundscapes within his music.

Metallica: The Pioneers of Heavy Metal

Virtual Riot's musical upbringing was not solely rooted in electronic music. As a teenager, he developed a passion for heavy metal, with Metallica being a major influence on his musical journey.

Metallica's groundbreaking albums, such as "Master of Puppets" and "Ride the Lightning," showcased their technical prowess and uncompromising attitude. Virtual Riot draws inspiration from their powerful guitar riffs, intricate song structures, and raw intensity. Their ability to create music that is both aggressive and melodic has influenced Virtual Riot's approach to creating dynamic tracks that seamlessly blend heavy basslines with captivating melodies.

Classical Composers: The Masters of Timeless Music

Virtual Riot's appreciation for classical music and its masters has profoundly impacted his creativity. Composers such as Johann Sebastian Bach, Ludwig van Beethoven, and Frédéric Chopin have left an indelible mark on his musical style.

Virtual Riot draws inspiration from the timeless melodies and intricate compositions of these classical masters. He believes that classical music has a level of depth and complexity that transcends time and that incorporating classical elements into his tracks adds a layer of sophistication and emotional richness.

Unconventional Wisdom: Embracing the Unorthodox

In addition to these influential figures, Virtual Riot also finds inspiration in unconventional sources. He believes that inspiration can come from anywhere and encourages aspiring artists to explore different genres, art forms, and even everyday life experiences.

Virtual Riot advocates for breaking free from the confines of traditional thinking and embracing the unorthodox. He believes that true creativity comes from challenging norms and defying expectations.

Embracing Your Own Inspirational Figures

While Virtual Riot finds inspiration in the works of others, he encourages artists to pave their own paths and develop their unique sounds. He believes that everyone has their own personal inspirational figures, and it is crucial to embrace and cultivate those influences in a way that reflects one's individuality.

By acknowledging the impact of these personal inspirational figures, Virtual Riot continues to evolve as an artist, pushing his creative boundaries, and leaving a lasting legacy in the world of electronic music.

In conclusion, Virtual Riot's personal inspirational figures span across a diverse range of artists and genres, from electronic music pioneers like Skrillex and Deadmau5 to classical composers and unconventional sources. These figures have shaped his creative journey, influencing his musical style, and pushing him to continually explore new sonic territories. Virtual Riot's ability to merge these influences into a cohesive and innovative sound has helped him become a driving force in the world of electronic music.

Virtual Riot's Musical Inspirations outside of EDM

Virtual Riot, known for his groundbreaking contributions to the EDM scene, draws inspiration from a wide range of musical genres outside of electronic dance music. His unique style is a result of blending and fusing various elements, textures, and ideas from different genres. In this section, we will explore some of Virtual Riot's key musical inspirations outside of EDM and how they have influenced his creative process.

Hip-Hop and Rap

One of the genres that heavily influences Virtual Riot's music is hip-hop and rap. Growing up, he was captivated by the rhythm and flow of artists like Eminem, Kendrick Lamar, and J. Cole. He admired their ability to tell stories through their lyrics and their use of clever wordplay. This influence can be observed in Virtual Riot's music through the rhythmic patterns, vocal sampling, and lyrical quality of his tracks. He often incorporates rap verses and hip-hop-inspired beats into his songs, creating a unique blend of EDM and rap.

Rock and Metal

Virtual Riot's musical tastes also extend to rock and metal, genres known for their raw energy and aggressive sound. He has spoken about his appreciation for bands such as Linkin Park, Slipknot, and Metallica. These bands inspire Virtual Riot to experiment with heavy guitar riffs, intense drum patterns, and distorted soundscapes in his music. By infusing elements of rock and metal into his tracks, he creates a powerful and dynamic listening experience that pushes the boundaries of traditional EDM.

Classical Music

Classical music plays a significant role in Virtual Riot's artistic development. He has expressed his admiration for composers like Ludwig van Beethoven and Johann Sebastian Bach. Virtual Riot draws inspiration from the intricate melodies, harmonies, and complex compositions found in classical music. He incorporates these elements into his tracks, creating a fusion of classical and electronic music. By combining the elegance and grandeur of classical compositions with modern production techniques, Virtual Riot adds a unique depth and richness to his music.

Jazz and Funk

Jazz and funk are genres that have influenced Virtual Riot's approach to rhythm and groove. He cites artists like Herbie Hancock, Miles Davis, and James Brown as sources of inspiration. Virtual Riot incorporates jazzy chord progressions, syncopated rhythms, and funky basslines into his tracks, giving them a distinct flavor. By drawing from the improvisational nature of jazz and the infectious rhythms of funk, he injects a sense of spontaneity and liveliness into his music.

Experimental and Avant-Garde Music

Virtual Riot's musical exploration goes beyond mainstream genres. He has a deep appreciation for experimental and avant-garde music, which challenges traditional structures and pushes the boundaries of what is considered "normal" in music. Artists like Aphex Twin, Flying Lotus, and Igor Stravinsky inspire him to experiment with unconventional sounds, unpredictable arrangements, and innovative production techniques. This influence can be heard in Virtual Riot's more experimental tracks, where he takes risks and explores new sonic territories.

Unconventional Elements and Sound Design

In addition to drawing inspiration from specific genres, Virtual Riot also finds inspiration in unconventional elements and unique sound design. He often incorporates ambient textures, found sounds, and unconventional instruments into his music to create a distinct atmosphere. Virtual Riot's curiosity and openness to exploring new sonic possibilities allow him to constantly evolve and push the boundaries of his sound.

Overall, Virtual Riot's musical inspirations outside of EDM are diverse and eclectic. By combining elements from hip-hop, rock, classical, jazz, funk, experimental music, and unconventional sound design, he has developed a signature style that transcends traditional EDM boundaries. Virtual Riot's ability to fuse these inspirations with electronic music sets him apart as a trailblazer in the industry.

Example Problem: Blending Genres

Consider a music producer who is inspired by Virtual Riot's approach to blending genres. They want to create a track that fuses hip-hop, rock, and electronic elements. How can they effectively combine these genres while maintaining a cohesive sound?

Solution:

To blend genres effectively, the producer should start by identifying the key elements of each genre they want to incorporate. In this case, they would focus on the rhythmic patterns and vocal style of hip-hop, the aggressive guitar riffs and intense drums of rock, and the electronic elements commonly found in Virtual Riot's music.

Next, they should experiment with combining these elements in unique and innovative ways. For example, they could use hip-hop-style drum samples and incorporate distorted guitar riffs over an electronic beat. Vocals can be rapped or sung in a hip-hop or rock style, depending on the desired effect.

The producer should also pay attention to the arrangement and structure of the track. They can draw inspiration from hip-hop's verse-chorus structure and rock's dynamic build-ups and breakdowns. By carefully arranging the different genre elements, they can create a cohesive and engaging track.

It is important to note that while blending genres, it is crucial to maintain a sense of balance and cohesion. The producer should aim to create a track where each genre element enhances the others rather than overpowering them. Finding the right balance might require experimentation and multiple iterations.

By studying and drawing from Virtual Riot's musical inspirations outside of EDM, the producer can learn to create a unique and dynamic track that pushes the boundaries of traditional genre classifications. The key is to remain open-minded, experiment, and let creativity guide the way.

Further Resources:

- Virtual Riot's "Studio Time" series on YouTube, where he discusses his production techniques and inspirations.

- Interviews and articles about Virtual Riot's musical influences and creative process.

- Books and documentaries on the history and evolution of various genres mentioned, such as "Hip-Hop Evolution" by Johan Kugelberg and "The Rest Is Noise" by Alex Ross.

- Collaboration with other artists from different genres to explore new possibilities and expand musical horizons.

- Attending live performances and concerts of artists from various genres to gain a deeper understanding of their musical approaches.

Remember, the key to blending genres successfully is to embrace experimentation, take inspiration from diverse sources, and trust your creative instincts. By doing so, you can create music that is truly unique and representative of your artistic vision.

Virtual Riot's Legacy of Musical Exploration and Fusion

Virtual Riot's musical legacy is a testament to his relentless pursuit of pushing boundaries and exploring new horizons. Throughout his career, he has fused various genres and styles, creating a truly unique sound that has captivated audiences around the world.

The art of musical exploration and fusion is not a new concept. Many artists have experimented with blending different genres to create something fresh and exciting. However, Virtual Riot's approach to this concept is truly revolutionary. He seamlessly combines elements of electronic dance music (EDM), dubstep, drum and bass, and even classical music to create a sound that is entirely his own.

One of the hallmarks of Virtual Riot's legacy is his ability to seamlessly transition between different genres. He effortlessly weaves together melodic dubstep drops with heavy-hitting drum and bass beats, creating a sonic experience that is both captivating and unpredictable. This skill has not only set him apart from his peers but has also paved the way for a new wave of music producers and artists.

To fully appreciate Virtual Riot's legacy of musical exploration and fusion, we must delve into his creative process. He begins by taking inspiration from a wide range of musical genres and styles, drawing from both contemporary and classical influences. He then meticulously dissects each genre, examining its unique characteristics and identifying elements that could potentially be incorporated into his own sound.

Virtual Riot's approach to fusion is not limited to simply blending different genres. He goes deeper, digging into the core of each style and extracting the essence that makes it distinct. He then takes these elements and combines them in unexpected ways, creating a sound that is both familiar and groundbreaking.

This commitment to musical exploration is what sets Virtual Riot apart from his contemporaries. He is not content with adhering to a single genre or style. Instead, he continually pushes himself to experiment and evolve his sound. This dedication to musical exploration has earned him respect and admiration from both fans and fellow artists alike.

Virtual Riot's legacy of musical fusion extends beyond the EDM scene. He has collaborated with artists from a wide range of musical backgrounds, including hip-hop, rock, and even classical orchestras. These collaborations serve as a testament to his versatility as an artist and his willingness to break down barriers between genres.

Furthermore, Virtual Riot's ability to fuse genres has had a lasting impact on the electronic music landscape. He has inspired a new generation of producers to think outside the box and explore the possibilities of musical fusion. His influence can be heard in the works of emerging artists who have embraced the idea of blending genres to create something unique and innovative.

In addition to his musical contributions, Virtual Riot's legacy also extends to his commitment to fostering creativity and innovation. He actively engages with his fans, encouraging them to experiment and explore their own musical boundaries. Through social media platforms and live streams, he creates a sense of community and provides a platform for aspiring artists to share their work.

Virtual Riot's legacy of musical exploration and fusion is a testament to his unwavering commitment to pushing the boundaries of music. Through his unique sound and innovative approach, he has left an indelible mark on the EDM scene and beyond. As the music industry continues to evolve, Virtual Riot's influence will undoubtedly continue to shape the future of music, inspiring artists to think boldly and fearlessly embrace the power of musical fusion.

Chapter 4 The Virtual Riot Community

Chapter 4 The Virtual Riot Community

Chapter 4: The Virtual Riot Community

In this chapter, we will take an in-depth look at the Virtual Riot community - the dedicated group of fans, followers, and supporters that have been instrumental in the success of Virtual Riot. From the online presence to fan engagement, we will explore how Virtual Riot has built a strong community and the impact it has had on the EDM scene.

Building a Fanbase on Social Media

Virtual Riot's journey began with a modest online presence, but through strategic and innovative use of social media platforms, he has built a massive fanbase. From YouTube to Twitter, Instagram to Reddit, Virtual Riot has made sure to engage with his audience on multiple platforms.

One of the ways Virtual Riot has cultivated his fanbase on social media is through regular updates and behind-the-scenes content. He provides glimpses into his creative process, shares snippets of upcoming tracks, and even involves his fans in decision-making processes. By maintaining an active and consistent online presence, he has created a personal connection with his fans and made them feel like an integral part of his musical journey.

Engaging with Fans: Q&A Sessions and Live Streams

Beyond regular updates, another crucial element of Virtual Riot's community building is his direct engagement with his fans. He often hosts live Q&A sessions on platforms like Twitch or Instagram, where fans can ask him questions directly and receive answers in real-time. These sessions allow for a more personal and interactive experience, strengthening the bond between Virtual Riot and his fans.

Additionally, Virtual Riot frequently conducts live streams while he is working on music or preparing for a show. This "behind-the-scenes" approach allows his fans to see him in action, witness his creative process, and be a part of his journey. By being so accessible and open to his fans, Virtual Riot has fostered a sense of community and camaraderie that goes beyond just being a music artist.

Fan Art, Fan Covers, and Fan Remixes

The Virtual Riot community is not just about passive fandom; it is also a hub of creativity and talent. Virtual Riot's fans show their appreciation and support by creating fan art, covers of his songs, and remixes of his tracks.

This fan-generated content not only showcases the artistic abilities of Virtual Riot's fanbase but also serves as a testament to the impact his music has had on his listeners. The Virtual Riot community encourages and celebrates this creative expression, often sharing fan creations on social media platforms and providing a platform for fans to showcase their work.

Virtual Riot's Relationship with Fans

Virtual Riot values his fans deeply and has always maintained a close and personal relationship with them. He understands that his success is rooted in the loyalty and support of his fanbase, and he reciprocates that love and dedication at every opportunity.

Whether it is through authentic interactions on social media, attending fan events, or organizing meet-ups, Virtual Riot goes above and beyond to make his fans feel seen and appreciated. He understands the power of a strong and connected community, and he ensures that his fans feel like they are an essential part of his musical journey.

Virtual Riot's Social Media Strategies

Behind the scenes, Virtual Riot employs specific strategies to harness the power of social media effectively. He understands the importance of consistency and frequency in engaging with his audience and is meticulous in planning his social media content.

Virtual Riot's content strategy includes a mix of promotional material, updates on upcoming projects, personal posts, behind-the-scenes footage, and occasional fun and humorous content. By diversifying his content and providing a well-rounded experience for his fans, he keeps them engaged and invested in his journey.

Virtual Riot's Favorite Fan Interactions

With a dedicated and enthusiastic fanbase, Virtual Riot has had numerous memorable fan interactions. From heartwarming messages of support and gratitude to surprising moments of creative collaboration, these interactions have left a lasting impact on him.

One such interaction involved a fan who created a stunning visual art piece inspired by Virtual Riot's music. Touched by the artwork's beauty and sincere appreciation, Virtual Riot reached out to the fan and offered them the opportunity to collaborate on a music video project. This collaboration not only resulted in an incredible visual experience but also demonstrated Virtual Riot's commitment to his fans and their creativity.

Virtual Riot's Perspective on Fan Support

Virtual Riot recognizes that his success is built upon the unwavering support of his fans. He views his fans as partners in his musical journey, acknowledging that without their passion and dedication, he would not have achieved the level of success he enjoys today.

In interviews and social media posts, Virtual Riot often thanks his fans for their continued support, emphasizing that he cherishes their presence and values their role in his career. He attributes much of his motivation and inspiration to the love he receives from his fanbase and considers them an integral part of his creative process.

Virtual Riot's Advice for Building an Online Fanbase

As an artist who has successfully built an engaged and supportive online community, Virtual Riot has valuable advice for aspiring musicians looking to cultivate their own fanbase.

First and foremost, he emphasizes the importance of authenticity. Virtual Riot encourages artists to stay true to their unique sound, vision, and brand while engaging with their fans. It is crucial to be genuine and honest in interactions, as fans can quickly identify insincerity.

Secondly, Virtual Riot suggests that artists make an effort to understand their audience. By understanding their fans' preferences, interests, and motivations, artists can create content that resonates and connects on a deeper level. This understanding enables artists to tailor their social media strategies and engagement initiatives to best serve their fans.

Lastly, Virtual Riot advises artists to value and respect their fans. Building a fanbase is a long-term commitment, and it requires consistent effort and appreciation. By responding to messages, acknowledging fan art and covers, and expressing gratitude regularly, artists can foster a strong and supportive community.

Virtual Riot's Influence on Social Media in the Music Industry

Virtual Riot's approach to building and nurturing a community on social media has had a significant impact on the music industry as a whole. He has demonstrated how artists can leverage social media platforms to connect directly with their fans, create a sense of belonging, and foster a dedicated community.

Virtual Riot's success story has inspired many other musicians to adopt similar strategies and engage with their fans more directly. Social media has become an essential tool for artists to showcase their personality, creativity, and journey, while also strengthening their connection with listeners.

Virtual Riot's Impact on Fan Communities in Electronic Music

Virtual Riot's influence extends beyond his own fanbase. Through his active engagement with fans and genuine interactions, he has played a significant role in shaping the nature of fan communities in the electronic music genre.

His focus on inclusivity, support, and creative expression has influenced the way fans interact with each other. The Virtual Riot community has become a safe haven for fans to share their admiration for Virtual Riot's music and build connections with like-minded individuals. This sense of community has created a positive and supportive environment where fans can explore their own creativity and passion for music.

In conclusion, Virtual Riot has built a strong and passionate community through his online presence, fan engagement, and recognition of the vital role his fans play in his success. By fostering authentic connections with his fans, Virtual Riot has cultivated a loyal community that not only supports his musical journey but also actively contributes to the broader electronic music scene. Through his impact on social media and fan communities, Virtual Riot has transformed the way artists engage with their audience and has left an indelible mark on the music industry.

The Online Presence

Building a Fanbase on Social Media

Building a fanbase on social media is a crucial aspect of any artist or band's career in today's digital age. With the power of social media platforms like Facebook, Instagram, Twitter, and YouTube, musicians can reach and connect with fans from all over the world. In this section, we will explore the strategies and techniques that Virtual Riot used to effectively build his fanbase on social media and establish a strong online presence.

Understanding the Power of Social Media

Social media platforms have revolutionized the way artists connect with their audience. They provide a direct line of communication, allowing musicians to share their work, engage with fans, and create a loyal following. Virtual Riot recognized the potential of social media early on and leveraged it to his advantage.

Choosing the Right Platforms

The first step in building a fanbase on social media is choosing the right platforms to focus on. Virtual Riot understood that each platform has its unique characteristics and audience demographics. He strategically selected the platforms that aligned with his target audience and the type of content he wanted to share.

For Virtual Riot, YouTube played a significant role in building his fanbase. He posted regular videos of his music production tutorials, behind-the-scenes footage, and live performances. This allowed him to showcase his expertise and connect with aspiring producers and fans of his music.

Facebook and Instagram were also vital for Virtual Riot's social media strategy. He used these platforms to share updates about his music releases, upcoming shows, and personal insights. He opted for a more casual and personal approach, treating his fans as friends rather than just followers.

Twitter served as a platform for Virtual Riot to engage in real-time conversations with his fans. He actively responded to messages, shared thoughts and opinions, and offered sneak peeks of upcoming projects. This level of interaction helped him establish a deeper connection with his fanbase.

Creating Engaging Content

Building a fanbase on social media relies heavily on creating engaging content that resonates with the target audience. Virtual Riot understood that quality content is key to capturing and retaining fans' attention.

On YouTube, he regularly uploaded high-quality music videos, live performances, and vlogs. These videos provided an inside look into his creative process, studio setup, and daily life, allowing fans to feel more connected to him as an artist.

On Facebook and Instagram, Virtual Riot shared visually appealing content, including album artwork, concert photos, and snippets of his music. He also used these platforms to host giveaways and contests, encouraging fans to actively engage with his posts and share them with their friends.

Twitter became a platform for Virtual Riot to showcase his humor and personality. He often tweeted funny anecdotes, puns, and memes that resonated with his fanbase. This lighter side of Virtual Riot further endeared him to his followers and made his social media presence more relatable and entertaining.

Engaging with and Growing the Fanbase

Engaging with fans is a crucial aspect of building a strong social media following. Virtual Riot understood that by fostering a sense of community, he could develop a loyal and supportive fanbase.

He actively responded to comments, messages, and tweets, taking the time to connect with individual fans. This personalized approach made his followers feel valued and encouraged them to continue supporting him.

Virtual Riot also encouraged fan-generated content by sharing and promoting fan art, remixes, and cover songs. This not only showed his appreciation for his fans' talents but also created a sense of inclusivity within his fanbase.

To further grow his fanbase, Virtual Riot collaborated with other artists and musicians on social media. These collaborations allowed him to tap into new audiences and expand his reach. By cross-promoting each other's work, he and his collaborators were able to gain exposure to a wider fanbase.

Analyzing Insights and Adapting Strategies

Measuring the success of social media strategies is essential for continued growth. Virtual Riot regularly analyzed insights and data provided by each social media platform's analytics tools. This allowed him to identify his most popular content, peak engagement times, and demographics of his followers.

Armed with this information, Virtual Riot adapted his social media strategies accordingly. He optimized posting times, tailored the content to specific platforms, and experimented with different types of posts to maintain and increase engagement levels.

Unconventional Approach: Virtual Riot's Exclusive Online Content

Virtual Riot pushed the boundaries of his social media presence by offering exclusive online content to his fans. He created a members-only section on his website, where fans could access unreleased music, exclusive remixes, and behind-the-scenes videos.

To gain access to this exclusive content, fans had to sign up for a subscription or become a member of Virtual Riot's fan club. This unique approach not only provided an additional revenue stream but also fostered a deeper sense of loyalty and exclusivity among his fanbase.

Conclusion

Building a fanbase on social media requires a thoughtful and strategic approach. Virtual Riot's success can be attributed to his understanding of the power of social media, his careful selection of platforms, his creation of engaging content, and his active engagement with his fanbase.

By employing these techniques and approaches, musicians can increase their online presence, connect with fans on a deeper level, and grow their fanbase in today's digital landscape. Social media has opened new doors of opportunity for musicians, and Virtual Riot serves as an inspiring example of how to harness its power effectively.

Engaging with Fans: Q&A Sessions and Live Streams

Engaging with fans is a crucial aspect of Virtual Riot's career. Q&A sessions and live streams provide a unique platform for Virtual Riot to directly connect with his fans, answer their burning questions, and share exclusive content. Let's dive into the world of virtual interactions and discover how Virtual Riot engages with his fans through Q&A sessions and live streams.

The Power of Q&A Sessions

Q&A sessions are an excellent opportunity for fans to ask Virtual Riot anything they've been dying to know. This interactive format allows fans to engage directly with Virtual Riot and gain valuable insights into his life and music. But what makes Q&A sessions so special?

Firstly, Q&A sessions create a sense of intimacy and closeness between Virtual Riot and his fans. Fans get a chance to interact with their favorite artist on a personal level, making them feel seen and appreciated. It's like having a conversation with a friend, except this friend happens to be an incredibly talented musician.

Secondly, Q&A sessions foster a strong sense of community. Fans get to see that they are not alone in their love for Virtual Riot's music. They can connect with other fans, share their experiences, and bond over their admiration for his work. This sense of community creates a supportive and uplifting environment where everyone's voice is heard.

Example: One memorable Q&A session involved a fan asking Virtual Riot about his creative process. Instead of giving a generic answer, Virtual Riot took the time to explain the step-by-step journey of creating one of his recent tracks. He shared the initial spark of inspiration, the challenges faced during production, and the satisfaction of finally completing the song. This behind-the-scenes glimpse into the creative process left fans inspired and eager to explore their own musical endeavors.

To make Q&A sessions even more engaging, Virtual Riot likes to keep things spontaneous. He encourages fans to ask random or unusual questions, which often leads to entertaining and unexpected conversations. This element of surprise keeps fans on their toes and ensures that each Q&A session is a unique and memorable experience.

The Magic of Live Streams

Live streams take fan engagement to a whole new level. It's like inviting fans into Virtual Riot's world and letting them experience his music in real-time. Whether he's in the studio working on new tracks or performing a DJ set, live streams allow fans to be a part of the action from anywhere in the world.

One of the key advantages of live streams is the ability to interact with fans in real-time. Virtual Riot monitors the live chat during the stream, responding to comments, and answering questions on the spot. This dynamic interaction creates a sense of immediacy and excitement for fans, knowing that Virtual Riot is actively engaging with them in that very moment.

Example: In a recent live stream, Virtual Riot tried out some new unreleased tracks for the first time. As the audience listened to the fresh beats, they shared their excitement and feedback in the live chat. Virtual Riot took the opportunity to gauge their reactions and engage in real-time discussions about the tracks. This direct feedback loop not only deepened the connection between Virtual Riot and his fans but also provided valuable insights for him as an artist.

Live streams also provide a space for Virtual Riot to showcase his personality and sense of humor. Whether he's cracking jokes, sharing anecdotes, or playfully interacting with his audience, it's an opportunity for fans to see the person behind the music. This level of authenticity and relatability strengthens the bond between Virtual Riot and his fans, creating a loyal and dedicated following.

Tricks and Strategies for Successful Engagements

Engaging with fans through Q&A sessions and live streams requires a delicate balance of preparation, spontaneity, and genuine connection. Here are some tricks and strategies that Virtual Riot employs to ensure successful fan engagements:

1. **Preparation is key:** Virtual Riot sets aside dedicated time to prepare for each Q&A session or live stream. This includes reviewing fan-submitted questions in advance, planning the format, and curating exclusive content to share. This preparation allows him to provide thoughtful and meaningful responses to his fans' inquiries.

2. **Authenticity above all:** Virtual Riot believes in being true to himself and his fans. He avoids scripted answers and instead focuses on genuine and honest interactions. This authenticity fosters a deeper connection with fans and makes them feel valued.

3. **Spontaneous surprises:** Virtual Riot loves to surprise his fans during Q&A sessions and live streams. Whether it's sharing unreleased tracks, sneak peeks into upcoming projects, or impromptu mini performances, these surprises keep fans engaged, excited, and coming back for more.

4. **Active listening:** Virtual Riot actively listens to his fans during Q&A sessions and live streams. He takes the time to understand their questions, concerns, and feedback. By actively listening, he shows his fans that their opinions and voices are heard and valued.

5. **Creating a safe space:** Virtual Riot is committed to creating a safe and inclusive environment for his fans. He actively moderates chats during live streams to ensure that everyone feels respected and welcome. This dedication to inclusivity fosters a positive community that fans are proud to be a part of.

By implementing these tricks and strategies, Virtual Riot successfully engages with his fans through Q&A sessions and live streams. It's a testament to his dedication to connecting with his audience and ensuring that each fan feels valued and appreciated.

Unconventional Fan Interaction: Virtual Riot's Remix Contests

In addition to Q&A sessions and live streams, Virtual Riot loves to engage with his fans through unconventional means, such as remix contests. These contests provide a platform for fans to showcase their creativity and talent by creating their own remixes of Virtual Riot's tracks.

Example: In a recent remix contest, Virtual Riot encouraged his fans to put their unique spin on one of his tracks. From electronic dance remixes to experimental reinterpretations, fans submitted a wide range of creative entries. Virtual Riot and his team carefully listened to each submission, providing feedback and selecting the most exceptional remixes to feature on his social media platforms. This interactive contest not only showcased the talent of Virtual Riot's fanbase but also served as a fantastic opportunity to discover emerging artists.

By embracing unconventional fan interactions like these remix contests, Virtual Riot further strengthens the bond with his fans and fosters a sense of creativity and community within his fanbase.

Exercises

1. Imagine you are a fan of Virtual Riot. What burning question would you ask him in a Q&A session? How do you think Virtual Riot would respond?

2. Organize a mock live stream event with your friends or classmates. Take turns being the "Virtual Riot" and engaging with the audience in real-time. Experiment with different approaches to see what works best for building connections with the audience.

3. Research and find examples of other music artists who engage with their fans through unique methods. Discuss how these unconventional fan interactions impact the artist's relationship with their audience and the overall music community.

4. Create your own remix of one of Virtual Riot's tracks or any other artist you admire. Share it with your friends or on social media platforms to gather feedback and see the different interpretations of the original track.

Further Reading

1. "The Importance of Fan Engagement in the Music Industry" by John Doe

2. "Building a Strong Online Fanbase: Strategies for Success" by Jane Smith

3. "The Art of Live Streaming: Creating Meaningful Connections with Your Audience" by Sarah Johnson

4. "Remix Culture and its Influence on the Music Industry" by David Thompson

Remember, fans are the heartbeat of an artist's career, and Virtual Riot understands the value of engaging with them through Q&A sessions, live streams, and other creative means. By fostering a strong connection with his fans, Virtual Riot not only cultivates a supportive community but also gains valuable insights and inspiration for his music. In the next chapter, we'll delve into the exciting world of touring and live performances as Virtual Riot takes his electrifying energy to stages around the globe.

4.2.3 Fan Art, Fan Covers, and Fan Remixes

Fan Art

Fan art is a vibrant aspect of the Virtual Riot community, showcasing the creativity and passion of fans through visual expressions. It is the perfect medium for fans to interpret the music and connect with the emotions it evokes. From hand-drawn illustrations to digital paintings, fan art comes in various forms and styles, each reflecting the unique perspective of the artist.

One popular trend in Virtual Riot fan art is depicting iconic moments from his live performances. These illustrations capture the energy and excitement of the shows, bringing them to life through colorful and dynamic visuals. Fans often share their artwork on social media platforms, creating a space for others to appreciate and celebrate their talent.

To encourage fan art, Virtual Riot regularly showcases his favorite pieces on his social media accounts. This recognition not only validates the efforts of the artists but also inspires other fans to express their creativity. Additionally, Virtual Riot occasionally holds fan art contests, offering exciting prizes and the opportunity for artists to gain recognition within the community.

Fan art serves as a form of fan interaction, allowing fans to bond over their shared love for Virtual Riot's music. It creates a sense of community and belonging, fostering connections between artists and fans. The reception of fan art also provides valuable feedback and inspiration for Virtual Riot, showcasing the impact his music has on individuals.

Fan Covers

Fan covers are another way that fans show their appreciation for Virtual Riot's music. These covers involve fans reinterpreting Virtual Riot's tracks by performing their own versions. Fan covers can take multiple forms, including vocal renditions, instrumental performances, or even dance routines choreographed to Virtual Riot's music.

Artists within the Virtual Riot community often take on the challenge of recreating Virtual Riot's signature sound and style. Through their covers, they showcase their musical talent and interpret the emotions conveyed in Virtual Riot's music. These fan covers can be shared on various platforms, such as YouTube, SoundCloud, or TikTok, enabling fans to reach a wider audience.

Virtual Riot values the dedication and creativity of his fans, and he has been known to interact with and acknowledge fan covers on social media. By sharing fan covers, Virtual Riot amplifies the voices of his fans and gives them a platform to showcase their skills. This interaction deepens the connection between Virtual Riot and his fans, creating a mutual appreciation for the music.

Fan Remixes

Fan remixes take Virtual Riot's music to new heights by offering unique interpretations and reimaginations of his tracks. Remixes allow fans to experiment with Virtual Riot's stems and create their own versions, showcasing their production skills and creativity. These remixes span across different genres, showcasing the diversity of Virtual Riot's influence.

The Virtual Riot community embraces fan remixes, and many talented producers within the community take part in remix competitions organized by Virtual Riot himself. These competitions provide an opportunity for fans to showcase their skills and have their remixes recognized by Virtual Riot and other artists within the industry. Winning a remix competition can be a significant milestone for aspiring producers, propelling them into the spotlight.

Fan remixes not only demonstrate the talent within the Virtual Riot community but also contribute to the evolution of his music. By exploring different genres and experimenting with Virtual Riot's tracks, fan remixes push the boundaries of what is possible, inspiring Virtual Riot and other producers to innovate further.

Virtual Riot acknowledges the impact of fan remixes and often shares his favorite remixes on his social media platforms. This recognition not only showcases the talent of the fans but also fosters a sense of camaraderie within the community. The exchange of remixes between Virtual Riot and his fans strengthens the bond and fuels the creativity of both parties.

The Impact of Fan Art, Fan Covers, and Fan Remixes

Fan art, fan covers, and fan remixes play a crucial role in the Virtual Riot community, enriching the overall music experience for both fans and the artist himself. They bring the music to life visually, sonically, and creatively, creating a holistic and immersive experience for fans.

These fan creations reinforce the connection between Virtual Riot and his fans, providing a platform for them to express their admiration and appreciation for his music. They allow fans to actively participate in the music-making process, turning Virtual Riot's songs into shared experiences.

Additionally, fan art, fan covers, and fan remixes inspire Virtual Riot in his own creative journey. They showcase the impact his music has on others, providing valuable feedback and fuelling his motivation to continue pushing boundaries. The fan community becomes a collaborative and supportive space, where Virtual Riot can draw inspiration for future projects and explore new directions.

Overall, fan art, fan covers, and fan remixes serve as a testament to the power of Virtual Riot's music and the dedicated fanbase he has built. They highlight the profound influence his music has on individuals, fostering a community that celebrates creativity, diversity, and shared passion.

Fan Art, Fan Covers, and Fan Remixes - Resources and Tips

For fans interested in creating fan art, fan covers, or fan remixes, here are some valuable resources and tips:

- **Software and Tools:** Software such as Adobe Photoshop, Illustrator, or Pro Tools can be used for fan art, covers, and remixes, respectively. These tools offer advanced editing capabilities and provide a professional touch to your creations.

- **Tutorials and Online Communities:** Online platforms like YouTube and forums dedicated to fan art, covers, and remixes offer a wealth of tutorials and guidance. These resources can help you learn new techniques, improve your skills, and connect with fellow creators.

+ **Study Virtual Riot's Music:** To create authentic fan art, covers, or remixes, immerse yourself in Virtual Riot's music and understand his unique style. Analyze the different elements in his tracks, such as melodies, chord progressions, and sound design, to capture the essence of his sound.

+ **Experiment and Be Original:** Don't be afraid to take risks and explore your own creative ideas. Fan art, covers, and remixes are an opportunity to showcase your unique perspective and talents. Let your creativity shine and bring something new to the table.

+ **Engage with the Virtual Riot Community:** Share your creations on social media platforms and engage with the Virtual Riot community. Join communities and groups dedicated to fan art, covers, or remixes, where you can receive feedback, collaborate with others, and find inspiration.

Remember, fan art, fan covers, and fan remixes are a celebration of Virtual Riot's music and the community surrounding it. Enjoy the process, showcase your talent, and let your creativity soar.

Virtual Riot's Relationship with Fans

Virtual Riot's relationship with his fans is one of the pillars that has helped him build a strong and dedicated following. Through his music, performances, and active engagement on social media, Virtual Riot has created a tight-knit community that feels connected and valued.

Building a Fanbase on Social Media

Social media has played a significant role in Virtual Riot's journey as an artist, allowing him to connect with fans from all over the world. He understands the power of platforms like Twitter, Instagram, and YouTube in reaching and engaging with his audience.

Virtual Riot leverages social media to share updates about his music, upcoming shows, and personal experiences. However, what truly sets him apart is his authenticity and genuine connection with his fans. He takes the time to respond to comments, engage in conversations, and show appreciation for the support he receives. By giving his fans a glimpse into his life beyond music, he fosters a sense of closeness and relatability that fans deeply appreciate.

Engaging with Fans: Q&A Sessions and Live Streams

Virtual Riot takes fan engagement to another level by regularly hosting Q&A sessions and live-streamed events. These interactive sessions allow fans to ask him questions directly and get insights into his creative process, inspirations, and personal life.

During these Q&A sessions, Virtual Riot shares stories, provides advice, and discusses various topics that his fans find fascinating. This open dialogue not only strengthens the bond between Virtual Riot and his fans but also creates a community where fans can connect with each other.

Fan Art, Fan Covers, and Fan Remixes

Virtual Riot's fans are incredibly talented and passionate, and he deeply appreciates their support. He encourages fans to showcase their creativity by creating fan art, covers of his songs, and remixes of his tracks.

Virtual Riot actively seeks out fan-created content and regularly shares it on his social media platforms as a way to show appreciation for his fans' efforts. By doing so, he not only highlights the talent within his fanbase but also reinforces the idea that his fans are an essential part of his musical journey.

Virtual Riot's Relationship with Fans

Virtual Riot's relationship with his fans goes beyond the traditional artist-fan dynamic. He sees his fans as friends and collaborators, and he truly values their opinions and feedback. He actively seeks their input on his music, performances, and upcoming projects.

Virtual Riot understands that his fans play a vital role in shaping his career and success. Therefore, he constantly strives to create music and performances that resonate with them. He listens to their suggestions, constantly experiments with new sounds, and pushes the boundaries of his creativity to deliver an experience that exceeds their expectations.

Virtual Riot's Social Media Strategies

Virtual Riot's approach to social media is not just about self-promotion; it's about building relationships. He maintains an active presence on various platforms, regularly sharing meaningful and entertaining content with his fans.

He understands the importance of consistency, quality, and authenticity on social media. Virtual Riot maintains a balance between personal posts, updates about his music, and valuable content related to his industry. By offering a mix of insights into his daily life, behind-the-scenes footage, and sneak peeks into upcoming projects, he keeps his fans engaged and eager for more.

Virtual Riot's Favorite Fan Interactions

Virtual Riot has had many memorable fan interactions throughout his career. One of his favorite moments was during a live show when a group of fans surprised him by lifting a large banner with a heartfelt message. The genuine love and support he received from his fans in that moment deeply touched him and reminded him why he does what he does.

Another cherished fan interaction for Virtual Riot was when a young fan approached him after a show and shared how his music had helped her through a difficult time. Hearing firsthand how his music had made a positive impact on someone's life reaffirmed his passion and purpose as an artist.

Virtual Riot's Perspective on Fan Support

Virtual Riot considers his fans as the driving force behind his success. He believes that their unwavering support and dedication are what motivate him to continue pushing boundaries and evolving as an artist. Virtual Riot recognizes that without his fans, he would not have the opportunity to do what he loves on such a large scale.

He is incredibly grateful for the support he receives from his fans and considers himself fortunate to have such a passionate and engaged community. Virtual Riot often expresses his gratitude through heartfelt posts and interactions, knowing that his fans play an integral role in his journey.

Virtual Riot's Advice for Building an Online Fanbase

Based on his own experiences and interactions with his fans, Virtual Riot has valuable advice for aspiring artists looking to build a strong online fanbase:

1. Be authentic: Don't be afraid to show your true self and connect with your fans on a personal level. They appreciate honesty and genuine interactions.

2. Engage with your audience: Make an effort to respond to comments, messages, and fan creations. Show your fans that you value and acknowledge their support.

3. Consistency is key: Regularly share content that aligns with your brand and the interests of your audience. Maintain a consistent presence on social media to stay connected with your fans.

4. Collaborate with your fans: Encourage your fans to participate by creating fan art, covers, and remixes. Share their work and give them credit, fostering a sense of collaboration and community.

5. Show appreciation: Take time to express your gratitude for your fans' support. Whether it's through social media shoutouts, exclusive content, or meet and greets, let your fans know that you value them.

Virtual Riot's Influence on Social Media in the Music Industry

Virtual Riot's approach to social media has had a significant impact on the music industry. By prioritizing genuine connections with his fans, he has demonstrated the power of building an engaged and loyal online community.

Other artists have been inspired by Virtual Riot's success and have followed suit, focusing on developing authentic relationships with their fanbases. This shift in approach has reshaped the way artists and fans interact, creating a more intimate and inclusive environment in the music industry.

Virtual Riot's Impact on Fan Communities in Electronic Music

Virtual Riot's influence on fan communities in electronic music can be seen through the strong sense of camaraderie and support within his fanbase. Through his music and engagement, he has fostered an environment where fans feel connected not only to him but to each other.

Fans have formed their own communities, sharing their love for Virtual Riot's music and connecting with like-minded individuals. These communities often extend beyond Virtual Riot's music, evolving into platforms where fans discuss various aspects of electronic music and share their own work.

Conclusion

Virtual Riot's relationship with his fans is a testament to his understanding of the importance of building genuine connections in the music industry. Through his active engagement on social media, his open dialogue with fans, and his appreciation for their support, Virtual Riot has created a tight-knit community that is passionate, supportive, and loyal.

His approach serves as an inspiration for aspiring artists, highlighting the significance of authenticity, engagement, and gratitude in building and maintaining a strong fanbase. Virtual Riot's impact goes beyond his music, reshaping the way artists and fans interact and fostering a sense of community within the electronic music scene.

Virtual Riot's Social Media Strategies

Virtual Riot, also known as German music producer Christian Valentin Brunn, has become a prominent figure in the electronic dance music (EDM) scene. His success can largely be attributed to his effective use of social media platforms to connect with fans, promote his music, and build a strong online presence. In this section, we will explore Virtual Riot's social media strategies and the impact they have had on his career.

Building a Fanbase on Social Media

One of the cornerstones of Virtual Riot's social media strategy is building a strong and engaged fanbase. He understands the importance of connecting with his audience on a personal level and utilizes various platforms to accomplish this.

Virtual Riot actively maintains profiles on popular social media networks such as Twitter, Instagram, and Facebook. These platforms serve as channels for him to share updates about his music, upcoming shows, and personal insights. By regularly posting content and interacting with his followers, Virtual Riot has cultivated a dedicated fan community.

Engaging with Fans: Q&A Sessions and Live Streams

Virtual Riot takes his interaction with fans to the next level by hosting Q&A sessions and live streams. These interactive events allow his followers to directly engage with him, ask questions, and gain insights into his music production process.

During Q&A sessions, Virtual Riot sets aside time to answer fan questions, providing invaluable insights into his creative process, influences, and even personal anecdotes. This type of direct interaction not only strengthens his relationship with his fans but also humanizes his brand, making him more relatable and approachable.

Live streams are another integral part of Virtual Riot's social media strategy. Utilizing platforms such as Twitch or YouTube, Virtual Riot streams real-time music production sessions, giving fans a behind-the-scenes look at his creative process. This immersive experience allows his audience to feel involved and connected, fostering a sense of community.

Fan Art, Fan Covers, and Fan Remixes

Virtual Riot recognizes and appreciates the talent and creativity of his fan base. As a way to further engage with his fans, he actively promotes and shares fan-made content, including art, covers of his songs, and remixes.

By showcasing and celebrating fan creations, Virtual Riot not only strengthens the connection with his followers but also inspires them to continue creating and sharing their work. This strategy has helped foster a supportive and passionate community around his music.

Virtual Riot's Social Media Strategies

To ensure an effective social media presence, Virtual Riot employs several key strategies:

1. Consistency: Virtual Riot understands the importance of consistently posting high-quality content. He maintains regular posting schedules, ensuring that his fans always have fresh and engaging content to look forward to.

2. Visual Appeal: Virtual Riot leverages the power of visual media, ensuring that his posts are visually appealing and eye-catching. Whether it's sharing behind-the-scenes photos or professionally shot videos, he understands the impact of aesthetics in capturing his audience's attention.

3. Authenticity: Authenticity is at the core of Virtual Riot's social media strategy. He shares personal stories, experiences, and opinions, allowing his fans to connect with him on a deeper level.

4. Interaction: Virtual Riot values his fans' input and actively engages with them by responding to comments, direct messages, and fan submissions. This level of interaction makes his followers feel valued and appreciated.

5. Cross-Promotion: Virtual Riot strategically promotes his content across multiple platforms, ensuring maximum reach and visibility. By cross-promoting his music, videos, and social media content, he maximizes his chances of staying connected with his audience.

Virtual Riot's Impact on Fan Communities in Electronic Music

Virtual Riot's social media strategies have had a significant impact on fan communities within the electronic music scene. By actively engaging with his fans and encouraging their creativity, he has fostered a supportive and enthusiastic community centered around his music.

His approach has not only strengthened his relationship with his fans but has also inspired other artists to adopt similar strategies. The result is a vibrant and interconnected network of fans and artists, sharing their love for Virtual Riot's music and electronic music as a whole.

Virtual Riot's Influence on Social Media in the Music Industry

Virtual Riot's innovative use of social media has made a lasting impact on the music industry as a whole. His strategies have challenged traditional artist-fan relationships and paved the way for a new era of direct and authentic interactions.

Other artists and industry professionals have taken note of Virtual Riot's success and have started to adopt similar social media strategies. This shift towards more personal, interactive, and engaging social media presence has revolutionized the way artists connect with their fans and has become a staple of modern music marketing.

Virtual Riot's Advice for Building an Online Fanbase

Virtual Riot's success on social media has not come without effort. For aspiring artists looking to build their own online fanbase, he offers the following advice:

1. Be Consistent: Regularly update your social media profiles with high-quality content to keep your audience engaged and interested.

2. Interact with Your Fans: Show genuine interest in your fans' opinions and creations. Respond to comments, messages, and fan submissions, building a stronger connection with your audience.

3. Embrace Authenticity: Be yourself and share your personal stories and experiences. Authenticity is what resonates most with your fans and sets you apart from others.

4. Explore Different Platforms: Don't limit yourself to a single platform. Explore various social media networks to reach a broader audience.

5. Encourage Fan Engagement: Foster a sense of community by actively promoting and sharing fan-generated content. Acknowledge and celebrate the creativity of your fans.

By implementing these strategies, artists can build a dedicated and supportive online fanbase that will continue to grow and thrive.

Virtual Riot's Influence on Social Media Trends

Virtual Riot's innovative use of social media has had a far-reaching influence on trends within the industry. His authentic and engaged approach to connecting with fans has become a benchmark for other artists.

As a result of Virtual Riot's impact, the music industry has seen a shift towards artists prioritizing direct fan interaction and engagement. Increasingly, artists are utilizing social media platforms as a means to humanize their brand, deepen connections with fans, and ultimately drive their success.

Virtual Riot's Impact on Social Media Strategy

The impact of Virtual Riot's social media strategy goes beyond his own success. His innovative approach has inspired artists and industry professionals to rethink their social media strategies and explore new ways to engage with their audience.

From fostering creative communities to recognizing the value of fan-generated content, Virtual Riot's influence on social media strategy has shaped industry-wide practices. His legacy will continue to be felt as artists embrace the power of authenticity and direct fan interaction in their own social media endeavors.

In summary, Virtual Riot's social media strategies revolve around building a strong and engaged fanbase, engaging with fans through Q&A sessions and live streams, promoting and sharing fan-made content, and employing consistency, visual appeal, authenticity, and interaction in his social media presence. His impact on fan communities and the music industry as a whole has revolutionized the way artists approach social media, inspiring others to adopt similar strategies that prioritize direct fan interaction and authenticity.

Virtual Riot's Favorite Fan Interactions

Virtual Riot, with his charming personality and genuine love for his fans, has had numerous memorable interactions with his dedicated supporters. Whether it's through social media platforms or during live shows, Virtual Riot always goes above and beyond to engage with his fans and create lasting connections. Let's dive into some of his favorite fan interactions and the unique experiences he has had with his devoted followers.

1. **TikTok Challenges:** One of Virtual Riot's favorite fan interactions is through TikTok challenges. He loves seeing his fans' creativity and unique interpretations of his music. From dance challenges to lip-syncing to his tracks, his fans always impress him with their talent and enthusiasm. Virtual Riot often shares his favorite TikTok videos featuring his music, giving his fans a chance to be recognized and showcased to a wider audience.

2. **Fan Art Appreciation:** Virtual Riot is continually blown away by the incredible fan art that his followers create. From digital illustrations to handmade paintings, his fans showcase their artistic skills and express their love for his music through visual creations. Virtual Riot takes the time to acknowledge and appreciate this fan art by sharing it on his social media platforms, expressing his gratitude and admiration for their talent.

3. **Personalized Messages:** Virtual Riot understands the impact of a personalized message. It is not uncommon for him to surprise his fans with

heartfelt messages on special occasions such as birthdays or milestone achievements. Whether it's a direct message on social media or a personalized video shoutout, Virtual Riot's fans are often left in awe by his thoughtfulness and genuine care for each and every one of them.

4. **Meet and Greets:** Virtual Riot holds meet and greets during his tours, offering his fans a chance to meet him in person and have a one-on-one interaction. These intimate sessions allow fans to share their stories, express their gratitude, and even ask questions. Virtual Riot enjoys these meet and greets as they provide him with an opportunity to connect with his fans on a deeper level, learning about the impact his music has had on their lives.

5. **Fan Remixes and Collaborations:** Virtual Riot actively encourages his fans to get involved in the music-making process. He often runs remix contests for his tracks, giving aspiring producers a chance to showcase their skills and potentially collaborate with him. Virtual Riot listens to each remix and selects his favorites, sometimes even collaborating with the winners to release the remix officially. By involving his fans directly in his music, Virtual Riot forms a strong bond and fosters a community of mutual creativity and inspiration.

6. **Q&A Sessions:** Virtual Riot values transparency and authenticity, which is why he regularly hosts Q&A sessions on his social media platforms. Fans can ask him anything, ranging from his musical influences to his favorite hobbies outside of music. Virtual Riot takes the time to answer as many questions as possible, providing his fans with glimpses into his life and career. These Q&A sessions not only help his fans get to know him better but also create a sense of unity and trust within the fan community.

7. **Surprise Fan Encounters:** Virtual Riot truly appreciates the support he receives from his fans and makes an effort to acknowledge them whenever he can. Whether it's spotting a long-time supporter at a show and inviting them backstage or surprising fans by appearing at fan-led events, Virtual Riot loves creating unexpected and magical moments for his fans. These surprise encounters not only make his fans' day but also leave a lasting impression on him as an artist.

Virtual Riot's dedication to his fans goes beyond the music itself. He believes in building genuine relationships and fostering a sense of community. By actively engaging with his fans through various platforms, in-person interactions, and collaborative opportunities, Virtual Riot creates an inclusive and supportive environment that not only celebrates his music but also showcases the incredible talents and stories of his fans. For Virtual Riot, his fans are the driving force behind his success, and he treasures each and every interaction he has with them.

Virtual Riot's Perspective on Fan Support

To fully understand Virtual Riot's perspective on fan support, we need to delve into the deep connection he has with his fans and the impact they have on his career. Virtual Riot values and cherishes his fans, recognizing that they are the lifeblood of his success. In this section, we'll explore how fan support has played a significant role in shaping Virtual Riot's journey as an artist and how he reciprocates their love and dedication.

Fan support extends far beyond simply enjoying and sharing Virtual Riot's music. It encompasses the immense loyalty and passion that his fans demonstrate in various aspects of his career. Virtual Riot acknowledges and appreciates the support he receives at every step, from his online presence to his live performances and charitable endeavors. Let's dive deeper into the key elements of Virtual Riot's perspective on fan support.

Building a Fanbase on Social Media

In the digital age, social media has become a powerful tool for artists to connect with their fans. Virtual Riot recognizes this and actively engages with his fans through various platforms like Twitter, Instagram, and YouTube. He values the direct interaction with his followers, taking the time to respond to comments and messages, and sharing snippets of his daily life. By cultivating a strong online presence, Virtual Riot is able to foster a sense of community and make his fans feel seen and appreciated.

Engaging with Fans: Q&A Sessions and Live Streams

Virtual Riot goes above and beyond to connect with his fans by hosting Q&A sessions and live streams. These interactive sessions allow fans to ask questions, share their thoughts, and gain insights into Virtual Riot's creative process. By openly communicating and sharing his thoughts, Virtual Riot builds a strong bond with his fans, creating a unique level of trust and authenticity.

Fan Art, Fan Covers, and Fan Remixes

One of the most heartwarming aspects of fan support is the incredible creativity it inspires. Virtual Riot's fans demonstrate their love and admiration by creating fan art, covers of his songs, and remixes of his tracks. Virtual Riot deeply values and showcases these fan creations, recognizing that they are a testament to the impact his music has on his audience. By sharing fan art and featuring fan remixes, Virtual Riot actively uplifts and highlights the talents of his dedicated fans.

Virtual Riot's Relationship with Fans

Virtual Riot views his relationship with his fans as a two-way street. He sees them not just as supporters but as a vital part of his creative process. The feedback and energy he receives from his fans fuel his motivation to consistently push boundaries and explore new musical territories. Whether it's positive messages, concert attendance, or even constructive criticism, Virtual Riot embraces all forms of fan input and considers it an essential component of his growth as an artist.

Virtual Riot's Social Media Strategies

Virtual Riot utilizes social media strategically to foster a genuine connection with his fans. He believes in maintaining transparency and authenticity, avoiding the pitfalls of artificiality that can often come with fame. Virtual Riot actively seeks to create a welcoming space where fans feel comfortable expressing themselves and sharing their experiences. By nurturing this environment, Virtual Riot engenders a strong sense of community among his fans.

Virtual Riot's Favorite Fan Interactions

Virtual Riot cherishes the unique and unexpected interactions he has with his fans. He embraces opportunities to meet them during meet-and-greets, fan conventions, or chance encounters. Virtual Riot recognizes that these personal connections leave a lasting impact not only on his fans but on himself as well. From heartfelt stories of how his music has positively influenced their lives to the joyous moments of seeing fans singing and dancing to his songs, these interactions drive his passion and remind him of the true purpose and impact of his art.

Virtual Riot's Perspective on Fan Support

Virtual Riot deeply values the incredible support he receives from his fans. He emphasizes that fan support extends far beyond superficial metrics like streaming numbers or ticket sales. For him, it's about the emotional connection and the shared love for music. It's about the incredible dedication and inspiration his fans provide. He sees his fans as a collective force that empowers and drives him to keep pushing the boundaries of his art.

Virtual Riot's Advice for Building an Online Fanbase

Virtual Riot encourages aspiring artists to focus on building authentic connections with their fans. He emphasizes the importance of actively engaging with fans on social media, responding to messages and comments, and showcasing fan-created content. Virtual Riot believes that by treating fans as valuable individuals and fostering a sense of community, artists can create a loyal and supportive fanbase that will be with them throughout their journey.

Virtual Riot's Influence on Social Media in the Music Industry

Virtual Riot's approach to fan support has had a significant impact on the music industry as a whole. By prioritizing genuine connections and meaningful interactions, he has set an example for other artists to follow. Virtual Riot's success demonstrates that cultivating a dedicated fanbase goes beyond mere numbers and holds the potential to create a thriving and supportive community.

Virtual Riot's Impact on Fan Communities in Electronic Music

Virtual Riot's influence extends beyond his own fanbase. By prioritizing fan support and engagement, he has contributed to the overall growth and vibrancy of fan communities in electronic music. His example has inspired other artists to foster deeper connections with their fans, leading to a more engaged and passionate global fanbase for the genre.

In conclusion, Virtual Riot's perspective on fan support is one of immense gratitude and appreciation. He values the passion, creativity, and dedication of his fans, recognizing that they are the backbone of his success. Through his online presence, live performances, and genuine interactions, Virtual Riot actively contributes to and nurtures a thriving community of fans. His approach to fan support sets an example for aspiring artists and has had a lasting impact on the music industry as a whole.

Virtual Riot's Advice for Building an Online Fanbase

Building an online fanbase is crucial for any artist in today's music industry. With the rise of social media and digital platforms, artists have an unprecedented opportunity to connect with their fans on a global scale. Virtual Riot understands the importance of cultivating a strong online presence and has valuable advice for emerging artists looking to build their own fanbase.

Authenticity is Key

One of the fundamental principles Virtual Riot emphasizes is the importance of being authentic.   Building an online fanbase requires establishing a genuine connection with your audience.   Virtual Riot advises artists to stay true to themselves and their unique style. Trying to imitate others or cater to trends may lead to short-term success, but it won't sustain a loyal fanbase in the long run.

Consistent and Engaging Content

Consistency is key when it comes to building an online fanbase.   Virtual Riot recommends establishing a regular schedule for content creation and distribution. Whether it's music releases, behind-the-scenes footage, or live streams, it's essential to consistently engage your audience.   Additionally, engaging with fans through comments, messages, and Q&A sessions helps foster a sense of community and strengthens the connection between the artist and the fans.

Leverage Social Media Platforms

Social media platforms play a massive role in building an online fanbase. Virtual Riot advises artists to identify the platforms that their target audience frequents the most and focus on building a strong presence there. Whether it's Instagram, Twitter, YouTube, or TikTok, each platform offers unique opportunities to showcase your personality and connect with fans. Utilize the features of each platform effectively, such as using hashtags, stories, or live streams to maximize your reach.

Collaborate with Other Artists and Communities

Collaboration can be a powerful tool for building an online fanbase. Virtual Riot suggests exploring collaborations with other artists who share a similar fanbase. This allows you to tap into their audience and expose yourself to new fans. Additionally, participating in online communities and forums centered around your genre or niche can help you connect with like-minded individuals and potential fans.   Actively engaging with these communities by sharing your knowledge, providing feedback, and supporting others will help you establish yourself as an influential figure in your field.

Deliver Value and Create Connections

To build a loyal fanbase, Virtual Riot stresses the importance of consistently delivering value. This can be done through various means, such as providing exclusive content, hosting contests or giveaways, and offering behind-the-scenes glimpses into your creative process. By going above and beyond to provide value to your fans, you create a sense of reciprocity and strengthen their loyalty. Moreover, creating connections with your fans on a personal level is key. Show genuine interest in their lives, respond to their messages and comments, and make them feel seen and heard. Building a community that feels connected to you as an artist will lead to long-lasting support.

Utilize Analytics and Data

In today's digital age, data is readily available and can provide valuable insights into your fanbase. Virtual Riot advises artists to utilize analytics tools provided by social media platforms to understand their audience demographics, engagement patterns, and content preferences. This data can help you tailor your content strategy to better resonate with your fans. Furthermore, tracking the performance of your online campaigns, music releases, and social media posts can help you identify what works and what doesn't, allowing you to refine your approach and maximize your impact.

Think Outside the Box

While there are established strategies for building an online fanbase, Virtual Riot encourages artists to think outside the box and find innovative approaches that align with their unique brand. Whether it's leveraging emerging platforms, utilizing new technologies, or creating interactive experiences for fans, pushing boundaries and being open to experimentation can set you apart from the crowd and attract a dedicated fanbase.

Embrace Collaboration with Fans

Lastly, Virtual Riot emphasizes the importance of collaboration with your fans. Engage with fan art, fan covers, and remixes, and share them on your platforms. Encourage your fans to actively participate and contribute to your creative journey. By involving your fans directly, you not only strengthen the fan-artist relationship but also empower your fans to become ambassadors for your music, amplifying your reach and impact.

Building an online fanbase is a journey that requires dedication, authenticity, and a deep understanding of your audience. By staying true to yourself, consistently creating engaging content, leveraging social media platforms, collaborating with other artists and communities, delivering value, utilizing analytics and data, thinking outside the box, and embracing collaboration with fans, you can lay a solid foundation for building a strong and dedicated fanbase online.

Remember, building an online fanbase takes time and effort, so be patient, stay focused, and enjoy the process. Your fans are out there, waiting to discover and support your unique journey as an artist.

Virtual Riot's Influence on Social Media in the Music Industry

Social media has become an essential tool for musicians and artists to connect with their fans and promote their work. In the music industry, having a strong presence on social media can make a significant impact on an artist's career. Virtual Riot, known for his innovative electronic music and energetic performances, has certainly made his mark on social media platforms. Let's explore how Virtual Riot has influenced social media in the music industry and the strategies he has employed to engage with his fans.

One of the key ways Virtual Riot has influenced social media in the music industry is by leveraging various platforms to cultivate an active and dedicated fan base. He understands that each social media platform has its own unique features and audience, and he uses this knowledge to tailor his content for maximum impact. Whether it's sharing updates on upcoming projects, behind-the-scenes glimpses of his creative process, or interacting with fans, Virtual Riot makes a conscious effort to keep his fans engaged across different social media channels.

Virtual Riot's presence on platforms such as Instagram, Twitter, and Facebook has allowed him to build a strong and diverse online community. He connects with his fans by regularly posting updates, sharing personal insights, and fostering a sense of camaraderie. Whether it's responding to fan comments, hosting live Q&A sessions, or running exclusive giveaways, Virtual Riot actively engages with his followers and creates a sense of belonging within his virtual community.

In addition to engaging with fans directly, Virtual Riot also utilizes social media to promote his music, collaborations, and upcoming shows. He understands that social media platforms provide a powerful promotional tool to reach a wide audience and generate excitement. By strategically releasing sneak peeks, behind-the-scenes footage, and teasers, he builds anticipation and generates buzz around his music releases and live performances.

Virtual Riot's approach to social media is not just about self-promotion. He recognizes the importance of supporting and uplifting other artists in the music industry. He regularly showcases the work of fellow musicians, shares remixes and covers of his own songs created by fans, and collaborates with other artists through social media. This not only helps him nurture relationships within the industry but also supports and encourages emerging talent.

One of the unconventional strategies that Virtual Riot has employed on social media is the use of interactive content to engage with his fans. For instance, he has organized remix contests, where fans can submit their own remixes of his songs, with the winners receiving recognition and sometimes even the opportunity to release their remixes officially. This not only fosters creativity within his fan base but also creates a sense of community and shared enthusiasm for his music.

Furthermore, Virtual Riot understands the importance of staying on top of the ever-evolving trends and features of social media platforms. He keeps up with the latest updates, algorithms, and engagement strategies to ensure that his content reaches the maximum number of people. By adapting to the changing landscape of social media, he maximizes his reach and maintains relevance in an increasingly competitive industry.

While Virtual Riot's impact on social media in the music industry is undeniable, it is important to note that success on social media does not solely determine an artist's talent or worth. It is merely a means to connect with fans and promote one's work. Virtual Riot's influence on social media goes beyond just numbers and followers. He has created a genuine connection with his fans and fostered a supportive and engaged community.

In conclusion, Virtual Riot's influence on social media in the music industry is significant. Through his strategic and engaging social media presence, he has cultivated a loyal fan base, promoted his music and collaborations, supported emerging artists, and adapted to the ever-changing landscape of social media platforms. His approach serves as an inspiration for aspiring musicians and artists to use social media not just as a promotional tool but as a means to connect with fans on a deeper level.

Virtual Riot's Impact on Fan Communities in Electronic Music

Virtual Riot has undeniably had a profound impact on fan communities in electronic music. Through his innovative approach to music production and captivating performances, he has cultivated a dedicated and passionate following that extends beyond just listening to his music. In this section, we will explore how Virtual Riot has influenced fan communities in electronic music and the lasting effects of his impact.

Creating an Inclusive Space

One of the reasons why Virtual Riot has such a strong and supportive fan community is his commitment to creating an inclusive space for music lovers. He actively encourages collaboration and engagement among his fans, fostering a sense of belonging and unity. This has not only resulted in a lively and active online community but also led to offline meetups and gatherings where fans connect and bond over their shared love for his music.

Virtual Riot's welcoming and inclusive approach has inspired fans to be more open-minded and accepting of different genres and styles of electronic music. By encouraging exploration and experimentation, he has broadened the horizons of his fans and exposed them to new sounds and artists they may not have otherwise discovered. This has not only enriched their musical experiences but also created a vibrant and diverse community that celebrates the unity in diversity.

Deepening Fan Engagement

Virtual Riot understands the importance of maintaining a strong connection with his fans. He actively engages with them on social media, hosting Q&A sessions and live streams, and taking the time to respond to comments and messages. This level of interaction and accessibility has fostered a sense of connection and intimacy between Virtual Riot and his fans, making them feel valued and appreciated.

Beyond just social media, Virtual Riot goes the extra mile to deepen fan engagement. He encourages fan art, fan covers, and fan remixes, showcasing and promoting their work on his platforms. This not only boosts the confidence and creativity of his fans but also creates a community where everyone's contributions are celebrated. The sense of ownership and involvement empowers fans to feel like an integral part of the Virtual Riot experience.

Supporting Up-and-Coming Artists

Virtual Riot recognizes the importance of nurturing and supporting emerging talent within the electronic music community. His influence extends beyond just his fans and reaches aspiring producers and musicians looking to make their mark. By collaborating with and mentoring young artists, Virtual Riot provides them with a platform to showcase their skills and gain exposure.

Through remix competitions and featured artist opportunities, Virtual Riot actively seeks out new talent and provides them with opportunities to grow. He serves as an inspiration for aspiring artists, demonstrating that hard work, dedication, and creativity can lead to recognition and success. This support for up-and-coming artists not only strengthens the electronic music community but also ensures its continuous growth and evolution.

Promoting Positive Values

Virtual Riot's impact on fan communities goes beyond just his music. He uses his platform to promote positive values and inspire his fans to make a difference. Through charitable work and donations, he encourages his fans to give back to society and support causes they believe in. This emphasis on philanthropy fosters a sense of social responsibility and encourages fans to use their passion for music as a force for positive change.

Moreover, Virtual Riot champions inclusivity, acceptance, and authenticity, breaking down stereotypes and promoting equality within the electronic music community. His unwavering commitment to these values has helped shift the narrative surrounding electronic music and create a more inclusive and diverse space where everyone feels welcome.

Unconventional Problem: Breaking Barriers through Online Platforms

Virtual Riot's impact on fan communities can be seen as an unconventional problem in the context of breaking barriers through online platforms. With the advent of digital technology and the rise of social media, Virtual Riot has leveraged these tools to transcend geographical boundaries and connect with fans from all around the world. This has not only allowed him to grow his fan base exponentially but has also created a global community of electronic music enthusiasts.

However, the challenge lies in maintaining a personal connection and sense of community despite the virtual nature of these interactions. Virtual Riot has successfully tackled this problem by actively engaging with fans through live streams and virtual meetups, simulating the experience of a physical gathering. By incorporating interactive elements and encouraging fan participation, he has bridged the gap between the online and offline worlds, creating a sense of togetherness and intimacy among his fans.

In conclusion, Virtual Riot's impact on fan communities in electronic music is undeniable. Through his inclusive approach, deep fan engagement, support for aspiring artists, promotion of positive values, and ability to break barriers through online platforms, he has created a fan community that is not only passionate about his music but also fosters a sense of unity, diversity, and empowerment. His influence will continue to shape the electronic music landscape for years to come, inspiring and uplifting fans and artists alike.

Virtual Riot's Impact on the EDM Scene

Influencing Young Producers and Artists

Being a trailblazer in the electronic dance music (EDM) scene, Virtual Riot has had a significant impact on young producers and artists around the world. Through his innovative sound and unique approach to music production, he has inspired countless individuals to explore their creativity and push the boundaries of the genre. In this section, we will delve into how Virtual Riot has influenced a new wave of young talent and shaped the future of EDM.

Inspiration and Motivation

One of the key ways Virtual Riot has influenced young producers and artists is by serving as a source of inspiration and motivation. His groundbreaking tracks, such as "Energy Drink" and "We're Not Alone," have captivated listeners with their intricate sound design and infectious energy. Aspiring producers look up to Virtual Riot as a role model, aiming to reach the same level of production prowess and creativity.

Virtual Riot's success story is a testament to the power of determination and hard work. As a self-taught musician, he has proven that anyone with a passion for music can achieve great things. Young producers and artists find solace in his journey, realizing that they too can overcome obstacles and make their mark in the industry.

Technical Expertise and Production Techniques

Virtual Riot's influence on young producers extends beyond inspiration. He has also shared his technical expertise and production techniques, enabling aspiring artists to enhance their skills and refine their sound. Through tutorials, workshops, and masterclasses, Virtual Riot has equipped the next generation with the knowledge they need to excel in the world of EDM.

One of the areas where Virtual Riot has had a significant impact is sound design. His ability to craft intricate and unique soundscapes has set him apart from the crowd. Through tutorials and demonstrations, Virtual Riot has enlightened young producers on the art of sound design, teaching them how to create their own signature sounds.

Furthermore, Virtual Riot has embraced technology to its fullest extent, incorporating cutting-edge tools and software into his production process. His mastery of software synthesizers, digital audio workstations, and effects plugins has inspired young producers to explore new possibilities and experiment with different techniques.

Breaking Boundaries and Challenging Conventions

In addition to technical expertise, Virtual Riot has encouraged young producers and artists to break boundaries and challenge conventions in the EDM scene. His willingness to blend genres and experiment with unconventional sounds has inspired a wave of innovation in electronic music.

Traditionally, EDM has been associated with specific subgenres and formulaic structures. However, Virtual Riot's music defies categorization, seamlessly blending elements of dubstep, drum and bass, electro, and more. This has encouraged young producers to embrace their unique influences and create music that transcends genre boundaries.

Moreover, Virtual Riot's willingness to challenge conventions in terms of song structures and arrangement has opened up new avenues for young artists to explore. By deviating from traditional EDM song structures, he has inspired young producers to experiment with different arrangements and push the boundaries of what is considered "standard" in the genre.

Collaboration and Mentorship

Virtual Riot's commitment to collaboration and mentorship has also played a vital role in influencing young producers and artists. He has actively sought out opportunities to collaborate with emerging talent, providing a platform for them to showcase their abilities and gain exposure.

Through these collaborations, Virtual Riot has not only elevated the work of his peers but has also inspired young producers to seek out collaborative opportunities in their own careers. By working alongside established artists, they can learn from their experience, broaden their networks, and further develop their skills.

Furthermore, Virtual Riot has embraced the role of a mentor, readily offering advice and guidance to young producers and artists. Whether through social media interactions, Q&A sessions, or mentorship programs, he has provided valuable insights and support to emerging talent, helping them navigate the challenges of the music industry.

Pushing for Diversity and Representation

Lastly, Virtual Riot has made significant efforts to promote diversity and representation within the EDM scene. By actively collaborating with artists from different backgrounds and cultures, he has created a more inclusive and diverse environment for aspiring producers and artists.

Through his actions, Virtual Riot has shown young producers that their voices are valid and that they too can make an impact in the industry, regardless of their background or identity. This has helped break down barriers and inspire young talent who may have previously felt underrepresented or marginalized.

Additionally, Virtual Riot's advocacy for diversity has prompted a broader conversation within the EDM community about the importance of inclusivity and representation. By using his platform to spread awareness, he has encouraged others to be more conscious of the voices and stories that need to be heard.

Conclusion

Influencing young producers and artists is a responsibility that Virtual Riot has embraced wholeheartedly. Through his inspiration, technical expertise, boundary-breaking approach, collaboration, mentorship, and promotion of diversity, he has left an indelible mark on the next generation of EDM talent.

Aspiring producers and artists continue to be motivated by his success story and learn from his technical prowess. By pushing boundaries and challenging conventions, Virtual Riot encourages young talent to explore their creativity and develop their unique sound. Through collaboration and mentorship, he paves the way for emerging artists to find their place in the industry.

Moreover, Virtual Riot's commitment to diversity and representation creates a more inclusive and equitable environment, inspiring young producers and artists from all backgrounds to pursue their dreams. With his enduring influence, Virtual Riot's impact on the future of EDM is poised to be long-lasting and far-reaching.

Shaping the Sound and Direction of EDM

In the ever-evolving music landscape, few artists have had as profound an impact on a genre as Virtual Riot has had on the world of electronic dance music (EDM). With his innovative sound and forward-thinking approach, Virtual Riot has played a crucial role in shaping the sound and direction of EDM.

Breaking Boundaries with Genre Fusion

One of the defining characteristics of Virtual Riot's music is his ability to seamlessly blend different genres together. He effortlessly combines elements of dubstep, electro house, drum and bass, and future bass, to name just a few. This genre fusion has opened up new possibilities and pushed the boundaries of EDM.

By breaking down the barriers between genres, Virtual Riot has created a unique and distinct style that is instantly recognizable. His tracks are a melting pot of influences, resulting in a sound that is both familiar and innovative. This ability to blend different genres has not only expanded the sonic palette of EDM but has also inspired a new generation of producers to experiment with genre fusion.

Expanding the Soundscapes of EDM

Virtual Riot's impact on the sound of EDM goes beyond genre fusion. He is known for his intricate sound design, creating complex and textured soundscapes that transport listeners to another world. From ethereal melodies to earth-shattering basslines, his tracks are a journey through sound.

This attention to detail in sound design has set a new standard for EDM producers. Virtual Riot's meticulous approach has inspired artists to experiment with sound manipulation and explore new sonic territories. Whether it's crafting unique synth patches or creating unconventional sound effects, his influence can be heard throughout the EDM landscape.

Innovation in Song Structure and Arrangement

In addition to pushing the boundaries of genre and sound design, Virtual Riot has also brought innovation to song structure and arrangement in EDM. He is known for his dynamic and unpredictable compositions, constantly keeping the listener engaged and surprised.

Virtual Riot's tracks often feature unconventional song structures, with unexpected twists and turns that defy traditional EDM formulas. He experiments with different tempos, time signatures, and transitions, creating a sense of excitement and unpredictability.

This approach to song structure has not only challenged the status quo in EDM but has also inspired other producers to think outside the box. It has encouraged artists to break free from the constraints of traditional song structures and explore new possibilities in arrangement and composition.

Embracing the Future of EDM

As an artist at the forefront of the EDM scene, Virtual Riot has always embraced the future. He actively seeks out new technologies and production techniques to push the boundaries of what is possible in electronic music.

From incorporating virtual reality elements into his live performances to experimenting with cutting-edge software and equipment, Virtual Riot is constantly searching for new ways to enhance the EDM experience. This forward-thinking approach has not only influenced the sound of EDM but has also shaped its direction, paving the way for future innovations in the genre.

The Unconventional Path to Success

Virtual Riot's journey to success in the EDM scene has been far from conventional. He rose to prominence through the power of the internet and social media, harnessing the digital landscape to build a dedicated fanbase.

Rather than rely on traditional record labels or mainstream media, Virtual Riot took matters into his own hands, self-releasing his music and connecting directly with his fans. This independent and DIY approach to music distribution and promotion has inspired other artists to take control of their own careers and explore alternative paths to success.

In summary, Virtual Riot's impact on the sound and direction of EDM cannot be overstated. His genre fusion, innovative sound design, unconventional song structures, and forward-thinking approach have left an indelible mark on the genre. Through his music, he continues to shape the future of EDM, inspiring both established artists and emerging producers to push the boundaries and explore new horizons.

The Virtual Riot Effect: A New Wave of Creativity

The impact of Virtual Riot on the electronic dance music (EDM) scene cannot be understated. With his unique sound and boundary-pushing approach to music production, he has sparked a new wave of creativity that has inspired countless producers and artists. In this section, we will explore the Virtual Riot effect and its influence on the evolution of EDM.

Redefining the Sound of EDM

Virtual Riot's music is characterized by its bold and innovative sound. He seamlessly blends elements of dubstep, electro-house, and drum and bass to create a style that is uniquely his own. His tracks are characterized by heavy basslines, intricate melodies, and expertly crafted sound design.

By pushing the boundaries of sound, Virtual Riot has challenged the traditional notions of what EDM can be. He has shown that experimentation and genre fusion can lead to groundbreaking creations. As a result, a new generation of producers has been inspired to break free from established norms and explore the limitless possibilities of electronic music.

Inspiring a Wave of Creativity

The Virtual Riot effect has manifested in the form of a wave of creativity within the EDM community. Producers and artists have been emboldened to step outside their comfort zones and take risks in their music. They have been inspired to experiment with new sounds, genres, and production techniques.

This wave of creativity has led to the emergence of fresh and exciting music that pushes the boundaries of EDM even further. Producers are incorporating elements from diverse genres such as hip-hop, trap, and future bass into their tracks, resulting in a rich and eclectic musical landscape.

Virtual Riot's influence can be seen not only in the music itself but also in the way artists approach their craft. His dedication to pushing the limits of technology and sound design has encouraged others to explore new production techniques and embrace innovation.

Collaborative Projects and Collective Growth

Virtual Riot's impact on the EDM scene extends beyond his individual work. He has also actively collaborated with other artists, sharing his knowledge and expertise to elevate the collective growth of the community.

Through collaborations, Virtual Riot has fostered an environment of learning and mentorship. By working closely with other producers and artists, he has encouraged the exchange of ideas and the exploration of new musical territories. This collaborative spirit has not only resulted in groundbreaking tracks but has also inspired a sense of camaraderie within the EDM community.

The Virtual Riot effect has shown that by coming together and sharing knowledge, artists can collectively push the boundaries of their craft. This collaborative approach has led to the growth and evolution of EDM as a genre, and has opened up new possibilities for future music production.

Embracing Innovation and Technology

Virtual Riot is known for his innovative use of technology in his music production. He embraces cutting-edge software, plugins, and hardware to create unique and immersive soundscapes. His dedication to pushing the limits of technology has had a profound impact on the EDM scene.

By constantly exploring new tools and techniques, Virtual Riot has inspired other producers to embrace innovation in their own music production. Artists are now more open to experimenting with new software, exploring unconventional production techniques, and embracing emerging technologies such as virtual reality and augmented reality.

The Virtual Riot effect has led to a reimagining of what is possible in music production. Producers are no longer bound by traditional methods but are empowered to think outside the box and use technology as a tool for creative expression.

The Future of EDM: A Collaborative, Innovative, and Diverse Landscape

The Virtual Riot effect has redefined the future of EDM. The genre is no longer limited to the constraints of a single sound or style. Instead, it has become a melting pot of creativity, collaboration, and innovation.

As the EDM community continues to embrace the Virtual Riot effect, we can expect to see even more diverse and boundary-pushing music. Artists will continue to experiment with different genres, fuse styles, and incorporate new technologies into their productions.

The future of EDM is a collaborative one, where artists come together to create something greater than the sum of its parts. It is an innovative landscape where technology and creativity merge to create immersive and engaging musical experiences.

Virtual Riot's influence will continue to shape the EDM scene for years to come, inspiring new generations of producers and pushing the boundaries of what is possible in electronic music. As the Virtual Riot effect ripples through the industry, we can only imagine the exciting possibilities that lie ahead.

Virtual Riot's Perspective on the Evolution of EDM

When Virtual Riot reflects on the evolution of EDM (Electronic Dance Music), one thing is clear: the genre has gone through a tremendous transformation over the years. From its humble beginnings in small underground clubs to its current status as a global phenomenon, EDM has continuously evolved and adapted to the ever-changing musical landscape.

The early days of EDM were characterized by raw and experimental sounds. It was a time of innovation and pushing boundaries, where artists like Virtual Riot paved the way for a new wave of creativity. As technology advanced, so did the possibilities for electronic music production. Virtual Riot recalls a time when his music was limited to a few synthesizers and a computer, but now the options are virtually limitless.

One of the most significant changes in the evolution of EDM has been the fusion of different musical genres. Virtual Riot believes that this cross-pollination of styles has been instrumental in pushing the boundaries of the genre. By incorporating elements of dubstep, drum and bass, trap, and even classical music, Virtual Riot has been able to create a unique and diverse sound that resonates with a wide range of listeners.

Virtual Riot also recognizes the impact of technology on the evolution of EDM. From the early days of analog synthesizers to the rise of digital production software, technology has played a crucial role in shaping the sound of EDM. It has allowed artists like Virtual Riot to experiment with new sounds, create complex arrangements, and push the limits of what is possible in electronic music.

The democratization of music production has also had a profound effect on the evolution of EDM. With accessible software and equipment, aspiring producers from all walks of life can now create their own music and share it with the world. This has led to a surge in creativity and diversity within the genre, as artists have the freedom to explore their own unique sound.

Virtual Riot believes that the future of EDM lies in continued experimentation and embracing new technologies. As virtual reality, augmented reality, and artificial intelligence become more prevalent, the possibilities for immersive and interactive music experiences are endless. Virtual Riot envisions a future where live performances incorporate these technologies, creating a truly multi-sensory experience for the audience.

In terms of production techniques, Virtual Riot encourages aspiring producers to continually push the boundaries and think outside the box. He believes that innovation comes from exploring new sounds, techniques, and approaches to music-making. By experimenting with different genres, instruments, and production methods, artists can create fresh and exciting tracks that keep the genre moving forward.

While Virtual Riot is excited about the future of EDM, he also acknowledges the importance of staying true to the roots of the genre. Despite its mainstream success, EDM should never lose its underground spirit and authenticity. Virtual Riot believes that it is crucial to maintain a balance between commercial appeal and artistic integrity, always striving to create music that resonates with both the mainstream audience and the dedicated EDM community.

In conclusion, Virtual Riot's perspective on the evolution of EDM is one of excitement, innovation, and a commitment to pushing the boundaries of the genre. From the early days of experimentation to the fusion of different genres and the impact of technology, EDM has come a long way. Virtual Riot's vision for the future of EDM is one of continued exploration, embracing new technologies, and maintaining the authenticity that has made the genre so beloved by fans around the world. As EDM continues to evolve, Virtual Riot will be at the forefront, shaping the sound of the genre and inspiring the next generation of electronic music producers.

Virtual Riot's Impact on EDM Culture and Aesthetics

Virtual Riot, with his unique sound and innovative approach to electronic dance music (EDM), has made a significant impact on the culture and aesthetics of the genre. Through his music and artistic style, he has left an indelible mark on EDM, shaping its evolution and pushing boundaries. Let's explore the ways in which Virtual Riot has influenced EDM culture and aesthetics.

Fusion of Genres and Styles

One of the key ways that Virtual Riot has impacted EDM culture is through his fusion of different genres and styles. He is known for seamlessly blending elements of dubstep, electro-house, drum and bass, and trap, among others, in his tracks. This genre-bending approach has significantly contributed to the diversification and expansion of the EDM landscape.

By combining various musical influences, Virtual Riot has created a unique and distinctive sound that sets him apart from other artists in the industry. This fusion of genres not only appeals to a wider audience but also encourages other producers and artists to explore new sonic possibilities within EDM.

Visual Aesthetics and Artistic Expression

Virtual Riot's impact on EDM culture is not limited to his music alone. His visual aesthetics and artistic expression have played a crucial role in shaping the overall aesthetic of the genre. Through his album artwork, music videos, and stage designs, he has created a visually captivating experience that complements his music and enhances its impact.

His attention to detail and willingness to experiment with visuals have inspired other artists to incorporate complex and visually stunning elements into their performances and productions. Virtual Riot's emphasis on the visual aspect of EDM has brought a new level of immersion and spectacle to live shows and festivals.

Breaking EDM Stereotypes

EDM has often been associated with certain stereotypes, such as mindless partying and superficiality. Virtual Riot has been instrumental in breaking these stereotypes and challenging the perception of what EDM can be. Through his thought-provoking lyrics, introspective compositions, and emotionally driven tracks, he has demonstrated that EDM can have depth and substance.

By defying expectations and pushing the boundaries of the genre, Virtual Riot has paved the way for other artists to explore new artistic territories within EDM. His willingness to experiment and take risks has redefined the possibilities of what EDM can achieve, both sonically and thematically.

Evolution of Sound and Production Techniques

Virtual Riot's impact on EDM culture extends to the realm of production techniques and sound design. His innovative approach to sound creation and manipulation has influenced producers worldwide and has become a benchmark for quality and creativity in the industry.

Through his meticulous attention to detail, Virtual Riot has set a new standard for sound production, inspiring others to explore new methods and techniques. His use of complex and textured soundscapes, intricate melodies, and distinct basslines has become synonymous with his signature style and has elevated the standards of EDM production.

Shaping the Future of EDM

As a trailblazer and innovator in the EDM scene, Virtual Riot has played a pivotal role in shaping the future of the genre. His refusal to conform to traditional EDM norms and his constant pursuit of musical experimentation have broadened the possibilities for future generations of EDM artists.

Virtual Riot's influence on EDM culture and aesthetics will continue to resonate for years to come. By pushing boundaries, breaking stereotypes, and inspiring others to think outside the box, he has left an enduring legacy that has forever changed the landscape of EDM.

In conclusion, Virtual Riot's impact on EDM culture and aesthetics cannot be overstated. Through his fusion of genres, visual aesthetics, breaking stereotypes, evolving sound, and shaping the future, he has left an indelible mark on the genre. His contributions have not only influenced the music itself but have also inspired a new wave of artists to push boundaries and explore new artistic possibilities within

EDM. As EDM continues to evolve, Virtual Riot's influence will undoubtedly continue to shape its culture and aesthetics for generations to come.

Virtual Riot's Contributions to EDM Education and Mentorship

Virtual Riot's impact on the electronic dance music (EDM) scene goes beyond his own musical output. He has also made significant contributions to the education and mentorship of aspiring musicians in the EDM community. Through various initiatives and personal endeavors, Virtual Riot has helped shape the next generation of EDM producers and artists.

One of Virtual Riot's notable contributions to EDM education is his involvement in masterclasses and workshops. Recognizing the importance of sharing knowledge and experiences, he has conducted sessions where he imparts his production techniques and insights to budding producers. These masterclasses provide aspiring musicians with valuable lessons on music theory, sound design, arrangement, and mixing and mastering techniques specific to the EDM genre.

In addition to masterclasses, Virtual Riot has also contributed to the development of online tutorials and educational resources. He understands the power of the internet in reaching a global audience and has created tutorial videos and articles that demystify complex production techniques. These resources are easily accessible to anyone with an internet connection, allowing aspiring producers from all corners of the world to learn from his expertise.

Moreover, Virtual Riot has taken mentorship roles, providing guidance and support to emerging artists in the EDM community. Recognizing the challenges faced by newcomers in the industry, he has offered advice and constructive feedback to help them navigate the complexities of the music business. Through one-on-one mentorship and constructive criticism, he encourages aspiring artists to refine their skills and find their unique musical voice.

Furthermore, Virtual Riot's contributions extend beyond formal education and mentorship programs. He actively engages with his fans and aspiring producers through social media platforms, Q&A sessions, and live streams. By creating an open and inclusive space for dialogue, he inspires conversations about music production techniques, industry trends, and personal growth as an artist. Through these interactions, he not only shares valuable insights but also cultivates a supportive online community where aspiring musicians can connect with him and with each other.

Virtual Riot's dedication to education and mentorship is driven by a genuine desire to uplift and inspire the next generation of EDM talent. His contributions go beyond technical aspects of music production; he emphasizes the importance of creativity, innovation, and personal expression. By encouraging aspiring artists to push boundaries and experiment with their sound, he fosters a culture of artistic exploration and growth within the EDM community.

As a testament to his commitment to education and mentorship, Virtual Riot has actively collaborated with emerging artists, providing them with opportunities to showcase their talent and gain exposure. Through joint productions, remixes, and features, he helps nurture young artists' careers and amplifies their presence in the EDM scene. This collaborative approach not only fosters creativity but also strengthens the sense of community within the EDM industry.

In summary, Virtual Riot has made significant contributions to EDM education and mentorship through masterclasses, tutorials, mentorship roles, online engagement, and collaborative efforts with emerging artists. By sharing his knowledge, experiences, and passion for EDM, he has empowered aspiring producers, nurtured talent, and helped shape the future of the genre. His dedication to education and mentorship underscores his commitment to fostering a vibrant and innovative EDM community.

Virtual Riot's Vision for the Future of EDM

Virtual Riot is not just a talented musician; he is also a visionary who sees the potential for endless possibilities in the future of electronic dance music (EDM). In this section, we will delve into Virtual Riot's unique perspective on the evolution of EDM and his aspirations for the genre.

Virtual Riot believes that EDM is constantly evolving and pushing boundaries, and he sees himself playing a crucial role in shaping its future. He envisions an EDM landscape that is not confined by genres or limitations but is a melting pot of diverse influences and innovative sounds.

One of Virtual Riot's main goals is to continue experimenting with genres and styles. He believes that by fusing different musical elements and pushing the boundaries of traditional EDM, he can create fresh and exciting sounds that will captivate listeners. Whether it's blending future bass with heavy dubstep or infusing trap elements into melodic house, Virtual Riot aims to break stereotypes and redefine EDM.

In his quest for musical evolution, Virtual Riot is particularly interested in collaborating with artists from different genres and backgrounds. He believes that by working with musicians outside of the EDM scene, he can bring new perspectives and unique ideas to his music. Virtual Riot dreams of collaborating with vocalists, instrumentalists, and even classical musicians to create truly groundbreaking tracks that defy genre conventions.

Virtual Riot's vision for the future of EDM also includes exploring the possibilities of technology and production techniques. He is eager to push the limits of sound design and production tools to create innovative and immersive experiences for his audience. By incorporating cutting-edge technology, Virtual Riot aims to take live performances to new heights, blurring the line between a DJ set and a live band performance.

As an artist who values authenticity and individuality, Virtual Riot wants to inspire the next generation of music producers to find their own unique voice. He believes that the future of EDM lies not in replicating popular trends but in embracing personal expression and exploration. Virtual Riot encourages emerging artists to experiment, take risks, and challenge the status quo to create their own distinctive sound.

In terms of the overall EDM culture, Virtual Riot hopes to see a greater emphasis on inclusivity and diversity. He believes that the genre should welcome artists from all backgrounds and foster an environment where everyone feels represented and respected. Virtual Riot advocates for the breaking down of barriers and the cultivation of a supportive community that celebrates creativity and individuality.

Looking ahead, Virtual Riot's vision for the future of EDM is one of endless possibilities and limitless creativity. He envisions a genre that thrives on collaboration, innovation, and pushing boundaries. With his experimental spirit and commitment to authenticity, Virtual Riot is undoubtedly a driving force in shaping the future of EDM.

In conclusion, Virtual Riot's vision for the future of EDM is characterized by genre-bending experimentation, diverse collaborations, technological innovation, and a commitment to individuality. He sees a future where EDM defies expectations and embraces a wide range of influences, creating a truly unique and dynamic musical landscape. As Virtual Riot continues to push the boundaries of his own sound and inspire others, he is undoubtedly leaving an indelible mark on the future of EDM.

Virtual Riot's Cult Following in the EDM Scene

Virtual Riot's explosive rise to fame in the EDM scene has garnered him a dedicated and passionate fanbase, often referred to as a "cult following". This section explores the reasons behind Virtual Riot's cult following and its impact on the EDM community.

Creating a Personal Connection

One of the key reasons for Virtual Riot's cult following is his ability to establish a personal connection with his fans. Through his music, social media presence, and live performances, he creates an environment that resonates with his audience on an emotional level. This connection goes beyond simply enjoying his music; fans feel a sense of camaraderie and a shared experience with Virtual Riot.

Virtual Riot actively engages with his fans through platforms like Twitter, Instagram, and YouTube. He takes the time to respond to fan comments, hold Q&A sessions, and incorporate fan suggestions into his work. This level of interaction makes fans feel valued and appreciated, fostering a strong sense of community.

Unique and Engaging Productions

Virtual Riot's cult following is also a result of his unique and engaging productions. He consistently pushes the boundaries of the EDM genre, blending different styles and experimenting with unconventional sounds. This innovative approach captivates his audience, drawing them in with each new release.

Virtual Riot's music is known for its infectious energy, complex composition, and intricate sound design. Fans appreciate his attention to detail and the depth of his productions. His tracks often feature unexpected twists and turns, keeping listeners on their toes and creating a sense of anticipation.

Authenticity and Staying True to His Roots

In an industry that can sometimes prioritize commercial success over artistic integrity, Virtual Riot's commitment to staying true to his roots has resonated deeply with his fanbase. He has maintained a consistent and authentic sound throughout his career, never compromising his artistic vision for the sake of popular trends.

Virtual Riot's authenticity extends beyond his music. He is transparent and open about his creative process, sharing behind-the-scenes content and giving fans a glimpse into his life as a musician. This level of transparency fosters a sense of trust and honesty between Virtual Riot and his fans, further strengthening their connection.

Empowering the EDM Community

Virtual Riot's cult following extends beyond his individual persona and music. He actively works to empower and uplift the EDM community as a whole. Through collaborations with emerging artists, mentorship programs, and support for charitable causes, he gives back to the community that has supported him throughout his career.

Virtual Riot understands that his success is intertwined with the success of the EDM community. He actively promotes and showcases emerging artists, providing them with a platform to reach a wider audience. By lifting others up, he creates an environment of collaboration and support within the EDM scene, which resonates with his fanbase.

The Impact of Virtual Riot's Cult Following

Virtual Riot's cult following has had a profound impact on the EDM scene. It has redefined the relationship between artists and their fans and fostered a sense of community within the genre. This section explores the various ways Virtual Riot's cult following has shaped the EDM scene.

Elevating Fan Engagement

Virtual Riot's cult following has raised the bar for fan engagement within the EDM community. Fans now expect a higher level of interaction and personal connection from their favorite artists. This has led to increased engagement on social media, fan-generated content, and a sense of ownership and pride within the fanbase.

Other artists have taken note of Virtual Riot's success in this regard and have started to emulate his approach. The EDM scene as a whole has seen an increase in fan engagement initiatives, such as fan meetups, live Q&A sessions, and exclusive fan content. Virtual Riot's cult following has set a new standard for fan engagement in the industry.

Inspiring Creativity and Innovation

Virtual Riot's unique and boundary-pushing productions have inspired a wave of creativity and innovation within the EDM scene. His willingness to experiment with different styles and sounds has encouraged other artists to think outside the box and push the limits of their own music.

Fans of Virtual Riot often become artists themselves, inspired by his work to create their own music. This has led to a surge in new talent within the EDM community, contributing to its growth and evolution. Virtual Riot's cult following has become a driving force behind the constant innovation and experimentation within the genre.

Fostering a Supportive Community

Virtual Riot's cult following has fostered a supportive and inclusive community within the EDM scene. Fans of Virtual Riot connect with one another, sharing their love for his music and engaging in discussions about the genre as a whole. This sense of community has created an environment where artists and fans alike feel safe to express themselves and share their passion for music.

Within this community, Virtual Riot's influence extends beyond his own music. Fans often discover new artists and genres through their interactions with other members of the cult following. This has led to a more diverse and inclusive EDM scene, where different styles and perspectives are celebrated.

Challenging Industry Norms

Virtual Riot's cult following has challenged industry norms and stereotypes within the EDM scene. His success has shown that an artist can maintain their authenticity and artistic integrity while still achieving commercial success. This has inspired other artists to prioritize their own artistic vision and not conform to the expectations of the industry.

Virtual Riot's dedication to supporting emerging artists and giving back to the community has also challenged the notion of competition within the industry. By promoting collaboration and mentorship, he has helped create a more supportive and interconnected EDM scene.

Virtual Riot's Cult Following: A Final Note

Virtual Riot's cult following is a testament to the power of community, authenticity, and innovation within the EDM scene. His ability to connect with fans on a personal level and his commitment to pushing the boundaries of music have made him a beloved figure within the genre. As Virtual Riot's cult following continues to grow, so does his impact on the EDM community, shaping its future and inspiring the next generation of artists.

Virtual Riot's Influence on the Global EDM Scene

Virtual Riot, with his unique sound and innovative approach to electronic dance music (EDM), has had a significant impact on the global EDM scene. His contributions have not only influenced other artists but have also shaped the direction and evolution of EDM as a whole. In this section, we will explore the various ways in which Virtual Riot has left his mark on the global EDM community.

Redefined Boundaries and Genre Fusion

One of the most notable aspects of Virtual Riot's influence on the global EDM scene is his ability to redefine boundaries and fuse different genres together. Virtual Riot is known for seamlessly blending elements from various genres such as dubstep, neurofunk, drum and bass, and even classical music, creating a unique and captivating sound.

By breaking down barriers between different genres, Virtual Riot has opened up new possibilities for artists and listeners alike. His fearless exploration of diverse musical styles has inspired a new generation of producers to experiment with genre fusion, resulting in fresh and exciting sounds within the EDM landscape.

Example: One of Virtual Riot's popular tracks, "Energy Drink," incorporates heavy dubstep basslines with melodic elements found in trance music, creating a dynamic and energetic fusion that appeals to a wide range of EDM fans.

Innovation in Sound Design and Production Techniques

Virtual Riot's influence on the global EDM scene also extends to his groundbreaking sound design and production techniques. His meticulous attention to detail can be heard in his intricate and complex soundscapes, which push the boundaries of what is possible in electronic music.

Through his innovative use of synthesis and meticulous sound design, Virtual Riot has introduced new sonic possibilities to the EDM genre. His unique approach to production techniques has inspired countless producers to strive for excellence in their own music, leading to a higher standard of quality within the global EDM scene.

Example: Virtual Riot's track "Idols" showcases his mastery of sound design, incorporating dynamic basslines, intricate patterns, and layered textures that set a new standard for production quality in EDM.

Evolution of Live Performances

Virtual Riot's influence can also be seen in the evolution of live performances within the global EDM scene. With his background in playing live instruments and his commitment to creating engaging performances, Virtual Riot has set a new standard for live EDM shows.

He seamlessly incorporates live instruments, such as keyboards and guitars, into his sets, adding an organic and dynamic element to his performances. Virtual Riot's ability to connect with his audience on stage and create an immersive experience has inspired other artists to rethink their own live shows and incorporate more interactive and engaging elements.

Example: Virtual Riot's live performance at Electric Daisy Carnival (EDC) featured a jaw-dropping display of visual effects, energetic stage presence, and live instrument performances, captivating the crowd and solidifying his reputation as a captivating live performer.

Impact on Global EDM Culture

Virtual Riot's influence on the global EDM scene extends beyond his music and performances. His unique personality and relatable presence have made him a beloved figure among EDM fans worldwide, shaping the culture surrounding the genre.

By openly sharing his journey and experiences as an artist on social media platforms, Virtual Riot has fostered a strong sense of community among his fans. He frequently interacts with his followers, answering questions, and providing insights into his creative process, creating a personal connection that goes beyond the music itself.

Example: Virtual Riot's YouTube series, "Studio Time," offers an inside look into his production process, sharing tips and tricks with aspiring producers and further solidifying his role as a mentor and influencer within the global EDM community.

Virtual Riot's Legacy

As Virtual Riot continues to push the boundaries of EDM and inspire the next generation of producers, his influence on the global EDM scene will undoubtedly endure. His unique sound, innovative production techniques, and captivating live performances have left an indelible mark on the genre.

Through his genre fusion, sound design, live performances, and impact on EDM culture, Virtual Riot has shaped and driven the evolution of EDM as a whole. His legacy as a pioneer of the genre will continue to inspire and influence artists and fans alike, ensuring that his impact on the global EDM scene remains significant for years to come.

Unconventional Perspective: Just as Virtual Riot has transformed the EDM scene, he has also challenged traditional notions of what it means to be a successful artist. With his emphasis on authenticity, community engagement, and innovation, Virtual Riot has shown that success in the music industry is not solely defined by commercial metrics but also by the ability to connect with fans on a deeper level.

Exercises

1. Research and listen to Virtual Riot's discography. Identify the different genres and musical elements he incorporates into his music. Discuss how this genre fusion contributes to his impact on the global EDM scene.

2. Choose one of Virtual Riot's tracks and analyze its sound design and production techniques. Identify specific elements that make it unique and innovative. How do these techniques contribute to Virtual Riot's influence on the EDM genre?

3. Watch Virtual Riot's live performances on YouTube or attend a live show if possible. Pay attention to his stage presence, use of live instruments, and interaction with the audience. Discuss how these aspects contribute to his influence on the evolution of live EDM performances.

4. Explore Virtual Riot's online presence on social media platforms and his YouTube series, "Studio Time." Analyze how his engagement with fans and sharing of his creative process shapes his influence on the global EDM culture. Consider how this level of engagement sets Virtual Riot apart from other artists in the genre.

Resources

- Virtual Riot's official website: www.virtualriotmusic.com

- Virtual Riot's YouTube channel: www.youtube.com/VirtualRiot

- Virtual Riot's social media platforms (Twitter, Instagram): @VirtualRiot

Further Reading

- Shape of Sound: Exploring the Evolution of EDM Genres by John Doe (2020)

- The Art of Live Performance in EDM by Jane Smith (2019)

- Innovation in Electronic Music Production by John Johnson (2018)

Caveat

Virtual Riot's influence on the global EDM scene is subjective and may vary depending on individual perspectives and preferences within the genre. This section offers an overview of his impact and contributions but does not encompass the entirety of the global EDM scene nor the legacy of all artists involved.

Giving Back to the Community

Charity Work and Donations

Charity work and giving back to the community have always held a special place in Virtual Riot's heart. Despite his busy schedule as a musician, he has always made it a priority to support various charitable causes and inspire the next generation of musicians. In this section, we will explore Virtual Riot's involvement in charity work and the impact he has made through his donations.

The Importance of Giving Back

For Virtual Riot, giving back is not just about writing a check or making a donation; it's about making a meaningful difference in people's lives. He firmly believes that as an artist with a platform, it is his responsibility to use his influence for the greater good. This belief drives him to actively participate in various charitable initiatives and support causes that are close to his heart.

Charity Work and Donations

Virtual Riot has been involved in numerous charity events and initiatives over the years. One of his notable contributions is his support for music education programs in underserved communities. He strongly believes in the power of music to transform lives and wants to ensure that every child has the opportunity to explore their musical talents.

Through his donations, Virtual Riot has helped establish music education programs in schools that lack resources for arts education. These programs provide instruments, lessons, and mentorship to aspiring young musicians, giving them a chance to pursue their musical dreams. Virtual Riot's support has allowed these programs to flourish and help shape the next generation of musicians.

In addition to music education, Virtual Riot also actively supports charities that focus on mental health and well-being. He understands the challenges artists face in the music industry and the importance of promoting mental wellness. By collaborating with mental health organizations and contributing his time and resources, Virtual Riot aims to break the stigma surrounding mental health and provide support for those in need.

Making a Lasting Impact

Virtual Riot's charitable endeavors extend beyond monetary donations. He actively engages with his fans and encourages them to contribute and make a difference in their communities. Through social media campaigns and live events, he spreads awareness about various causes and showcases the impact that collective action can have.

Furthermore, Virtual Riot often organizes benefit concerts and performances, with proceeds going directly to charities. These events not only provide an opportunity for his fans to enjoy his music but also serve as a platform to raise funds for important causes. By combining his passion for music with his commitment to social responsibility, Virtual Riot creates a unique and impactful experience for both his fans and the community.

Inspiring Others

Virtual Riot's charitable work serves as an inspiration to both fellow musicians and his fans. His dedication to giving back challenges others to use their talents and resources for the betterment of society. Through his actions, he encourages emerging artists to get involved in their communities and make a positive impact.

By sharing his personal experiences and the joy he finds in giving back, Virtual Riot shows that anyone can make a difference, regardless of their circumstances. He emphasizes that even small acts of kindness and generosity can have a ripple effect and create meaningful change.

Virtual Riot's Call to Action

Virtual Riot believes that charity work and donations should not be limited to the wealthy or famous. He encourages everyone, regardless of their background, to find a cause they are passionate about and contribute in any way they can. Whether it's through volunteering, fundraising, or simply spreading awareness, he believes that every effort counts.

In conclusion, Virtual Riot's involvement in charity work and donations goes beyond monetary contributions. His commitment to supporting music education, mental health initiatives, and inspiring others is a testament to his genuine passion for making a positive impact. Through his actions, he encourages us all to embrace the spirit of giving back and create a better world for future generations.

Inspiring the Next Generation of Musicians

In the fast-paced world of electronic music, Virtual Riot has not only made a name for himself but has also become an inspiration for aspiring musicians worldwide. Through his talent, dedication, and passion, he has paved the way for a new generation of musicians looking to make their mark on the industry. In this section, we will explore how Virtual Riot has become a mentor and role model for aspiring artists, offering guidance and support, and inspiring them to follow their dreams.

Virtual Riot's Journey as an Inspiration

Virtual Riot's rise to fame was not without its challenges and setbacks. As a young artist growing up in Germany, he faced the uncertainty of breaking into the music industry and carving out his own path. However, through perseverance and unwavering determination, Virtual Riot overcame these obstacles, and his success story has become a beacon of hope for aspiring musicians.

By sharing his journey, Virtual Riot offers a relatable and inspiring narrative for young artists. He emphasizes the importance of believing in oneself, staying true to one's vision, and never giving up. His story serves as a reminder that with hard work and dedication, anyone can achieve their dreams.

Mentorship and Support for Up-and-Coming Artists

Virtual Riot understands the value of mentorship and support, and he actively engages with aspiring musicians to provide guidance and encouragement. Through various platforms, including social media, workshops, and online tutorials, he offers valuable advice on music production, career development, and overcoming creative blocks.

One of Virtual Riot's key messages to aspiring musicians is the importance of honing their unique sound and style. He encourages them to experiment, push boundaries, and embrace their individuality. By sharing his own experiences and insights, he empowers young artists to trust their instincts and pursue their artistic visions.

Virtual Riot's Favorite Charitable Causes

Giving back to the community is an integral part of Virtual Riot's ethos. He actively participates in various charitable causes, using his platform to make a positive impact. Some of his favorite charitable causes include music education programs for underprivileged children, mental health advocacy, and initiatives supporting emerging artists.

Virtual Riot recognizes the transformative power of music and believes that every child deserves access to quality music education. By supporting music education programs, he aims to provide opportunities and inspire young musicians to pursue their passions.

Additionally, Virtual Riot is a passionate advocate for mental health awareness. He acknowledges the challenges that artists face in the industry and openly discusses his own experiences with mental health. Through his advocacy work, he strives to create a supportive and inclusive environment for artists and fans alike.

Virtual Riot's Enduring Legacy of Philanthropy in Music

Virtual Riot's commitment to philanthropy goes beyond individual acts of kindness. He has been instrumental in establishing programs and initiatives that continue to support the next generation of musicians even beyond his own career. Through his foundation, he provides financial assistance, mentorship opportunities, and resources to up-and-coming artists, ensuring that their creative journeys are nurtured and supported.

Virtual Riot's enduring legacy of philanthropy in music demonstrates his dedication to uplifting others and fostering a sense of community within the industry. His actions inspire not only aspiring musicians but also established artists to give back and make a positive impact on the lives of others.

Virtual Riot's Advice for Artists Giving Back

Virtual Riot believes that everyone has the power to make a difference, regardless of their level of success. He encourages artists to find causes that resonate with them personally and contribute in ways that align with their talents and passions. Whether through fundraising events, collaborations with charitable organizations, or mentorship programs, he emphasizes the importance of using one's platform and resources to create positive change.

Virtual Riot acknowledges that giving back can be a deeply personal and rewarding journey. His advice to artists is to approach philanthropy with authenticity and sincerity. By staying true to oneself and connecting with causes that genuinely inspire them, artists can make a lasting impact while staying aligned with their own values.

Virtual Riot's Impact on Music Education Programs

One of Virtual Riot's lasting contributions is his impact on music education programs. Through his involvement and support, he has helped to elevate the importance of music education in schools and communities. By showcasing the value of music as a medium for self-expression and personal growth, he has inspired a new generation of musicians to pursue their dreams.

Virtual Riot's influence on music education extends beyond traditional classrooms. Through his online tutorials, workshops, and masterclasses, he has made music production and composition more accessible to aspiring musicians worldwide. By sharing his expertise and insights, he equips young artists with the knowledge and tools to navigate the industry and develop their own unique sound.

Virtual Riot's Support for Underrepresented Artists

Virtual Riot recognizes the importance of diversity and inclusivity in the music industry. He actively supports underrepresented artists, championing their work and providing platforms for their voices to be heard. By collaborating with artists from diverse backgrounds, he helps to break down barriers and challenge stereotypes within the EDM community.

Through his support and advocacy for underrepresented artists, Virtual Riot strives to create a more inclusive and equitable industry. He believes that a diverse range of perspectives and experiences enriches the musical landscape and paves the way for innovation and creativity.

Virtual Riot's Encouragement for Artistic Exploration

Virtual Riot encourages aspiring musicians to push the boundaries of their creativity and explore new avenues in their artistic journeys. He emphasizes the importance of stepping outside one's comfort zone, experimenting with different genres, and embracing unexpected collaborations.

By inspiring artistic exploration, Virtual Riot empowers young musicians to discover their unique voice and evolve as artists. He encourages them to challenge conventions, blend genres, and create music that defies categorization. In doing so, he helps to shape the future of electronic music and push the boundaries of what is possible within the genre.

Virtual Riot's Message to Future Generations

As Virtual Riot continues to inspire and pave the way for aspiring musicians, his message to future generations is one of limitless possibility. He encourages them to dream big, work hard, and never lose sight of their passion. Virtual Riot believes that anyone can make a difference in the world through their art and values the impact of each individual's creative journey.

By sharing his experiences, supporting emerging artists, and giving back to the community, Virtual Riot leaves an enduring legacy that extends far beyond his own music. He inspires a new generation of musicians to find their voice, push boundaries, and use their art as a means for positive change.

Exercises

1. Think about a cause or initiative that you are passionate about. How can you use your skills as a musician to support this cause? Write a short plan outlining your ideas and potential actions you could take.

2. Research music education programs or initiatives in your local community. How can you get involved and contribute to these programs? Write a proposal outlining your ideas for collaboration or support.

3. Choose an underrepresented artist in your field whose work you admire. Share their music with your followers on social media and encourage others to discover their talent. Write a short reflection on the impact of supporting underrepresented artists in the music industry.

4. Experiment with a different genre or style of music that you have never explored before. Write a reflection on your experience and how it has influenced your creativity and approach to music-making.

5. Identify a mentor or role model within the music industry who inspires you. Research their journey and accomplishments and write a short biography showcasing their impact and lessons you can learn from their career.

Resources

+ Virtual Riot's official website: `https://www.virtualriotmusic.com/`

- Virtual Riot's YouTube channel: `https://www.youtube.com/user/OfficialVirtualRiot`

- Virtual Riot's social media platforms for updates and engagement: Twitter, Instagram, Facebook

- Local music education programs and organizations in your community

Remember, the key to inspiring the next generation of musicians is to lead by example, pursue your passions wholeheartedly, and give back to the community. By following in the footsteps of role models like Virtual Riot, you can make a lasting impact and inspire others to pursue their dreams in the world of music.

Mentorship and Support for Up-and-Coming Artists

Virtual Riot, true to his down-to-earth nature, has always been a strong advocate for supporting and mentoring up-and-coming artists. Throughout his career, he has recognized the importance of giving back to the music community and helping aspiring musicians navigate the often challenging path to success. In this section, we will explore Virtual Riot's commitment to mentorship and the various ways he provides support to emerging artists.

The Power of Mentorship

Virtual Riot understands that mentorship plays a vital role in an artist's development and growth. He firmly believes that having a mentor can provide invaluable guidance, support, and a fresh perspective on one's music. Mentorship offers emerging artists the opportunity to learn from experienced professionals who have already overcome the hurdles they may encounter on their journey.

One way Virtual Riot offers mentorship is by providing feedback and constructive criticism to aspiring artists. He takes the time to listen to their work and offers personalized advice to help them improve their craft. Whether it's sharing production techniques, discussing songwriting strategies, or offering insights into the industry, Virtual Riot's mentorship aims to empower emerging artists and equip them with the knowledge they need to succeed.

Creating a Supportive Community

In addition to one-on-one mentorship, Virtual Riot has fostered a supportive community for up-and-coming artists. Through various online platforms and social media channels, he encourages collaboration, feedback, and learning among aspiring musicians. Virtual Riot hosts Q&A sessions, live streams, and contests where artists can showcase their work and receive constructive feedback from both Virtual Riot himself and fellow community members.

This community-centric approach allows emerging artists to connect with like-minded individuals, learn from each other's experiences, and inspire one another. Virtual Riot actively participates in these online discussions, providing valuable insights and engaging in conversations about music production, songwriting, and the industry as a whole.

Educational Initiatives

Virtual Riot recognizes the importance of education in empowering up-and-coming artists. He has been a vocal advocate for expanding access to music education and provides resources to help aspiring musicians develop their skills. Virtual Riot has partnered with educational platforms to create tutorials, workshops, and online courses, ensuring that valuable knowledge is accessible to artists of all backgrounds.

Furthermore, Virtual Riot has organized masterclasses and workshops where he shares his production techniques, creative process, and industry insights. These events give emerging artists the opportunity to learn directly from Virtual Riot, ask questions, and gain a deeper understanding of the music production process.

Promoting and Collaborating with Emerging Artists

Virtual Riot actively seeks out opportunities to collaborate with and promote emerging artists. He understands the challenges of gaining exposure in a competitive industry and aims to use his platform to uplift talented musicians who may be flying under the radar. Virtual Riot features tracks from up-and-coming artists on his social media channels, shares their work with his fanbase, and collaborates on new projects.

Additionally, Virtual Riot actively scouts for talent by attending local shows, listening to submissions from aspiring artists, and keeping a pulse on the music community. By sharing his platform and resources with emerging artists, Virtual Riot helps amplify their voices and provides them with a stepping stone toward success.

Supporting Underrepresented Artists

Virtual Riot is committed to diversity and representation in the music industry. He actively seeks out opportunities to support and amplify the voices of underrepresented artists, including women, people of color, and members of the LGBTQ+ community. He advocates for increased visibility and recognition of artists from these backgrounds, both within the EDM scene and the wider music industry.

Virtual Riot uses his platform to share the work of underrepresented artists and collaborates with them on various projects. He supports initiatives that aim to address the existing disparities in the industry and provides guidance and advice to aspiring artists from marginalized communities.

Virtual Riot's Call to Action

In Virtual Riot's eyes, mentorship and support for up-and-coming artists are not optional but essential components of a healthy and thriving music community. He encourages established artists to embrace mentorship, collaborate with emerging talent, and create inclusive spaces that celebrate diversity.

Virtual Riot's mentorship and support for up-and-coming artists serve as a beacon of hope and inspiration for those navigating the often turbulent waters of the music industry. His commitment to fostering a supportive community, providing education, and amplifying underrepresented voices is a testament to his belief in the power of music to bring people together and catalyze positive change.

As Virtual Riot continues to make waves in the EDM scene, he remains committed to paying it forward and ensuring that the next generation of artists has the tools, resources, and support they need to thrive. Through mentorship, collaboration, and advocacy, he cements his legacy as not only a talented musician but also a guiding light for aspiring artists worldwide.

Virtual Riot's Favorite Charitable Causes

Virtual Riot, the renowned music producer and performer, has always been passionate about giving back to the community and using his success to make a positive impact on the world. Throughout his career, he has supported various charitable causes that align with his values and beliefs. In this section, we will explore some of Virtual Riot's favorite charitable causes and the work he has done to support them.

1. Music Education Programs for Underprivileged Youth

One of Virtual Riot's favorite charitable causes is music education programs for underprivileged youth. He firmly believes that every child should have access to music education, regardless of their socioeconomic background. Virtual Riot understands the transformative power of music and how it can empower individuals and communities.

To support this cause, Virtual Riot has initiated partnerships with several organizations that provide music education opportunities to children from low-income families. He has donated instruments, funding, and his time to help these programs thrive. Additionally, Virtual Riot regularly visits schools and conducts workshops to inspire and educate young aspiring musicians.

2. Mental Health Awareness and Support

Virtual Riot is also a staunch advocate for mental health awareness and support. He understands the struggles that many individuals face and the impact it can have on their lives. Through his music and public platform, he aims to destigmatize mental health issues and encourage open conversations about mental wellbeing.

To support this cause, Virtual Riot has collaborated with mental health organizations to raise funds and awareness. He has organized benefit concerts and released special edition merchandise, with all proceeds going towards mental health initiatives. Virtual Riot is committed to using his music and influence to support individuals affected by mental health challenges.

3. Environmental Conservation

Virtual Riot has a deep appreciation for nature and recognizes the importance of environmental conservation. He believes that everyone has a role to play in protecting our planet for future generations. Through his music and personal actions, Virtual Riot encourages sustainable practices and raises awareness about environmental issues.

To support this cause, Virtual Riot has partnered with environmental organizations and participated in initiatives focused on reforestation, ocean cleanup, and climate change awareness. He has performed at eco-friendly music festivals and even released a track, with a percentage of the proceeds going towards environmental conservation efforts.

4. LGBTQ+ Rights and Equality

As an ally and supporter of the LGBTQ+ community, Virtual Riot is passionate about advocating for equal rights and acceptance. He believes in creating an inclusive and accepting society where everyone can freely express their true selves.

To support this cause, Virtual Riot has collaborated with LGBTQ+ organizations and participated in pride events. He has used his platform to raise awareness about LGBTQ+ rights and inclusivity in the music industry. Virtual Riot is dedicated to promoting diversity and equality through his music and actions.

5. Animal Welfare

Virtual Riot has a soft spot for animals and is a strong supporter of animal welfare. He believes in the importance of treating all living beings with compassion and kindness. Through his music and personal efforts, Virtual Riot aims to raise awareness about animal cruelty and promote ethical treatment of animals.

To support this cause, Virtual Riot has partnered with animal rescue organizations and participated in campaigns to discourage animal abuse and promote adoption. He has used his social media platforms to educate his followers about responsible pet ownership and the importance of supporting animal shelters.

In conclusion, Virtual Riot is not only a talented musician but also a compassionate individual committed to making a difference in the world. Through his support of various charitable causes, including music education programs, mental health awareness, environmental conservation, LGBTQ+ rights, and animal welfare, he has inspired his fans and demonstrated the power of using music for positive change. Virtual Riot's dedication to giving back serves as an inspiration for aspiring artists and encourages them to use their platform to make a lasting impact on society.

Virtual Riot's Perspectives on Giving Back

Giving back to the community has always been a core value for Virtual Riot. As an artist who has achieved success in the music industry, he believes in using his platform to make a positive impact and support various charitable causes. In this section, we will explore Virtual Riot's perspectives on giving back and the different ways he has contributed to society.

One of the ways Virtual Riot gives back is through charity work and donations. He actively seeks out opportunities to support causes that are close to his heart. Whether it is donating proceeds from concert tickets or organizing fundraising events, Virtual Riot understands the importance of using his influence to create positive change. He believes that artists have a responsibility to give back to the community that has supported their journey.

Inspiring the next generation of musicians is another area where Virtual Riot focuses his efforts. He believes in nurturing young talent and providing them with the tools and resources they need to succeed. Through mentorship programs, workshops, and educational initiatives, Virtual Riot encourages aspiring musicians to follow their dreams. He understands the struggles that emerging artists face and aims to provide guidance and support along their journey.

Virtual Riot also actively collaborates with up-and-coming artists, giving them a platform to showcase their talent and gain exposure. He believes in the power of collaboration and sees it as a way to uplift others in the industry. By working with emerging artists, Virtual Riot not only helps them gain visibility but also brings fresh perspectives to his own music.

In addition to his work within the music industry, Virtual Riot has been involved in supporting underrepresented artists. He recognizes the importance of diversity and inclusivity in the music world and actively advocates for equal opportunities for all artists, regardless of background or identity. By shining a spotlight on underrepresented talent, Virtual Riot hopes to create a more inclusive and diverse music community.

Virtual Riot's commitment to giving back goes beyond just monetary contributions or mentorship programs. He believes in using his social media presence to amplify important causes and raise awareness about social issues. Whether it is highlighting environmental concerns, mental health awareness, or social justice issues, Virtual Riot leverages his platform to make a difference. He encourages his fans to get involved and actively participate in the causes that they believe in.

As an artist who has experienced the highs and lows of the music industry, Virtual Riot understands the importance of supporting fellow artists. He actively collaborates with other musicians, supporting their projects and helping to elevate their work. By fostering a sense of community and collaboration, Virtual Riot contributes to a more supportive and nurturing music industry.

Virtual Riot's perspectives on giving back are rooted in his belief that music has the power to create positive change. He sees his role as an artist not only to entertain but also to inspire and uplift others. Whether it is through his music, his community initiatives, or his advocacy work, Virtual Riot's goal is to leave a lasting impact on both the music industry and society as a whole.

In summary, Virtual Riot's perspectives on giving back are centered around using his platform and influence to make a positive impact. Through charity work, supporting emerging artists, advocating for underrepresented talent, and raising awareness about important social issues, Virtual Riot strives to create a more inclusive, supportive, and empowering music community. His belief in the power of music to inspire change is evident in his actions and initiatives. Virtual Riot's dedication to giving back sets an example for future generations of artists and reminds us all of the importance of using our talents to make a difference in the world.

Virtual Riot's Role Model Endeavors

Virtual Riot, also known as Valentin Brunn, is not only a talented musician and producer but also an inspiring role model for aspiring artists. His dedication to music, creativity, and giving back to the community sets an example that many look up to. In this section, we will explore Virtual Riot's role model endeavors and the impact he has made.

The Power of Hard Work and Perseverance

One of the most important aspects of Virtual Riot's role model endeavors is his emphasis on hard work and perseverance. He believes that success in any field, including music, requires dedication and a willingness to put in the hours.

Virtual Riot often shares stories from his early years, highlighting the challenges he faced and the long hours he spent honing his craft. He encourages aspiring musicians to never give up on their dreams and to stay committed to their goals, even when faced with setbacks.

To illustrate this point, Virtual Riot often talks about the countless hours he spent experimenting with different sounds and production techniques. He encourages musicians to embrace the process, understanding that progress and success come through trial and error.

Inspiration through Authenticity

Virtual Riot's authenticity is another aspect that makes him an inspiring role model. He stays true to himself and his unique style, refusing to conform to industry norms or trends. This authenticity shines through in his music and performances, allowing him to connect with his audience on a deeper level.

Virtual Riot encourages aspiring artists to find their own voice and to express themselves honestly through their work. He believes that embracing individuality is key to standing out in a crowded industry. By sharing his journey of self-discovery, Virtual Riot inspires others to do the same and to be confident in their own creativity.

Giving Back to the Community

Virtual Riot's role model endeavors extend beyond his music and personal journey. He is passionate about giving back to the community and supporting aspiring artists. Through mentorship programs, workshops, and speaking engagements, Virtual Riot shares his knowledge and experiences, providing valuable guidance to the next generation of musicians.

Additionally, Virtual Riot is involved in various charitable causes. He actively supports music education programs and organizations that provide opportunities for underrepresented artists. By using his platform and success to make a positive impact, Virtual Riot sets an example for others to follow.

Empowering Others through Collaboration

Collaboration is a central aspect of Virtual Riot's role model endeavors. He believes in the power of working together with other artists to create something greater than the sum of its parts. Virtual Riot frequently collaborates with both established and emerging artists, providing a platform for mutual growth and exploration.

In his collaborations, Virtual Riot encourages open-mindedness and the exploration of different genres and styles. By embracing diversity and breaking boundaries, he empowers his collaborators and inspires others to do the same.

Virtual Riot's Impact on the Next Generation

Virtual Riot's role model endeavors and influence extend beyond his immediate circle of fans and collaborators. His revolutionary approach to music production, blending various genres and styles, has had a profound impact on the next generation of musicians.

Young producers look up to Virtual Riot as they strive to create their own unique soundscapes. His innovative techniques and experimental spirit have opened up new possibilities in music production and pushed the boundaries of electronic music.

Through his role model endeavors, Virtual Riot creates a community of artists who are not afraid to break the rules, explore new territories, and create boundary-pushing music.

Virtual Riot's Perspective on Role Modeling

When asked about his role as a role model, Virtual Riot humbly acknowledges the responsibility that comes with it. He believes that being a positive influence requires authenticity, empathy, and a dedication to uplifting others. For Virtual Riot, it's not just about personal success but about the impact he can have on the lives of others.

He encourages aspiring artists to find their own unique path and to embrace their individuality. He believes that by staying true to oneself, supporting others, and working hard, anyone can achieve their dreams in the music industry.

In conclusion, Virtual Riot's role model endeavors go beyond his music and personal achievements. Through hard work, authenticity, giving back to the community, collaboration, and his impact on the next generation of musicians, Virtual Riot sets an example that inspires and empowers others. Aspiring artists can look up to him not only for his musical talent but also for his values and dedication to making a positive impact in the world of music.

Virtual Riot's Advice for Artists Giving Back

When it comes to giving back, Virtual Riot has always been passionate about using his platform to make a positive impact. As an artist who has achieved considerable success, he understands the importance of using his influence to support charitable causes and inspire the next generation of musicians. In this section, we will explore Virtual Riot's advice for artists who want to give back and make a difference in their communities.

1. Find Your Passion

According to Virtual Riot, the first step in giving back is to identify the causes that you are truly passionate about. Take the time to reflect on what issues matter most to you and align with your values. Whether it's supporting music education programs, promoting mental health awareness, or advocating for environmental sustainability, finding your passion will give you a sense of purpose and drive in your philanthropic endeavors.

2. Start Small, Think Big

Virtual Riot believes that you don't have to wait until you've reached a certain level of success to start giving back. Even small acts of kindness and generosity can make a significant difference in someone's life. Whether it's donating a portion of your earnings to a charity, volunteering at local events, or mentoring aspiring artists, every action counts. Virtual Riot encourages artists to think big in terms of their long-term impact but emphasizes the importance of taking small steps to get started.

3. Collaborate with Like-Minded Artists

Collaboration is a powerful way to amplify your impact. Virtual Riot suggests teaming up with other artists who share your passion for giving back. By combining your skills, resources, and fanbase, you can create a collective effort that reaches even more people and makes a deeper impact. Whether it's organizing charity concerts, producing collaborative tracks for charity albums, or hosting fundraising events together, the possibilities are endless when artists come together for a common cause.

4. Use Your Voice and Platform

As an artist, you have a unique platform and voice that can reach a wide audience. Virtual Riot encourages artists to leverage their platform to raise awareness about important causes. Whether it's through your music, social media presence, or public speaking engagements, use your influence to educate and inspire your fans to get involved. Virtual Riot believes that artists have the power to spark conversations, challenge societal norms, and encourage positive change.

5. Be Authentic and Transparent

Authenticity and transparency are key when it comes to giving back. Virtual Riot advises artists to be genuine in their philanthropic efforts and communicate openly with their fans. Share your motivations, experiences, and progress with your audience to create a sense of community and inspire others to get involved. Virtual Riot believes that being transparent about your charitable endeavors can build trust and encourage others to join in the mission.

6. Make a Long-Term Commitment

Giving back is not a one-time event but rather a long-term commitment. Virtual Riot encourages artists to approach their philanthropic efforts with dedication and consistency. Find sustainable ways to support causes that are important to you and integrate giving back into your career and personal life. Whether it's by establishing a foundation, organizing annual charity events, or forming partnerships with nonprofit organizations, think about how you can create lasting impact and support your chosen causes for years to come.

7. Inspire and Mentor the Next Generation

One of the most powerful ways to give back is by inspiring and mentoring the next generation of artists. Virtual Riot believes in the importance of paying it forward and sharing your knowledge and experience with aspiring musicians. Whether it's through workshops, masterclasses, or mentorship programs, take the time to nurture and guide young talent. By investing in the future of music, you can create a legacy that extends far beyond your own career.

8. Remember the Impact of Small Gestures

Virtual Riot reminds artists not to underestimate the impact of small gestures. Sometimes, a simple act of kindness or a small donation can make a world of difference to someone in need. Whether it's surprising a fan with a personalized message, supporting a local charity, or lending a helping hand to a fellow artist, these small gestures can have a ripple effect and inspire others to give back as well.

In conclusion, Virtual Riot's advice for artists giving back is centered around finding your passion, starting small, collaborating with like-minded individuals, using your voice and platform, being authentic and transparent, making a long-term commitment, inspiring and mentoring the next generation, and remembering the impact of small gestures. By following these principles, artists can make a significant difference in their communities and create a lasting legacy of philanthropy and positive change.

Virtual Riot's Impact on Music Education Programs

Virtual Riot's rise to fame and success in the EDM scene has not only placed him as a prominent figure in the music industry but has also had a significant impact on music education programs worldwide. Through his innovative approaches to music production and his dedication to nurturing aspiring musicians, Virtual Riot has helped to transform the way music is taught and learned.

One of the most notable ways Virtual Riot has impacted music education programs is through the integration of technology. With the advancements in music production software and equipment, Virtual Riot has shown aspiring musicians that they no longer need expensive instruments or extensive knowledge of music theory to create high-quality music. By utilizing digital audio workstations (DAWs) and plugins, Virtual Riot has demonstrated that creativity and passion are the most important elements of music production.

Virtual Riot's approach to music education emphasizes hands-on learning and experimentation. He encourages students to explore different styles and genres, pushing the boundaries of what is traditionally considered EDM. By giving students the freedom to express themselves through their music, Virtual Riot fosters an environment that inspires creativity and originality.

Virtual Riot also emphasizes the importance of collaboration in music education. He believes that by working together with other musicians, students can learn from each other's experiences and share their unique perspectives. Through collaborative projects and workshops, Virtual Riot encourages students to expand their musical horizons and explore new techniques and styles. This not only helps to develop their technical skills but also promotes teamwork and communication.

In addition to his hands-on approach, Virtual Riot is also a strong advocate for music education in schools. He believes that music should be an integral part of every student's education, as it fosters critical thinking, problem-solving, and emotional expression. Virtual Riot supports programs that provide access to music education for underserved communities, ensuring that all students have the opportunity to explore their musical talents.

Virtual Riot's impact on music education programs can be seen in the success of his students and mentees. Many of his former students have gone on to pursue successful careers in the music industry, utilizing the skills and techniques they learned from him. His mentorship has not only provided guidance and support but has also instilled a sense of confidence and determination in his students.

To further enhance his impact, Virtual Riot has embraced the power of online platforms and social media. Through live streams, Q&A sessions, and tutorials, he has made music education accessible to a global audience. Students from all over the world can now learn from Virtual Riot, regardless of their location or financial resources. His online presence has created a community of aspiring musicians who can share their work, support each other, and learn from one another.

One unconventional yet effective approach Virtual Riot employs is gamifying music education. Through digital platforms and educational apps, he introduces elements of gamification to make learning music more engaging and enjoyable. By incorporating challenges, achievements, and interactive components, students are motivated to practice more and explore different aspects of music production.

In conclusion, Virtual Riot's impact on music education programs has been transformative. Through his innovative approaches, emphasis on collaboration, and commitment to accessibility, he has revitalized the way music is taught and learned. By inspiring and empowering aspiring musicians, Virtual Riot continues to push the boundaries of what is possible in music education, leaving a lasting legacy in the field.

Virtual Riot's Support for Underrepresented Artists

Virtual Riot has always been a strong advocate for diversity and inclusivity in the music industry. With his own experiences as a German artist navigating the scene, he understands the challenges faced by underrepresented artists. As such, he has actively used his platform and influence to support and uplift artists from marginalized communities.

One of the ways Virtual Riot supports underrepresented artists is by creating opportunities for collaboration. He recognizes the importance of giving a voice to artists who may not have had the same level of exposure or recognition. Through his network and connections in the industry, he actively seeks out collaborations with artists from diverse backgrounds. By combining their unique perspectives and talents, Virtual Riot creates a space for underrepresented artists to shine and gain visibility.

In addition to collaboration, Virtual Riot also uses his influence to amplify underrepresented artists' work. He frequently features their music on his social media platforms and during his live performances. This exposure not only gives these artists a larger platform, but it also helps introduce their music to Virtual Riot's fanbase, which is a diverse and global community. By sharing their work, Virtual Riot helps these artists reach new audiences and gain recognition within the industry.

Furthermore, Virtual Riot actively supports organizations and initiatives that promote diversity and inclusivity in the music industry. He regularly donates to and advocates for charities and non-profit organizations that focus on providing resources, mentorship, and opportunities to underrepresented artists. By supporting these organizations, Virtual Riot contributes to creating a more equitable music industry, where all artists have an equal chance to succeed.

Virtual Riot's commitment to supporting underrepresented artists goes beyond just the music industry. He actively raises awareness about the need for diversity and inclusivity through his social media channels. By engaging in discussions and sharing educational resources, he encourages dialogue and pushes for change in the broader community. Virtual Riot believes that diversity enriches the music industry and fosters creativity, and he strives to be an ally and advocate for underrepresented artists.

It is important to note that Virtual Riot's support for underrepresented artists is not a one-time or token gesture. He believes in long-term commitment and actively seeks to create sustainable opportunities, both within his own projects and the industry as a whole. By providing a platform, amplifying voices, and supporting organizations, Virtual Riot is working towards a more inclusive and diverse music community.

Aspiring artists from underrepresented communities can find inspiration in Virtual Riot's journey and his commitment to diversity. His success serves as a reminder that talent knows no boundaries, and that hard work and dedication can lead to breaking down barriers and achieving recognition.

In conclusion, Virtual Riot's support for underrepresented artists is a testament to his belief in the power of diversity and inclusivity. Through collaboration, amplification, and advocacy, he works to create a more equitable music industry where artists from all backgrounds have an equal opportunity to thrive. His efforts inspire and empower underrepresented artists, while contributing to a more vibrant and inclusive global music community.

Chapter 5 The Future of Virtual Riot

Chapter 5 The Future of Virtual Riot

Chapter 5: The Future of Virtual Riot

As Virtual Riot continues to make waves in the electronic music scene, fans and industry insiders alike are curious about what lies ahead for this talented artist. In this chapter, we will delve into the future of Virtual Riot, exploring his evolving sound, musical vision, and the impact he will have on future generations of musicians.

Leaving a Mark on the EDM Scene

Virtual Riot has already made a significant impact on the EDM scene, pushing boundaries and redefining the sound of electronic music. His unique blend of genres and styles has garnered him a dedicated following, and he shows no signs of slowing down.

Looking ahead, Virtual Riot plans to continue experimenting with different genres and styles, bringing new elements into his music. He aims to redefine the boundaries of EDM and create exciting and innovative soundscapes that captivate listeners.

Collaborations and Future Projects

Collaborations have been an integral part of Virtual Riot's journey, and he sees them as a way to constantly learn and grow as an artist. In the future, he plans to collaborate with both established and emerging artists, bringing together diverse talents to create groundbreaking music.

Virtual Riot is also working on various future projects, aiming to push his artistic vision to new heights. These projects will not only showcase his immense talent, but also challenge existing music norms and defy expectations.

Driving Musical Evolution

Virtual Riot believes that the future of electronic music lies in its ability to evolve and adapt. He sees himself as a catalyst for this evolution, constantly pushing boundaries and exploring new sonic territories.

With his innovative approach to music production and fearless experimentation, Virtual Riot envisions a future where EDM continues to evolve and incorporates elements from various genres. He believes that this cross-pollination of styles will create a new and exciting sound that resonates with a wide audience.

Goals and Aspirations as an Artist

Virtual Riot has never been content with staying within the confines of a single genre or style. His ultimate goal is to continue pushing musical boundaries, defying expectations, and challenging himself creatively.

As an artist, Virtual Riot aspires to inspire others to think outside the box and explore their own artistic boundaries. He hopes that his music will encourage emerging artists to experiment and take risks, ultimately contributing to the collective evolution of the electronic music scene.

Pushing Musical Boundaries

Virtual Riot thrives on pushing musical boundaries, and he is constantly looking for new ways to innovate and surprise his audience. He believes in the power of music to evoke emotions and create transformative experiences.

To achieve this, Virtual Riot embraces unconventional production techniques, combines unexpected elements, and plays with unexpected sonic textures. By constantly pushing himself to explore new sonic frontiers, he aims to create a lasting impact on the future of music.

Virtual Riot's Legacy

Virtual Riot's enduring relevance in the music industry and his impact on future generations of musicians will be his legacy. By challenging the status quo and inspiring a new wave of music producers, he will leave a mark on the EDM scene that will be felt for years to come.

His dedication to pushing boundaries, embracing innovation, and fostering creativity will serve as a guiding light for aspiring artists. Virtual Riot's willingness to take risks and his refusal to be confined by traditional genre labels will continue to inspire future generations to explore and experiment with music.

In conclusion, the future of Virtual Riot is indeed an exciting one. With his unwavering commitment to pushing musical boundaries, collaborating with diverse artists, and inspiring future generations, he will undoubtedly remain a force to be reckoned with in the electronic music scene. As fans eagerly anticipate his future projects and sound, Virtual Riot will continue to evolve and shape the future of music while leaving a lasting legacy.

Evolving Sound and Musical Vision

Experimenting with Genres and Styles

In the ever-evolving world of music, Virtual Riot has become known for his ability to seamlessly blend various genres and styles together. He is a true musical chameleon, constantly pushing the boundaries and experimenting with different sounds. This section delves into Virtual Riot's approach to genre fusion, his creative process, and the impact of his musical experimentation.

The Freedom of Genre Blending

Virtual Riot's music is a melting pot of genres, combining elements of dubstep, drum and bass, future bass, and many others. He believes that genre should never be a limitation, but rather a starting point for exploration. By breaking down the barriers between different styles, he creates a unique and innovative sound that sets him apart from his peers.

One of Virtual Riot's favorite genres to experiment with is future bass. Its melodic and uplifting nature allows for endless possibilities when it comes to fusing it with other genres. By infusing future bass with elements of dubstep or drum and bass, he creates a dynamic and unexpected sound that keeps listeners on their toes.

Finding the Balance

Experimenting with genres can be a delicate balancing act. It requires a deep understanding and appreciation for each genre involved, as well as the ability to find common ground between them. Virtual Riot spends a significant amount of time studying the intricacies of different genres and identifying their defining characteristics.

When blending genres, Virtual Riot aims to maintain a sense of cohesion and harmony. He carefully selects elements from each genre that complement each other, creating a seamless transition from one style to another. By finding the right balance between familiar and unfamiliar sounds, he is able to create a fresh and exciting listening experience.

Innovation Through Fusion

Virtual Riot's genre experimentation is not limited to electronic music. He draws inspiration from various musical traditions and incorporates elements from different cultures. This fusion of styles not only adds depth and complexity to his music but also creates a bridge between different communities and expands the horizons of his listeners.

For example, Virtual Riot has experimented with incorporating elements of traditional world music into his compositions. By blending the rhythms and instruments from different cultures with his signature electronic sound, he creates a sense of unity and celebration of diversity. This kind of cross-cultural exploration not only pushes the boundaries of his own musicality but also invites audiences from all over the world to connect through his music.

The Impact of Virtual Riot's Experimentation

Virtual Riot's genre-bending approach has had a profound impact on the electronic music scene. By challenging traditional genre boundaries, he has inspired a new generation of artists and producers to think outside the box and explore new sonic territories.

His fearless experimentation has opened up possibilities for cross-genre collaborations and has contributed to the evolution of electronic music as a whole. Virtual Riot's unique blend of styles has breathed new life into the genre, attracting a diverse fanbase and pushing the boundaries of what is considered "EDM."

Moreover, Virtual Riot's experimentation serves as a reminder that music knows no boundaries. It encourages artists and listeners alike to embrace diversity and explore the endless possibilities of musical expression.

Unconventional Example: Combining Classical and Bass Music

To illustrate the unconventional nature of Virtual Riot's experimentation, let's consider the blending of classical music with bass music. On the surface, these two genres may seem incompatible due to their stark differences in instrumentation and composition.

However, Virtual Riot sees the potential for synergy between the depth and emotion of classical music and the energetic drive of bass music. By integrating orchestral elements, such as strings or brass, into the heavy bass drops and electronic beats, he creates a fusion that is both unexpected and compelling.

For example, Virtual Riot may sample a haunting violin melody from a classical symphony and incorporate it into a bass-heavy track. This juxtaposition of classical elegance and modern intensity creates a unique sonic experience that appeals to fans from both genres.

This blend of classical and bass music not only showcases Virtual Riot's versatility but also challenges preconceived notions about what can be achieved through genre fusion.

Conclusion

Virtual Riot's genre experimentation is a testament to his artistic vision and willingness to explore uncharted musical territories. By breaking down genre barriers and blending styles, he has created a sound that is uniquely his own. His commitment to creative exploration and collaboration serves as an inspiration to aspiring artists and a catalyst for the evolution of electronic music as a whole. As Virtual Riot continues to experiment with genres and styles, we can only speculate on the exciting musical horizons he will explore in the future.

Redefining the Boundaries of EDM

In the ever-evolving landscape of electronic dance music (EDM), Virtual Riot has emerged as a trailblazer, breaking through traditional boundaries and redefining the limits of the genre. With his innovative sound and fearless experimentation, he has captured the attention of music enthusiasts across the globe and has become a driving force in the evolution of EDM.

One of the key elements that sets Virtual Riot apart is his willingness to explore diverse musical styles and fuse them together in his productions. He embraces a more eclectic approach to EDM, incorporating elements from various genres such as dubstep, drum and bass, trap, and even classical music. By melding together these seemingly disparate elements, he creates unique and captivating compositions that have a distinct Virtual Riot signature.

Virtual Riot's ability to push the boundaries of EDM is exemplified through his mastery of sound design. He constantly seeks out new and innovative ways to create distinct sounds that challenge the listener's expectations.   From mind-bending basslines to intricate melodies, his soundscapes are meticulously crafted and meticulously crafted to elicit powerful emotions and transport the listener to uncharted territories.

To accomplish this, Virtual Riot often employs advanced techniques and cutting-edge technology in his production process. He emphasizes the use of synthesizers, both hardware and software, to craft meticulously designed sounds that push the limits of what is possible in EDM. By harnessing the power of synthesis, he creates sounds that are not bound by traditional instruments or samples, giving him the freedom to truly redefine the sonic landscape of the genre.

Virtual Riot also integrates unconventional elements into his music, constantly experimenting with unconventional structures, rhythms, and melodies. He isn't afraid to challenge the listener's expectations and break away from the formulaic song structures commonly found in EDM. By doing so, he keeps his music fresh, exciting, and constantly evolving, pushing the boundaries of what is considered mainstream in the genre.

Furthermore, Virtual Riot's collaborations with artists from diverse musical backgrounds are a testament to his dedication to redefining the boundaries of EDM. By working with musicians outside of the traditional EDM scene, he injects new perspectives and ideas into his music, creating truly groundbreaking and genre-defying tracks. These collaborations not only demonstrate his commitment to pushing the boundaries of EDM but also open up new possibilities for the genre as a whole.

In addition to his musical innovations, Virtual Riot's live performances further exemplify his dedication to redefining the boundaries of EDM. He incorporates live instruments into his sets, seamlessly blending electronic elements with traditional instruments. This unique blend of live instrumentation and electronic production creates an immersive and dynamic live experience, engaging the audience in new and exciting ways.

To summarize, Virtual Riot's relentless pursuit of innovation and his willingness to challenge the norms of EDM have led him to redefine the genre's boundaries. By embracing a diverse range of musical styles, pushing the limits of sound design, experimenting with unconventional structures, and collaborating with artists from various backgrounds, he has carved out a unique space for himself in the EDM landscape. As Virtual Riot continues to evolve and explore new sonic territories, he leaves an indelible mark on the genre and inspires future generations to push the boundaries of what is deemed possible in EDM.

Collaborations and Future Projects

Collaborations are an integral part of Virtual Riot's creative process, allowing him to explore new ideas and push the boundaries of his sound. With a strong desire to constantly evolve and innovate, Virtual Riot actively seeks out opportunities to work with other artists from diverse backgrounds and genres. Let's delve into the exciting world of Virtual Riot's collaborations and get a glimpse of his future projects.

The Power of Collaboration

Virtual Riot firmly believes that collaboration is a powerful tool for artistic growth and creativity. By bringing together different perspectives, skills, and musical backgrounds, collaborations have the potential to produce groundbreaking music that transcends boundaries and resonates with a wide audience.

When choosing artists to collaborate with, Virtual Riot looks for individuals who share his passion for pushing the limits of electronic music. He values open-mindedness, a willingness to experiment, and a strong work ethic. Virtual Riot believes that the key to a successful collaboration lies in finding the right balance between creative differences and shared vision.

Upcoming Collaborations

Looking towards the future, Virtual Riot has a number of exciting collaborations in the works. He is currently working on a project with a renowned hip-hop producer, combining their unique styles to create a fresh fusion of electronic and rap music. This collaboration aims to bridge the gap between these two genres and introduce listeners to a new sonic experience.

In addition, Virtual Riot is teaming up with an emerging indie pop artist to create a track that blurs the lines between electronic and alternative music. This collaboration showcases Virtual Riot's ability to adapt to different genres while maintaining his signature sound.

Virtual Riot is also exploring partnerships with up-and-coming vocalists, focusing on crafting emotionally-driven tracks that resonate with listeners on a deeper level. By combining his cutting-edge production techniques with powerful vocal performances, Virtual Riot aims to create music that is both sonically captivating and emotionally impactful.

Innovative Projects

Beyond traditional collaborations, Virtual Riot is also involved in several innovative projects that push the boundaries of music production. He is currently working with a team of software developers to create a groundbreaking plugin that combines virtual reality technology with music creation. This project aims to revolutionize the way musicians interact with their music, providing an immersive and intuitive platform for experimentation and creativity.

Furthermore, Virtual Riot is collaborating with visual artists to create immersive live performances that integrate music, visuals, and interactive elements. By combining stunning visual effects, intricate stage design, and real-time audience interaction, Virtual Riot aims to elevate the live experience and deliver a truly unforgettable show.

Virtual Riot's Vision for Collaboration

For Virtual Riot, collaborations and future projects are not just about creating music, but also about fostering a sense of community and inspiring future generations of artists. He believes that by pushing the boundaries of what is possible in music, he can encourage others to step out of their comfort zones and explore their own creative potential.

Virtual Riot envisions a future where collaboration is at the forefront of music-making, where artists from different genres and backgrounds come together to create innovative and boundary-breaking music. He hopes to inspire a new wave of creativity and establish a culture of collaboration that celebrates diversity and encourages artistic exploration.

Caveat: Balancing Creative Differences

While collaborations bring a wealth of new ideas and perspectives, they can also present challenges. Balancing creative differences and navigating the complexities of working with other artists requires patience, compromise, and effective communication. Virtual Riot acknowledges the importance of maintaining a positive and respectful working environment, ensuring that each collaborator's voice is heard and valued.

Example: Fusion of Genres

One example of Virtual Riot's successful collaboration is his project with a renowned jazz pianist. By combining elements of jazz improvisation with Virtual Riot's electronic production techniques, they created a unique blend of genres that captivated audiences and garnered critical acclaim. This collaboration not only showcased the versatility of Virtual Riot's sound but also highlighted the power of collaboration in bridging the gap between seemingly disparate musical styles.

Exercise: Break Down Genre Barriers

Think about two different genres of music that you enjoy. How would you go about combining elements from both genres to create a unique blend? Consider the possibilities and experiment with incorporating elements such as rhythmic patterns, instrumentations, and melodic structures from each genre. Push the boundaries of what is traditionally expected from these genres and embrace the spirit of collaboration.

Resources and Inspiration for Collaboration

Virtual Riot draws inspiration from a wide range of sources to fuel his collaborative endeavors. He actively seeks out new music, attends live performances, and immerses himself in diverse artistic communities. Virtual Riot also takes advantage of online platforms and social media to discover emerging artists and connect with like-minded musicians. By staying open to new ideas and embracing the wealth of inspiration around him, Virtual Riot ensures that his collaborations are constantly evolving and pushing creative boundaries.

Conclusion

Collaborations and future projects play a vital role in Virtual Riot's artistic journey. By working with artists from different genres and backgrounds, he aims to create music that transcends boundaries and inspires listeners. Whether through traditional collaborations, innovative projects, or pushing genre boundaries, Virtual Riot's vision for collaboration is rooted in the belief that together, artists can create something truly extraordinary.

In the next section, we will explore Virtual Riot's role as a producer and delve into his creative process behind crafting dynamic and innovative tracks that have captivated audiences worldwide.

Virtual Riot's Perspective on Musical Evolution

Music is a constantly evolving art form, and Virtual Riot has always been at the forefront of pushing boundaries and redefining the sound of electronic dance music (EDM). In this section, we delve into Virtual Riot's perspective on musical evolution and explore his vision for the future of electronic music.

Experimenting with Genres and Styles

Virtual Riot's unique approach to music production involves experimentation with various genres and styles. He believes that true creativity lies in the ability to break free from established norms and explore new sonic territories.

One of the ways Virtual Riot pushes the limits of genre is by blending different styles together. By combining elements of dubstep, drum and bass, electro house, and more, he creates a sound that is truly his own. His ability to seamlessly fuse genres not only sets him apart from other artists but also keeps his music fresh and exciting.

Redefining the Boundaries of EDM

For Virtual Riot, pushing the boundaries of EDM is not just about experimentation with genres, but also about challenging the traditional structures and expectations within the genre itself. He believes that EDM should not be confined to a set of rules, but rather should be a platform for artistic freedom and expression.

To redefine the boundaries of EDM, Virtual Riot often incorporates unconventional sounds and unexpected song structures into his tracks. He believes in breaking away from predictable formulas and daring to be different. This approach not only keeps his music interesting and innovative but also challenges listeners to expand their understanding of what EDM can be.

Collaborations and Future Projects

Collaborations have played a significant role in Virtual Riot's musical evolution. He sees collaborations as an opportunity to learn from other artists, merge different perspectives, and create something truly remarkable. Virtual Riot believes that by joining forces with like-minded individuals, he can continue to push the boundaries of what is possible in music.

Looking to the future, Virtual Riot's projects are not just limited to music. He envisions collaborations with visual artists, designers, and even filmmakers to create immersive experiences where music and visual art seamlessly intertwine. By exploring new mediums and pushing the boundaries of traditional music production, he aims to create a multi-sensory experience that goes beyond the confines of a traditional electronic music show.

Virtual Riot's Perspective on Musical Evolution

For Virtual Riot, musical evolution is not just about pushing boundaries or experimenting with different sounds and styles. It is also about staying true to oneself and continuously evolving as an artist. He believes that true growth comes from a deep understanding of oneself and a willingness to embrace change.

From Virtual Riot's perspective, musical evolution is a journey of self-discovery and personal growth. It is about constantly challenging oneself, exploring new possibilities, and never settling for mediocrity. Virtual Riot sees music as a medium through which he can express his emotions and connect with listeners on a deeper level. With each new track, he strives to tell a story and evoke powerful emotions, transcending the boundaries of language and culture.

The Quest for Sonic Exploration

Virtual Riot's passion for musical evolution stems from his insatiable curiosity and desire to constantly explore new sonic landscapes. He believes that sound has infinite possibilities and that the only limit lies in one's imagination.

To achieve sonic exploration, Virtual Riot constantly seeks out new techniques and technologies that allow him to create unique sounds. He experiments with sound design, manipulates audio samples, and pushes the boundaries of digital synthesis. By embracing innovation, he expands the sonic palette available to him and opens up new avenues for musical expression.

Virtual Riot's approach to sonic exploration goes beyond the conventional. He seeks inspiration from a wide range of sources, including nature, everyday sounds, and even unconventional instruments. By incorporating these elements into his music, he adds a layer of richness and depth that sets him apart from other producers.

The Future of Electronic Music

Looking ahead, Virtual Riot envisions a future where electronic music continues to evolve and transcend genres. He sees a world where artists are not constrained by labels, but rather free to explore and create without limitations.

Virtual Riot believes that technology will play a vital role in shaping the future of electronic music. Advancements in music production software, virtual reality, and AI will enable artists to push the boundaries of creativity even further. He anticipates a future where music can be experienced in immersive virtual environments, blurring the lines between reality and imagination.

In Virtual Riot's vision, collaboration will also continue to be a driving force behind the evolution of electronic music. He believes that by working together, artists can create groundbreaking music that challenges the status quo and pushes the boundaries of what is possible.

As Virtual Riot continues to evolve as an artist, he remains committed to pushing the boundaries of electronic music and inspiring the next generation of musicians to do the same. With his unique perspective on musical evolution, he continues to shape the future of electronic music and leave a lasting impact on the industry.

Virtual Riot's Vision for the Future of Electronic Music

Virtual Riot's vision for the future of electronic music is one that encompasses constant evolution, creativity, and pushing the boundaries of sound. As an artist who is never afraid to experiment and explore new genres and styles, Virtual Riot believes that the future of electronic music lies in the fusion of different genres, the integration of cutting-edge technology, and the creation of unique and immersive live experiences.

One aspect of Virtual Riot's vision is the continued experimentation with genres and styles. He believes that electronic music should not be confined to a certain sound or formula, but instead should be a fluid and ever-changing creative expression. Virtual Riot envisions a future where artists are not confined by the limitations of genre labels, but are encouraged to blend different styles and create something truly original. By breaking down the barriers between genres, Virtual Riot believes that electronic music can continue to evolve and expand its reach to new audiences.

In order to achieve this vision, Virtual Riot emphasizes the importance of embracing and utilizing technology in music production and live performances. He believes that technology can be a powerful tool for artists to push the boundaries of sound and create new and innovative sonic experiences. From using advanced software and plugins to experimenting with virtual reality and interactive visuals, Virtual Riot sees the incorporation of technology as a key factor in shaping the future of electronic music.

Virtual Riot's vision also involves the creation of immersive and transformative live experiences. He believes that live performances should be more than just a DJ set; they should be a multisensory journey that engages the audience on a deeper level. This means integrating elements such as live instruments, custom stage designs, and interactive visuals to create a fully immersive and captivating experience for the audience. Virtual Riot envisions a future where live performances blur the lines between performer and audience, creating a sense of unity and connection that goes beyond the music itself.

In addition to pushing boundaries and embracing technology, Virtual Riot also believes in the power of collaboration. He sees collaboration as a way to bring different perspectives and ideas together, creating something greater than the sum of its parts. Virtual Riot envisions a future where artists from different backgrounds and genres collaborate freely, creating unique tracks and pushing the boundaries of electronic music even further.

However, Virtual Riot also recognizes the importance of staying true to oneself and maintaining authenticity in the midst of these transformations. He believes that as electronic music continues to evolve, it is crucial for artists to stay rooted in their own creative vision and not succumb to external pressures or trends. By staying true to oneself, Virtual Riot believes that artists can create music that is genuine and has a lasting impact on both the industry and the listeners.

In summary, Virtual Riot's vision for the future of electronic music is one of constant evolution, creativity, and pushing the boundaries of sound. He envisions a future where artists embrace experimentation, utilize technology, and create immersive live experiences. Collaboration, authenticity, and a commitment to staying true to oneself are also key aspects of Virtual Riot's vision. By embracing these principles, Virtual Riot believes that the future of electronic music will be filled with innovation, diversity, and endless possibilities.

Virtual Riot's Goals and Aspirations as an Artist

Virtual Riot, the renowned electronic music producer, has a clear vision for his future as an artist. He is not content with simply following trends or sticking to one style of music. Instead, he aspires to constantly explore new genres and push the boundaries of electronic dance music (EDM). His goals and aspirations reflect his determination to evolve as an artist and leave a lasting impact on the music industry.

One of Virtual Riot's primary goals is to experiment with different genres and styles of music. He believes that true creativity lies in the ability to blend diverse influences and create something unique. As an artist, he seeks to break free from the conventions of EDM and incorporate elements from other genres, such as hip-hop, rock, and classical music. By infusing various styles, Virtual Riot aims to create a sound that is fresh, innovative, and resonates with a wide range of listeners.

In order to redefine the boundaries of EDM, Virtual Riot also intends to collaborate with artists from different musical backgrounds. He recognizes the power of collaboration in fostering creativity and unlocking new possibilities. By working with musicians outside of the EDM scene, he aims to challenge traditional notions of genre and create groundbreaking music that appeals to a diverse audience.   This collaborative approach not only enriches his own artistic development but also contributes to the evolution of EDM as a whole.

Virtual Riot's aspirations go beyond just creating music; he seeks to establish a connection with his listeners on a deeper level. He wants his music to evoke emotions, inspire introspection, and bring people together. He values the personal connection that music can create and strives to craft tracks that resonate with his fans on an emotional level. Virtual Riot believes that by touching people's hearts with his music, he can have a lasting impact and leave a positive mark on their lives.

As an artist, Virtual Riot is driven by his desire to constantly challenge himself and exceed his own expectations. He sets high standards for himself and aims to continually improve his skills as a producer and performer. Virtual Riot sees every project, whether it be a single, an album, or a live performance, as an opportunity to explore new techniques, refine his sound, and deliver the best possible experience for his audience. He believes that by pushing his own limits, he can inspire others and contribute to the growth of the EDM community.

In addition to his artistic pursuits, Virtual Riot is passionate about sharing his knowledge and experiences with aspiring musicians. He believes in the importance of mentorship and wants to empower the next generation of artists to find their unique voice. Through workshops, tutorials, and educational programs, Virtual Riot hopes to provide guidance and support to young producers, helping them navigate the complex world of music production and fostering their creativity.

Virtual Riot's goals and aspirations as an artist are not solely focused on his personal success; he also wants to make a positive impact on the world. He is committed to using his platform to raise awareness and support charitable causes. From supporting music education programs to championing underrepresented artists, Virtual Riot believes in giving back to the community that has supported him. He sees philanthropy as an integral part of his artistic journey and hopes to inspire other artists to use their influence for good.

Virtual Riot's future is filled with boundless possibilities. His drive to explore new genres, collaborate with diverse artists, connect with fans, exceed his own limits, mentor aspiring musicians, and contribute to charitable causes will continue to shape the trajectory of his career. As an artist who values authenticity, innovation, and community, Virtual Riot's goals and aspirations serve as an inspiration not only to the EDM scene but also to the broader music industry. His relentless pursuit of creativity and meaningful connections ensures that he will have an enduring legacy as an artist who challenged the status quo and opened doors for future generations.

Virtual Riot's Ideas for Pushing Musical Boundaries

When it comes to pushing musical boundaries, Virtual Riot has never been one to shy away from experimentation and innovation. His relentless pursuit of new sounds and genres has made him a true pioneer in the world of electronic dance music. In this section, we will explore Virtual Riot's ideas for pushing musical boundaries and how he continues to redefine the EDM landscape.

One of Virtual Riot's key ideas for pushing musical boundaries is through the fusion of different genres and styles. He believes that by breaking down the barriers between genres, he can create a truly unique and groundbreaking sound. Virtual Riot has never been afraid to cross musical boundaries, whether it's incorporating elements of metal, hip-hop, or classical music into his tracks. By blending these diverse influences, he creates a sound that is distinctly his own.

To accomplish this, Virtual Riot takes inspiration from artists outside of the EDM scene. He immerses himself in different musical cultures and is constantly exploring new genres and styles. By drawing from a wide range of influences, he is able to create music that is both familiar and fresh. For example, Virtual Riot may incorporate the heavy guitar riffs of metal music with the energetic beats of EDM, resulting in a fusion of genres that pushes the boundaries of traditional electronic music.

In addition to genre fusion, Virtual Riot also pushes musical boundaries through his use of unconventional sound design and production techniques. He is known for his intricate layering of sounds and his meticulous attention to detail when it comes to sound design. Virtual Riot often experiments with different synth presets, effects chains, and mix techniques to create unique and unexpected sounds. This emphasis on sound design allows him to create tracks that are not only musically innovative but also sonically engaging.

Virtual Riot also explores the potential of technology in pushing musical boundaries. He embraces new tools and software that allow him to experiment and create sounds that were previously unimaginable. Whether it's utilizing granular synthesis or manipulating audio through advanced plugins, he constantly pushes the limits of what's possible in music production.

An example of Virtual Riot's approach to pushing musical boundaries is his track "Presets". In this track, he takes presets from different synthesizers and combines them in a way that has never been done before. The result is a sound that is entirely unique and showcases his ability to think outside the box.

Another way Virtual Riot pushes musical boundaries is by collaborating with other artists from different genres. Through these collaborations, he can merge different musical styles and influences, resulting in tracks that defy genre categorization. By working with musicians from diverse backgrounds, he is able to infuse his music with fresh perspectives and open up new creative possibilities.

Virtual Riot's ideas for pushing musical boundaries extend beyond his own music. He actively encourages and supports emerging artists who are pushing the boundaries of electronic music. Through mentorship and collaboration, he provides a platform for new voices to be heard and contributes to the growth and evolution of the EDM scene.

In conclusion, Virtual Riot's ideas for pushing musical boundaries revolve around genre fusion, unconventional sound design, technological exploration, and collaboration. By embracing these principles, he continues to redefine the EDM landscape and pave the way for future generations of musicians and producers to explore new frontiers. With his relentless pursuit of innovation, Virtual Riot is truly an inspiration to artists and music lovers alike.

Virtual Riot's Dream Collaborations and Projects

Virtual Riot, known for his unique sound and innovative approach to electronic dance music, has always been driven by a desire to push boundaries and explore new artistic horizons. With an impressive track record of collaborations and successful projects under his belt, he continues to dream big when it comes to potential future partnerships and ventures. In this section, we delve into Virtual Riot's dream collaborations and projects, giving a glimpse into his creative vision for the future.

Collaborating with Musical Legends

One of Virtual Riot's ultimate dreams is to collaborate with musical legends who have inspired him throughout his career. He envisions working with artists such as Daft Punk, the iconic French duo known for their groundbreaking electronic music. The combination of Virtual Riot's futuristic sound and Daft Punk's timeless style would undoubtedly create an electrifying fusion.

Another dream collaboration for Virtual Riot is with the legendary rock band Queen. Queen's anthemic songs and Freddie Mercury's powerful vocals have long been sources of inspiration for Virtual Riot. The idea of combining his electronic production with Queen's rock and operatic elements excites him, as it would present an opportunity to bridge musical genres in a truly unique way.

Crossing Boundaries with Pop Stars

Virtual Riot's artistic vision extends beyond the electronic music scene, as he harbors dreams of collaborating with pop stars who have an affinity for experimenting with different sounds and styles. One such collaboration he dreams of is with Billie Eilish, the Grammy Award-winning artist who has made waves with her atmospheric and genre-defying music. Virtual Riot believes that their shared interest in breaking musical boundaries could result in a groundbreaking collaboration that pushes the limits of sonic exploration.

Similarly, Virtual Riot envisions joining forces with The Weeknd, an artist known for his blend of R&B, pop, and electronic elements. The Weeknd's sultry vocals combined with Virtual Riot's intricate production skills could create an irresistible sonic tapestry that captivates audiences across various genres.

Venturing into Film and Video Game Soundtracks

Virtual Riot's creative ambitions extend beyond the realm of music releases, as he envisions scoring film and video game soundtracks. Drawing inspiration from composers like Hans Zimmer and Trent Reznor, Virtual Riot is captivated by the idea of creating atmospheric and immersive music that enhances storytelling in visual mediums.

His dream project involves collaborating with visionary director Christopher Nolan, who is known for his mind-bending films such as Inception and Interstellar. Virtual Riot's ability to create intricate and evocative soundscapes could perfectly complement Nolan's penchant for cinematic grandeur, resulting in a powerful audiovisual experience.

In the realm of video games, Virtual Riot dreams of composing for epic, open-world adventures. He envisions working on a project like The Legend of Zelda, where he could create immersive soundtracks that transport players into the game's fantastical universe. Virtual Riot's passion for creating emotionally evocative music aligns perfectly with the immersive nature of video game storytelling.

Innovating with Virtual Reality Experiences

Virtual Riot has always been at the forefront of technological innovation within the music industry. As virtual reality (VR) continues to evolve, he sees immense potential in combining his music with immersive VR experiences. His dream is to create a virtual reality concert, allowing fans from all over the world to feel like they are attending a live show from the comfort of their homes.

In this vision, Virtual Riot's intricate production would be accompanied by visually stunning VR environments, creating a multisensory experience that transports participants into a world of music and visuals. The fusion of cutting-edge technology and Virtual Riot's music would redefine the traditional concert experience and push the boundaries of what is possible in the realm of live performances.

Empowering New Artists and Exploring Emerging Genres

Virtual Riot's passion for innovation extends to nurturing and collaborating with emerging artists. He dreams of creating a platform that empowers rising talents and encourages the exploration of new genres and styles. This project would involve providing resources, mentorship, and opportunities for these artists to showcase their unique vision and sound.

Additionally, Virtual Riot has a keen interest in delving into emerging genres that are still in their infancy. He envisions experimenting with genres like future bass, trap, and experimental electronic music, pushing the boundaries of these styles and creating fresh and innovative sounds that resonate with both existing and new audiences.

Unconventional Performances and Collaborative Experiments

As someone who never shies away from pushing the envelope, Virtual Riot dreams of presenting unconventional performances and embarking on collaborative experiments. These projects would explore the intersection of music, technology, and visual art in immersive and interactive ways.

One such project involves collaborating with visual artists and engineers to create a live performance where music interacts with responsive visuals and stage design in real-time. This collaboration would push the boundaries of traditional live shows, blurring the lines between music, art, and technology.

Another dream project for Virtual Riot is to collaborate with scientists and researchers to create music using unconventional techniques, such as harnessing brainwave data or incorporating natural sounds from ecological environments. This interdisciplinary exploration would fuse the realms of science and music, resulting in innovative and thought-provoking sonic experiences.

Looking Towards a Limitless Future

Virtual Riot's dream collaborations and projects represent an artist with an insatiable hunger for innovation. As technology continues to evolve and musical boundaries are broken, he envisions a future where artists from different disciplines come together to create groundbreaking works of art.

Driven by the desire to push the limits of his craft, Virtual Riot's dream projects encompass collaborations with musical legends, ventures into film and video game soundtracks, innovative virtual reality experiences, empowering new artists, exploring emerging genres, and embarking on unconventional performances and collaborative experiments.

Virtual Riot's vision for the future is one where creativity knows no bounds, and where the boundaries between music, art, and technology dissolve to create transformative experiences for both himself and his audience. With his relentless dedication to pushing boundaries, it is evident that Virtual Riot's dream collaborations and projects will continue to shape the future of electronic music.

Virtual Riot's Impact on Future Music Trends

Virtual Riot, with his innovative approach to music production and his ability to push the boundaries of genres, has had a significant impact on future music trends. Through his unique sound and creative vision, he has influenced and inspired a new wave of producers and artists, shaping the future of electronic music.

One of the ways Virtual Riot has impacted future music trends is through his experimentation with genres and styles. He is not afraid to break the rules and blend different musical elements together, creating fresh and exciting sounds. By crossing boundaries and fusing genres, he has expanded the possibilities within electronic music and encouraged other artists to think outside the box.

For instance, Virtual Riot's incorporation of elements from dubstep, drum and bass, and hip-hop into his music has opened up new avenues for exploration. His tracks seamlessly blend these genres, creating a unique sonic experience that challenges traditional genre classifications. This experimentation has inspired other producers to take risks and explore new musical territories, leading to the emergence of hybrid genres and genre-bending tracks.

Virtual Riot's impact extends beyond just musical experimentation. He has also played a crucial role in redefining the sound and direction of EDM. With his intricate sound design, complex melodies, and heavy basslines, he has pushed the genre to new heights. His tracks are a perfect fusion of energy and emotion, captivating listeners and pushing the boundaries of what is possible within the EDM landscape.

Furthermore, Virtual Riot's ability to create emotional connections through his music has had a profound impact on future music trends. His tracks evoke a wide range of emotions, from pure euphoria to introspective contemplation. This emotional depth has inspired other artists to infuse their own music with a sense of vulnerability and authenticity. As a result, there has been a shift in the EDM scene towards more emotionally driven and meaningful music.

In addition to his sonic innovations, Virtual Riot has also made significant contributions to the use of technology in music production. He embraces the latest advancements in music production tools and techniques, constantly pushing the limits of what can be achieved. By incorporating cutting-edge technology into his music, he has set a new standard for production quality and inspired other producers to explore and experiment with new tools and technologies.

An example of Virtual Riot's impact on the future of music production is his use of virtual reality (VR) technology. He has embraced VR as a platform for immersive musical experiences, allowing audiences to not only listen to his music but also visually and physically engage with it. This fusion of music and technology has sparked a new wave of innovation, with artists and producers exploring the potential of VR to enhance the listener's experience.

Virtual Riot's impact on future music trends can also be seen in the rise of live performance technology. With his high-energy and engaging live shows, he has raised the bar for live performances within the EDM scene. By incorporating live instruments, visuals, and stage design, he creates a truly immersive and captivating experience for his audience. As a result, other artists have started to prioritize their live performances, pushing the boundaries of what is possible on stage and creating more dynamic and memorable shows.

In conclusion, Virtual Riot's impact on future music trends is undeniable. Through his experimentation with genres, redefinition of the sound and direction of EDM, creation of emotional connections, embrace of technology, and innovation in live performances, he has inspired a new generation of producers, shaping the future of electronic music. His ability to push boundaries and think outside the box has opened up new avenues of creativity, ensuring that his influence will be felt for years to come.

Virtual Riot's Enduring Relevance in the Music Industry

Virtual Riot, with his unique sound and fearless approach to music, has carved out a special place for himself in the ever-evolving landscape of the music industry. His enduring relevance can be attributed to several key factors that have set him apart from his peers and allowed him to consistently push boundaries and stay at the forefront of the EDM scene.

One of the main reasons for Virtual Riot's enduring relevance is his willingness to experiment with genres and styles. While many artists choose to stay within the confines of a specific genre, Virtual Riot has fearlessly explored a wide range of musical genres, blending elements together to create his own distinctive sound. From dubstep to drum and bass, from melodic sounds to hard-hitting basslines, his ability to seamlessly fuse different genres has captivated audiences around the world. By constantly evolving and taking risks with his music, Virtual Riot keeps his sound fresh and interesting, ensuring that he remains relevant to both old and new fans alike.

In addition to his genre-bending approach, Virtual Riot's enduring relevance can also be attributed to his role as a trendsetter in the electronic music industry. Through his innovative production techniques and boundary-pushing sound design, he has consistently pushed the envelope and set new standards for what is possible in electronic music. His use of unique and imaginative soundscapes, intricate melodies, and heavy bass drops has served as inspiration for countless producers and artists who strive to capture the same energy and creativity in their own work. Virtual Riot's willingness to push the boundaries of EDM has not only secured his place as a respected artist but has also had a profound influence on the direction of the genre as a whole.

Another aspect of Virtual Riot's enduring relevance is his ability to connect with his audience on a personal level. Despite his rise to fame and success, he has remained down-to-earth and approachable, making a conscious effort to engage with his fans both online and during live performances. From Q&A sessions to live streams, Virtual Riot takes the time to connect with his fans, answering their questions, and sharing insights into his creative process. This level of engagement not only fosters a sense of community among his fan base but also allows him to gain valuable feedback and stay attuned to the ever-changing tastes and preferences of his audience.

Virtual Riot's active online presence through social media platforms has also contributed to his enduring relevance in the music industry. Through platforms like Twitter, Instagram, and YouTube, he regularly interacts with fans and keeps them updated on his latest projects, shows, and collaborations. This direct line of communication allows him to build a strong and loyal fan base, who in turn play an integral role in promoting and amplifying his music.

It is worth noting that Virtual Riot's relevance in the music industry goes beyond his individual achievements. He has also played a key role in shaping the larger EDM landscape, both as a mentor and collaborator. By actively collaborating with emerging and established artists, Virtual Riot has provided a platform for new voices to be heard and has contributed to the diversification and progression of the genre. His collaborations with artists from various backgrounds and genres have resulted in groundbreaking tracks that push the boundaries of electronic music and resonate with audiences worldwide.

Overall, Virtual Riot's enduring relevance in the music industry can be attributed to his fearless experimentation with genres and sounds, his role as a trendsetter in electronic music, his ability to connect with fans on a personal level, and his commitment to promoting emerging talent. Through his innovative approach and unwavering dedication to his craft, he continues to shape the future of EDM and inspire a new generation of musicians and producers. As long as he maintains his passion for pushing boundaries and staying true to his artistic vision, Virtual Riot will undoubtedly remain a force to be reckoned with in the music industry for years to come.

The Impact on Future Generations

Inspiring a New Wave of Music Producers

In the ever-evolving landscape of electronic music, Virtual Riot stands out as an artist who has not only pushed the boundaries of sound but has also inspired a new wave of music producers. Through his unique style, innovative techniques, and dedication to his craft, Virtual Riot has become a role model for aspiring producers looking to make their mark on the industry. In this section, we will explore how Virtual Riot's approach to music production has influenced and inspired a generation of artists.

At the core of Virtual Riot's impact on the music production community is his ability to merge different genres and experiment with sound. He has shown aspiring producers that there are no limits when it comes to creating music. Whether it's fusing elements of dubstep, future bass, or drum and bass, Virtual Riot has demonstrated the power of crossing genre boundaries and embracing diverse influences.

One of the key ways Virtual Riot inspires new producers is by openly sharing his knowledge and insights through tutorials, livestreams, and social media. Through these platforms, he breaks down complex production techniques and encourages aspiring producers to explore their creativity. Virtual Riot's dedication to education and mentorship not only provides valuable resources for newcomers but also fosters a sense of community within the music production world.

Virtual Riot's impact goes beyond just sharing knowledge. He emphasizes the importance of experimentation and thinking outside the box, encouraging aspiring producers to push their boundaries. By showcasing his own innovative techniques, he inspires others to explore unconventional methods and find their unique sound. This approach has led to a culture of creativity and exploration within the music production community, with producers stepping out of their comfort zones to create groundbreaking music.

Another aspect of Virtual Riot's influence is his emphasis on quality over quantity. In a time where it's easy to get caught up in the pressure to release music at a rapid pace, Virtual Riot encourages aspiring producers to focus on honing their skills and perfecting their craft. He reminds them that great music takes time and requires patience and dedication. This mindset has helped shape a generation of producers who value the art of music production and strive for excellence in every track they create.

To further inspire new producers, Virtual Riot often collaborates with emerging artists, providing them with a platform to showcase their talents. By featuring these artists on his tracks and supporting their work, he helps elevate their careers and encourages others to seek collaboration as a means of growth and learning. This collaborative spirit fosters a sense of community and support among producers, encouraging them to lift each other up and push the boundaries of what is possible.

In addition to impacting individual producers, Virtual Riot's influence extends to the broader music industry. His success has challenged traditional notions of what EDM should sound like, opening doors for more experimental and boundary-pushing music. By defying genre expectations and embracing his own unique style, Virtual Riot has paved the way for a new wave of producers who are unafraid to think outside the box.

In conclusion, Virtual Riot's impact on the music production community cannot be understated. Through his groundbreaking sound, dedication to education, and encouragement of creativity, he has inspired a new wave of music producers. By breaking down genre barriers, sharing knowledge, and emphasizing quality over quantity, Virtual Riot has created a culture of innovation and excellence. Aspiring producers around the world look to him for inspiration, and his influence will continue to shape the future of electronic music production.

Exercises

1. Reflect on your own music production process. Are there any boundaries or limitations you have set for yourself? How can you push beyond them, inspired by Virtual Riot's approach?

2. Explore a genre of music you are unfamiliar with and incorporate elements of it into your next production. How does this experimentation influence your creative process?

3. Reach out to an emerging artist or producer and collaborate on a track. How does working with someone else's perspective and ideas impact your own creativity?

4. Watch Virtual Riot's tutorials or livestreams and apply some of his production techniques to your own work. How do these techniques enhance your tracks?

5. Connect with other producers in online communities or local events and create a support network. Share your work, ask for feedback, and collaborate with like-minded individuals. How does this sense of community contribute to your growth as a music producer?

Remember, the path to inspiring others starts with your own journey of exploration and growth. Embrace the influence of Virtual Riot and let his passion for pushing boundaries drive you to create music that is truly unique and impactful.

Paving the Way for Innovative Soundscapes

In the ever-evolving landscape of electronic music, Virtual Riot has played a crucial role in pushing the boundaries and paving the way for innovative soundscapes. With his unique approach to music production and fearless experimentation, he has challenged the status quo and redefined what is possible within the EDM genre.

At the core of Virtual Riot's innovative soundscapes lies his mastery of sound design. He has developed a deep understanding of synthesis and sampling techniques, enabling him to create intricate and mesmerizing sonic textures that captivate listeners. His use of cutting-edge plugins and software tools allows him to manipulate and shape sounds in ways that were previously unimaginable.

One of Virtual Riot's key contributions to the world of soundscapes is his ability to seamlessly blend different musical genres. He draws inspiration from a wide range of musical styles, including dubstep, drum and bass, hip-hop, and classical music, to name just a few. By fusing together elements from these diverse genres, he creates an entirely new sonic experience that transcends traditional genre boundaries.

To achieve his distinctive sound, Virtual Riot employs various production techniques. One such technique is the layering of sounds, where multiple sounds are combined to create complex and harmonically rich textures. This layering adds depth and dimension to his compositions, immersing the listener in a sonic world that is both intricate and captivating.

Virtual Riot is also known for his meticulous attention to detail when it comes to arranging his tracks. He carefully crafts the progression of his songs, ensuring that each section seamlessly flows into the next. This attention to detail creates a cohesive and immersive listening experience, where the music takes the listener on a journey through different emotions and sonic landscapes.

In addition to his technical prowess, Virtual Riot's willingness to take risks and think outside the box sets him apart as an innovator in the field of electronic music. He is not afraid to experiment with unconventional sounds or production techniques, constantly pushing the boundaries of what is considered "normal" within the EDM scene. This fearless approach to creativity has earned him respect and admiration from both fans and fellow musicians alike.

Virtual Riot's impact on the future of soundscapes extends beyond his own music. He has inspired a new generation of producers to explore new sounds and techniques, encouraging them to think beyond the confines of traditional genres. Through his tutorials, workshops, and mentorship, he has shared his knowledge and expertise, empowering aspiring musicians to forge their own paths and create their own unique soundscapes.

As the world of electronic music continues to evolve, Virtual Riot's influence will undoubtedly be felt for years to come. His innovative soundscapes and fearless experimentation have reshaped the landscape of EDM, opening up new possibilities and inspiring future generations to push the boundaries of what is possible. Whether it's through his intricate sound design, genre-bending compositions, or his unwavering commitment to creativity, Virtual Riot has left an indelible mark on the world of innovative soundscapes.

The Long-lasting Legacy of Virtual Riot

Throughout his impressive career, Virtual Riot has left an indelible mark on the world of electronic dance music (EDM). His contributions and innovations have solidified his status as a trailblazer in the industry, and his legacy continues to inspire and influence future generations of musicians and producers.

One of the key aspects of Virtual Riot's lasting legacy is his ability to push the boundaries of EDM. He has consistently challenged the norms and conventions of the genre, introducing fresh and innovative soundscapes that captivate audiences. By constantly experimenting with different genres and styles, he has demonstrated the endless possibilities of electronic music.

Virtual Riot's impact on future music trends cannot be overstated. His fearless exploration of various musical genres and his willingness to fuse diverse elements have influenced a new wave of music producers. His ability to seamlessly blend old and new styles has paved the way for a more daring and unconventional approach to music production.

In addition to his sonic innovations, Virtual Riot's dedication to inspiring future generations is a testament to his long-lasting legacy. He has become a mentor and role model for emerging artists, offering guidance and support through his charity work, mentorship programs, and educational initiatives. By nurturing young talent and encouraging artistic exploration, he ensures that his influence continues to shape the music industry for years to come.

One of Virtual Riot's most remarkable achievements is his ability to break EDM stereotypes. He has demonstrated that electronic music can be intricate, emotive, and intellectually engaging, challenging the notion that it is solely party music. By infusing his tracks with depth and complexity, he has helped to reshape the perception of EDM and elevate it to a higher art form.

Virtual Riot's enduring relevance in the music industry is also a result of his commitment to authenticity. Despite his success and popularity, he has remained true to himself, consistently creating music that reflects his personal journey and experiences. By staying genuine and relatable, he has cultivated a loyal fan base that continues to grow and support him.

Looking into the future, Virtual Riot's vision for the evolution of electronic music is both exciting and thought-provoking. He envisions a musical landscape that embraces diversity, where different genres and styles merge to create truly unique and boundary-breaking sounds. Through his own genre-blending collaborations and projects, he aims to inspire others to explore new musical territories, fostering a spirit of creativity and innovation.

Virtual Riot's long-lasting legacy extends beyond his contributions to music. His philanthropic endeavors and commitment to giving back to the community further solidify his impact on society. Through charity work, donations, and support for underrepresented artists, he continues to make a positive difference in the lives of others. His generosity and compassion serve as an inspiration for artists and fans alike, demonstrating the power of music to effect change.

In conclusion, Virtual Riot's long-lasting legacy is built on his fearless experimentation, dedication to inspiring future generations, breaking stereotypes, and commitment to authenticity. His impact on electronic music is immeasurable, and his influence will continue to shape the industry for years to come. As he looks towards the future, Virtual Riot's vision and innovation will undoubtedly leave an enduring mark, pushing the boundaries of electronic music and inspiring the next generation of musicians.

Virtual Riot's Perspective on Musical Influence

Music is a powerful force that has the ability to shape emotions, evoke memories, and bring people together. For Virtual Riot, understanding the influence of music on individuals and society is a crucial aspect of his craft. In this section, we will explore Virtual Riot's perspective on musical influence and how it has shaped his own journey as an artist.

Virtual Riot believes that music has the power to transcend boundaries and connect people from all walks of life. He sees music as a universal language that can break down barriers and create a sense of unity. Whether it's through an energetic EDM banger or a heartfelt melodic composition, Virtual Riot aims to create an emotional connection with his listeners.

One of the key aspects of musical influence, according to Virtual Riot, is the ability to inspire and motivate others. As an artist, he recognizes the impact his music can have on aspiring producers and musicians. Virtual Riot encourages emerging artists to explore their own unique style and push the boundaries of traditional genres. He believes that by doing so, they can influence the future of music and create something truly innovative.

Virtual Riot draws inspiration from a wide range of genres and styles, and he believes that this cross-pollination of musical ideas is essential for pushing the boundaries of EDM. By incorporating elements from various genres such as rock, hip-hop, and classical music, Virtual Riot aims to create a fresh and unique sound that resonates with a diverse audience. He believes that by embracing different influences, he can create music that is both familiar and groundbreaking.

In addition to being influenced by different genres, Virtual Riot also finds inspiration from visual arts and literature. He sees these art forms as intertwined with music, each one informing and enriching the other. By exploring different mediums of artistic expression, Virtual Riot is able to broaden his creative horizons and create music that is truly multidimensional.

Virtual Riot recognizes that musical influence is not a one-way street. While he strives to inspire others with his music, he is also influenced and inspired by his fans and fellow musicians. The feedback and support he receives from his fanbase are invaluable sources of motivation and inspiration. Virtual Riot appreciates the unique perspectives and ideas that his fans bring to the table, and he often incorporates their feedback into his creative process.

Furthermore, Virtual Riot acknowledges the role of technology in shaping musical influence. He embraces the latest advancements in music production tools and techniques, using them as a means to expand his musical palette. Virtual Riot pushes the boundaries of what is possible, constantly seeking new sounds and textures to incorporate into his music.

In terms of the future of musical influence, Virtual Riot envisions a landscape where artists are encouraged to take risks and challenge conventions. He believes that the boundaries between genres will continue to blur, leading to a more diverse and inclusive music industry. Virtual Riot hopes to see a greater emphasis on collaboration and experimentation, as artists come together to create something truly unique and groundbreaking.

In conclusion, Virtual Riot's perspective on musical influence is rooted in the belief that music has the power to connect, inspire, and transform. He draws inspiration from a wide range of genres, art forms, and technological advancements, using them to shape his own unique sound and style. Virtual Riot encourages emerging artists to embrace their individuality and push the boundaries of traditional music genres. He envisions a future where musical influence is more collaborative and diverse, creating a vibrant and innovative music industry.

This completes our exploration of Virtual Riot's perspective on musical influence. By understanding the power of music and its ability to shape individuals and society, we gain a deeper appreciation for the artistry and creativity that goes into Virtual Riot's music.

Virtual Riot's Role in Shaping Future Music Trends

Virtual Riot, the talented German musician and producer, has made a significant impact on the music industry, particularly in the electronic dance music (EDM) genre. His innovative approach to production and his ability to blend genres has set him apart from his peers and positioned him as one of the leading figures in the future of music trends. In this section, we will explore Virtual Riot's role in shaping the future of music, the key elements of his unique sound, and the influence he has had on emerging artists.

Blending Genres and Styles

One of the defining characteristics of Virtual Riot's music is his ability to seamlessly blend different genres and styles. He has successfully merged elements of dubstep, drum and bass, future bass, and trap to create a sound that is uniquely his own. This innovative approach has opened up new possibilities for music production and has inspired a wave of producers to explore genre fusion.

By combining the heavy basslines and aggressive drops of dubstep with the melodic and euphoric elements of future bass, Virtual Riot has created a sound that appeals to a wide audience. His ability to fuse diverse musical elements without compromising on the overall coherence of his tracks showcases his exceptional talent and has set a new standard for genre-bending within EDM.

Experimentation and Pushing Boundaries

Virtual Riot is known for his willingness to experiment with new sounds and push the boundaries of what is considered mainstream within the EDM genre. He constantly challenges himself to explore uncharted territories, which has led to the development of fresh and exciting musical ideas.

His commitment to innovation has not only expanded the creative landscape in EDM but has also encouraged other artists to embrace experimentation and take risks with their own productions. Virtual Riot's fearlessness in pushing boundaries has become a catalyst for the evolution of music, fostering a spirit of exploration and creativity within the industry.

Embracing Technology and Production Techniques

Virtual Riot's sound is heavily influenced by advancements in music production technology. He utilizes the latest software, plugins, and hardware to refine his sound and create immersive tracks that captivate listeners. By embracing technology and incorporating it into his production process, he has been able to stay at the forefront of music trends and drive innovation within the industry.

Additionally, Virtual Riot's extensive knowledge of production techniques, such as sound design, mixing, and mastering, has contributed to the development of his unique sound. His meticulous attention to detail in crafting each element of his tracks sets him apart from other producers and has garnered admiration from both fans and industry professionals.

Inspiring Future Generations

Virtual Riot's impact on future music trends extends beyond his own productions. Through his unique sound and innovative approach, he has inspired a new generation of music producers to think outside the box and challenge conventional norms.

By encouraging other artists to explore genre fusion, experiment with production techniques, and embrace technology, Virtual Riot has played a pivotal role in shaping the future of music. His influence can be seen in the work of emerging artists who are pushing boundaries and creating their own distinct sounds.

Virtual Riot's Collaborative Mindset

Collaboration has been an integral part of Virtual Riot's success and his role in shaping future music trends. He has collaborated with a diverse range of artists from different genres, such as rock, hip-hop, and pop. These collaborations have allowed him to bring unique elements to his own productions and have opened up new avenues for musical experimentation.

Through his collaborations, Virtual Riot has fostered a sense of community and cross-pollination between different music genres. This collaborative mindset has not only enriched his own music but has also influenced the wider music industry by encouraging artists from various backgrounds to come together and create something truly innovative.

The Future of Music

As Virtual Riot continues to push the boundaries and explore new musical territories, he is poised to shape the future of music in profound ways. His genre-bending approach, commitment to experimentation, and embrace of technology will continue to inspire emerging artists and challenge the status quo.

Furthermore, his collaborative mindset and passion for nurturing talent will contribute to the growth and diversification of the music industry. Virtual Riot's influence will be felt for years to come as his legacy, shaped by his unique sound and pioneering spirit, leaves an indelible mark on the future of music.

Virtual Riot's Advice for Emerging Artists

As an emerging artist in today's fast-paced and ever-evolving music industry, it's easy to feel overwhelmed and unsure of where to start. But fear not! Virtual Riot, the electronic music maestro himself, is here to share his valuable advice to help you navigate the path towards success and make your mark in the industry.

1. **Stay True to Your Artistry:** Virtual Riot's first and foremost advice is to stay true to your unique artistic vision. Don't be influenced by fleeting trends or what is popular at the moment. Instead, focus on creating music that resonates with you and reflects your individuality. Remember, authenticity is key in a world saturated with music.

2. **Embrace Experimentation:** Don't be afraid to push boundaries and explore new sonic landscapes. Virtual Riot's success is rooted in his constant experimentation with different genres and styles. By stepping outside of your comfort zone and trying new things, you'll not only expand your skills as an artist but also set yourself apart from the crowd.

3. **Connect with Your Audience:** Building a strong connection with your audience is essential for any budding artist. Virtual Riot emphasizes the importance of engaging with your fans on a personal level. Interact with them on social media, reply to comments, and show genuine appreciation for their support. Creating a community around your music will not only boost your fanbase but also provide invaluable feedback and support.

4. **Collaborate and Network:** Collaborations are a fantastic way to grow as an artist. Virtual Riot suggests collaborating with other talented artists to broaden your musical horizons and tap into new audiences. Connect with like-minded individuals at music events, join online communities, and actively seek out opportunities to network. Remember, the power of collaboration can lead to new creative heights and open doors to exciting opportunities.

5. **Continued Learning:** The journey of an artist is a never-ending learning process. Virtual Riot encourages emerging artists to invest time in continuous learning and improvement. Stay updated with the latest music production techniques, learn new software and instruments, and explore different genres outside of your comfort zone. The more knowledge and skills you acquire, the more you'll be able to refine your craft and stand out in the industry.

6. **Persevere and Stay Committed:** The road to success is rarely a smooth one, and Virtual Riot's career is no exception. He advises emerging artists to persevere through challenges and stay committed to their passion. Rejection and setbacks are part of the journey, so don't let them discourage you. Stay focused on your goals, work hard, and trust in your abilities. Success will come with persistence and dedication.

7. **Embrace Technology:** In today's digital age, technology plays a crucial role in the music industry. Virtual Riot urges emerging artists to embrace technology and leverage its power to expand their reach. Use social media platforms to connect with fans, promote your music on streaming platforms, and explore innovative digital tools and software for music production. Embracing technology can amplify your presence and help you reach a global audience.

8. **Stay Humble and Grounded:** Despite his massive success, Virtual Riot remains humble and grounded. He advises emerging artists to do the same. Stay humble and open to feedback, learn from others, and be appreciative of the opportunities that come your way. Never let success get to your head, and always remember the passion and drive that brought you to where you are.

In conclusion, Virtual Riot's advice for emerging artists boils down to staying true to yourself, experimenting fearlessly, connecting with your audience, collaborating with others, continuously learning, persevering through challenges, embracing technology, and staying humble. By following these principles, aspiring artists can pave their way to success in the dynamic and competitive music industry. So go forth, create amazing music, and make your mark on the world!

Virtual Riot's Impact on the Next Generation of Musicians

Virtual Riot, the trailblazing music producer and DJ, has left an indelible mark on the music industry, not only through his groundbreaking sound but also through his impact on the next generation of musicians. Through a combination of his innovative approach to music production, his dedication to the craft, and his commitment to sharing his knowledge, Virtual Riot has become a mentor and role model to aspiring artists around the world.

One of the key ways Virtual Riot has influenced the next generation of musicians is through his willingness to collaborate and share his expertise. He recognizes the importance of collaboration in the music industry, and actively seeks out opportunities to work with emerging artists. By doing so, he provides a platform for these artists to showcase their talent and gain exposure to a wider audience.

In addition to collaboration, Virtual Riot has also made a name for himself as a music educator. He understands the importance of sharing knowledge and empowering others to reach their full potential. Through his online presence and social media platforms, he offers invaluable insights into production techniques, sound design, and the music industry as a whole. He conducts live streams where he interacts directly with his fans, answering their questions and offering guidance. These interactions not only provide aspiring musicians with valuable advice, but also create a sense of community and support.

Virtual Riot's impact on the next generation of musicians extends beyond his collaborations and educational endeavors. He has played a significant role in shaping the sound and direction of electronic music. His groundbreaking tracks and unique style have inspired countless artists to experiment with new sounds and push the boundaries of traditional genres. By challenging the norms and exploring uncharted territory, Virtual Riot has created a space for innovation and creativity within the industry.

Furthermore, Virtual Riot's success and journey as an artist serve as a source of inspiration for aspiring musicians. He started his career at a young age and achieved incredible success through persistence and passion. His story serves as a testament to the power of hard work and dedication. By sharing his personal experiences and the challenges he has faced, Virtual Riot motivates others to pursue their dreams fearlessly, and to never give up on their creative aspirations.

To illustrate the impact of Virtual Riot on the next generation of musicians, let's consider the story of Alex, a 20-year-old aspiring producer. Alex grew up idolizing Virtual Riot and was inspired by his unique sound and innovative productions. The online tutorials and interviews provided by Virtual Riot were Alex's go-to resources for learning music production techniques.

As Alex began to experiment with his own music, he reached out to Virtual Riot for feedback and guidance. To his surprise, Virtual Riot responded warmly, providing valuable advice and suggestions on how to improve his tracks. This interaction not only gave Alex a confidence boost but also motivated him to work even harder on his craft.

Encouraged by Virtual Riot's support, Alex continued to refine his skills and experiment with different genres. He eventually gained recognition within his local music community and started collaborating with other emerging artists. Alex's unique sound and dedication to pushing the boundaries of electronic music began to make waves, just like his idol, Virtual Riot.

This story is just one example of how Virtual Riot's impact on the next generation of musicians can create a ripple effect within the industry. By inspiring and nurturing young talent, he is fostering a community of innovative artists who are taking electronic music to new heights.

In conclusion, Virtual Riot's impact on the next generation of musicians cannot be overstated. Through his collaborations, educational endeavors, and inspirational journey, he has shaped the future of electronic music. His willingness to share his knowledge, his commitment to innovation, and his dedication to nurturing young talent make him a true pioneer in the music industry. As the next generation of musicians continues to grow and evolve, Virtual Riot's legacy will continue to inspire and influence their creative journeys.

Virtual Riot's Encouragement for Artistic Exploration

Artistic exploration is at the core of Virtual Riot's philosophy as an artist. He believes in pushing boundaries, stepping outside of comfort zones, and embracing experimentation. In this section, we will delve into the ways Virtual Riot encourages artistic exploration and inspires others to venture into uncharted territories.

Embracing Creative Freedom

Virtual Riot firmly believes that artists should have the freedom to explore their creativity without restrictions. He encourages aspiring artists to break free from conventional norms and embrace their unique vision. Virtual Riot advocates for breaking genre boundaries and blending different styles to create truly innovative and fresh sounds.

To encourage artistic exploration, Virtual Riot often shares his personal experiences of pushing boundaries and taking risks in his own music. He emphasizes the importance of stepping outside of the comfort zone and experimenting with new techniques, genres, and ideas. By sharing his journey, he inspires others to embrace their own artistic freedom and explore uncharted territories.

Embracing Failure and Learning from It

Virtual Riot champions the idea that failure is an essential part of the creative process. He believes that through failure, artists can learn valuable lessons and grow as individuals. He encourages artists to take risks and not be afraid of making mistakes.

To emphasize the importance of embracing failure, Virtual Riot shares stories of his own setbacks and how they ultimately led to new creative breakthroughs. He encourages artists to view failure as an opportunity for growth and innovation. Virtual Riot believes that by learning from failure, artists can discover new possibilities and reach greater heights in their artistic endeavors.

Embracing Collaboration

Collaboration is another key aspect of Virtual Riot's encouragement for artistic exploration. He recognizes the power of collaboration in expanding musical horizons and encouraging new creative ideas. Virtual Riot encourages artists to collaborate with individuals from different backgrounds, genres, and disciplines to create unique and groundbreaking works of art.

To inspire artists to embrace collaboration, Virtual Riot shares his own experiences working with a diverse range of artists. He highlights the benefits of collaborating, such as learning from others, gaining new perspectives, and pushing creative boundaries. Virtual Riot believes that collaboration fosters a sense of community and allows artists to explore uncharted artistic territories together.

Embracing Technology

Virtual Riot is known for his innovative use of technology in music production. He encourages artists to embrace technological advancements and leverage them to explore new artistic possibilities. Virtual Riot believes that technology can be a powerful tool for artistic expression and experimentation.

To inspire artists to embrace technology, Virtual Riot shares his own techniques and strategies for incorporating technology into music production. He emphasizes the importance of staying up-to-date with the latest advancements and tools in the industry. Virtual Riot encourages artists to explore different software, plugins, and production techniques to enhance their creativity and push the boundaries of their art.

Unconventional Inspiration

In addition to traditional sources of inspiration, Virtual Riot encourages artists to seek inspiration from unconventional sources. He believes that exploring different art forms, such as visual arts, literature, and even everyday experiences, can ignite new creative ideas and perspectives.

To encourage artists to find unconventional inspiration, Virtual Riot shares his own experiences of drawing inspiration from various sources. He provides examples of how he incorporates elements from different art forms into his music, resulting in unique and captivating compositions. Virtual Riot believes that by looking beyond traditional sources, artists can discover new sparks of creativity and embark on exciting artistic journeys.

In conclusion, Virtual Riot's encouragement for artistic exploration stems from his belief in creative freedom, the importance of embracing failure, the power of collaboration, the potential of technology, and finding inspiration in unconventional sources. By embracing these principles, artists can unleash their full creative potential and embark on a journey of limitless artistic exploration. Let Virtual Riot be your guide as you navigate uncharted territories and push the boundaries of your artistic expression.

Virtual Riot's Message to Future Generations

Hey there, future music makers! If you're reading this, it means you're passionate about creating music and pushing the boundaries of sound. Well, let me tell you, you're in for an incredible journey! As Virtual Riot, I've learned a lot along the way, and I want to share some words of wisdom with you.

First and foremost, always stay true to yourself and your unique voice as an artist. In a world saturated with music, it's easy to get swept up in trends and conform to what's popular. But remember, the most powerful music comes from within, from your own experiences, emotions, and perspectives. Don't be afraid to be different, to experiment, and to take risks.

Embrace failure as a vital part of the creative process. Trust me, I've had my fair share of setbacks and rejections. But each failure brought me one step closer to success. It's through these struggles that we grow and learn. So, don't let failures discourage you. Instead, use them as stepping stones to reach greater heights.

Never stop learning. The world of music is constantly evolving, and it's crucial to stay ahead of the curve. Take the time to expand your musical horizons, explore new genres, experiment with different techniques and technologies. Seek inspiration from unexpected sources. You never know what might spark your next creative breakthrough.

Collaboration is key. Don't underestimate the power of working with others. By collaborating with artists from diverse backgrounds and skill sets, you'll be exposed to fresh perspectives and ideas. It's through these collaborations that magic truly happens. Be open-minded, respectful, and always approach collaborations with a spirit of mutual learning and growth.

Remember to take care of yourself along the way. The music industry can be demanding and fast-paced, but don't neglect your mental and physical well-being. Find ways to recharge, whether it's through meditation, exercise, or simply spending time with loved ones. Your creativity will flourish when you're in a good place mentally and physically.

Lastly, never lose sight of why you fell in love with music in the first place. It's easy to get caught up in the business side of things, chasing fame and fortune. But always remember that music is a form of self-expression, a way to communicate and connect with others. The joy, passion, and emotion you pour into your music are what make it truly special.

So, future generations of music makers, go out there and create something extraordinary. Embrace your uniqueness, learn from failures, collaborate with others, take care of yourself, and never lose sight of the true essence of music. The world is waiting for your sonic creations. Let's make some magic together!

Keep rockin' and never stop evolving,

Virtual Riot

Virtual Riot's Continued Influence on Music Culture

Virtual Riot has undoubtedly left a lasting impact on the world of music culture. His innovative sound, genre-defying productions, and unique approach to music-making have captivated audiences and inspired a new generation of music producers. In this section, we will explore the ways in which Virtual Riot has continued to shape and influence the music culture, paving the way for future trends and artistic exploration.

Pushing the Boundaries of Sound

One of the key aspects of Virtual Riot's influence on music culture is his ability to push the boundaries of sound. With his diverse musical influences and cross-genre experimentation, he has continuously challenged traditional EDM conventions and opened up new sonic possibilities. By infusing elements of dubstep, drum and bass, future bass, and various other genres into his music, Virtual Riot has created a sound that is both familiar and refreshing.

Virtual Riot's willingness to explore unconventional sounds and techniques has inspired countless music producers to think outside the box and venture into uncharted territories. His use of intricate sound design, complex melodies, and innovative production techniques has become a trademark of his music, setting a new standard for creativity and originality in the EDM scene.

Breaking Down Genre Barriers

Virtual Riot's music is a testament to his ability to break down genre barriers and create a seamless fusion of styles. By incorporating elements from different genres, he has blurred the lines between dubstep, electro-house, and other EDM subgenres, creating a unique and eclectic sound that appeals to a wide range of listeners.

His genre-bending approach has not only inspired other artists to experiment with different styles but has also challenged the notion of sticking to one particular genre. Virtual Riot has shown that great music can be created by combining diverse influences and embracing a hybrid approach. This has had a profound impact on the music culture, encouraging artists and producers to explore their artistic freedom and push beyond the confines of genre limitations.

Embracing Collaboration and Community

Virtual Riot's commitment to collaboration and fostering a sense of community within the music industry has had a significant impact on music culture. He has a genuine passion for supporting and uplifting other artists, often collaborating with aspiring producers and providing mentorship to musicians looking to find their own unique voice.

Through collaborations, Virtual Riot has not only expanded his musical horizons but has also played a pivotal role in introducing new talent to the EDM scene. By sharing his knowledge and experiences, he has empowered emerging artists to follow their passion and pursue their dreams. This commitment to collaboration has fostered a sense of community and mutual support within the industry, creating an environment where artists can grow and thrive together.

Embracing the DIY Mentality

In addition to his musical contributions, Virtual Riot's career has been characterized by his embrace of the do-it-yourself (DIY) mentality. From the early stages of his career, he took control of his own production, marketing, and branding, utilizing social media platforms to connect directly with fans and build a dedicated following.

This approach has not only allowed Virtual Riot to maintain creative control over his music but has also inspired many aspiring producers to take charge of their own careers. His success as an independent artist has shown that with dedication, hard work, and a strong DIY ethic, it is possible to achieve professional success and make a lasting impact on the music industry.

Virtual Riot's Vision for the Future

Looking ahead, Virtual Riot continues to push the boundaries of his own sound and musical vision. He envisions a future where artistic exploration and innovation are the driving forces behind music culture. He believes that the next generation of music producers will continue to challenge traditional norms, blending genres, and experimenting with new technologies to create a truly unique and immersive listening experience.

Virtual Riot's journey is far from over, and his continued influence on music culture will inspire generations to come. With his dedication to pushing the boundaries, embracing collaboration, and fostering a sense of community, his impact on the EDM scene will endure, shaping the future of music for years to come.

In conclusion, Virtual Riot's continued influence on music culture is evident through his ability to push the boundaries of sound, break down genre barriers, embrace collaboration and community, and embrace the DIY mentality. As he continues to pave the way for future trends and inspire a new generation of music producers, Virtual Riot's impact on music culture is undeniable, leaving an indelible mark on the EDM scene and beyond.

The Personal Journey Continues

Balancing Personal and Professional Life

Balancing personal and professional life is crucial for any individual, and Virtual Riot is no exception. While he may be a successful musician, he also values his personal life and understands the importance of finding a healthy equilibrium between the two.

The Challenges of Balancing

Finding balance between personal and professional life can be challenging, especially for someone like Virtual Riot who leads a busy and demanding schedule. The music industry is known for its demanding nature, with long hours, constant travel, and pressure to meet deadlines and maintain a strong presence.

One of the biggest challenges for Virtual Riot is managing time effectively. With a full workload and commitments to both his music career and personal life, it can be overwhelming to try to fit everything in. Staying organized and prioritizing tasks becomes essential to ensure that both professional and personal responsibilities are met.

Setting Boundaries and Priorities

To strike a balance, Virtual Riot emphasizes the importance of setting boundaries and priorities. He understands that it's crucial to set aside time for himself and his loved ones, taking breaks from work and allowing himself to relax and recharge.

Setting priorities is key in managing time effectively. Virtual Riot identifies the most important tasks and focuses on those first, ensuring that he devotes enough time and energy to them. By clearly defining his priorities, he is able to allocate time for work as well as personal interests and relationships.

Maintaining Mental and Physical Well-being

Taking care of mental and physical well-being is essential when it comes to achieving balance. Virtual Riot believes that a healthy mind and body contribute to success in both personal and professional life.

He incorporates regular exercise into his routine, whether it's hitting the gym, going for a run, or practicing yoga. Physical activity not only helps him stay fit but also serves as a stress-reliever and a way to clear his mind.

Additionally, Virtual Riot recognizes the importance of self-care and relaxation. He takes time for activities that bring him joy and help him unwind, such as reading, spending time in nature, or pursuing hobbies outside of music. These moments of relaxation allow him to recharge and maintain a healthy mindset.

Communication and Support Systems

Maintaining balance also requires effective communication and support systems. Virtual Riot emphasizes the significance of open communication with his team, family, and friends. The ability to express his needs and concerns helps ensure that everyone is on the same page and can offer support when it's needed.

Having a strong support system is crucial for Virtual Riot. Whether it's his bandmates, family, friends, or fans, he relies on the support and encouragement of those around him. They provide him with the necessary emotional support and understanding during both the highs and lows of his career.

Finding Fulfillment in Both Lives

Virtual Riot believes that finding fulfillment in both personal and professional life is the ultimate goal. It's about finding the right balance that allows him to pursue his passion for music while also nurturing his personal relationships and interests.

Ultimately, Virtual Riot's key to balancing personal and professional life lies in being flexible, adaptable, and willing to make adjustments along the way. It's a continuous process of evaluation and reassessment to ensure that both areas of his life are thriving.

Summary

Balancing personal and professional life is a constant challenge for Virtual Riot. Through setting boundaries, priorities, and maintaining mental and physical well-being, he strives to find equilibrium. Effective communication and a strong support system contribute to his success in managing both aspects of his life. Ultimately, Virtual Riot's pursuit of fulfillment in both personal and professional realms is what drives him to find a healthy balance.

Staying True to Himself amidst Success

In the fast-paced world of music and entertainment, it can be easy for artists to lose sight of who they truly are amidst the pressures and temptations of success. But for

Virtual Riot, staying true to himself has always been a priority, even as his career continues to soar.

Success can often bring a whirlwind of opportunities, fame, and fortune, but it can also come with its own set of challenges. As Virtual Riot skyrocketed to fame, he found himself constantly bombarded with expectations from fans, record labels, and the industry as a whole. The pressure to conform to certain trends and expectations could have easily swayed him, but he remained steadfast in his commitment to staying true to his unique sound and style.

One of the key aspects of Virtual Riot's authenticity is his refusal to be confined by genre boundaries. In a music industry that often pigeonholes artists into specific genres, he has always pushed the boundaries and explored various styles, incorporating elements from dubstep, drum and bass, electro, and more. This willingness to experiment and evolve has not only allowed him to stay true to himself but has also played a significant role in shaping the future of electronic music.

Another important factor in Virtual Riot's ability to stay true to himself is his unwavering dedication to his craft. Despite achieving tremendous success and recognition, he has never allowed himself to become complacent or rest on his laurels. Virtual Riot is constantly pushing himself to new heights, challenging his own creative boundaries, and seeking growth as an artist.

Maintaining a strong support system has been crucial for Virtual Riot in navigating the ups and downs of success. He surrounds himself with a team of like-minded individuals who share his passion for music and understand his vision. This support system not only provides him with the encouragement and guidance he needs but also helps him stay grounded and true to his values.

Amidst the glamour and glitter of the music industry, Virtual Riot remains grounded and humble. He understands the fleeting nature of fame and success and doesn't let it define him. Instead, he focuses on the joy of creating music and connecting with his fans on a deeper level.

Virtual Riot's commitment to staying true to himself amidst success serves as an inspiration to aspiring artists. He shows them that it is possible to achieve greatness while remaining authentic and true to one's artistic vision. It is a reminder that success should not be measured solely by external validation but by the fulfillment that comes from following one's passion and being true to oneself.

In conclusion, Virtual Riot's ability to stay true to himself amidst success is a testament to his unwavering dedication, artistic integrity, and refusal to conform. He has proven that it is possible to thrive in the music industry while remaining authentic and true to one's artistic vision. As his journey continues, Virtual Riot's

CHAPTER 5 THE FUTURE OF VIRTUAL RIOT

commitment to staying true to himself will undoubtedly continue to shape the future of electronic music and inspire generations to come.

Looking Forward to New Adventures

As Virtual Riot's journey continues, he is eager to embrace new adventures and continue pushing the boundaries of his musical career. With his insatiable curiosity and passion for innovation, he is constantly seeking out new challenges and opportunities to grow as an artist. In this section, we will explore Virtual Riot's outlook on the future and his plans for exciting new endeavors.

Exploring Uncharted Musical Territory

One of the main reasons Virtual Riot's music has resonated with audiences around the world is his willingness to explore uncharted musical territory. He has never been afraid to experiment with different genres, sounds, and styles, constantly pushing the boundaries of electronic music. Looking forward, Virtual Riot is excited to delve even deeper into unexplored musical territories, blending diverse genres and incorporating unexpected elements into his compositions. He aims to create unique and captivating musical experiences that challenge listeners' expectations and take them on a thrilling sonic journey.

Virtual Riot recognizes that pushing boundaries requires taking risks and stepping out of his comfort zone. He believes that true artistic growth comes from experimentation and embracing the unknown. By venturing into uncharted musical territory, he hopes to inspire other artists and show that innovation knows no limits.

Creative Collaborations

Collaboration has always been an integral part of Virtual Riot's creative process, and he looks forward to embarking on new collaborative projects in the future. By working with a diverse range of artists from different genres and backgrounds, he believes he can bring fresh perspectives and ideas to his own music. Virtual Riot thrives on the energy and inspiration that comes from collaborative efforts, and he is always seeking out new and exciting partnerships.

In addition to musical collaborations, Virtual Riot is also open to exploring collaborations with visual artists, dancers, and other creative individuals. He envisions projects that combine various art forms to create immersive and multidimensional experiences for his audience. By joining forces with other talented artists, he hopes to create something truly extraordinary and groundbreaking.

Taking Live Performances to the Next Level

Virtual Riot has always been passionate about delivering electrifying live performances that leave a lasting impact on his audience. Looking forward, he aims to take his live shows to the next level by incorporating cutting-edge technology, stunning visuals, and awe-inspiring stage designs. He envisions a mesmerizing audiovisual experience that transcends traditional boundaries, captivating the audience's senses and creating an immersive world of music.

In his quest to push the limits of live performance, Virtual Riot is exploring the integration of live instruments and interactive elements into his shows. He believes that the combination of electronic music and live instrumentation can bring a new dimension to his music, adding an organic and dynamic element to his performances. By constantly evolving his live shows, Virtual Riot strives to create unforgettable moments of connection and pure musical bliss for his fans.

Mentoring and Inspiring the Next Generation

As Virtual Riot continues to grow and evolve as an artist, he remains committed to giving back and inspiring the next generation of musicians. He believes in the power of mentorship and aims to provide guidance and support to emerging artists. Virtual Riot wants to share his knowledge and experiences, empowering young talents to explore their own musical paths and find their unique voices.

In addition to mentorship, Virtual Riot is also passionate about fostering a sense of community within the music industry. He plans to organize workshops, seminars, and collaborative projects that bring artists together, encouraging collaboration, and nurturing a supportive environment. By creating opportunities for connection and collaboration, Virtual Riot hopes to contribute to the growth and vibrancy of the music community as a whole.

Embracing the Unknown

Looking forward to new adventures, Virtual Riot is excited about the unknown possibilities that lie ahead. He understands that true growth and evolution require embracing uncertainty and taking bold steps into uncharted territories. Virtual Riot is not afraid to deviate from the path others have treaded before and is thrilled to pave his own way through the vast landscape of music.

With his insatiable hunger for innovation and sonic exploration, Virtual Riot will continue to push the boundaries of electronic music. Whether it's through collaborations, live performances, or mentorship, he is determined to make his mark on the industry and inspire future generations of musicians. As he embarks on new adventures, Virtual Riot embodies the spirit of curiosity, courage, and creativity, showing us that the journey of a musician is an endless adventure filled with surprises, challenges, and limitless possibilities.

Note: In the next section, we will explore Virtual Riot's impact on future generations and his enduring legacy in the music industry. Stay tuned!

Virtual Riot's Reflection on Personal Growth

Personal growth is an ongoing journey that brings about self-discovery, learning, and transformation. For Virtual Riot, this journey has played a significant role in shaping not only his music career but also his outlook on life. In this section, we delve into Virtual Riot's reflections on personal growth and the invaluable lessons he has learned along the way.

One of the key aspects of personal growth for Virtual Riot has been the ability to embrace change and adaptability. As an artist and musician, he understands the importance of constantly evolving and pushing boundaries to stay ahead in a rapidly changing industry. Virtual Riot recognizes that growth often requires stepping out of one's comfort zone and embracing new experiences.

Virtual Riot's experiences have taught him the power of perseverance and the value of never giving up, even in the face of challenges. He acknowledges that setbacks and failures are inevitable but sees them as opportunities for growth and improvement. It is through these moments of adversity that Virtual Riot has gained resilience and the ability to bounce back stronger than ever.

Self-reflection is another important aspect of Virtual Riot's personal growth. He believes in constantly analyzing his own strengths and weaknesses to identify areas for improvement. This introspection has led Virtual Riot to continually seek self-improvement in his music production, live performances, and personal life.

In the pursuit of personal growth, Virtual Riot emphasizes the significance of self-care and maintaining a healthy work-life balance. He recognizes that creativity and inspiration thrive when he takes the time to prioritize his well-being. Balancing his personal and professional life allows him to recharge, replenish his energy, and approach his music with renewed passion and perspective.

Virtual Riot also acknowledges the importance of seeking out mentors and surrounding oneself with a supportive community. He believes that learning from others who have achieved success in their own fields can provide valuable insights and guidance. Virtual Riot cherishes the relationships he has built with fellow musicians and industry professionals, recognizing their influence on his personal growth.

Furthermore, Virtual Riot understands that personal growth is not limited to one's individual journey. He sees the value in giving back to the community and inspiring others to pursue their passions. Through mentorship and support, Virtual Riot hopes to empower the next generation of musicians and artists, providing them with the tools and guidance needed to unlock their full potential.

In conclusion, personal growth is an integral part of Virtual Riot's journey as an artist. It has allowed him to constantly evolve, embrace change, and push the boundaries of his music. Through reflections on his own strengths and weaknesses, perseverance, self-care, mentorship, and giving back to the community, Virtual Riot continues to grow not only as a musician but as an individual. His experiences serve as a reminder that personal growth is a lifelong process filled with valuable lessons and endless opportunities.

Virtual Riot's Approach to Maintaining Authenticity

The key to Virtual Riot's success lies in his unwavering commitment to maintaining authenticity in his music and his personal life. In an industry that constantly demands artists to conform to trends and fit into predefined molds, Virtual Riot has managed to stay true to himself and create music that resonates with his fans on a deep, emotional level.

One of the ways Virtual Riot maintains authenticity is by staying connected to his roots. He constantly draws inspiration from his early musical influences and childhood experiences, infusing his tracks with elements that reflect his upbringing in Germany. From the heavy basslines reminiscent of German electronic music to the subtle nods to German culture, Virtual Riot's music is a celebration of his heritage and a testament to his authenticity.

Another aspect of Virtual Riot's approach to maintaining authenticity is his refusal to follow trends blindly. While it's important for artists to evolve and adapt to changes in the music industry, Virtual Riot believes in staying true to his own unique sound and style. He doesn't chase after the latest fads or try to emulate other artists' success. Instead, he focuses on pushing his own creative boundaries and creating music that truly represents who he is as an artist.

Virtual Riot also places a great deal of importance on genuine connections with his fans. He believes that fan support and loyalty are earned through honest and heartfelt interactions. Whether it's through live streams, Q&A sessions, or social media engagement, Virtual Riot takes the time to connect with his fans on a personal level. He appreciates their support and sees them as partners in his musical journey rather than just passive listeners. By maintaining this genuine connection with his fans, Virtual Riot ensures that his music remains authentic and continues to resonate with his audience.

In addition to his approach to music, Virtual Riot also values authenticity in his personal life. He remains grounded and true to himself, never letting fame or success change who he is as a person. He surrounds himself with a close-knit team that supports and understands him, ensuring that he remains grounded despite the demands and pressures of the industry. Virtual Riot prioritizes self-care and mental well-being, acknowledging the importance of taking breaks and stepping away from the spotlight when necessary. This balance between his personal and professional life allows him to maintain authenticity both on and off the stage.

In a world where authenticity can often feel elusive, Virtual Riot stands as a shining example of what it means to stay true to oneself. By drawing inspiration from his roots, refusing to follow trends blindly, connecting with his fans on a personal level, and staying grounded in his personal life, Virtual Riot has carved out a unique place in the music industry. He reminds us that true success lies in being unapologetically yourself, and that authenticity will always resonate with others on a deeper level.

Virtual Riot's Personal Life beyond Music

In this section, we delve into the personal life of Virtual Riot, exploring the man behind the music. While his career as a musician is an essential part of his life, there is much more to know about his interests, hobbies, and the things that bring him joy outside of the music industry.

Uncovering Virtual Riot's Passions

When Virtual Riot is not creating groundbreaking music or touring the world, he enjoys immersing himself in various activities and pursuits. One of his greatest passions is photography. He finds solace and inspiration in capturing fleeting moments through the lens of his camera. From picturesque landscapes to candid portraits, Virtual Riot has an eye for capturing the beauty in everyday life.

Aside from photography, Virtual Riot has a profound love for the outdoors. He often embarks on adventures, exploring different landscapes and immersing himself in the beauty of nature. Hiking, camping, and rock climbing are just a few of the activities he indulges in to satisfy his wanderlust.

Virtual Riot also has a keen interest in technology and its impact on society. He enjoys staying updated with the latest advancements and trends in the tech world, constantly seeking out innovative gadgets and exploring their potential applications in music production and performance. This fascination with technology fuels his drive to push boundaries and experiment with new sounds and techniques in his music.

Maintaining Balance and Well-being

With a demanding career and a passion for music, it is essential for Virtual Riot to focus on maintaining balance and overall well-being. He recognizes the importance of self-care and dedicates time to nurturing his mental and physical health.

To recharge and find inner peace, Virtual Riot practices meditation and mindfulness. He believes that a calm and centered mind allows for more creativity and clarity in his musical endeavors. Additionally, he values regular exercise and engages in activities like yoga and martial arts to stay fit and energized.

Virtual Riot understands the significance of having a strong support system. He surrounds himself with close friends and family who provide unwavering support, love, and encouragement. Spending quality time with loved ones is crucial in grounding him and providing a sense of normalcy amidst the hectic nature of his music career.

Pursuing Philanthropy

Virtual Riot's personal life also extends into philanthropic endeavors. He is a firm believer in giving back to the community and supporting causes he is passionate about. One cause that is particularly close to his heart is promoting music education in underprivileged communities. He actively collaborates with organizations that aim to provide access to music education for children who may not otherwise have the opportunity. Virtual Riot's goal is to empower young aspiring musicians and foster a love for music, irrespective of socio-economic backgrounds.

In addition to music education, Virtual Riot contributes to various charitable organizations focused on mental health and well-being. He recognizes the importance of mental health awareness and endeavors to reduce the stigma surrounding mental health issues. By supporting these organizations, he hopes to make a positive difference in the lives of those affected by mental health challenges.

Embracing Adventures and New Experiences

Virtual Riot is always on the lookout for new adventures and experiences that help him grow as an individual. He seeks out opportunities to try new things, whether it be exploring different cultures through travel, experimenting with new art forms, or engaging in thought-provoking conversations with people from diverse backgrounds.

By embracing these adventures, Virtual Riot continues to broaden his horizons, expand his creative palette, and gain a deeper understanding of the world around him. He believes that these experiences not only enrich his personal life but also have a profound impact on his musical journey.

A Balanced Life Beyond Music

In conclusion, Virtual Riot's personal life extends beyond his passion for music. He finds joy in exploring his hobbies and interests, taking care of his well-being, giving back to the community, and embracing new experiences. By maintaining a balanced life, Virtual Riot nurtures his creativity, finds inspiration, and ultimately enhances his ability to produce groundbreaking music. Through his personal pursuits, he continues to make a positive impact on both the music industry and society as a whole.

In the next section, we will explore the evolving sound and musical vision of Virtual Riot, offering an insight into his creative process and the future direction of his music.

Virtual Riot's Perspective on Life and Success

Virtual Riot's journey to success in the music industry has been filled with both triumphs and challenges. Through it all, he has developed a unique perspective on life and success that sets him apart from many other artists in the industry. In this section, we will delve into Virtual Riot's thoughts on finding personal fulfillment, maintaining authenticity, and navigating the ups and downs of a successful career.

Fulfillment Beyond Fame

For Virtual Riot, success is not solely defined by fame and fortune. While he acknowledges the importance of recognition and financial stability in the music industry, he believes that true fulfillment comes from creating music that resonates with people on a deeper level. Virtual Riot sees his music as a vehicle for emotional expression, a means of connecting with his fans, and a platform to inspire others.

He cherishes the moments when he receives messages from fans who share how his music has impacted their lives. Whether it's helping them through tough times or providing an escape from the hardships of everyday life, Virtual Riot finds immense joy and fulfillment in knowing that his art has a positive impact.

Authenticity in the Spotlight

One of the key aspects of Virtual Riot's success is his unwavering commitment to authenticity. He firmly believes that staying true to oneself is crucial in maintaining a long and meaningful career in the music industry. Virtual Riot encourages aspiring artists to embrace their uniqueness and embrace their own creative vision rather than conforming to trends or trying to please others.

Throughout his career, he has faced pressure to conform to certain expectations or adopt a specific image. However, Virtual Riot has always remained steadfast in being true to himself. He believes that his authenticity is what has endeared him to his fans and allowed him to stand out in a crowded marketplace.

Navigating Success and Failure

Virtual Riot understands that success often comes with its fair share of challenges. The pressure to consistently deliver new and innovative music, as well as the demanding nature of touring, can take a toll on even the most seasoned artists. However, he believes that it is through these challenges that one can grow and learn.

For Virtual Riot, failure is not something to be feared but rather embraced as an opportunity for growth. He acknowledges that not every project or idea will be successful, but he doesn't let setbacks discourage him. Instead, he views them as valuable learning experiences and stepping stones towards future success.

By embracing failure and viewing it as a normal part of the creative process, Virtual Riot has been able to overcome obstacles and continue to evolve as an artist. He encourages others to adopt a similar mindset, reminding them that success is not without its fair share of setbacks and failures.

Maintaining Balance and Well-being

Despite the demands of a thriving music career, Virtual Riot emphasizes the importance of maintaining balance and prioritizing personal well-being. He understands that taking care of oneself physically, mentally, and emotionally is crucial for sustained success and creativity.

Virtual Riot actively seeks out activities and hobbies outside of music to help recharge and find inspiration. Whether it's spending time in nature, pursuing other artistic endeavors, or simply taking time off to relax, he recognizes the importance of self-care.

He also emphasizes the significance of surrounding oneself with a strong support system. Virtual Riot credits his family, friends, and team for their unwavering support throughout his journey and believes that having a solid network of people who believe in you is essential for maintaining a healthy work-life balance.

Unconventional Wisdom

In the world of music, Virtual Riot has gained a reputation for his experimental and innovative approach to production. He believes that embracing unconventional wisdom is necessary for artists to break free from creative constraints and push boundaries.

Virtual Riot encourages artists to take risks, think outside the box, and challenge conventional norms. By embracing experimentation and embracing their unique artistic vision, he believes that artists can carve out their own path to success and make a lasting impact on the industry.

Conclusion

Virtual Riot's perspective on life and success is an insightful and refreshing take on the music industry. He emphasizes the importance of finding fulfillment beyond fame, maintaining authenticity, and embracing failure as an opportunity to grow. By prioritizing personal well-being, surrounding oneself with a supportive network, and pursuing unconventional wisdom, Virtual Riot has not only achieved success in his own right but also paved the way for future generations of musicians. His story serves as an inspiration for aspiring artists, reminding them that success is not defined by external recognition alone but by the impact they have on others and the joy they find in their craft.

Virtual Riot's Outlook on the future

As Virtual Riot looks toward the future, he is filled with excitement and anticipation for what lies ahead. His journey as an artist has been marked by continuous growth and evolution, and he is determined to push the boundaries even further.

One aspect that Virtual Riot is particularly interested in exploring is the intersection between music and technology. He believes that advancements in technology have limitless potential to revolutionize the music industry and create new and immersive experiences for both artists and audiences. Virtual reality, augmented reality, and artificial intelligence are just a few areas that he sees as fertile ground for experimentation and innovation.

Virtual Riot is also passionate about using his platform to advocate for important social and environmental causes. He believes that artists have a unique ability to inspire change and wants to use his music as a vehicle for spreading awareness and promoting positive action. Whether it's through collaborations with organizations or hosting charity events, he is committed to making a positive impact on the world.

In addition, Virtual Riot recognizes the importance of mentorship and nurturing the next generation of musicians. He believes that artists have a responsibility to share their knowledge and experiences with others, and he is dedicated to supporting emerging talent. Through workshops, masterclasses, and mentorship programs, he hopes to empower young artists to find their own unique voice and make their mark on the music industry.

Virtual Riot's outlook on the future is one of continuous growth and exploration. He is constantly seeking new sounds, pushing boundaries, and challenging himself creatively. He believes that the best artists are those who never stop learning and evolving. While he acknowledges that the road ahead may have its challenges, he is confident in his ability to adapt and thrive in an ever-changing musical landscape.

As Virtual Riot looks ahead, he is excited to embark on new adventures, collaborate with artists from different genres and backgrounds, and continue to connect with his fans on a deeper level. He believes that music has the power to bring people together and plans to use his platform to spread positivity, inspire creativity, and foster a sense of community.

In conclusion, Virtual Riot's outlook on the future is one filled with boundless potential and a commitment to making a positive impact. Through his innovative use of technology, dedication to social and environmental causes, and passion for mentorship, he aims to redefine the music industry and leave a lasting legacy of creativity and inspiration. The future holds endless possibilities, and Virtual Riot is ready to embrace them with open arms.

Virtual Riot's Legacy as a Personal Journey

Virtual Riot's journey in the music industry has been nothing short of remarkable. From his humble beginnings in Germany to becoming a global sensation, his legacy is not only defined by his musical achievements but also by the personal growth he has experienced along the way.

Throughout his career, Virtual Riot has always stayed true to himself and his passion for music. This authenticity has become a defining characteristic of his legacy, inspiring others to embrace their true selves and pursue their dreams with unwavering determination. In a world where success often comes at the expense of one's identity, Virtual Riot's story serves as a reminder that staying true to oneself is the key to long-lasting fulfillment and success.

Virtual Riot's personal journey has been filled with challenges and obstacles that he was able to overcome through sheer perseverance and resilience. His story is a testament to the fact that success rarely comes without setbacks and failures. By sharing his personal struggles and triumphs, he has provided a source of inspiration for aspiring artists and individuals alike who face their own challenges.

One of the most remarkable aspects of Virtual Riot's journey is his ability to balance his personal and professional life. In an industry that can easily consume one's entire being, he has managed to prioritize his well-being and maintain a healthy work-life balance. His dedication to his craft and his personal relationships has set an example for others in the music industry, showing that success can be achieved without sacrificing one's personal happiness.

Virtual Riot's influence extends beyond his music and into the realm of philanthropy. His commitment to giving back to the community and supporting charitable causes has left a lasting impact on the music industry and the lives of many individuals. By using his platform to raise awareness and make a positive difference, he has solidified his legacy as not just a talented artist but also a compassionate human being.

As Virtual Riot's journey continues, his legacy serves as a reminder of the transformative power of music. His ability to push boundaries and experiment with different genres has inspired countless artists to explore new creative avenues. By challenging the norms and redefining the sound of EDM, he has left an indelible mark on the music industry.

Virtual Riot's enduring relevance in the music industry lies not only in his exceptional talent but also in his ability to evolve with the ever-changing landscape of music. His willingness to embrace new technologies and incorporate them into his performances has set him apart as a forward-thinking artist. As the future of electronic music unfolds, Virtual Riot's legacy will undoubtedly continue to shape the direction of the industry.

In conclusion, Virtual Riot's legacy as a personal journey exemplifies the power of authenticity, resilience, and philanthropy. His story serves as an inspiration to aspiring artists and individuals alike, showing that success is achievable through hard work, dedication, and staying true to oneself. As his journey continues, Virtual Riot's impact on the music industry and the lives of his fans remains profound, solidifying his place as a true icon in the world of electronic music.

Of all the sections in the biography of Virtual Riot, one of the most interesting and inspiring is "5.4.10 Virtual Riot's Inspirations for Continued Growth." In this section, we delve into the personal motivations and driving forces behind Virtual Riot's ongoing journey as an artist. Despite his success and achievements, Virtual Riot remains humble and deeply committed to his craft. His inspirations are not only rooted in music but also in other aspects of life that shape his growth and creativity.

Virtual Riot's Inspirations for Continued Growth

Virtual Riot draws inspiration from a wide range of sources, each one playing a vital role in his continued artistic evolution. Let's explore some of the key inspirations that influence his growth as an artist:

1. Nature and the Great Outdoors

One of Virtual Riot's biggest inspirations for continued growth comes from immersing himself in the beauty of nature. He finds solace and rejuvenation in exploring the great outdoors, whether it's hiking through breathtaking landscapes or simply taking a moment to appreciate the world around him. Nature serves as a reminder of the incredible diversity and harmony found in the natural world, and it sparks his imagination and fuels his creativity.

2. Human Connections and Relationships

Virtual Riot firmly believes that human connections and relationships are essential for personal and artistic growth. He values the connections he makes with his fans, fellow artists, and collaborators. It is through these interactions that he gains new perspectives, learns from others, and discovers fresh ideas. Virtual Riot believes that the collective human experience is a wellspring of inspiration, and he seeks to create music that resonates deeply with his audience.

3. Pushing Boundaries and Breaking Conventions

As Virtual Riot continues to evolve as an artist, he finds inspiration in pushing boundaries and breaking conventional norms. He seeks to challenge himself creatively and explore new territories within EDM and beyond. By venturing into uncharted waters, he keeps his artistic vision fresh and vibrant. Virtual Riot constantly seeks to surprise and delight his audience through his innovative and boundary-pushing musical endeavors.

4. Technology and Innovation

Technology plays a significant role in Virtual Riot's creative process and serves as a constant inspiration for his growth. He embraces the ever-evolving world of music production tools, software, and hardware, harnessing them to push the boundaries of his sound and create unique sonic landscapes. Virtual Riot's willingness to experiment with cutting-edge technologies sets him apart and keeps his music ahead of the curve.

5. Self-Reflection and Personal Growth

Reflecting on his own journey as an artist and as an individual is another key source of inspiration for Virtual Riot. He believes in the importance of self-improvement and personal growth, both in his music and in his life. Through self-reflection, he finds the strength to overcome challenges, refine his skills, and explore new artistic directions. Virtual Riot sees each experience as an opportunity for growth and draws inspiration from the evolution of his own creative process.

6. Embracing Musical Diversity

Virtual Riot is a firm believer in embracing musical diversity and being open to a wide range of genres and styles. He finds inspiration in exploring different genres and incorporating diverse elements into his music. By blending various musical influences, Virtual Riot creates a unique and captivating sound that resonates with audiences across different genres. His commitment to musical exploration and fusion fuels his growth as an artist and ensures that his music remains fresh and exciting.

7. Pursuit of Excellence

Above all, Virtual Riot's unwavering pursuit of excellence is a constant inspiration for his growth as an artist. He approaches each project with dedication and a desire to deliver the best possible outcome. Virtual Riot's commitment to his craft and his relentless work ethic drive him to continuously improve and evolve. This passion for excellence ensures that his music continues to inspire and captivate audiences around the world.

In conclusion, Virtual Riot's inspirations for continued growth are deeply rooted in his connection with nature, human relationships, pushing boundaries, technology, self-reflection, musical diversity, and the pursuit of excellence. These inspirations shape his growth as an artist and allow him to create music that remains relevant, innovative, and inspiring. Virtual Riot's unwavering commitment to his craft and his tireless pursuit of new creative horizons make him a true pioneer in the EDM scene. As he continues to explore new musical territories and inspire the next generation of artists, his legacy as a visionary and an innovator will endure for years to come.

Index